Pesticides, a Love Story

Pesticides, a Love Story
America's Enduring Embrace of Dangerous Chemicals

Michelle Mart

UNIVERSITY PRESS OF KANSAS

Published by the University Press of Kansas (Lawrence, Kansas 66045), which was organized by the Kansas Board of Regents and is operated and funded by Emporia State University, Fort Hays State University, Kansas State University, Pittsburg State University, the University of Kansas, and Wichita State University

Library of Congress Cataloging-in-Publication Data

Mart, Michelle, 1964–
Pesticides, a love story : America's enduring embrace of dangerous chemicals / Michelle Mart.
pages cm — (CultureAmerica)
Includes bibliographical references and index.
ISBN 978-0-7006-2128-6 (hardback : alkaline paper) — ISBN 978-0-7006-2157-6 (ebook)
1. Pesticides—United States—History. 2. Agricultural chemicals—United States—History. 3. Pesticides—Social aspects—United States—History. 4. Pesticides—United States—Public opinion—History. 5. Public opinion—United States—History. 6. United States—Social conditions—1945– 7. Nature—Effect of human beings on—United States—History. 8. United States—Environmental conditions. I. Title.
SB950.2.A1M37 2015
363.738'498—dc23

2015020380

British Library Cataloguing-in-Publication Data is available.

Printed in the United States of America

10 9 8 7 6 5 4 3 2 1

The paper used in this publication is recycled and contains 30 percent postconsumer waste. It is acid free and meets the minimum requirements of the American National Standard for Permanence of Paper for Printed Library Materials Z39.48-1992.

Contents

Introduction

"Presto! No More Pests," read a 1955 article in *Coronet* magazine introducing the new pesticides aldrin and dieldrin to readers. These synthetics were not only easy to use, the article emphasized, they were "sister miracle-workers for the housewife and back-yard farmer" that did not harm other living things when used properly. This type of article was common in the mid-1950s, and similar messages were found in advertisements from chemical manufacturers. News stories and ads alike not only highlighted how easy it was to use pesticides or how powerful they were but also emphasized that American bounty was inextricably linked to the wonders of chemical agriculture. Readers, for instance, opened their *Saturday Evening Post* from 1952 to see a full-page Dow Chemical Company ad showing grocery-store customers buying large, lushly colored fruits and vegetables that were "not the work of Mother Nature alone."[1]

Who wouldn't love synthetic pesticides?

Apparently, most Americans did. At least there was evidence that they had been embracing these chemicals since news of them had first burst on the scene during World War II and continued to do so into the twenty-first century. More than 90 percent of soybeans grown in the United States in 2008, for example, were "Roundup Ready" genetically modified organisms (GMOs), dependent on the generous use of the herbicide glyphosate to control weeds.[2] Such statistics reveal the enduring commitment to pesticides. It is also revealed over several decades from the mid–twentieth century to early twenty-first century in the marketing of products that appealed to the idea that humans could easily control nature, eradicating troublesome species with no ill effects. An Ortho advertisement from spring 2014 is illustrative:

suburban consumers learned that Weed B Gon "kills weeds without harming your lawn." Similar, magical names were found on pesticide products sixty years earlier, and the rhetoric was also familiar, as shown by a 1946 herbicide ad encouraging homeowners to "get rid of weeds—now that chemistry had developed an easy, economic method for their destruction."[3]

This book is a story about this remarkable continuity, about how attitudes toward pesticide use remained relatively stable from the 1940s to the present day. Why did synthetic pesticides become so pervasive, and, more importantly, why did they remain so? Why did popular and political attitudes toward pesticide use change so little over six decades, even in the face of numerous criticisms and crises that offered opportunities to rethink the commitment to synthetic pesticides?

Silent Spring, with the rise of environmentalism that was ushered in by its publication, was the most obvious turning point when faith in pesticides might have weakened. And it did—but only to a certain extent. The persistent insecticide DDT (dichlorodiphenyltrichloroethane) and its chlorinated hydrocarbon cousins were banned a decade after *Silent Spring* was published, and the name "DDT" became synonymous with human abuse of the environment. But, contrary to the dominant story that we tell about the revolutionary impact of Rachel Carson's 1962 book, the overall commitment to pesticides did not lessen. Indeed, their use went up. Farm use in the United States more than doubled in the thirty years after *Silent Spring* was published. By the beginning of the twenty-first century, more than 5.2 billion pounds of pesticides were used annually throughout the world at a cost of $40 billion, with the United States accounting for 22 percent of the total amount used and 32 percent of the money spent.[4] What accounts for this paradox: the rejection of DDT *and* a strengthened commitment to pesticide use? One way to solve this puzzle is to uncover the origins of the story we tell about modern pesticides and their use.

Average Americans first learned of a new delousing powder, DDT, in early 1944 with news stories that the Allies had brought a raging typhus epidemic in Naples to a standstill. Within a few months, more stories reached the United States about DDT's successes against the malarial mosquito—although it was "harmless to man, so far as the evidence goes," reported the *New York Times*. Hailed as "the greatest single weapon in the war against [malaria]" from 1944 on, DDT had a powerful effect on the American imagination.[5] The story of modern American pesticides usually starts here, during World War II, with the embrace of DDT by most Americans as a chemical miracle bringing improved health and agricultural bounty. The real significance of this wartime moment thus lay in the transformation of American life that would follow.

DDT and its pesticide cousins were part of a technological revolution that reshaped American life, most visibly changing the operation of the nation's farms. After the war, farmers used an array of mechanized equipment as well as mass-produced feed, seed, fertilizer, and synthetic pesticides.[6] These changes, along with genetic innovations in crops and livestock, increased agricultural productivity. Such success, in turn, encouraged greater reliance on the new innovations. So widespread was DDT use by the mid-1950s that journalists referred to it as "familiar as orange juice" and toothpaste.[7] Total usage of all pesticides continued to climb. In the three decades after World War II, for example, pesticide use in the United States went up tenfold.[8] The embrace of pesticides (which took many forms, including insecticides, herbicides, nematocides, fungicides, and rodenticides, among others) during this period reflected the start of a chemical era in all areas of American life as well as continued innovation and research into new products.[9] More broadly, the chemical revolution symbolized the confidence many Americans felt in their ability, through modern science, to tame and control nature, just as the United States was taming the rest of the world militarily, politically, and economically in the postwar era.

By the end of the twentieth century, the chemical age was no longer revolutionary; it was entrenched. Evidence that chemicals were woven into every aspect of modern life was well illustrated in the enduring power of pesticides. The types of pesticides used and the way that they were used had changed in half a century, but their ubiquity had not—even if they seemed less *visible* than in an earlier age. DDT was a powerful insecticide whose immediate effects were clear, as was its persistence. By the start of the twenty-first century, DDT was no longer sprayed across US fields; it had long been eclipsed by the herbicide glyphosate, better known to ordinary citizens by its brand name, Roundup. The shift from insecticides to herbicides had been going on for years and was accelerated by the introduction of genetically modified crops in the 1990s. Although one of the arguments in favor of GMOs had been that they would reduce pesticide use by modifying crops internally instead of having to douse them with chemicals, at the beginning of the twenty-first century, the GMOs that dwarfed all others in acres planted were Roundup Ready varieties of grain—crops that could be safely sprayed with glyphosate and suffer no damage. The use of glyphosate doubled from 1996 to 2003, with the majority of soybeans and corn planted in the United States being Roundup Ready by 2008, and it had become the world's largest-selling herbicide by 2004, with $400 million in sales annually. The whole point of chemical companies investing in herbicide-resistant GMOs was clear. Back in 1982, an article in *Chemical Week* had described the motivation: "The theory is that farmers would then be willing to use even more of the weedkillers, safe in the knowledge that their crop won't be damaged."[10]

Most Americans probably cared little about the bottom line of the chemical and seed companies; the appeal of GMOs was more in the ease of a modern technology that could master nature. For example, although far less prevalent than Roundup Ready soybeans, "Golden Rice" garnered much more publicity. Golden Rice had been engineered to contain more vitamin A than other rice, thus having the potential to erase a common nutritional deficiency in the developing world. Golden Rice landed on the cover of *Time* magazine in July 2000 with an article that exaggerated its possibilities by proclaiming that it could save 1 million children a year.[11] Such an innovation reflected the confidence that technology could control nature, whether through insecticides or gene manipulation. In the face of such momentous possibilities—from insecticides in 1950 to GMOs in 2000—most people did not look too closely at the downsides, even if increasing amounts of chemicals were needed to achieve the desired results.

Modern synthetic pesticides are a legacy of government-supported research and investment during World War II. Their image as miraculous innovations was strengthened by the stories of DDT helping to save soldiers and civilians alike from deadly diseases. These stories—combined with the effectiveness of the new chemical—laid the foundation for the positive postwar images of pesticides and eased their transition to civilian use. The first brilliant glow of DDT symbolized modernity, scientific prowess, and the idea that the environment was a resource to be harnessed. Such was the power of DDT's image that it is worth asking: What if the foundation of American attitudes had been *not* the Allies' miracle chemical but, instead, the organochlorines stockpiled by the Nazis for possible use as chemical weapons? Alternatively, what if the postwar American image of pesticides had been shaped by the legacy of the cyanide-based insecticide Zyklon-B, used to exterminate humans in the concentration camps?

It would be foolhardy to push such counterfactual concepts too far, and it would be illogical to argue that the foundational images of pesticides in 1945 shaped all that followed. Nevertheless, it makes sense to consider the starting point of some of the cultural images associated with the growth in synthetic pesticides after the war. First impressions can be powerful, at least as they set the stage for what is to follow. Material motivations and constraints are essential for understanding pesticide use in the post–World War II United States, but they don't provide a complete explanation unless they are understood within a broader cultural discourse. Cultural discourses make up the framework or paradigm we use to give our lives structure and meaning. They help us interpret the world around us and make choices about our material lives. In order to understand the cultural discourse surrounding pesticides, we need to examine how people viewed the chemicals: when they debated their use and when they did not. Did the discussions and images found in the press and in public-opinion polls mirror or contrast with the views of scientists, businesspeople, and government officials? Did opinions about pesticides reinforce contemporary cultural trends and discourses or go in a new direction? Investigating these questions reminds us that although the American embrace of pesticides was enduring, it was not inevitable.

There was of course good reason for Americans to first embrace pesticides. DDT *had* been responsible for fighting typhus and malaria, saving American soldiers in World War II and civilians in the years after from deadly diseases. This was not an abstraction for most Americans in the mid–twentieth century. Although the greatest dangers from such diseases after the war were in the developing world, many adults had clear memories of malaria as a danger in the continental United States; it was not until 1949 that the US Centers for Disease Control declared that malaria was no longer a significant public health problem.[12] In addition, the dramatic increase in crop yields after World War II, due in part to all sorts of chemical inputs, was obvious and led many, logically, to embrace pesticide use. Such results cannot be denied. But they are not the whole story.

It's also worth noting that interpreting material motivations or evaluating the effectiveness of pesticides is not as straightforward as it might at first appear. There are different ways to measure success. If per-acre commodity output rises in the short term, but per-acre costs also go up dramatically and drive some farmers off the land, is that a successful outcome? If consumers have ready access to relatively cheap, out-of-season food, but the variety of flora overall declines, is that a successful outcome? If insect and weed resistance to pesticides increases dramatically but can then be controlled by the introduction of new pesticides, is that a successful outcome? If pesticides that help boost output harm human and animal health in previously unforeseen ways, should they still be widely used? This book will not attempt to provide definitive answers to these or related environmental questions, but such questions remind us that we should not automatically accept the contention that the material benefits of pesticides outweigh their costs.

However we evaluate the material costs and benefits of pesticides, the primary focus of this book is the *story* that we tell about those costs and benefits. Most especially, these pages will argue that there has been a remarkably consistent and strong embrace of synthetic pesticides, a strength of feeling that in other human endeavors could be characterized as a love story. Characterizing this relationship as a love story is, of course, a metaphor, not a literal description. I'm aware of the provocative potential of the image, especially in a work of history, not literature. Nevertheless, the metaphor is chosen as a deliberate reminder of three main themes in this narrative. First, like love, the attachment to pesticides was not necessarily rational; a sober assessment of costs and benefits might have weakened American confidence in pesticides. Instead, cultural conceptions, even emotions, often blinded people to the dangers of pervasive pesticide use. Second, as in many a love story, widespread pesticide use fostered what was at times an unhealthy dependency, a treadmill from which there seemed little chance of escape. Finally, love stories can turn to tragedy, even if they begin with great promise. The benefits of pesticides have been both miraculous, such as vanquishing malaria, and tragic, such as causing the deaths of thousands of people in Bhopal, India.

Pesticides, a Love Story is a cultural history of pesticide use in postwar America arguing that the popular and political embrace of the chemicals remained strong despite accidents, controversies, rising expense, and declining effectiveness. The book outlines the appeal of pesticides and how they fit into a broader postwar discourse, promising modernity, sophisticated technologies, and increased productivity as well as the possibility that humans could control nature. In addition, the appeal of pesticides reinforced assumptions of Western economic and material superiority during the Cold War. The expression of these appeals changed over the decades, prominently foregrounded in the middle of the twentieth century and less visible, but still assumed, toward the end of the century. Second, the book discusses various challenges to the prevailing consensus about pesticides and why these challenges, in the end, were muted, moderated, defeated, or co-opted. In several examples spanning half a century, the tendency to favor industrial solutions, traditional scientific explanations, and the status quo strengthened the American embrace of pesticides. Finally, the book argues that despite the popular flowering of a new environmental sensibility in the late twentieth and early twenty-first centuries, one of the core principles of many modern environmentalists—"the precautionary principle"—was never widely embraced by Americans when it came to pesticides because it clashed with stronger cultural ideals about modernity, progress, and the desire to triumph over natural "enemies."

As a cultural survey of popular and political attitudes toward pesticides, this book synthesizes scholarly work on familiar turning points in the history of pesticides and juxtaposes these with contemporary media and political discussions. I argue that the embrace of pesticides in the United States has been enduring even while there have been regulations on use, the banning of particular chemicals, and growth in the organic-food industry. Thus, the attachment to pesticides has been long lasting, but the relationship has not been static. By the early 1970s, there was a broad consensus that persistent chlorinated hydrocarbon insecticides should no longer be widely sprayed. Moreover, for many people, one of the reasons to favor the widespread adoption of a herbicide such as glyphosate was that it was much less acutely toxic than a chemical such as dieldrin. On another front, growing discomfort with pesticides has led to the dramatic growth of organic food. By the early 2000s, organic food was the fastest-growing sector of the food economy and accounted for 4 percent of food sold in the United States. But just as important as figuring out what accounted for the growth of organic food is figuring out why such growth coincided with increased herbicide use on food crops throughout the nation. Herein we find that the embrace of pesticides has been stronger than one might expect at first glance.

If this book focuses upon the story we tell about pesticides, it necessarily asks: What shapes that narrative? Who wrote the love story? The tale has various authors, including the companies that make the pesticides, government officials who establish regulations for their use, ordinary citizens who both support and object to pesticides, and the press that reports upon the views of the other constituencies and frames the ensuing debates. This book will compare the contributions of the various groups, though it will give less attention to the manufacturers because their interest is self-evident and inevitable: to convince others to use pesticides and to sell as much as possible. The focus here is on the narrative about pesticides found in the *public culture* and, most especially, how it was shaped by mainstream media. In particular, the book will look at whether the rhetoric in news stories circumscribed the way that many Americans understood pesticides and to what extent the debates over regulation, environmental protection, and food safety were determined through the narratives penned by journalists. In addition, it will explore the connection between the story that journalists *shaped* and the stories they *reported upon* from policymakers, activists, scientists, and other citizens. To what extent did these groups reinforce each other's messages? To what extent did the narratives work at cross-purposes?

Due to the messy nature of trying to unpack cultural discourses, a few more words about methodology are in order. Although one starting point of this book is the assertion that mainstream press stories are a good way to understand prevailing common opinions about various topics, I am under no illusion that the "press" is monolithic. There are—among others—national-circulation newsmagazines or network-television news programs presenting themselves as balanced, big-city papers with ambitious news-gathering agendas, lifestyle magazines aimed at particular groups such as suburban homeowners, and journals focused on a political issue or niche. Uncovering prevalent themes and widely held cultural beliefs among such a collection of sources is not an exact science. Nor is it always clear how to isolate a direct causal relationship between a news story and a public opinion or between a government policy and how it is portrayed in the media. Thus, the aim of this book is to look for dominant themes and attitudes reflected in a sampling of mainstream press and, at times, of more specialized publications. I will discuss mutually reinforcing discourses found in these media examples as well as in the policies and language of government officials, environmental organizations, chemical companies, and individual citizens. The goal of these comparisons is to uncover the dominant paradigm that helped to shape the American relationship with pesticides.

Some significant topics—each of which could merit a book of its own—are not discussed here. This study does not focus on debates within the agrichemical industry or the views of its leaders except as they have been reflected in the press and the public culture. In addition, the following discussion reflects the perspective of many Americans for whom the interests of chemical or agricultural workers have been invisible; it does not examine the effects of pesticides on workers' health or how people in those communities viewed the chemicals. Similarly, since this book focuses on public American discourse, it does not delve into the impact of pesticides exported throughout the world except when the American press addressed particular policies or crises such as the Green Revolution, Bhopal, or Agent Orange use.

Many scholars and other observers have provided examples of how the welfare of poor workers, whether in India or Mexico or California, has been disregarded in public discussions, even during periods when pesticide use was criticized and environmentalism was on the rise. Instead, criticisms of pesticides usually arose over the question of how they might affect American consumers or, occasionally, the environment. This bias is evident in comparing the relative impact of Rachel Carson and United Fruit Workers leader Cesar Chavez in the 1960s. Although both highlighted the dangers of pesticides in modern life, Carson focused on the impact on American citizens, consumers, and wild animals, whereas Chavez worked to protect fruit pickers and other farm laborers who were exposed to dangerous chemicals daily as they grew fruit for the mass market. The impact of each in modern American culture was vastly different: Rachel Carson became the godmother of modern environmentalism, while the plight of farmworkers remained largely invisible.[13] Moreover, one of the lasting legacies of Carson's work was the shift away from persistent, less acutely toxic organochlorines to less persistent, more acutely toxic organophosphates that endangered agricultural workers. The banning of many broad-spectrum persistents was hailed as a triumph by policymakers and environmentalists, although the organophosphates that replaced them posed a greater hazard to farmworkers.

The impact of Rachel Carson's book was powerful and helped to change the discourse about pesticide use. There were other turning points in people's attitudes toward the chemicals, such as the revulsion over Bhopal or the growth of organic-food consumption. Nonetheless, this book will argue that even in the midst of various crises that led to growing environmentalism, there was *not* a fundamental, permanent paradigm shift to reject ubiquitous pesticide use or to reimagine the relationship between humans and nature, between risk and caution, between short-term gain and long-term harm. Synthetic pesticide use in the United States remained as entrenched in 2014 as it had been in 1945. This book is one attempt to understand that paradox.

CHAPTER 1

Falling in Love: The Golden Age of Synthetic Pesticides

By many measures, life was good in post–World War II America. It was truly a golden age. The United States that emerged victorious from the war was transformed in extraordinary ways politically, militarily, and economically. For many ordinary Americans, economic change was most clearly demonstrated by their ever-improving material well-being—including access to plentiful, inexpensive food. Such bounty, moreover, seemed attributable to the triumph of modern industrial agriculture, which was increasingly reliant on synthetic pesticides.

Pesticides, thus, were revolutionary. They symbolized much about American modernity, superiority in the Cold War, and the ability to control nature. Most Americans embraced the chemicals and all that they represented—one could say they fell in love. Was it inevitable that people would embrace the revolution? Or were attitudes shaped by particular political and cultural forces? This chapter seeks to answer these questions, looking especially at the role of the press in framing this nascent love story and the reasons that positive attitudes toward pesticides would prove to be enduring.

One starting point in understanding the postwar embrace of chemical pesticides is to recognize how strongly many Americans supported economic growth and new technologies. Many, including politicians such as Harry Truman, had a fundamental bias in favor of development and scientific innovation. Such a bias was as natural as the embrace of modernity, progress, and the scientific revolution. For liberals who favored environmental projects such as those that were part of the New Deal, pesticides and the modernization of agriculture were an obvious continuation of that legacy. Truman's Fair Deal agenda included large-scale dam and irrigation projects like those before World War II, and the president remained committed to the idea that human mastery over the landscape would bring prosperity to more Americans and benefit the nation as a whole in its Cold War competition with the Soviet Union.[1] Truman viewed nature pragmatically as a collection of resources waiting to be tamed and exploited.[2] Moreover, he and other American leaders worried that anything short of robust economic development could plunge the country back into its prewar depression.

The imperative of development was strong for philosophical, political, and economic reasons. Few people questioned possible environmental consequences of the chosen path. This perspective counters some of the criticisms from the late twentieth century of those who enthusiastically embraced pesticide use. Just as a certain inertia and inevitability led to the use of the atomic bomb on Hiroshima once the technology had been successfully mastered, so the discovery of chlorinated hydrocarbon pesticides compelled their use. It would have been shocking, indeed, if American policymakers had prevented the use of the atomic bomb—or the civilian adoption of synthetic pesticides.

Another aspect of the postwar embrace of synthetic pesticides was the assumption that increased agricultural output was by definition good and that this bounty was inextricably tied to modern techniques. A cursory look at the transformation of postwar farming bolstered widespread faith in new technologies. The amount produced on farms skyrocketed, dwarfing all previous output. Grain, dairy, and animal production all increased.[3] Postwar productivity rested on an array of mechanized equipment as well as mass-produced feed, seed, fertilizer, and synthetic pesticides, with pesticide use increasing tenfold from 1945 to 1972.[4] There were also genetic innovations in crops and livestock even before World War II; the most visible example was the spread of hybrid corn, going from just a few acres in Iowa in 1930, for example, to 90 percent of corn planted there a decade later.[5] These and other innovations were the natural outgrowth of the industrial ideal that had taken hold in the prewar years and begun to reshape how people viewed agriculture.[6]

The infrastructure for the widespread mechanization of agriculture in the decade after the war was great. Not only was the American chemical industry large and thriving coming out of the war but there were numerous war-surplus planes and discharged pilots who could be cheaply and easily set to work spraying chemicals over fields (and forests).[7] The complete package of modern farming, including a "bumper crop of chemicals," as described in a 1955 *New York Times* article, along with mechanization, conservation, and improved technology generally, led to a 42 percent increase in output and a 13 percent increase in food consumption for the average American compared with the period before World War II.[8]

The technological revolution in agriculture was more accessible for some than for others. Many small family farmers could not afford the heavy investment needed for the new technologies, nor did they have the vast swaths of land that made the technologies economically feasible. By 1955, total operating costs for the average farm had tripled from just fifteen years before, precipitating a decline in the number of farms and in the number of people who worked on the land. From 1939 to 1959, the number of farms in the United States fell 40 percent, and the number dropped almost another 50 percent from 1950 to 1970, while the size of an average farm went up 2 acres each year. By 1959, the earnings of the top 6 percent of farms equaled those of the bottom 94 percent. And, finally, the number of Americans employed on farms went from 25 percent in 1945 to 6 percent in 1965 to 2 percent by the end of the century.[9] Mechanized industrial agriculture took the place of the small family farms that had dominated earlier American history.

Newspaper and magazine articles did not dwell on those left out of the agricultural revolution. They lauded the ballooning output and the technology that brought it. For example, a 1946 article in the *New York Times* on Iowa's 100th birthday began with a large photo of a fertile cornfield, noting that the state enjoyed "the best corn crop prospects in history" and that farmers carried with them "cans of DDT for their cattle and pamphlets on artificial insemination for their cows."[10] Similarly, a *New York Times Magazine* photo essay three years later—titled "Another Bumper Harvest"—showcased lush fields with large threshing machines and combines.[11] One 1949 story in *U.S. News & World Report* observed that even if there was a decline in farm labor, with more machinery and new techniques, farmers raised "40 per cent more food and fiber than before the war."[12] Another article in the *New York Times* extolled wide-ranging improvements in agriculture, from new hybrids with higher outputs per acre to a more efficient use of fertilizers.[13] Although the fruits of agricultural innovation were everywhere in evidence, journalists made a point of celebrating them and thus increasing their readers' awareness of the revolution in their midst.

Press stories most often highlighted the benefits brought by mechanization. For example, an article in *Barron's* boasted that "the mechanical picker may give American cotton a new lease on life." The article went on to explain that the picker, along with the flame weeder, might bring a revolution in the South and perhaps allow the region's cotton to regain the market share that it had lost to that grown abroad and synthetics such as rayon produced at home.[14] Articles in the *Nation's Business* and *New York Times Magazine* described how mechanization in places such as Indiana had brought prosperity to average farmers, whose income and quality of life had increased since the war. Even those displaced from farm labor due to mechanization, the articles added, had new opportunities in factory jobs coming to small towns and rural America.[15]

Another way in which the press celebrated modern agricultural techniques—ranging from the development of hybrids to the more scientific management of livestock to the application of chemicals—was to describe them in almost miraculous terms. For example, a 1954 article in the *Saturday Evening Post* observed, "Airplanes swooping over a field leaving a trail of vapor of dust, are engaged in chemical warfare against crop-destroying insects. . . . You'll also see spray machines squirting selective chemicals which kill weeds but don't harm the crops."[16]

Such press articles helped to strengthen a widespread feeling of confidence in the ability of modern American farmers to produce more-than-adequate food for the nation's needs. With new technologies, new chemicals, and new science—"the factories in the fields," as described in a *Saturday Evening Post* editorial—there was little worry for Americans about the food shortages that plagued the rest of the world.[17] Even after the outbreak of the Korean War in 1950, there was no expectation of rationing or other wartime measures. As the same editorial phrased it, "Short of atomic disaster, it is hard to see how Americans can be seriously threatened by hunger."[18]

It's worth pausing to consider the impact of such confident press pronouncements. After all, if, as this chapter asserts, the mainstream press played a foundational role in the American love affair with pesticides, we cannot think of journalists as merely chroniclers of an objective reality, self-evident to all. Nor were journalists simply cheerleaders for attitudes that were inevitable. Instead, modern news media have both a political role in shaping government actions and a cultural role in establishing the common discourse of the public sphere.[19]

Despite the protests of journalists who frequently assert their independence from the political subjects about which they write, many communications scholars have observed that the relationship between media and government is, as described by Timothy Cook, "intertwined," "interactive and interdependent."[20] Thus, those with political and institutional power help determine what issues are most important, most newsworthy, by virtue of their authority. Journalists are dependent on the access and information granted by such elites, and elites are dependent on journalists to frame the discussion—and hopefully public support—that they seek. All are aware of the symbiotic relationship and the outsized role played by government sources in the news that makes its way into the public sphere.[21]

Along with government and official sources, other elite actors whose interest is to protect the status quo play an influential role in shaping the news. Communications scholar Julia Corbett argues that there is an important cultural consequence to this relationship: "Media decisions about what to publish by and large protect dominant cultural values such as existing power and class arrangements. . . . In general, there [i]s a lack of news that might appear offensive to the values of family, religion, community, patriotism, and business."[22] In this way, media sources can be seen as fairly conservative institutions due to their dependence not only on official sources but also on the advertising and other interests that support them. These relationships help to shape mainstream environmental news, as reflected in the frequency with which news media champion technological developments that favor economic and business growth.

Such an outcome stems not only from media conservatism but also from the widely held cultural assumption that technological progress and mastery over the natural world are inherent goods.[23] Those who suffer the consequences of what sociologist Ulrich Beck labeled a "risk society" have been marginalized, and only occasionally are these social and economic norms challenged in mainstream media.[24] Regarding the environment and pesticides, in particular, such examples are found when there are acute crises or events in which journalists can expose oppositional forces. As will be discussed in the following chapters, these occasions are rare, as when the chemical industry attacked Rachel Carson; Vietnam veterans were sickened by Agent Orange; or people fell dead in the streets of Bhopal, poisoned by pesticide gas.[25] In these cases, press stories seemed to challenge the protechnology ethos that supported widespread pesticide use. More often, though, mainstream news stories uphold the environmental trade-offs made in support of a modern risk society.

Coupled with the mainstream media biases in favor of elite and technological interests, the environment has proven to be an elusive subject because its "newsworthiness" is not always apparent. Most often, newsworthiness is determined by immediacy, novelty, and conflict. Environmental stories often call for complex historical and scientific context and are difficult to pin down as particular events in time.[26] The human relationship to the environment is more fluid and expansive than can always be contained within a clearly defined news story. In addition, what Timothy Cook calls the "ritual of objectivity" has often led mainstream journalists to reduce complex situations to two sides that are expected to "balance" each other—even when they are far from equal.[27]

In sum, mainstream media have often been a poor vehicle for understanding the environmental consequences of human technologies—in this case pesticides. First, the close relationship between media and government, business, and other institutions has led to the political and economic starting point that pesticides are beneficial or at least benign. A corollary assumption is that pesticides represent technological and scientific progress, which is also inherently beneficial. Second, the complexities of history and science necessary to understand the impact of pesticides have often been left out of mainstream news stories, or at least simplified into a clear binary. A third, related point is that environmental stories are often seen as not newsworthy because they may lack the requisite markers of immediacy, novelty, and conflict. Thus, it is no surprise that the press stories on pesticides surveyed in this chapter are celebratory rather than critical and encourage readers to admire the wonders of modern technology. Though it is difficult to measure the exact impact of such messages, as communications scholars have long agreed, mainstream media help to frame our cultural discourse and act as gatekeepers to what is shared in the public sphere. Thus, the news media have played a crucial role in establishing cultural attitudes toward the new synthetic pesticides of the postwar era.

Let us return to those attitudes found in the press and elsewhere in the public sphere.

It was not only journalists who expressed confidence that American agricultural technology would produce unprecedented bounty. Such assertions were also found in advertisements placed by agricultural chemical companies. Moreover, these ads linked agricultural success with the definition of modernity. For example, a 1951 Dow Chemical Company ad in the *Saturday Evening Post* read, "Modern farms depend on modern knowledge." A similar ad from Dow one year later, illustrated with beautiful close-up color drawings of fruits and vegetables, told readers that "the modern farmer and food packer have worked wonders in adding to our food supply. Today they are feeding 27 million more people than a decade ago." Such technological prowess, according to Dow, had implications for American privilege and national identity. The 1952 ad captioned the colorful produce "Food . . . Fit for an American," and the 1951 ad read, "The strength of the nation begins on the farm—and the farmer shapes the future for us all."[28]

The theme of American abundance and agricultural modernity was prominent in many advertisements and news articles in the late 1940s and 1950s, and some articles suggested to readers that a more rational use of technology could provide even greater output. For example, a 1949 article in the *New York Times Magazine* dismissed the visions of neo-Malthusians worried about the exploding worldwide population.[29] The author noted with approval that with a reduction of soil loss, replenishment of weak soils, and the application of new technologies, crop output per acre had gone up 30 percent since 1940; he confidently predicted that food production in the coming decade could go up another 50 percent, outstripping the projected population growth of 10 percent. The article highlighted a prediction by the US Department of Agriculture (USDA) that the explosion of grain grown, especially corn, which had already increased the production of meat, would continue in the future.

Even while some commentators might have worried about the dilemmas of feeding a growing world, confidence in American abundance dominated public discourse. Abundance, moreover, was inherently something to be celebrated—and was in places such as the pages of *Time* magazine, where an article concluded in 1953, "The U.S. is fast piling up the biggest agricultural surplus in history."[30] Several magazine articles in 1950 had observed with wonder that despite the conventional wisdom about food shortages during wartime, the start of the Korean War seemed to have had no effect on the mounting surpluses.[31] In numerous examples, then, journalists told their readers that the technological achievement of ongoing surpluses was an unalloyed good.

But the case was not so clear-cut when it came to the political and economic impact of such bounty. It should be noted that in some ways, the agricultural situation in the late 1940s and early 1950s was not unusual. As historian Nick Cullather has noted, the "paradox of plenty"—increased yields, decreased crop prices, and reduced earnings for farmers—was a dilemma of domestic agriculture from the 1930s to the 1970s.[32] Even though government programs beginning with the New Deal addressed the issue of stabilizing farmers' income, the surpluses remained.

Amid the celebratory articles about agricultural surpluses, many journalists could not help but remark on the double edge to this "golden glut," in the phrase of *Time* editors in 1953, or what a *Newsweek* journalist a year later called a "tyranny of plenty."[33] Press descriptions of the downsides of agricultural success almost all focused on the political and economic policies coming out of Washington—*separate* from the actual technological achievement of growing so much food. *U.S. News & World Report* observed in 1949 that there was a danger of returning to the falling commodity prices of the Depression and that "old days of superabundance are returning."[34]

The downsides of agricultural abundance were not imagined by the press. Since the end of World War I, the great expansion of commodity output had led to the collapse of grain prices and bankruptcy for countless farmers, helping to usher in, eventually, the Great Depression. One of the centerpieces of New Deal policy had been federal efforts to heal the agricultural sector through various subsidies to cut commodity production. After World War II, fears of returning to a weak agricultural sector led the Truman administration to propose the continuation of farm subsidies, but now through direct payments to farmers computed by an "income standard." This proposal put forward by Secretary of Agriculture Charles Brannan in mid-1949 engendered more controversy than support.[35] Facing charges that the proposal was too complicated and too expensive, it failed to pass Congress.

As the debate about the plan unfolded in 1949 and 1950, many articles criticized it, including some in *U.S. News & World Report*, *Fortune*, *Collier's*, *Reader's Digest*, and *Life*.[36] Press stories about the Brannan Plan and other dilemmas of postwar agriculture provide an example of how government policies were fodder for debate, whereas the technological and economic systems that created overabundance and consolidation were seldom questioned.[37] The press did *not* question the imperative to produce as much as possible or the industrial agricultural system that brought such bounty. Journalists were cheerleaders for technological success and critics of fumbling government policies.

The political dilemmas of agricultural overproduction remained a problem for the new Republican administration in 1953. Huge surpluses were still being produced when Dwight Eisenhower took office, while the price of crops had fallen and farmers' costs remained relatively fixed.[38] Although consumption in the United States had risen, it did not take the place of falling demand from abroad, and growing capacities had rebounded to prewar levels. As with earlier coverage of the agricultural sector, magazine articles continued to highlight the political and economic problems associated with agricultural surpluses, or what was referred to as a "headache" and the "farm problem."[39] The debates over Washington's agricultural policies were linked to food prices, which had increased sharply after World War II, with the greatest rates of increase between 1945 and 1947 and 1950 and 1954.[40] A spate of articles in 1953 and 1954 bemoaned the higher costs faced by housewives and also argued that the farmer was getting a declining share of food dollars.[41] Despite such sympathy for farmers, it's interesting that an unspoken assumption in these articles was that food prices *should* be low and that something was wrong when they weren't. By the early 1950s, the expectation was that booming agricultural production would continue into the foreseeable future, and food for American consumers should, therefore, remain relatively cheap.

Surveying magazine and newspaper articles about American agriculture in the late 1940s and into the 1950s leads to a few conclusions. Journalists consistently celebrated the technological success of greater output and, by implication, the broader industrial system that it represented. There seemed to be little disagreement that increased production and modern industrial agriculture were inherently good. In contrast, news stories about the political and economic side of industrial agriculture focused more on controversies over government policies, the welfare of farmers, and the price of food for consumers. Although different opinions of these issues were presented, government policies inevitably came off poorly. Thus, to the extent that mainstream press articles were influencing the opinions of their audience, the average reader was likely to believe that modern agriculture had successfully harnessed technology to improve people's lives and that bumbling government programs had not been able to properly address the political and economic implications of such bounty. In this view, agricultural technology was politically neutral and an objective good.

Amid all of the positive stories that celebrated the bounty of American technology were numerous articles that specifically extolled the virtues of

DDT and other chemicals and invited readers to use them. Before examining the positive news stories, it is important to understand how these pesticides differed from their predecessors.

In many ways, the new synthetic pesticides were products of the war: they had been refined or their use accelerated due to wartime exigencies. DDT was a chlorinated hydrocarbon, or an organochlorine. It had been synthesized in the late nineteenth century but not until 1939 were its remarkable insecticidal properties discovered by Paul Müller of the Swiss chemical company J. R. Geigy. Importantly, DDT was a persistent, broad-spectrum insecticide and had a low acute toxicity for humans. The existing insecticide, pyrethrum, used to control body lice that carried typhus was in short supply during the war, so the military began using DDT widely with great success. Other—though more toxic—organochlorines that were synthesized and used by civilians in the late 1940s and early 1950s included aldrin, dieldrin, toxaphene, and endrin.

Organophosphates were another category of insecticides adopted after World War II, and their use increased as scientists and governments moved to reduce the use of and eventually ban many of the persistent, broad-spectrum organochlorines. Organophosphates, which had been synthesized in the 1930s by a research team under Gerhard Shrader at I. G. Farben in Germany, were more acutely toxic than DDT and its cousins. The chemical-weapons potential of this category of nerve-agent insecticides was quickly apparent, and the Nazi government appointed Shrader and his team to continue research on the pesticides. One of the first organophosphates to be marketed to civilians after the war, parathion, remained one of the most widely used insecticides by the end of the twentieth century and was the cause of numerous acute poisonings.[42]

One more category of pesticides that grew from wartime research and use was the phenoxy herbicides, artificial plant hormones that overstimulated growth, thus killing the plant. The herbicides were discovered by independent teams in both the United States and the United Kingdom in 1941 and quickly transitioned to civilian use at the war's end to combat broadleaf weeds. The best-known phenoxy herbicide—and still one of the most widely used herbicides in the world at the start of the twenty-first century—was 2,4-D. It was paired with another herbicide, 2,4,5-T, to make Agent Orange, the defoliant used by the US military in the Vietnam War. The former survived the notoriety of the military campaign, but the latter was blamed for the numerous health effects associated with Agent Orange and largely banned. At the beginning of the twenty-first century, herbicides were integral to industrial agriculture, accounting for the majority of pesticide use in the United States.

The three categories of pesticides that grew from military research and use (organochlorines, organophosphates, and phenoxy herbicides) were quickly adapted to civilian use when the guns stopped. Wartime news stories had already heightened expectations among farmers and others that the chemicals were dramatically more effective and apparently less toxic than prewar, inorganic pesticides. Postwar press built upon these assumptions.

Newspaper and magazine stories about DDT and other new pesticides did not just celebrate their effectiveness—they domesticated the chemicals. Manufacturers led the way with advertisements intended for farmers and others in the agricultural industry. To emphasize the effectiveness of the pesticides, these ads detailed how much yields per acre would be increased with their use.[43] In addition to these ads in trade journals, articles and ads in mainstream publications told nonfarmers that the pesticides would more than triple agricultural output and invited consumers to identify with the chemicals. One pesticide manufacturer was quoted as saying that "housewives can kill more insects this spring and summer than ever before."[44] Press stories also highlighted other new, nonagricultural uses for pesticides such as impregnating drawer and closet lining paper with DDT.[45]

The view of DDT as a miracle cure was sometimes taken to extremes. For example, the *New York Times* told its readers in 1945 and 1946 about local governments in New Jersey, New York, and Maryland that were choosing to spray entire towns with DDT to get rid of Japanese beetles, flies, and mosquitoes. At the same time, towns in Illinois and Texas were aerially sprayed in the belief that DDT would get rid of flies believed to carry polio.[46] These stories did not raise any doubts about the wisdom or effectiveness of such schemes. Rather, they naturalized them as inventive, modern solutions to persistent problems.

The press stories about DDT from during the war and immediately after are striking for the unbridled enthusiasm and the lack of any caution or skepticism in many of the articles. Statements from the manufacturers were liberally quoted and helped to shape the positive coverage. The director of research for J. R. Geigy, a maker of DDT, for example, predicted that DDT might save 1 to 3 million lives a year from malaria and that DDT-impregnated paint and wallpaper might soon make mothballs obsolete and keep homes free of pests for several years. Stories about DDT were joined by those that extolled a new stage in pest control with an "avalanche of new compounds with striking insect-killing abilities." Many articles gave details about the new compounds steadily reaching the market: what they were best for and how they measured up against DDT.[47]

The triumphalist rhetoric in discussions about new pesticides drew on the military discourse of World War II, emphasizing the ongoing need to fight and win a *war* against pests.[48] Such sentiments were common from many sources, including government scientists. One brief newspaper article opened with a quotation from a presentation before the American Chemical Society in early 1946 by the chief insecticide chemist of the USDA's Bureau of Entomology and Plant Quarantine: "War-developed products gave man new and important weapons in his ageless war against insects, but unless we devote less of our energy to killing each other and more of it to annihilating pests, the insect may win out in the long run and inherit the earth."[49] Articles frequently referred to the "battle" against pests or the "onslaught" faced by farmers.[50] More than a decade after the end of World War II—and beyond—military rhetoric to describe the human relationship with insects continued to be frequently used. For example, one 1960 advice article for gardeners gave prescriptions against "plant enemies" and spoke about planning the use of "ammunition" against pests.[51]

It was not only journalists and USDA officials who used military rhetoric to frame the relationship between humans and insects. Manufacturers of pesticides consistently used such language in their advertisements, both those for farmers and others in the agricultural industry and those for ordinary consumers. For example, Hercules pesticide ads for those in the industry emphasized a "quick knockdown" and a "high kill."[52] In addition to the common descriptors in consumer ads of pesticides as different varieties of "killers," they were also said to thwart "invasions" and bring "doomsday" to pests.[53] Chemical companies used similar military language in pamphlets for government officials (such as one in 1956 to convince municipalities to launch spray programs against mosquitoes) and for broadcasters (such as one to accompany a public service television announcement on the threat of insect pests).[54]

In their liberal use of military rhetoric, the advertisements aimed at professionals and consumers emphasized that the new products would win the war against pests because they were highly *effective*—much more so than earlier pesticides had been. At times the manufacturers still selling some prewar pesticides even tried to piggyback their marketing on the reputation of the new formulations. For example, Hercules offered new-product combinations of its older Thanite with DDT to bring together the "kill power" of one with the persistence of the other.[55]

Importantly, the military rhetoric that permeated mainstream newspaper and magazine articles emphasized that this was a war to be waged not just by experts but by ordinary citizens as well. Thus, the combination of military rhetoric and enthusiastic celebration of pesticide effectiveness further naturalized the embrace of these chemicals and the assumption that they were unquestionably good. Moreover, naturalized chemicals were domesticated chemicals, ready for home use. Manufacturers worked to encourage the idea that these domesticated chemicals should be widely used by all consumers. For example, a 1947 Hercules ad for agricultural professionals pictured ten different people—ranging from an insecticide salesman to a hotel housekeeper to a housewife—who all liked a particular pesticide sold by the company. Another way that manufacturers emphasized the domestication message was to gender the images. Numerous ads included pictures of housewives using pesticides with ease, thus emphasizing that no expertise was needed.[56]

The message of domestication resonated with growing legions of suburbanites. The exploding numbers of suburbs in America were particularly fertile fields for new pesticide products. More than 1 million acres per year were being absorbed by suburban expansion in the 1950s, fueled by the construction of more than 15 million homes in that decade.[57] As urbanites relocated out of cities, they were presented with their own private patches of earth to tame, beautify, and conform to the model yards of their neighbors—or, as historian Christopher Sellers phrased it, to engage in a "more or less artful *rearrangement*" of nature.[58] The mysteries of accomplishing such feats were greatly simplified if one could go to the hardware store, buy a product, and use it according to the label directions. Manufacturers such as Hercules knew that this was their target audience when they boasted to wholesalers that with their ad campaign, 2.4 million consumers would be reading about their products in the pages of *Better Homes and Gardens* in July 1946.[59]

The unnatural ecosystems at the center of suburban living were exemplified by the importance placed upon the lawn. The lawn, the ultimate symbol of the efforts to domesticate nature, led to greatly increased pesticide use as well as spawning a whole economy, culture, and ideology.[60] However, taming the lawn was just one example of mastery over nature. Magazine and newspaper stories contained tantalizing visions of what an ordinary person could accomplish. For example, an article on the chemicals dieldrin and aldrin in *Coronet* tempted readers with the possibilities by reflecting the excitement of new discoveries and hubris about the power of modern science to improve on nature. The piece liberally quoted one entomologist who mused that because subsoil and surface pests had always attacked plants, "we have never really known what a *perfect* plant should be. How big will a tomato grow? How beautiful can a rose become? After thousands of years, we are just beginning to find out."[61]

The extent to which pesticides were domesticated after World War II was apparent in the newspaper and magazine articles that went beyond enthusiastic descriptions to give detailed instructions for use. Basic articles shortly after the war attempted to sort through the confusing rash of new information. For example, one in 1946 tried to reassure readers that the "enthusiastic publicity about DDT [that] has left many people with the impression that this chemical is the answer to every problem of insect control" could be confusing. The author carefully described what DDT was good for and what it was not good for.[62]

Magazines expressly for the suburban homeowner, such as *Better Homes & Gardens*, preached the gospel of pesticide use from shortly after World War II through the 1950s. For example, two articles in 1947 cheered on readers by describing—in military rhetoric—new chemicals that would "provide sure death for red spider mites" and would "blitz more bugs than last year's DDT bomb." A decade later, popular articles such as one in *American Home* still spoke of "waging a great war on bugs" with "the wonders of modern chemistry." Another in *Sunset* reminded readers to "check the arsenal" each spring to make sure that their pesticide stores were well stocked for all uses.[63] In their enthusiastic recommendations, these and other articles sometimes had a confusing message about hazards. For example, one article in *Better Homes & Gardens*, which clearly stated that DDT was harmful to humans, reassured readers that the two new products it recommended had very little DDT, so "you can use them safely anywhere."[64]

Articles with detailed explanations about chemicals were a standard feature through the 1950s.[65] A popular item in home magazines was a handy chart with separate columns and rows listing different types of vegetation, pests, diseases, and recommended chemicals.[66] The magazines were sometimes even more prescriptive, providing a basic shopping list for garden care or a cut-out chart of a "complete pesticide shelf." Similarly, articles sometimes featured a series of photos or drawings to illustrate pesticide application methods and proper care of equipment. Some articles were accompanied by large, detailed drawings of insects.[67] *Consumer Reports* couched its how-to articles in crisp, rational prescriptions of which pesticides represented the best value for the homeowner and gardener.[68]

Magazines and newspapers gave detailed descriptions of new pesticides as they became available. The enthusiasm of such profiles mirrored the tone in the original articles about DDT, giving no hint of the evidence of health and environmental dangers that would be publicized a decade later. For example, the magazine article that introduced aldrin and dieldrin as "sister miracle-workers for the housewife and back-yard farmer" asserted that the chemicals did not harm beneficial organisms in the soil, nor humans or animals. Like other articles, it included detailed application instructions for outdoor and indoor use of these "wonder drugs." At the same time, it mentioned only minimal precautions, such as not letting children walk across a wet, newly sprayed lawn. Finally, the article also advised painting the kitchen with paint impregnated with dieldrin whose insect-killing powers would last more than two years.[69]

Many articles placed great emphasis on a carefully planned schedule for lawn and garden care, as one piece in *House & Garden* summarized: "Proper timing of applications still remains the important key to success with garden insecticides."[70] For some, proper timing was synonymous with *prevention* of pest problems: "Ideal pest control is preventative—every two weeks for most plants," declared one 1958 article in *American Home.* Pesticides were not the cure for a problem but "health insurance," as one article described them.[71] "Garden Upkeep" necessitated prophylactic use of pesticides.[72]

Thus, the many articles that detailed careful, rational ways to control pests and emphasized timing and prevention all reinforced the idea that pesticides were a permanent and necessary part of lawn and garden care. This idea, in turn, encouraged naturalized chemical use and increased pesticide consumption. Magazine and newspaper articles thus were shaping popular attitudes toward pesticides and reinforcing their embrace by average Americans.

The content of the magazine articles was reinforced by ads extolling the virtues of various chemicals. "Expello" brought "sudden death to moths" but was "harmless to human beings and sweet smelling."[73] Meanwhile, the herbicide "Weedone" would bring "new, undreamed-of beauty! Spray away weeds easily, quickly, safely" in order to get "a lawn your neighbors will envy!" To emphasize the message of effectiveness and safety, the ad was illustrated with a preschool-aged girl playing on a verdant lawn.[74] An ad for "End-o-Weed" feminized the product with a cartoon drawing of a husband who manually tried to remove weeds from the lawn, only to fall over with injuries from the effort. His scantily clad, pretty wife sprayed away the problem: "No work! No weeds!"[75] There were also ads for the tools needed for the most efficient pesticide use. For example, "Hudson Sprayers and Dusters" were touted as "best for applying any pesticide."[76]

The ubiquitous primers for chemical use paid careful attention to safety—although that message was not as simple as it first appeared. One article, for example, reminded readers that the newer pesticides were not as safe as the rotenone and pyrethrum that were most common before the war. Gardeners needed to break their habit of ignoring the labels and instead read all warnings and follow directions carefully. Safety, this and other articles added, included making sure there were not excessive residues left on foods.[77]

Information about toxicity, though, was sometimes inconsistent from one magazine article to the next and changed over time. Wartime news stories about DDT emphasized its lack of toxicity. By the time that home gardeners were using it in 1947, articles instructed readers not to use it on fruits and vegetables because it was toxic to humans, but there remained no precautions about breathing or touching it. Similarly, different articles gave different information about the same chemicals. For example, one 1953 *House & Garden* article describing the then new insecticide malathion noted that it had a "low order of toxicity to man"; the same magazine a year later cautioned that malathion should "be treated with respect," that users shouldn't breathe in the dust or the spray drift and should wash well after using it.[78] Warnings about safety were often quite specific to a particular substance or method. For example, one consumer article in 1953 directly told readers not to use insecticide vaporizers in homes.[79] One article framed the issue in a way that would become familiar in the 1960s, when defenders of chemical pesticides would place most of their safety message on the importance of following directions and being careful. Misuse of pesticides, said a 1956 article in *American Home*, could be fatal, but so could the careless use of "your iodine, your razor, your stepladder, or power saw." Thus, everyone's lives and houses were full of potentially dangerous items and substances; it all depended on how they were used. Presumably, readers would never dream of giving up these useful tools, so why would they give up pesticides, their "Dangerous Friends"?[80] Moreover, these cautionary tales—read in conjunction with articles that focused on pesticides' modernity, ease of use, and necessity—were overwhelmed by the latter messages.

Even the articles that warned readers to be careful about safety never implied that there was any danger if *all* directions were followed. There was also a presumption, sometimes explicit, that the government was testing each new insecticide. For example, a brief announcement of the new pesticides dieldrin and aldrin in a 1950 *Science News Letter* noted that "each new insecticide is carefully tested by the Department of Agriculture and other agencies before the product is put on the market."[81]

Taken together, certain themes in these early postwar articles on the new pesticides stand out. First, there were detailed descriptions of new chemicals on the market and careful classifications of what product should be used for what pest. Second, this level of detail emphasized the scientific aspects of pest control and the precision with which humans could shape their personal environments. Third, the articles often contained a healthy dose of caution about hazards and the importance of following label directions. Fourth, the message of caution was overshadowed by one promising ease and simplicity, thus undermining the idea that these chemicals were dangerous. And, finally, the articles usually incorporated military rhetoric to frame the control of pests and thus built on the wartime language that first introduced DDT to the public and conveyed the urgency of the struggle against pests. As a group, these types of articles promoted the ability of individual Americans to tame their own houses and gardens by banishing pests and maintaining landscapes of their own design, and that the best way to achieve these goals was to use the modern chemicals available to them. In sum, magazine and newspaper articles—despite occasional words of caution—shaped popular attitudes toward pesticides by celebrating their effectiveness and advocating their use.

Even when there were cautions about the use of chemical pesticides, it is interesting that there were still strong presumptions about the *necessity* of their use. For example, in its June 1949 issue, *Consumer Reports* included an article criticizing the lack of adequate government safeguards to prevent misuse and overuse of DDT.[82] The article charged that warnings in USDA bulletins were sometimes too general and that those on container labels were also too general or mild. It called for sped-up research and better government regulations and enforcement and raised the issue of chronic poisoning due to ingestion of small amounts of DDT over time. Yet, despite these calls for action, the same issue of the magazine contained a detailed how-to article whose takeaway was that a variety of pesticides should be stocked at home and actively used.[83] Surprisingly, the juxtaposition of these articles had not led the writers or editors to question the necessity of pesticide use.

An intermittent theme in the press coverage about pesticides was the problem of resistance. One 1951 article in *Business Week* worried that declining effectiveness of DDT was a big concern for farmers, and a 1953 article in the same magazine said that one of the reasons the pesticide business was growing so fast was that annual marketing of new products was necessary to combat resistance.[84] The 1953 article quoted a USDA entomologist looking to the future and the use of more specific, targeted pesticides instead of more general ones, which led to more resistance. A decade later, such recommendations would be part of the popular wisdom, but they were not common in 1953.

One other theme in the press discussions of agriculture at midcentury is worth noting: amid record-breaking harvests—the fruits of American know-how—worries about the threat from insects, surprisingly, increased. There were alarmist articles in the press, written in familiar militaristic language, about the onslaught from six-legged foes and what new chemicals should be deployed to defeat them. The winter of 1950 was particularly mild, and spring brought predictions in the press of horrific crop losses to the "worst insect onslaught in years." And although "insecticide manufacturers are rushing into the breach," increasing shipments to farmers by 40 percent over the previous year, crop losses, articles warned, might reach as high as $2 billion.[85] Press stories—that year and at other times—featured close-up photos or drawings of the foes so that readers could readily identify with the fight.[86] With irony, one unusual article in *Business Week* commenting on the possible $2 billion crop loss in 1950 pointed to the contradictions of worrying about losses from insects while the government spent billions for surpluses: "The crop destroyers . . . may cut down on price support payments by eating up the crops."[87] Despite such an example of critical insight, the dominant message in numerous articles was to favor continued, unquestioned pesticide use.

Warnings about ongoing insect threats were found not just in popular newspaper and magazine articles. Trade advertisements from chemical manufacturers emphasized that insects were a great danger that "might strike anywhere."[88] Similarly, USDA officials often spoke about the ongoing threat from insect outbreaks. For example, Undersecretary of Agriculture True Morse spoke before the National Agricultural Chemicals Association meeting in 1955 to discuss the huge annual losses that persisted from weeds, diseases, and insects. He told the attendees that Americans looked to the chemical industry to address this problem. The newspaper article on the meeting adopted Morse's perspective: "The farmer—and the chemical industry—still have a long battle to fight against agricultural scourges."[89] Thus, readers learned from USDA officials, advertisers, and journalists that the war against pests was dire and likely to continue for a long time to come. Under such a threat, who would slacken their embrace of the chemicals that might bring salvation?

Conclusion

Newspaper and magazine articles from the first decade after World War II conveyed a healthy ardor for the new synthetic pesticides that were blanketing agricultural fields and suburban backyards throughout the country. The press attention to the chemicals and the agricultural progress that they represented was celebratory and often unquestioning. Similar sentiments and rhetoric came from USDA officials and the manufacturers who profited from the pesticides. Journalists were part of a mutually reinforcing discursive loop and were, in part, responsible for the enduring love story that began in the first heady years after World War II.

As with any good narrative, the story of pesticides found in the press—and in the public culture more generally—emphasized particular themes, including the importance of progress and technological advancement, the belief that increased production and efficiency were necessarily good, the need for victory over nature's pests, and the idea that the ease and safety of synthetic pesticides made them domesticated for the ordinary person. Thus, the enthusiasm for increased production and the wealth it brought was predictable and straightforward. Similarly, the embrace of scientific wonders and technological prowess was uncomplicated.

But stories are rarely simple and can often be interpreted in more than one way. The love story with pesticides was complicated from the outset. This can be seen, for example, in the way that American agriculture was described. Newspaper and magazine stories worried that there might not be enough food to feed the world, first in war-weary Europe and then in the developing world, whose population was exploding and whose resources seemed to shrink in proportion. In response, Americans seemed confident about their own agricultural know-how and their ability to continue increasing productivity; many press stories predicted that the export of new agricultural technology would feed the world. At the same time, the hopefulness about American agricultural abundance was marred both by the fear that surpluses might soon overwhelm the domestic economy, bringing debt to the government and a collapse of the farm sector, and by the irrational fear that threatening insect hordes might diminish that abundance.

Such concern about the double-edged impact of agricultural success was not the only challenge to the pesticide love story. As the next chapter will discuss, challenges came from all sides and sometimes from unexpected directions.

CHAPTER 2

Trouble in Paradise: The USDA and the Rise of Critical Voices

The appeal of synthetic pesticides was seductive. They seemed to be dramatically effective, modern, easy to use, safe, and inexpensive. Yet, almost immediately, there were some who challenged this narrative. From the end of World War II on, there were individuals, activists, and scientists who criticized the quick adoption of agricultural chemicals because of questions about their safety and their declining effectiveness over time. Moreover, some challenged the assumption that nature could be manipulated by human will. What would be the result of these challenges? Would they moderate or curtail pesticide use?

This chapter addresses these questions, examining the arguments made against pesticides in the years before Rachel Carson published *Silent Spring* and considering whether or not they had a lasting impact. The USDA was the most consistent voice (aside from chemical companies) defending pesticides against criticisms, and, thus, the role of the USDA provides a window into the arguments that were made to quiet the growing clamor of critical voices as well as into the justifications used to strengthen the embrace of pesticides. By the late 1950s, although criticisms of pesticides had greatly increased since 1945, they had not done much to dislodge industrial agricultural systems or the expectation that people could effectively control the environment through chemicals. In this first set of challenges to pesticides, the chemicals triumphed.

As discussed in chapter 1, popular knowledge about and interest in pesticides was great by 1945—largely due to extensive and overwhelmingly positive newspaper and magazine stories. The publicity even moved some citizens to write to their congressmen and senators asking for information about where they might acquire the "wonderful insecticide used by the army."[1] Farmers, gardeners, and those wanting their towns to be generally sprayed for mosquitoes wrote to Washington. Invariably, the congressmen forwarded the letters to the USDA to help them draft appropriate responses. The earliest of these—signed by Secretary of Agriculture Clinton Anderson or his assistant Charles Brannan—emphasized that almost all available DDT was still needed by the military in 1945. The responses also contained a mild admonition that DDT should be used only when properly prepared and with caution because it was a poison.[2] Such USDA caution was in evidence in other public forums. In October 1945, the chief of the Bureau of Entomology and Plant Quarantine, Dr. P. N. Annaud, spoke at the National Audubon Society convention, explaining that much still had to be learned about the health and environmental safety of DDT before the USDA could recommend its widespread use on food or forage crops.[3]

Another example of cautious optimism from the government agency was reflected in a query from a *Newsweek* editor, E. Tomlinson, who was preparing "DDT and Your Community" for an upcoming issue in mid-1946. In response to publicity about DDT and its rapid adoption, *Newsweek* sought to clear up misconceptions about the chemical for amateur gardeners and others. Tomlinson noted that both he and the undersecretary knew that DDT was "*not* a panacea for all pest control problems."[4] Although it's unlikely that any USDA officials viewed DDT as a miracle cure-all, it is still difficult to find any indication that they doubted the chemical's ultimate value, although testing of its effectiveness was ongoing. For example, by 1946, one response from Secretary Anderson to Senator Robert Wagner observed that because responsible agencies had been using DDT for fly control, "it was inconceivable that its efficacy can be questioned."[5]

Agency messages to ordinary citizens sometimes emphasized caution more than confidence. For example, when DDT first became available for civilian use in September 1945, agency statements said it should be used only in small areas, that formulations should be carefully checked, that it should be washed off if it came in contact with skin, and that sprayed fruits and vegetables should be washed. Statements from the USDA's Bureau of Entomology and Plant Quarantine also told gardeners that they should not see DDT as a panacea.[6] Nevertheless, the timidity of the recommendations is apparent when compared with those coming from other government agencies. Officials from the Department of the Interior, for example, were more worried about the implications of civilian use of DDT. The director of the Fish and Wildlife Service wrote to Secretary of the Interior Ickes in September 1945 that "uncontrolled broad-scale use of DDT may be a serious threat to fish populations, both game and commercial species, and to birds and mammals."[7]

Beyond the immediate postwar period, the USDA continued to receive many queries about the effects of synthetic pesticides. In contrast to the earliest responses, by about mid-1947, agency officials became more consistently reassuring and confident about the necessity of using synthetic pesticides. Responses from the assistant secretary, the undersecretary, or the chief of the Bureau of Entomology and Plant Quarantine argued that when DDT was used according to the directions and in the concentrations needed for particular uses, it would not be harmful to humans or animals. Even if people consumed fruits or vegetables with residue or ate livestock from treated pastures, there would undoubtedly be no injury.[8] Interestingly, as USDA officials became stronger supporters of the use of synthetic pesticides within a few years of the war, officials from the Department of the Interior became more cautious. For example, in August 1950, Secretary of the Interior Oscar Chapman wrote to Secretary of Agriculture Charles Brannan with concern about the "promiscuous use" of the new chemicals.[9]

In their responses to citizen complaints about the safety of chemical pesticides, USDA officials charged that one of the causes of the unnecessary worry was "irresponsible stories" in the press, as Annaud argued in spring 1948.[10] Criticizing press articles charging that DDT upset the "balance of nature," Annaud countered that nature was "out of balance when there are extensive outbreaks of insect pests."[11] A year later, Undersecretary A. J. Lowland twice responded to Senator Irving Ives that the senator's constituents had been influenced by "sensational and misleading articles," citing in particular ones in the *New York Post* by Albert Deutsch, and that reports of contamination of milk due to spraying of grazing fields and dairy barns could not be substantiated.[12]

USDA responses to complaints about pesticides from beekeepers also illustrated the agency's policy to support growing use of the chemicals and to reassure citizens about their safety. For example, in response to 1945 resolutions from the National Federation of State Beekeepers Associations protesting bee losses from pesticides, the assistant to the secretary merely said that the USDA was investigating the issue with respect to DDT—even though some agency scientists at the time were raising the same worry about the effects on bees.[13] Over the next few years, the USDA told beekeepers that if the chemical was used according to directions—in the right concentrations, on the right crops, and at the right time—then it was less damaging to bees than were the arsenical pesticides widely used before the war. In the end, though, Undersecretary Lowland asserted to a beekeeper in 1950 that it was inevitable that insecticides would sometimes have to be used to save a crop even if it meant destroying pollinators.[14]

By the early to mid-1950s, USDA responses to citizen queries or complaints about pesticides contained common themes. First, there were frequent references to the necessity of various chemicals for one purpose or another. There were no examples questioning the use of chemical pesticides or whether agriculture in the United States could function without them. Such views were illustrated in a letter from Undersecretary True Morse in September 1954 when he explained that pesticides "are essential in the endless fight against insects, weeds and rodents."[15]

Second, USDA officials continued to emphasize, as they had done from 1945 on, the importance of following label directions. Increasingly, the use of the term "careless" seemed to imply that the blame for any ill effects lay with the user, not the product. For example, in 1952, Assistant Secretary B. T. Hutchinson responded to the concerns of a citizen about the ill effects of pesticides, specifically referring to an article published in the *Journal of the American Medical Association* on vaporizing devices for pesticides. He wrote back to the congressman who had forwarded the letter that "there would appear to be no danger to human health involved in the use of these vaporizing devices as long as the approved directions for use are followed." In addition, he asserted that the fault lay with users: "[The] greatest danger is from carelessness and the improper use of such materials."[16] In subsequent decades, the emphasis on carelessness would continue to be a prominent theme when USDA officials and others defended pesticides.

Another frequent rhetorical strategy was to compare pesticides with other commonly used products that had the potential to harm people. Undersecretary Morse summed up this perspective in 1954: "We regret that accidents occur with pesticides as they do with drugs, spot removers, silver polishes, lye and a host of other common household items. . . . Accidents with pesticides could be prevented by strict compliance with the precautionary label on the part of the person handling or storing the material."[17] Placing the blame for any problems on "carelessness" was also a favorite theme of the pesticide industry from the mid-1940s onward. For example, a 1948 article in the trade journal *Agricultural Chemicals* bemoaned how "the manufacturer is too often criticized for the misdeeds of persons who misuse his products."[18] To be sure, in written materials that came with pesticides, manufacturers were careful to provide detailed instructions to those who used their products, including cautions about toxicity.[19] So their frustration if users did not abide by such warnings was understandable, and the USDA adopted the perspective of the manufacturers in this regard.

Two more common themes in USDA responses to complaints about pesticides referred to the role of the federal government, and especially the USDA, in pesticide regulation. USDA officials asserted that existing government regulations under the 1947 Federal Insecticide, Fungicide, and Rodenticide Act (FIFRA) supplied all necessary regulations because under the law, administered by the Plant Pest Control Branch at USDA, all pesticides shipped interstate had to be registered with the agency and include proper labeling and directions.[20]

But officials were also quick to assert that their jurisdiction under FIFRA was limited. According to the federal law, products made and sold within one state were not subject to any federal regulation, even if claims on their packages were erroneous.[21] In addition, USDA officials made it clear that in the agency's regulation of interstate commerce, it was empowered to prohibit products only if they were ineffective or not properly labeled. Undersecretary Morse wrote to Senator Thomas Kuchel in 1954, for example, "There is no provision in the Federal law which permits this Department to prohibit the marketing of a pesticide provided it is properly labeled."[22] Another letter from Morse a year earlier further illustrated that the philosophy behind FIFRA was about efficacy and labeling, not safety: "Even though a product may be inherently prone to misuse which may cause serious health hazard to the public it must be registered," providing it was effective and properly labeled. Morse explained that registration was an affirmation that a product met legal requirements but was not an endorsement by the USDA.[23] USDA officials freely admitted that "no federal legislation or regulation . . . directly governs the spraying of crops with insecticides."[24] USDA officials were certainly accurate in asserting that the impact of FIFRA was limited, as manufacturers had to do little more than submit accurate formulations and labeling to the agency to assure registration.

A brief survey of the status of pesticide regulations in the 1940s and 1950s bears out the USDA contention that FIFRA was limited in scope and that responsibility for regulation was fragmented among different government agencies. The Food, Drug, and Cosmetic Act of 1938—which regulated the interstate shipment of adulterated or contaminated products or those with illegal residue—was under the jurisdiction of the Food and Drug Administration (of the Food Security Administration in the Department of Health, Education, and Welfare), and the USDA referred exaggerated claims in pesticide ads to the Federal Trade Commission. One USDA official reminded a congressman in 1954 who forwarded constituent concerns about pesticide-contaminated milk that this was an issue that should be dealt with by the Food and Drug Administration and the Public Health Service.[25]

Although the state of pesticide regulations remained weak, there were some changes following lengthy hearings in a House Select Committee chaired by James Delaney regarding chemicals (including pesticides) in foods.[26] In a pattern that would be repeated in later years, chemical manufacturers and farm lobbyists objected to the hearings, asserting that existing legislation was sufficient to protect Americans. Although the hearings received a lot of publicity and spanned the 1950 and 1951 sessions, their impact was narrow, resulting in just two amendments to the federal Food, Drug, and Cosmetic Act of 1938, which regulated the interstate shipment of adulterated or contaminated products.[27]

First was the Pesticide Control Amendment (the Miller Amendment after Representative A. L. Miller), which mandated that the USDA could not register any pesticide for use that left residues on foods unless the Food and Drug Administration (FDA) had determined a safe tolerance level for such residue. On the one hand, this could be seen as a measure of protection for human health and a way to give power over pesticides to an agency other than the USDA. On the other hand, it codified the idea that it was acceptable for pesticide residues to remain on food that people ate—as long as the residues fell below a supposedly safe limit. Moreover, the regulation applied only to pesticides deliberately applied to food, not to chemicals such as herbicides sprayed on the ground around crops. Finally, the amendment did not resolve issues of accountability because it allowed USDA officials to further assert that they were not wholly responsible for the regulation of pesticides.[28]

Within the USDA, the passage of the Miller Amendment also prompted the realization that further coordination among divisions within the department was needed. Director of the Crops Regulatory Programs Avery Hoyt headed an informal task force of various USDA officials to act as a clearinghouse for new questions that arose regarding administration of FIFRA following passage of the Miller Amendment. The ad hoc group began meeting in spring 1955 in response to an alarmed letter from the dean of the New York State College of Agriculture at Cornell University to Undersecretary True Morse. Dean William Myers predicted that the Miller Amendment would present serious problems for farmers as well as agricultural colleges. He called on the USDA to provide leadership on the issue of spray residues. Myers was worried about whether then-current spray schedules were in compliance with the new law and about ensuring that farmers' crops did not get confiscated due to excessive residues. The Miller Amendment was, Myers wrote, "a real emergency, and I trust we will be able to meet it by united and intelligent action."[29]

The other amendment to the Food, Drug, and Cosmetic Act, the Food Additives Amendment, came four years later. This contained what came to be known as the Delaney Clause, which banned any carcinogenic food additives; although there were ambiguities as to whether it addressed deliberate or inadvertent additives, it became a tool used by the FDA to ban pesticides that left residues on foods if they were known carcinogens.

Overall, responses from USDA officials to questions about pesticide use and regulation were reassuring with respect to the general safety and necessity of pesticides, careful to point out that the department was not wholly responsible for this issue, and sometimes dismissive of comments from ordinary citizens. For example, Undersecretary Morse assumed that the complaints of a Utah woman who wrote of ill effects of insecticide spraying in her area were imagined or unrelated to the chemicals.[30] Another citizen a year later concerned about DDT contamination in milk elicited the response from Assistant Secretary J. Earl Coke that there was no evidence of even "a single case of illness in man caused by repeated exposures to small amounts of DDT."[31] And, finally, amid their reassurances about the benefits of modern pesticides, USDA officials sometimes sidestepped the actual issues of concern raised by citizens. For example, when the vice president of a local organic gardening club in Colorado wrote to his senator protesting aerial spraying for grasshoppers, a "reckless and irresponsible action being perpetuated on an unsuspecting public" by government officials and pesticide manufacturers, the answer from Assistant Secretary Coke simply asserted that grasshoppers were a serious problem in Colorado and that insecticides were necessary.[32]

At this moment of regulatory reform, when there was great potential to challenge the growing dominance of chemical agriculture, not a lot changed. Pesticides were not limited, and government power to regulate them remained weak and fragmented. The USDA, whose officials had been cautious about the domestication of DDT and its cousins in 1945, had become an advocate for their use and a critic of those who questioned their safety. Here was an example of how the embrace of pesticides endured even when it was challenged.

Perhaps it was not surprising that USDA officials were defensive about criticisms regarding pesticide safety. In addition to the political challenges raised by congressional hearings and legislative amendments and to letters from individual citizens, others were questioning pro-pesticide assumptions, including scientists and physicians. One of the earliest organizations to raise questions in public about the safety of DDT was the American Medical Association (AMA). In spring 1949, articles in the press questioned whether or not DDT residues in food supplies were causing mild human poisoning. The AMA joined the debate by having a representative announce at the annual meeting of the American Chemical Society in March 1949 that it would establish a special committee to study the problem.[33] The presumption of the AMA was that pesticide use had been adopted too quickly. The AMA spokesman at the American Chemical Society meeting observed that manufacturers had "placed powerful pesticides on the market for general use before compiling full information about their toxicity." A year later, the AMA Pesticide Committee warned the public that there had been 198 documented cases of poisoning by the new insecticides HETP, TEPP, and parathion and that they should be used with caution.[34] This standing committee of the AMA remained in existence the following year, when it issued yet another tepid word of caution, telling the public not to be careless with DDT or to spray edible parts of a plant, or cattle shortly before slaughter.[35] The AMA was clearly concerned, though not leading any crusade against widespread pesticide use.

Nevertheless, AMA criticisms were taken note of elsewhere in the press. One article in *Hygia* in 1949, for example, asked "Are Pesticides Making Your Food Unsafe?"—referring to the AMA warning against indiscriminate use.[36] Although the article concluded that "the situation [of residues on food] is dangerous," it did not condemn pesticide use outright because "pesticides like fire are both useful and dangerous."

Along with the AMA, other organizations raised questions about pesticide use. In 1949, a ten-day meeting at the United Nations (UN) headquarters of the International Technical Conference on the Protection of Nature included many papers with a variety of opinions on DDT and other new insecticides.[37] The conference ended with a call for a permanent standing committee on pesticides formed by the UN's Food and Agriculture Organization (FAO), World Health Organization, and Educational, Scientific, and Cultural Organization as well as the recommendation that spray airplanes and powerful sprayers not be available to private individuals without special permission and scientific controls by an official body.

Such criticisms from the UN and the AMA made the news in mainstream magazines and newspapers. This coverage made it clear that although articles that celebrated the use of synthetic pesticides predominated in news about the issue, some articles were more skeptical about the new wonder chemicals, even as early as 1944.[38] For instance, *New York Times* journalists in 1945 wrote about when DDT failed to work against particular insect populations, when it may have caused unexpected fish kills, and when bees might have been harmed by it.[39] Another example is found in *Better Homes & Gardens* two years later, when an article described how a DDT application intended to kill mites ended up leaving them unharmed but killed off the natural enemies of the pests.[40]

After more than a decade of widespread use, debates about the downsides of synthetic pesticides became more common in the public sphere. The contributions of Yale professor Albert Worrell represent an attempt to engage in a genuine debate on the issue. The associate professor of forest economics published a lengthy examination in the journal *American Forests* in July 1960, "Pests, Pesticides and People."[41] His article was sponsored by the Conservation Foundation and published by the American Forestry Association. Although he asserted that it was his intention to provide a balanced discussion, in the end, he favored continued pesticide usage patterns. In his frank acknowledgment of the toxicity of some pesticides and his admission that this could not be judged just by the immediate effects because a slow buildup in animal tissues over time could affect reproduction and other health issues, he was clearly not an uncritical booster. But in his emphasis on the idea that the "poison is in the dose" ("since table salt is also lethal in large quantities") and on the need to perform a rational cost/benefit analysis to determine whether or not pesticides should be used, he sounded like strident critics of Rachel Carson and environmentalism would just a couple of years later. He wrote that carelessness was most often the cause of poisonings and that as long as reasonable precautions were taken, there was no evidence that people would be poisoned by current exposure levels.

In his effort to take stock of the debate over pesticides, Worrell observed that agriculture, forestry, and related interest groups had predictably emphasized the damage caused by insects and the need to control them while nature, wildlife, organic gardening, and similar groups had emphasized the side effects of the pesticides but paid little attention to the insect problem. He asserted that the latter groups had "served a useful function" in encouraging debate over important issues.[42]

Observations about the pesticide issue also changed in the popular press. In contrast to the articles of the immediate postwar years, those published in the mid- and late 1950s sometimes had a more nuanced discussion of pesticides. Pesticides were no longer the surprising miracle substances of the immediate postwar period. They were naturalized as part of the modern agricultural system and were tools that the mature homeowner used to wrestle his suburban landscape into submission. News articles freely acknowledged that pesticides were dangerous. Danger, though, asserted manufacturers quoted in the articles, was most often found when people did not use the chemicals as directed.

A *Saturday Evening Post* article from 1956 provides an example of how magazine stories both highlighted the dangers of pesticides and were nevertheless decidedly favorable toward their use.[43] "Bad Year for Bugs"—with the intriguing subtitle "Insect pests don't stand a chance against lethal new insecticides, which first were used to kill people, and sometimes still do"—began with three dramatic photos: one of a worker in extensive protective clothing and a gas mask spraying in a greenhouse, one of two scientists in a lab watching mosquitoes bite one of their arms, and a close-up of a mournful-looking little girl who apparently had suffered from malathion poisoning but recovered completely. Far from scaring readers away from pesticide use, the article described the evolution of the new class of organophosphates from Nazi nerve gas, meaning the highly effective agents needed to be used with proper precautions. The article began with the story of a deadly outbreak of encephalitis in California's Central Valley and the need to kill the mosquitoes that carried it. The article also described many examples of human "carelessness" that had led to "tragedies" all over the country. In affirming that carelessness was to blame for the accidents, the author also noted that too much of many substances could poison someone, even "common salt," and concluded that the benefits of organophosphates were "incalculable."

Other articles that acknowledged the possible danger of pesticides also laid the responsibility of preventing poisoning on the individual and condemned carelessness. Different examples of commonly used substances that could be lethal in high enough doses were also given. Along with table salt, aspirin was a frequently cited example.[44]

There were more ponderous magazine articles about pesticide use that were not anti-pesticide but instead framed the issue as an unresolvable dilemma. Ralph Martin in *Harper's Magazine* asked "How Much Poison Are We Eating?" in 1955.[45] At the outset, he introduced the tremendous increase in agricultural production from pesticide use as well as the lax safety regulations that governed the field. But he reasoned, "With the exception of the really convinced believer in compost, or 'organic' gardening, few people deny the importance of insect poisons in checking pests." His observations about the naturalization of pesticide use and the as yet unexplored questions of chronic health effects were keen. Regarding DDT, he wrote, "Here is an insecticide that had been almost wholly integrated into our way of life, as familiar as orange juice." (An article by a different journalist a year later likened the omnipresence of DDT to that of toothpaste.[46]) In terms of health effects, Martin wrote, "The reason for all this anxiety is not the microscopic bit of insecticide residue on any one apple you eat. It is fear of the unknown cumulative effect, the long-range build-up inside your body of the vast variety of toxic materials that may crop up in every meal."

To explain the usual disregard for the question of chronic toxicity, he quoted Dr. Morton Biskind, who had written in *American Journal of Digestive Diseases*, "No matter how lethal a poison may be for all forms of animal life, if it doesn't kill human beings instantly [then we think] it is safe. . . . [But the increasing use of insecticides was] the most intensive campaign of mass poisoning in known human history." To be sure, Martin's questions were not unique, but they were rare when most of the public discussion around pesticides focused on acute toxicity. Yet, despite Martin's critical insights, he affirmed that all except fringe organic types knew pesticides to be necessities.

Criticisms of pesticide use from different quarters continued to build. *American Mercury* ran an article in mid-1956 beginning with the image of a skull and crossbones next to the title.[47] Author Jack Scott explained that DDT was a neurotoxin, listed by the AMA as causing hyperexcitability, tremors, spastic or flaccid paralysis, and convulsions. He criticized the fact that before the Miller Amendment, the burden of proof had rested with the government to prove that a pesticide was harmful instead of with the manufacturer to prove that a pesticide was safe. Scott noted that one of the problems with the quick adoption of various pesticides was that substances originally thought not to be harmful had been discovered to be so. He cited beta-hexachlorocyclohexane (BHC) as having been introduced with great fanfare as "harmless to humans" only to be found to cause cancerous growths in test animals and thus be taken off food crops.[48] Scott gave some of the blame for contaminated food to consumers who were addicted to modern food systems: "We're conditioned to the easy way of life, to the instant mixes and drinks, to the quick work-saving way of doing things." Two years later, *American Mercury* ran another story by a different author that was an even more detailed and damning condemnation of synthetic pesticides. Also headlined with a skull and crossbones, the article by William Longgood described the serious and extensive health effects of DDT as well as the political and regulatory history of responses since World War II.[49]

Magazines such as *Outdoor Life*, directed at those interested in nature and conservation, became increasingly concerned about pesticides by the late 1950s. Readers of *Field & Stream*, for example, were reminded that there was confusion and differing opinions on this issue. One short article in 1957—headlined with a skull and crossbones raining granules over an unsuspecting bird—noted that ever since World War II, "the interested public had been alternately alarmed and reassured by reports on the indirect effects of spraying originating from one source or another."[50]

Two years, later, the skeleton figure of death was pictured spraying pesticides over the land in a *Field & Stream* article that described the unusually controversial meetings of the National Wildlife Federation and the Wildlife Management Institute, both of which had various presentations on pesticides and their effects on game populations.[51] Magazine editor Harold Titus ended up endorsing the idea that pesticide use should continue but that much more research on its effects was needed. Nevertheless, he rejected the idea that pesticides should be abandoned: "Those wildlifers who want to ban use of all the newer pesticides are not realistic and are just banging their heads against a stone wall."

In articles such as these in the late 1950s, journalists were primarily encouraging their readers to be cautious about pesticide use. They presented their assessments as antidotes to unthinking attitudes that were heedless of the dangers inherent in the chemicals. But they did not challenge the overall status quo of industrial agriculture or a technological approach to manipulating the environment. In fact, these articles advocated continued pesticide use and ridiculed those who thought otherwise.

In the late 1950s and early 1960s, four highly visible, failed pesticide campaigns became symbols of growing unease over the environmental and health effects of the chemicals. These were events that captured the public imagination, were widely covered in the press, and started to raise serious questions about pesticides. But, in the end, they failed to fundamentally challenge ideas about the human role in nature; instead, the news stories told readers that poorly designed government programs and careless commercial growers were at fault, not the chemicals themselves or the goal of having mastery over the natural world. Two of these stories were about massive government initiatives, and two were about commercial use of pesticides impacting human food.

The two large USDA spraying programs that began to make national headlines in 1957 were the campaigns to eradicate the fire ant in the Southeastern states and the gypsy moth in the Northeastern, Mid-Atlantic, and Midwestern states. For many reasons, the negative image of these two campaigns was not surprising. Their grandiose scale demonstrated hubris and overreach; they sought not just to control but to eradicate on a vast scale. The methods imposed by a federal Big Brother left many feeling powerless, with aerial spraying spreading poisons far and wide. The programs' cost was enormous and their failures highly visible in dramatic wildlife kills after the same land was repeatedly sprayed.

The plan to eradicate the gypsy moth was not new in the United States, as there had been intermittent efforts to stamp out the European insect accidentally released in Massachusetts in 1869. A large-scale campaign involving the spraying of arsenical pesticides in the last decade of the nineteenth century had failed to achieve its goals, leading to a renewed effort against the moth in the early twentieth century. After World War II, the campaign against the insect continued with the new weapon of DDT, and when it, too, proved less than successful, the USDA planned to greatly increase its program. By 1955, the effort to eradicate the moth had escalated, and pilots were paid by the number of gallons used. They were thus perfectly willing to repeatedly overspray particular swaths of land. In 1957, an even larger program was launched by the USDA and coordinated with state agencies in New York, Pennsylvania, New Jersey, and Michigan to spray more than 3 million acres of forest. Spraying was also carried out in Connecticut and other states.[52]

The objections to the programs were not just rhetorical. In the case of the gypsy moth campaign, the USDA had the ill fortune to send spray planes over Brookhaven, Long Island, where one of the nation's foremost ornithologists, Dr. Robert Cushman Murphy, lived. Murphy organized neighbors to sue in federal court to stop the campaign.[53] Murphy also organized the Committee against Mass Poisoning (CAMP) as a special committee of the New York Zoological Society and thus raised tax-deductible contributions for the opposition campaign.[54] In his many statements to the press (including participation in a televised debate), Murphy described the harm to wildlife; the number of fish, birds, and other animals killed; and the crops damaged. He described this issue as a direct threat to human health: "How many Long Islanders are right now swallowing vegetables and fruits similarly filled up with a debilitating and cumulative poison?" He also raised the emotional stakes by likening pesticide threats to those from radiation: "'Tolerance' of DDT, as of radioactive substances, properly begins not as seven parts per million or any other arbitrary figure, but at zero."[55] He left no doubt of "the social irresponsibility" of the USDA program and stated that, although they liked to deny it, government officials—not ordinary citizens—should have the burden of proof that the campaign did no harm. Most criticisms of pesticides continued to focus on acute effects (as they would do in the future), but in this case, Murphy argued that chronic effects were actually the more significant question: "Don't fear that the DDT we are ingesting will strike us down abruptly, as it did the caterpillar-eating cukoo [*sic*]. Not at all; it will merely weaken our resistance to other ills and shorten our lives, especially if we are not young."[56]

Other scientists also protested the gypsy moth campaign. One biologist and biochemist from Maryland, E. E. Pfeiffer, sent a letter and paper to his congresswoman explaining why aerial DDT spraying in the gypsy moth campaign was "a potential health hazard to the innocent." He reasoned that even if DDT had been beneficial when it first came into use, "its disadvantages have shown up so clearly that one wonders how anybody can still be in favor of its use." Outlining the most important arguments that would be made against DDT in the 1960s, Pfeiffer wrote that the key problems from DDT use were insect resistance, accumulation in fat cells, and destruction of beneficial and predatory insects. In terms of human health, Pfeiffer, like Murphy, raised the issue of chronic accumulation in people and the unknown effects of DDT working in combination with other chemicals in human bodies. And, in a preview of the images that Rachel Carson would make famous in her 1962 book, Pfeiffer wrote that "the day before the spraying, there was the spring song of all the song birds; the day after—almost dead silence."[57]

Following the federal court's finding in June 1958 that the federal and state governments had the right to aerially spray for the gypsy moth, spraying continued with the concession that a new, non-DDT spray would be used in dairy-farming areas and that the spray areas would be smaller. The fourteen plaintiffs led by Murphy and including the son of Theodore Roosevelt, Archibald Roosevelt, appealed up to the Supreme Court after the Second Circuit Court of Appeals ruled that the issue of an injunction was moot because the USDA said it did not plan to repeat the spraying. The Supreme Court denied hearing the case in March 1960.[58]

Robert Murphy's message was echoed in contemporaneous press stories that were not about his group or the court case in particular but that repeated details about the wildlife devastation wrought by the aerial DDT spraying.[59] Other press stories were less critical of the program, and still others were sympathetic with the aim of the USDA to control the destructive pest but critical of the execution of the government campaign.[60] For example, one 1958 story in *Outdoor Life* called the gypsy moth campaign successful in terms of pest control but noted that many sportsmen were alarmed at the fish kills in its wake.[61] The same column also described the fire ant campaign, reprinting the erroneous rhetoric from the USDA to justify the massive effort: "This ant does ruinous damage to growing crops and fruit trees, gangs up on and devours newly born calves and pigs, chases hens off nests and eats their broods." The story raised questions about the use of such potent pesticides as heptachlor and dieldrin, worrying about the impact on fish and game. *Nature Magazine* ran an editorial in 1958 saying that it had warned about the widespread use of DDT in 1945 and now had been proven right.[62] Citing the escalating production of more powerful pesticides, the editors condemned the ill effects on human health and the more spectacular devastation of wildlife. The editors credited the publicity given the gypsy moth and fire ant campaigns with the final public awakening to these dangers.

The publicity about the gypsy moth campaign, in turn, touched off more generalized criticism about pesticides and their effects. For example, a 1958 article in the *Nation* described the court challenge to the gypsy moth campaign but also gave details about the fatty-tissue storage of DDT in humans and listed the serious diseases and cancers that some doctors charged were caused by DDT.[63] The author, David Cort, pointed out that following two years of testimony in 1951 and 1952 before the House Select Committee concerning the use of chemicals, Congress had had detailed information about the effects of DDT for years. Interestingly, despite the satirical disdain with which Cort described the gypsy moth campaign and the defense offered up by government officials in the Long Island trial, he nevertheless would not go so far as to reconsider the necessity of pesticides or the agricultural system that had spawned them. He allowed that some pesticides when used properly would be washed off crops before harvest and that the public demanded blemish-free food, so "the pesticide, properly used, is indispensable to the job of feeding the world." In this magazine article and in others of the time, even criticisms of how pesticides were used still asserted that they were necessary.

Although the campaign against the fire ant had some similarities to that against the gypsy moth—it was a massive effort undertaken by the USDA to eradicate an insect—it also had some differences with the program in the Northeast and Midwest. The fire ant had been inadvertently imported into the United States around 1918, landing first in Mobile, Alabama. Within forty years, it had spread to some 20 to 30 million acres, though in all likelihood it would remain in the Southeast due to climatic restrictions. Although the USDA asserted otherwise once it decided to launch its eradication campaign in 1957, there was little evidence that the fire ant harmed humans or wildlife or that it was any more than a minor nuisance in agriculture when farmers had to work around large ant mounds in their fields. The campaign was accompanied by lurid propaganda films and pamphlets exaggerating the fire ant menace. Ironically, the decision to launch the eradication campaign was made just as public criticism over the gypsy moth campaign was growing.

From 1958 to 1962, the USDA sprayed more than 20 million acres in nine states with dieldrin and heptachlor. Although these insecticides were many times more toxic than DDT, the ants were not eradicated.[64]

Criticisms of both programs came from many quarters, including environmentalists, scientists, gardeners, and the mainstream press. For example, the director of the Welder Wildlife Foundation and former US Fish and Wildlife Service (FWS) official Clarence Cottam wrote to the secretary's office at the USDA that in his twenty-five years with the FWS, he had never seen such a poorly handled program with "such a lack of intellectual honesty." Even while they defended the goals of the fire ant program, current members of the FWS and the Department of the Interior criticized the methods used and worried about the public criticisms that both Interior and USDA would face if there were large losses of fish and wildlife.[65]

With increasing debates over these two programs, the divergent views of the Agriculture and Interior departments were obvious by the end of the decade. The assistant secretary of the interior was up-front about this as he answered a congressman's query in 1959, explaining that the departments had "different interpretations" of studies that investigated pesticide effects on wildlife. Although he agreed that harmful pests had to be controlled, he argued that wildlife was not being adequately protected from pesticides.[66] Two years later, the secretary of the interior wrote to a senator that conservationists were concerned about the harmful effects of pesticides, including increasing bird mortality from the Dutch elm spray program.[67] Outside Washington, many news publications had stories critical of the gypsy moth and fire ant programs, including *Field and Stream*, the *New York Times*, *Reader's Digest*, *Saturday Evening Post*, *Life*, and *Sports Illustrated*. The method of aerial spraying also came in for particular complaint.[68] Thus, some magazine and newspaper stories were encouraging a negative public image of the government programs.

As the criticisms of the gypsy moth and fire ant campaigns heated up in the press, USDA officials faced an increasing number of complaints about these programs from individual citizens, forwarded from various congressmen. Responses from agency officials early on (in 1957) cast doubt on the reported damage from spraying and said that the gypsy moth program was being carried out with careful planning and specific guidelines. Among the complaints was a telegram from the governor of New York, Averell Harriman, saying that there had been widespread fish kills in three counties following gypsy moth spraying. The response of Assistant Secretary Ervin L. Peterson was that the situation would be investigated but that pilots had been specifically told to avoid spraying near bodies of water. Increasingly, USDA responses to complaints followed a formula that included descriptions of the discovery of DDT in World War II, how it had successfully stopped dangerous epidemics of typhus and malaria while being applied directly to the skin of soldiers, and how it had a long history of safe use since then.[69] Like the responses to complaints about spraying for Dutch elm disease, officials asserted that when pesticides were used according to USDA recommendations, there was little or no loss of wildlife.[70]

USDA responses to criticisms of the fire ant program also became formulaic.[71] Since the two pesticides used in the fire ant program were many times more toxic than was DDT, the responses were changed accordingly from those in response to gypsy moth letters the previous year. Assistant Secretary Peterson, among others, emphasized that every precaution was taken in the application of the program to minimize any effects on wildlife and that the program was in response to the major threat posed by the fire ant in nine Southern states. USDA responses repeated the assertion that the ant was a threat to both rural and city dwellers and that citizens had demanded that action be taken against the threat. And, putting the program in a broader context, the USDA responses also noted that combating agricultural pests had become a major—expensive—international problem. This last commonly used response from 1958 was even inserted into a letter about the gypsy moth program, though clearly the gypsy moth was not an agricultural pest.[72]

The increased number of criticisms that reached the USDA in 1959 continued to elicit similar responses, with some additions. USDA officials began asserting that pesticides were widely "accepted" in forestry, agriculture, and public health programs. Thus, questioning pesticide use presumably put one outside the mainstream and was counter to scientific and technical facts. The agency defenses also asserted that there were no wildlife losses, or if there were, they were "negligible." A third common assertion was that it would be "impossible" to produce basic food, feed, and fiber crops without pesticides. Finally, the USDA letters said that when possible, of course, nonchemical means of pest control were used. The agency responses sometimes had a condescending tone, assuring recipients that officials valued hearing the views of the public, and they often enclosed USDA publications to educate the public, such as "Pests or Pesticides."[73]

At the same time that the massive USDA campaigns against the fire ant and gypsy moth were coming under attack, magazines and newspapers also focused public attention on the possible consequences to human health from pesticide residues in food. Stories about the USDA campaigns with their highly visible die-offs of wildlife were most prevalent, but an increasing number of news articles questioned the effects of pesticides on human health; they centered on the issue of contaminated milk and, in 1959, Thanksgiving cranberries. Both sets of stories had an extra emotional resonance, touching national symbols (cranberries on Thanksgiving and milk for children) and raising more serious questions about human health (not just the issue of dead fish).[74] Milk was also in a unique category for health reasons, since it was a large percentage of the diet of babies or sick people.[75]

Back in 1949, the problem of pesticide contamination of milk was already apparent to government officials. The USDA and FDA issued a joint statement calling on dairy farmers to stop spraying their barns with DDT because it was showing up in milk; the statement set a "zero tolerance" for DDT residues in milk, the only food to have such a designation. Dairy farmers turned to alternative chemicals to rid their barns of flies, including lindane, pyrethrum, and methoxychlor, but by the mid-1950s, new concerns were raised about the safety of residues from these chemicals, especially methoxychlor. In 1956, the FDA set a zero tolerance for methoxychlor in milk, leading DuPont to launch an unsuccessful petition to get the tolerance set at 0.25 parts per million (ppm). The FDA, meanwhile, declared that the margin of safety for milk should be greater than that for any other food.[76]

A year later, news stories of FDA officials announcing residues of pesticides and penicillin found in milk showed that milk contamination remained a problem despite the policy.[77] Although FDA head George Larrick kept up the pressure on farmers throughout 1959, warning them that they had to have better safeguards for milk, meat, eggs, and poultry, the cooperative efforts of the farming industry remained merely educational. By the end of the year, Larrick asserted that the FDA would have to take legal actions when needed for milk shipped interstate and that an educational effort alone was not enough. But, despite findings of contamination in milk, by December 1959, no milk had yet been seized as contaminated.[78] That year, many news articles had reported on the controversy over milk. Articles in papers such as the *New York Times* and the *Chicago Tribune* helped to make some readers feel that the basic, "pure" food of milk was being threatened by pesticides.

Milk was not the only emotionally resonant food under siege. The scare over aminotriazole-contaminated cranberries in November 1959 was a powerful wake-up call to many who might previously have not given much thought to pesticides. Two years before, the USDA had approved aminotriazole to control weeds in cranberry bogs, with the instructions that the chemical was to be used only after harvest. Some growers had ignored this guideline, so part of the harvest had reached stores contaminated with the herbicide, which had been shown to cause thyroid cancer in rats. Secretary of Health, Education, and Welfare (HEW) Arthur Fleming gave a press conference telling people not to buy cranberries for Thanksgiving, infuriating the growers. He was acting under the Delaney Clause of the 1958 Food Additives Amendment, which gave authority to the FDA to ban the use of any carcinogenic additive to food or drugs. Following criticism that the HEW action was too drastic, Secretary of Agriculture Ezra Taft Benson and Vice President Richard Nixon tried to help the cranberry market recover by very publicly eating multiple servings of cranberries, asserting that they were safe.[79]

Press coverage of the crisis was mixed in its message. Some articles referred in a disbelieving way to "supposed[ly] contaminated cranberries" and "an allegedly harmful residue," whereas others said that the episode raised questions about the "scientific and technological revolution" in American agriculture. The contrasting tone of articles was illustrated in two examples: one article noted that the federal government already had in place extensive checks to ensure safety before a chemical could be marketed, and another emphasized that the USDA had "no police power once it clears a chemical for use on the farm."[80] Despite the range of tone from alarmed to skeptical, the news coverage highlighted for readers the dangers of pesticides—but also kept consideration of those dangers focused on cranberries. Thus, pesticides, per se, were not a danger; only pesticide residues on cranberries were. This slant helped to ensure that the aminotriazole controversy would be short-lived and would not seriously undermine faith in pesticides that were used on a variety of food crops.

Meanwhile, in response to the cranberry scare, the chemical industry asserted that use of chemicals was absolutely necessary in modern American food production. One DuPont vice president, for example, criticized the Delaney Clause and how it had been used to seize contaminated cranberries because it seemed to hold out the vision of having no risk whatsoever. "To eliminate risk completely is to forgo progress," asserted Dr. David Dawson.[81]

Unlike those in Washington who pushed for and supported maximum economic growth after the war, some environmentalists believed that the United States had the opportunity to take stock of past environmental mistakes and to make rational plans for the future. For example, editor of Missouri's state conservation magazine and future National Audubon Society president Charles Callison wrote in 1945 that "nothing strips a man's thinking down to fundamentals like fighting a war." His call for reassessing values included "a new conception of the function of wildlife in a modern civilization."[82] He argued that many of his fellow Americans shared his belief in the necessity of wild creatures and the natural environment for the health and morale of the nation. In the immediate aftermath of the war, the environmental issue that concerned many conservationists was Truman's push for new water development projects beginning in 1946 and Congress's support for these projects.[83] By the end of the 1950s, the focus had shifted. Environmental organizations increasingly criticized the growing use of pesticides as a serious problem. Of the mainstream environmental organizations, the National Audubon Society became a leading voice on this issue.

Back in October 1945, at the organization's annual meeting, government and university scientists and administrators discussed the effect of DDT on wildlife, and Audubon president John Baker called for further study of DDT's effects, saying that the use of the chemical for mosquito control had "created serious problems."[84] Nevertheless, the relatively conservative organization—dubbed by some as a group of "old ladies in tennis shoes"—did not seem overly interested in the pesticide issue in 1945.[85] Slowly, this began to change. In 1949, Baker issued a press release calling for more research into the new insecticides and their residual and cumulative effects on birds and other animals. He further invited "entomologists and other qualified individuals" to write to Audubon with their experiences of insecticides and effects on animal populations.[86] Several years later, *Audubon* magazine published the account of FWS biologist Paul Springer to ask the question: "Insecticides, Boon or Bane?"[87] At its annual meeting in 1957, Audubon called for a long-range study on the effects of insecticides, to be paid for by a 5 percent federal tax on chemical manufacturers.[88]

A year later, the Audubon position was no longer tentative, and the gloves were off. The organization's leaders became more outspoken about pesticide use. In spring 1958, Audubon, criticizing in particular the fire ant program, called upon the USDA to immediately stop all insect-control programs using toxic chemicals unless there was evidence that the pesticides did no harm.[89] John Baker used an image of danger with which ordinary Americans were very familiar: "Insecticide hazards may well rank in seriousness of adverse effects with the dangers of radioactive fallout." Like Robert Cushman Murphy in his criticisms of the gypsy moth campaign, Audubon raised the danger of chronic, cumulative poisoning and argued that the burden of proof for safety lay with the USDA.[90]

A couple of months later, *Audubon* magazine reprinted an excerpt from another publication in which the Alabama Department of Conservation had called on federal and state agricultural agencies to cease all spraying for the fire ant within Alabama's borders.[91] The drum beat against the fire ant program continued as *Audubon* editors wrote that "almost all wildlife species in the areas treated were affected."[92] At its 1958 annual meeting, Audubon leaders urged members to petition Congress to stop the broadcast spraying of DDT, heptachlor, and dieldrin. At the meeting, the president of the Garden Club of America urged attendees to lobby Congress "just the same way the chemical industry does."[93] *Audubon* soon published a report on the fire ant program condemning the USDA policy as "ill-conceived, unnecessary, poorly handled, and extremely destructive to wildlife."[94]

Negative publicity against insecticides continued to pile up in the late 1950s—and not just about the fire ant program. Some ornithologists announced that the national bird, the bald eagle, was in "a serious and mysterious decline."[95] The scientists found that large numbers of the birds were sterile and suspected that increased use of insecticides could be the cause. Evidence of the pesticide relationship to bird sterility increased when zoologist Dr. George Wallace published in the January–February 1959 issue of *Audubon* the results of his four-year study of declining robins on the Michigan State University campus following repeated spraying for elm bark beetles, which transmitted Dutch elm disease. At least one *Audubon* reader was moved to write in about his own experience of having his house and garden sprayed from the air and without warning. The letter concluded that such treatment of fellow humans and the natural world was immoral.[96] The editor of *Audubon* then wrote an article for the *New York Times* on the bird story to try to reach a wider audience.[97]

The Audubon president who succeeded John Baker, Carl Buchheister, remained outspoken on the pesticide issue. In spring 1960, he told society members that "the pesticide problem is so vast and complex that we could most advantageously maintain a field staff of *several* trained biologists to help us keep up with developments." He proceeded to describe the documented heavy losses of birds in Michigan due to aldrin spraying and to confirm the continued heavy losses of robins in Wisconsin and Michigan due to DDT spraying. In the next issue of the magazine, he argued that the United States needed a new law requiring consultation with the FWS and thorough testing of materials and methods before any large pesticide program could be undertaken.[98]

Among the conservation organizations, scientists, and scattered journalists who had become outspoken critics of the agricultural status quo was University of California zoologist Robert Rudd, who remained vocal on the issue through the 1970s and beyond. Coauthor of the 1956 report *Pesticides: Their Use and Toxicity in Relation to Wildlife*, Rudd sought to educate readers about how current pesticide use interfered with the interrelated systems of the natural world. Three years before Rachel Carson published *Silent Spring*, Rudd was telling *Nation* readers about the balance of nature—though he did not use that term.[99] He wrote that four controversies (the gypsy moth and fire ant campaigns, use of Compound 1080 in Western rodent-control programs, and the cranberry scandal) had brought pesticide use to public attention but that it would nevertheless be difficult to change current policy for a number of reasons. Rudd argued that narrowly focused specialists who pushed for pesticide use did not look at how biological systems worked as a whole, ignoring the species unintentionally killed by pesticides, the insect resistance that developed, and the many other benefits that humans derived from nature aside from production of food and fiber. Indeed, he charged that many were gripped by a "production fetish" as "overproduction has settled on us like a plague." Unquestioning, many embraced chemical use to increase production without asking "'Why?' or 'What do we lose in the process?'"

Rudd condemned the results of dependence on chemical controls, including contamination of the environment and food, destruction of natural controls, the wasteful costs of overproduction, and the harmful impact on different parts of the world. Yet he asserted that with then-current land-use policies and agricultural systems, chemical pest control was necessary. Unlike earlier arguments, which had asserted that the unfortunate use of chemicals was necessary in order to feed the world, Rudd argued that the environment had become unbalanced due to "simplification" and that this spelled the need for chemicals. The ecosystem, he wrote, was a "total living complex" with a diversity of organisms; this diversity brought relative stability. Throughout human history, agriculture had simplified ecosystems to a certain extent by controlling them, but it was not until the mechanization and chemicalization of agriculture that simplification had been radically increased and much diversity destroyed. The only solution, Rudd argued, was to reverse course and complicate the system. People should cultivate diversity with biological controls and reduce alien species with quarantine measures so that "for the good of us all, chemical techniques must give way to ecological emphasis."

Another outspoken critic of pesticide use who would become better known and more widely quoted in the 1960s was conservationist and biologist Clarence Cottam. After many years with the FWS, Cottam became the first director of the Welder Wildlife Foundation in Texas. In December 1960, the *Chicago Tribune* wrote about his presentation at a conference in which he warned that the widespread use of pesticides was causing them to get into water systems and poison drinking water.[100] At the same time that a former government official such as Cottam was speaking out, occasional voices from Congress, such as Leonard Wolf from Iowa and John Dingell from Michigan, began to propose legislation to change pesticide regulations.[101] Although such proposals did not pass in 1960, they hinted at the political shift that would come by the end of the decade.

Conclusion

By the end of the 1950s, had the powerful arguments in the press waged by the National Audubon Society, Robert Rudd, and others won? The answer was a clear no. There were some changes in the public consensus about pesticides, even in a conservative publication such as *Reader's Digest*. A 1959 article in *Reader's Digest* condemned the damage done by aerial spraying of pesticides, citing the failed gypsy moth and fire ant campaigns as well as the record of dead robins in Michigan after spraying for Dutch elm disease.[102] The article reprinted a listing from the Garden Club of America's Conservation Committee detailing the many insects consumed by just one of various types of birds and quoted zoology and entomology experts to attest that the fire ant did not do any damage to crops. The article's conclusion did not oppose all pesticide use but condemned the wildlife damage that was caused by aerial spraying.

Elsewhere, there was also evidence that the naive, one-sided stories of the immediate postwar period had given way to a somewhat more nuanced understanding that pesticides had to be used with caution. Nevertheless, positive views of pesticides still predominated. Military rhetoric continued to be used to express the human relationship with pests and to argue for the necessity of pesticide use. For instance, DDT spraying programs by municipalities and counties in the summer of 1959 were described as waging a "war on mosquito[es]" and defeating "mosquito plague[s]."[103] In 1960, newspapers carried stories of caterpillars being "on the march" and "invad[ing]" suburbs.[104]

Meanwhile, the assumption that pesticides were harmful to human health was far from a majority position. As the USDA and other agencies of the federal government defensively asserted the safety of their pesticide programs, experts from some nongovernmental groups also argued that pesticides were not a great danger to humans. A panel from the American Public Health Association in November 1960, for example, said that the biggest danger of pesticide use in food crops was accidental poisoning of those using the chemicals.[105] Meanwhile, the main concern of the general public remained cheap and plentiful food; thus, many ignored the debates about dangers from pesticides and other food additives. Political scientist Christopher Bosso observed that lack of immediate, extreme danger lulled people into ignoring the risk presented by chemicals in their foods. He argued, "Missing from the food additives controversy, to put the matter baldly, were bodies. Death is much more dramatic to the mass public than some uncertain claim about future effects—a fact understood viscerally by every newspaper editor."[106]

Despite some bad publicity for pesticides, by the end of the 1950s, the economic health of the industry was looking up. A 1959 article in *Barron's* observed that although pesticide sales had been on the rise since the war, the profit margins had remained small, especially due to increased competition as more chemical companies entered the postwar market.[107] Thus, the increased volume of sales (from $120 million in 1947 to $300 million in 1959) was shared among more companies. With this type of economic motivation, some companies were leaving the field and improving the future prospects for those left behind. For example, although fifteen companies had produced DDT after the war, in 1959, just eight did. *Barron's* predicted—correctly, as it turned out—that the new growth area in the field would be in herbicides. Although they comprised just 15 percent of the physical volume sold in 1959, they accounted for 20 percent of the value of sales. Use of herbicides had grown rapidly and was predicted to continue to do so.

Seemingly, the public, economic, and political commitment to pesticides had withstood the publicized crises of the late 1950s, but that was no guarantee that this would remain the case in the future. Don Paarlberg, special assistant to Dwight Eisenhower, drafted a prescient memo to other administration officials in October 1959.[108] He wrote that although the residue tolerances established by the FDA had a wide margin of safety, it was possible that the buildup of small residues over time could pose a serious human health risk. He said that some scientists and those in the regulatory agencies and food trade were aware of this. Since there had been no publicity on the issue, "confidence in the safety of the food supply remains at a high level."

Paarlberg worried, though, about the effects of "sensational" journalism in the future. He wrote that the administration could face severe criticism because much more was spent on research about pesticide effects on animals than on humans. Paarlberg noted that he had already discussed with several officials a recommendation to greatly increase research into the effects of pesticides on human health and to establish an interagency committee to look at the "whole problem of chemical agriculture and human food." Indicating that his foremost concern was political, Paarlberg concluded, "If these two steps are taken, a bad news break would not catch us flat-footed. . . . The problem grows faster than our knowledge concerning it so that in the absence of some action . . . our posture progressively worsens." Three years later, the publication of *Silent Spring* would bring just such a "bad news break."

CHAPTER 3

Breakup? The Cultural Impact of Rachel Carson's *Silent Spring*

Rachel Carson's 1962 *Silent Spring* is one of the most famous books of the twentieth century and one of the most politically and culturally influential in American history. Often compared to the nineteenth-century antislavery novel *Uncle Tom's Cabin*, which strengthened support for abolition, *Silent Spring* contributed to a new cultural understanding of the human place in the natural world as well as policies to clean up the environment.[1] Thus, Rachel Carson deserves credit for being the godmother of the Environmental Protection Agency (EPA); the ban on DDT and other pesticides; Earth Day; the 1972 Federal Insecticide, Fungicide, and Rodenticide Act; and indeed of "environmentalism" as a philosophy and political movement. When we think about American attitudes toward pesticide use over half a century, there is probably no more important turning point than the publication of *Silent Spring*.

Due to the pivotal political and cultural role of the book, the historiography on it and Rachel Carson is both broad and deep.[2] The dominant interpretation in these works is that Carson and *Silent Spring* were path-breaking and influential despite the onslaught of criticism from the chemical industry and groups within the government. On the face of it, there seems little new to say about Carson or her book, yet there are apparent contradictions between the narrative about the effects of *Silent Spring* and environmental developments in the years that followed. DDT and other potent pesticides were banned, but overall reliance on pesticides increased after 1962, with farm use doubling by 1994.[3] On balance, then, we can say that Rachel Carson did *not* fundamentally weaken the American attachment to synthetic pesticides.

This brings us back to the question posed at the start of this book: Why did American farmers, corporations, regulators, and consumers continue down one environmental road and not another? Why did the embrace of pesticides remain relatively stable and strong even in the face of a challenge such as Carson's? Of course, there are different answers to this complex question, including political and economic forces that favored continued pesticide use. This chapter focuses on how many Americans responded to Carson's argument and the implications of her study. Moreover, it poses the counterintuitive question of not why was the impact of *Silent Spring* so great, but why was it *so limited*?

The most revolutionary aspect of Rachel Carson's argument was her challenge to readers to understand that they were part of the "balance of nature" and that the delicate interweaving of life on earth was under assault because of the arrogant assumption that humans could manipulate the natural world.[4] In particular, she turned her attention to the cavalier use of pesticides, heedless of any consequences. As I argued in chapter 2, Carson's framework was not completely new. Indeed, others had raised these questions as part of a backlash against the technocratic confidence of the early Cold War.[5] Carson's synthesis, though, was uniquely accessible and served as a cultural touchstone. The subsequent wide acceptance of the balance-of-nature formulation was borne out in the birth of environmentalism and in more than a generation of reform. This impact was *not* limited but great and fundamental.

If we ask, though, whether Carson achieved all that she intended or whether the embrace of a balance-of-nature ideal determined the direction of environmental politics and the scale of pesticide use, the answer would have to be no. This chapter examines why we can read the impact of *Silent Spring* as both a triumph and a disappointment and will focus upon two key reasons for this seeming contradiction. First, the rhetorical strategies used by Carson as well as her supporters, opponents, and the press highlighted the conservative aspects of her argument and thus made those aspects a safer fallback position from overly radical change. Second, the pesticide status quo was powerful enough to adapt to and co-opt critiques but still withstand their challenges. Ultimately, this is a story of frustration and why the political and economic reality following *Silent Spring* did not match its philosophical ideal.

Reacting to *Silent Spring*

By the early 1960s, readers were well primed for Rachel Carson's environmental challenge. In particular, the controversies over the massive USDA spraying programs for the fire ant and the gypsy moth and the press attention to contaminated cranberries and milk gave a lot of publicity to the idea that using synthetic chemical pesticides could have dangerous consequences. Thus, many readers might have listened to Carson's argument with greater openness than they would have a decade earlier.

Discussion of *Silent Spring* should begin with the understanding that its message was discursively constructed not only by Carson but also by its defenders and critics. The bulk of scholarship on Rachel Carson has sought to explain the complete argument that lies within *Silent Spring*'s covers and the political movement it spawned. Other studies, such as those by Craig Waddell, Gary Kroll, and Priscilla Coit Murphy, focused on the rhetoric of Carson's work, whose meaning was established through the media and audience reactions.[6] For example, both Kroll and Murphy highlighted the differences of the serialization of Carson's work in the *New Yorker* in June 1962 and the complete book published by Houghton Mifflin three months later. The structure of the argument was different in those venues, as was the intended audience of the urban elite magazine and the nationally published Book of the Month Club selection. (Kroll added a discussion of how the framing of the argument for viewers of a *CBS Reports* broadcast on Carson in June 1963 differed once again.) Interestingly, the two authors disagreed on the meaning of the *New Yorker* serialization: Kroll maintained that the argument was conservative because it focused on pesticide effects on humans, not on the centrality of the balance of nature, whereas Murphy argued that because many cautions and sources were left out of the serialization, it could have been read as a radical statement calling for the complete ban of all pesticides. The conflicting interpretations of these two authors make sense as we uncover the multiple impacts of *Silent Spring*.

Press attention to Carson's work on pesticides began in the summer of 1962 with the *New Yorker*'s three-part excerpt from the forthcoming book. By the middle of August 1962, numerous editorials, news stories, columns, and letters to the editor had been published referring to or discussing the articles. Three members of Congress and one senator read selections from the articles into the congressional record, and Carson received more than 400 fan letters. By the official publication date at the end of September, the number of news stories, columns, and editorials had grown extensively, and letters to the editor were so numerous that Carson's agent had stopped keeping track of them.[7] The book quickly became a best seller throughout the country and even abroad (in England) and remained on the best-seller lists into 1963.[8] It was selected as the Book of the Month Club selection in October 1962 and was soon translated into all languages in the industrialized world.[9] The majority of the press stories first on the *New Yorker* articles and then on the book itself were overwhelmingly positive, even if some were more enthusiastic and some more cautious.

A number of clear themes emerged in the articles and columns about *Silent Spring*. Both supporters and critics addressed the question of Carson's qualifications and approach to the subject. Those who celebrated her analysis called her "a realist," a "trained biologist," and "thoroughly scientific" and concluded that there was no doubt about her qualifications.[10] Some reviews or articles noted that Carson provided extensive documentation for her study.[11] Those who longed for sober judgments wanted it to be clear that they, too, were scientific. As one journalist who gave reserved support for Carson's argument concluded, "I am not an alarmist. . . . But I am concerned [about pesticide use]."[12]

Not surprisingly, critics, especially those from the chemical industry, challenged Carson's qualifications as well as her objectivity. As Carson's editor at Houghton Mifflin, Paul Brooks, observed, "The industry spent enormous sums to ridicule both the book and its author."[13] Carson was painted as an "alarmist," "hysterical," emotional, and someone who "just doesn't know what she is talking about."[14] She was described as the antithesis of a scientist. For example, she was dismissed as one who "disregard[ed] the rubrics of evidence."[15] Letters to the editor critical of *Silent Spring* came to similar conclusions about Carson's qualifications.[16] Those who agreed with Carson were sometimes derisively referred to as "disciples," seemingly having a religious, irrational devotion to the writer.[17]

Supporters of Carson saw the charge that she lacked objectivity and was biased as an illegitimate criticism. As her good friend and fellow environmentalist Irston Barnes wrote in a September 1962 newspaper column, the facts should speak for themselves; a scientist could not "give two sides to the law of gravity."[18] William Shawn, editor of the *New Yorker*, had earlier told his prospective contributor that she should let her research and argument speak. "After all," he said, "there are some things one doesn't have to be objective and unbiased about—one doesn't condone murder!"[19] Thus, argued her defenders, a fair, scientific consideration of the evidence did not mean that one could not draw conclusions from that evidence.

It is not surprising that critics of *Silent Spring* would want to paint Carson as an unscientific crusader. And it is probable that some of her partisans saw her in a heroic, passionate light. For example, the assistant to the president of the National Audubon Society who wrote to Carson in 1963 congratulating her on the Wildlife Society Award observed, "All beleaguered wildlifers who have been fighting the pesticides battle see in you, I think, a new embodiment of Jeanne d'Arc."[20] This trend increased after 1964. After her untimely death that year, the construction of Rachel Carson as an iconic saint was endemic in the communities of environmental activists and historians.[21]

Carson, as well as her agent and publisher, was determined that she not be dismissed as part of an unscientific environmental fringe. Her agent, Marie Rodell, anticipating attacks on Carson as a "crackpot and subversive," believed that if prior to publication many "highly respectable people . . . had read the book and discussed it [it] would be an enormous help." Consequently, Rodell sent out advance proofs to numerous scientific experts and social leaders, and planned at least one high-profile luncheon with Carson presenting her research.[22] The publisher of *Silent Spring*, Houghton Mifflin, was also determined to place the book in the mainstream debate. Advertisements, for example, included extensive endorsements from scientific experts and effusive praise from Supreme Court Justice William O. Douglas, who called the book "the most important chronicle in this century for the human race."[23]

Carson, too, wanted to ensure that she was depicted as a sober scientist. For example, in an interview shortly after the book's publication, she told a writer for the *Saturday Review* why she was not inclined to grant many interviews: "I don't want to make this a Carrie Nation crusade. As I see it, my job was to present the facts. Now it's up to the public."[24] In her many responses to critics, Carson kept her arguments moderate and rational. For example, in a January 1963 speech, she told her audience that one reason pesticides were undesirable was that they were inefficient. She explained that crop losses to insects before DDT had been 10 percent; after, they were 25 percent.[25] As scholar Peter McCord observed, Carson "walked a tightrope, trying to appeal to the sentimentality of the public while at the same time maintaining her authority as a rational scientific researcher."[26]

From her background, Carson might be seen as an unlikely crusader.[27] She was born in 1907 outside Pittsburgh in a poor family of Scots-Irish ancestry. From early in life, she spent much time outdoors learning about nature and writing. Following completion of a baccalaureate degree in biology and a master's in zoology, she joined the US Fish and Wildlife Service as a biologist and writer. During her sixteen years of government service, Carson launched her career as a popular science writer. Her success was ensured in 1950 with the smash best seller *The Sea around Us*, which was a Book of the Month Club selection. Becoming what biographer Linda Lear described as "an overnight literary sensation," Carson captivated readers with her synthetic, poetic tale of the history and life of the sea.[28] Following this success, her earlier 1941 book *Under the Sea Wind* also emerged as a best seller upon reissue, and she completed her trio of books on the sea with *The Edge of the Sea* in 1955. Thus, by the time of *Silent Spring* in 1962, Carson was a highly respected popular writer, well known to the reading public as well as to naturalists and government scientists.

Although Carson spent the early part of her writing career focusing on the sea, she had long been interested in pesticides and their effects on nature. Upon reading and editing reports on the effects of DDT from biologists in the FWS in 1945, she proposed an article on the subject to *Reader's Digest*—though she was turned down. Also in 1945, other scientists were speaking out about the dangers of the new miracle pesticide; critical articles on DDT—although drowned out by the loud chorus of pesticide boosters—appeared in *Harper's*, *The New Yorker*, *Atlantic Monthly*, and *Time*.[29] Carson focused again on the subject of pesticides in 1957 with the controversies over the USDA's fire ant and gypsy moth programs. She disagreed with those who said that the fire ant was a threat to agriculture and thus questioned the whole premise of the USDA actions.[30] She was joined by some in the press and public who decried these ill-considered programs, though few questioned the necessity of pesticide use. The real issue that seems to have piqued public concern at this time was the overly ambitious, expensive, and ineffective government campaigns that were based on the overuse—often sprayed on wide swaths of land—of persistent chemical pesticides. The aminotriazole cranberry scandal in 1959 further inflamed public and press alarm about pesticide use. That same year, *Reader's Digest*, which had previously turned down Carson's idea for an article on the dangers of pesticides, published a critical article on the issue.[31]

Rachel Carson became increasingly concerned about pesticide use in general, contracting in 1958 with Houghton Mifflin to write a book on the subject and committing to a three-part series in the *New Yorker*.[32] Thus, Carson was a pioneering voice against many pesticide uses, but she was in good company, writing at a time when scientists had discussed the dangers of pesticides and when the public was sensitized to the controversy. By 1962, the message of *Silent Spring* was not wholly unfamiliar, even though the book's comprehensiveness and lyric presentation gave it a unique power for the general audience. As *Consumer Reports* observed in January 1963, "There was little that was new in Miss Carson's book. But heretofore, most of the critical material had been scattered through pamphlets, survey reports, speeches by technicians, and scientific and statistical tracts. . . . . Until 'Silent Spring' . . . mounting concern . . . was uneasily contained within the ranks of a particular business-scientific-governmental community."[33] Most scholars who have written about the impact of *Silent Spring* would not disagree with this assessment, but it has been overshadowed by the dominant narrative that Rachel Carson's message was revolutionary and unprecedented, changing ideas about the landscape and the human place in nature.

Unquestionably, Carson's ability to synthesize a vast body of scientific and technical information was impressive. It also led some contemporary observers to grapple with her sex. As historians have discussed in a number of contexts, most contemporaries viewed Carson and her controversial book through a gendered lens. Carson was painted as an emotional woman romanticizing nature, not truly understanding the reality of the insect threat.[34] As Michael Smith observed, Carson's critics chided her "soft approach" to the natural world as decidedly sentimental and unscientific.[35] Along with her critics, many in the sympathetic press judged Carson's credentials in this way, highlighting her femininity. For example, one article observed in early 1963 that Carson was "a gentle little woman, too shy to answer questions after she talked about her book." Many other articles commented on Carson's femininity and delicacy.[36]

Although observers might have attempted to use a gendered discourse to denigrate or at least interpret *Silent Spring*, Rachel Carson's carefully structured argument proved to be more powerful. Her strategy of maintaining a moderate voice, both in the text and in publicity, paid off. A few months after the book's publication, one newspaper observed that *Silent Spring* had inaugurated a mainstream public debate over chemical pesticides, whereas not long ago this had taken place only on the fringe (for example, among organic gardeners, environmentalists, and natural food fans); the paper dismissed the impact of these groups: "They may have preached and screamed, but their voices were small."[37] Another article from a Massachusetts newspaper noted with approval that Carson was part of the mainstream and didn't use evidence from environmentalists. She didn't quote from any "bio-dynamic organizations, the organic gardeners or the natural food associations. . . . Instead her facts are gathered from such sober documents as medical journals, Audubon Society bulletins, fish and game journals, and, of course, the U.S. Department of Agriculture farmers' bulletins."[38]

Carson's sober argument, based on mainstream sources, was still passionate. Notwithstanding Carson's public comments, she was of course a crusader, albeit a scientific and thoughtful one. She wrote to her friend Dorothy Freeman in June 1962 with "deep satisfaction" about the news that *Silent Spring* had been selected as Book of the Month for October, which would give the book "an irresistible initial momentum. And the BOM will carry it to farms and hamlets all over the country that don't know what a bookstore looks like—much less the *New Yorker*."[39] She was clearly eager for the message in *Silent Spring* to influence people's opinions.

Beyond the question of Carson's scientific credentials and motivations, the most prominent theme in the articles on *Silent Spring* was the reassurance that she was not calling for the cessation of all pesticide use. For example, in September 1962, Brooks Atkinson noted in the *New York Times* that "Miss Carson understands that chemical sprays are a permanent part of technology."[40] Other reviews observed, "She was not advocating the overnight abolition of all chemical pesticides"; "She does not suggest that we suddenly stop using all pesticides"; "She does not suggest that modern pest control be abandoned."[41] Letters to the editor also highlighted the point that *Silent Spring* did not call for the abandonment of all chemical pesticides.[42]

Instead, the most important recommendation in *Silent Spring*, according to the many articles that praised the book, was to curb the "misuse," "indiscriminate" use, "irresponsible" use, and "overuse" of pesticides.[43] One editorial that agreed with Carson's apparent call to curb only the "promiscuous use of pesticides" further explained that the public agreed: "The growing public demand is . . . for greater caution, stricter regulation."[44] Most importantly, the press, both favorable to and critical of *Silent Spring*, used the language of Carson's book as well as her own interviews to answer charges against her. For example, one newspaper article quoted Carson as asserting that "she's rapidly getting tired of explaining for the zillionth time that she does not want to stop the use of all pesticides."[45]

In favorable reviews, the most widely quoted passage from *Silent Spring* highlighted this theme of reasonable moderation in the face of irresponsible excesses:

> It is not my contention that chemical insecticides must never be used. I do contend that we have put poisonous and biologically potent chemicals indiscriminately into the hands of persons largely or wholly ignorant of their potentials for harm. We have subjected enormous numbers of people to contact with these poisons, without their consent and often without their knowledge. If the Bill of Rights contains no guarantee that a citizen shall be secure against lethal poisons distributed either by private individuals or by public officials, it is surely because our forefathers, despite their considerable wisdom and foresight, could conceive of no such problem.[46]

Moreover, Carson's straightforward charge that individuals deserve to be protected against poison was beyond challenge.

A fourth theme emerged in the public and press reaction to *Silent Spring:* a new environmental outlook. This nascent environmentalism reflected Rachel Carson's own intention. In the *New York Times*, Brooks Atkinson's review of the *New Yorker* articles gave voice to this outlook: "The basic fallacy—or perhaps the original sin—is the assumption that man can control nature. Nature returns with a massive assault from an unexpected quarter. . . . Miss Carson's articles . . . prove the case for ecology, which is also the case for mankind."[47] Another review simply concluded that "you can't tamper too much with nature and get away with it."[48] Outside the press, policymakers who supported *Silent Spring* also focused on the idea of respecting nature's own systems. For example, in the dedication of a new wildlife laboratory devoted to the effects of pesticides on the environment, Secretary of the Interior Stewart Udall told his listeners in April 1963 that Rachel Carson "has reminded us with compelling urgency that Man is part of the balance of nature."[49]

A contrasting fifth theme was interwoven in the press and public debate about *Silent Spring*: the extent to which efficient, modern agriculture was synonymous with the use of pesticides. Several articles focused on the *necessity* of using pesticides. As a scientist from St. Louis observed in South Bend's *Tribune* in the summer of 1963, "Any reduction in the use of chemical weed killers might tip the balance toward starvation for many people."[50] Also that month, a West Virginia newspaper agreed that pesticides were needed in the "never-ending battle against insects, plant diseases, and rodents."[51] There were also dire predictions in the press; for example, the *Shreveport Times* in September 1962 said, "The human race could wither and die without pesticides—for lack of food."[52] Underlying these assessments was the assumption that the human relationship with insects was a constant battle.[53]

Although many observers agreed that pesticides' initial triumph over insects was partly responsible for the dramatic increases in postwar agricultural output, the shrill warnings that starvation loomed if the chemicals were not used seemed unwarranted at a time of unprecedented consumption. It was unlikely that the dire predictions of catastrophe stemmed from actual fears for American survival. *Silent Spring* was published at a time when faith in technology was at its height and confidence in human ability to control nature was solid. Thus, by challenging current pesticide practices, *Silent Spring* questioned the ideology of progress and modernity of which modern agriculture was one small representative. Historian Linda Nash observed that Carson also challenged ideals of modernity in her assertion of a fluid relationship between human technology and the natural world: "Purveyors of modernity have assumed and relied on clear boundaries between culture and nature, bodies and environments, humans and animals. But the movement of chemicals from the laboratory to the soil, from rivers to bloodstreams, from fish into breast milk all suggested that those boundaries were more fictional than real."[54]

Importantly, and perhaps surprisingly, this central theme in the critical press, that pesticides were necessary and emblematic of modernity, did not contradict a central theme of the supportive articles, which held that Carson was not calling for the banning of all pesticides. Thus, many could embrace aspects of Carson's message and still believe that some pesticide use was necessary. The pivotal cautionary section in Carson's book and the defense she offered in interviews was a moderate fallback position, a contrast to the radical questioning of modern technology and industrial agriculture.

Articles that stressed the centrality of pesticides to modern agriculture closely reflected and quoted extensively from industry or government arguments. Many scholars examined the industry and government responses (especially from the USDA and congressional supporters of the farm bloc) to *Silent Spring*.[55] It is worth reviewing the main themes of those responses in the context of public discussion of the book. Indeed, one of the chief criticisms of *Silent Spring* from the pesticide industry and its government supporters was that modern agriculture depended on these newly synthesized chemicals. For example, Thomas Harris of the USDA Pesticide Division was quoted in an Associated Press article from September 1962 as charging that Carson "fails to point out the vital need of continuing to use these materials."[56] Similarly, a representative from the chemical company Rohm and Haas pointed out that pesticides were a necessity because a third of productive potential was lost each year due to pests.[57] One prominent opponent of Carson, Dr. William Darby, a biochemist from Vanderbilt University, broadened these views. He argued that following the recommendations of Carson would lead to "the end of all human progress."[58] Another criticism from industry that made its way into many articles on and reviews of the book was that people confronted worse hazards than pesticides. This point was most commonly made with a familiar trope from the late 1950s that had sought to answer criticisms of pesticides by arguing that people faced many hazards of equal or greater risk. Thus, articles and reviews noted that more people died each year from aspirin poisoning and bee stings than from pesticides.[59]

The most visible critic of *Silent Spring* was industry spokesman Dr. Robert White-Stevens, who was assistant to the manager of research and development at American Cyanamide Co. Agricultural Division. As a representative of the pesticide industry, he was tapped by CBS to debate Carson in a *CBS Reports* program in April 1963. On the program, he charged that following Carson's prescriptions would return humans to "the Dark Ages, and the insects and diseases and vermin would once again inherit the earth."[60] Even when he was not warning of a return to the premodern past, White-Stevens repeated the basic, though less dramatic, corollary argument from the industry that the risks of using chemicals in food production were simply outweighed by the necessity of their use to feed the starving and banish epidemic diseases. Like his colleagues, White-Stevens also relied on the aspirin/pesticide comparison, telling the press in a series of appearances in December 1962 to debunk *Silent Spring* that although 89 people had died in 1961 from the misuse of pesticides, 128 had died from aspirin poisoning that same year.[61]

Dr. White-Stevens's argument on *CBS Reports* backfired. Whereas Carson was rational, calm, and earnest, White-Stevens appeared abrasive and, in the words of Linda Lear, "wild-eyed." Moreover, the television show drew a large audience, 10 to 15 million people, many of whom had not read the book but had heard about the controversy in the media. The program helped raise environmental awareness dramatically while sowing distrust of the chemical industry and government officials.[62]

A number of scientists and physicians joined with the chemical industry and some in government to criticize Carson's book. The basis of their attack was similar to that of the other critics, foremost that pesticides were necessary and Rachel Carson was raising needless alarm.[63] Some scientists also criticized *Silent Spring* because it was a synthesis of other scientific studies but did not provide detailed information about studies and experiments on pesticides. For example, an editorial in the *Archives of Internal Medicine* charged that Carson "quotes all kinds of statistics without giving any indication of how they were collected, the numbers represented, control evidence, standard deviations, and other information a respectable scientist is expected to provide."[64]

Scientists, academics, and industry representatives critical of *Silent Spring* also had an impact on the popular reception of the book. A number of local meetings or lectures hosted an "expert" reviewing the book—often critically, such as when a University of Tennessee zoologist told the Knoxville Science Club that the book was "one-sided" or an author of gardening books told a local alumni meeting that Carson was wrong on a number of points.[65] Yet perhaps more significant as an indicator of the grassroots reception of *Silent Spring* were the numerous garden clubs (women's clubs) throughout the country that discussed it and held meetings about it. Based on the newspaper accounts, these club discussions seemed quite favorable.[66] Moreover, Carson was invited to give a major speech at the national meeting of the Garden Club of America—indicating the respect with which many garden clubs viewed her work.[67] Similarly, local papers carried columns from women librarians commenting on new books and what was popular; these brief items included many references to *Silent Spring* and appeared favorable.[68] A number of women's organizations thus helped to build popular support for the book.[69]

Among the many different responses to *Silent Spring* inside and outside government were those from the Department of the Interior. As noted in chapter 2, officials at Interior had been increasingly critical in the 1950s about the environmental impact of pesticides. When Carson's book was published, Interior officials supported her argument, in stark contrast to the voices from the USDA. For example, a lengthy analysis from the director of the Resources Program Staff, Charles Stoddard, to Secretary of the Interior Stewart Udall critiqued the industry responses and explained that *Silent Spring* was much more nuanced than they allowed. Stoddard wrote that the industry responses were using a "straw man technique" by asserting that Carson was calling for the elimination of all pesticides (which he explained she wasn't) and then further bolstered their argument by repeating that food cannot be grown without pesticides. Thus, he argued, the industry was deliberately obscuring "the central proposition" of the book. Although Stoddard might have been defending Carson, he wrote that she was also supported by "cultists and faddists" such as "anti-fluoridationists and the organic gardening fanatics," who he also worried were "certain to confuse the issue." He concluded that the "basic problem" outlined in the book was "environmental contamination" and that scientists need to gather more data "to assess the danger."[70] Within a couple of years, one of the leading establishment voices in Washington supporting Rachel Carson had become Secretary Udall.

The Rhetoric of *Silent Spring*

Despite what Carson said in interviews following the publication of her study, it is difficult today to come away from *Silent Spring* with the impression that the "indiscriminate" use of pesticides was the most serious issue discussed. Naturally, I make such an assessment following more than fifty years of hindsight and accolades for the book as the spark of the modern environmental movement. Yet an examination of the book supports this conclusion. Carson was cautious at times, especially in the beginning as she eased her readers into the subject: "It is not my contention that chemical pesticides must never be used."[71] Moreover, Carson's tone throughout was not emotional or exaggerated; the language was one of quiet logic with numerous references to scientific research. But Carson's qualifications that she did not seek to ban all chemical pesticides were outweighed by her ingeniously woven tale of widespread poisoning. *Silent Spring*'s starting point was the assumption that nature was a harmonious system. Slowly, Carson built a case to demonstrate how people were threatening all aspects of the natural world, climaxing in the most dramatic point: the threat to humans.

The book opened with the controversial "A Fable for Tomorrow," a vivid description of a hypothetical town and its sick and dying animals, apparently afflicted by a "strange blight." Following the rain of "white granular powder," the birds were silenced and other life poisoned. Yet, Carson concluded, "no witchcraft, no enemy action had silenced the rebirth of new life in this stricken world. The people had done it to themselves."[72] Carson's dramatic scenario was the subject of ridicule from critics and used as evidence that all of *Silent Spring* was unscientific exaggeration. This prologue also served as the model for Monsanto's parody of the book, "The Desolate Year" (a horrific imagining of a world without pesticides and overrun by bugs, famine, and disease). Nevertheless, the fable of an uninviting future was an effective and compelling way to pull readers into the book.

Carson's discussion of the reality of pesticides began with an overview of their effect on nature, their origins, how they worked, and how they affected insects. She then proceeded to discuss the myriad unintended consequences from the widespread use of pesticides in forests and on farms, roadsides, and suburban lawns. She discussed the dangers of mass spraying and acute consequences, but she was careful not to let readers feel the complacency of their own removal from such circumstances. "Each . . . recurrent exposure," she reasoned, "no matter how slight, contributes to the progressive buildup of chemicals in our bodies and so to cumulative poisoning." Ordinary Americans found themselves exposed in a variety of situations. She wrote, for example, that "gardening is now firmly linked with the super poisons."[73]

The power of Carson's indictment of pesticides came in part from the thematic structure of the book as well as from the language she used. Before any details about pesticides and how they work, Carson painted a picture of harmonious nature under attack from chemicals, including pesticides. She then introduced chlorinated hydrocarbons and organic phosphates and how they functioned. Next she discussed how pesticides impacted each aspect of nature (water, soil, plant life, insects, birds, and fish). The book moved to more direct criticism of indiscriminate aerial spraying and slow, cumulative poisoning. Only then did Carson turn to what she had told editor Paul Brooks was her most important theme: the impact on humans, at a cellular level and in actual diseases.[74] Her discussion of cancer referred to that with which her readers were already familiar. More than once, Carson likened the damage of pesticides to that caused by radiation: "The parallel between chemicals and radiation is exact and inescapable." In the years before *Silent Spring* was published, there had been many discussions in the public culture about the dangers of radioactive fallout, including its contamination of milk. Carson used this public awareness to lay the groundwork for her message about pesticides.[75]

Readers could not help but think of the dangers of radiation when Carson argued that some pesticides had been demonstrated to cause genetic mutations, disrupt reproduction, interact dangerously with other chemicals, and lead to malignancies. And just as it was difficult to escape the dangers of radiation in the atmosphere, so it was difficult to escape exposure to pesticides that seemed to be on most foods Americans ate.[76] Carson concluded that when it came to pesticides, society must err on the side of caution; since scientists did not yet understand chemical interactions within people, there was no such thing as a "safe" level of human contact when it came to carcinogens.[77] The book returned to the big picture of pesticides in nature with two chapters on species imbalance and insect resistance.

The impact of the thematic progression was enhanced by Carson's language, most pithily illustrated in her chapter titles. The introduction of pesticides and their properties ("Elixirs of Death") was contrasted with the majesty of nature ("Earth's Green Mantle") under attack from humans' arrogance ("Needless Havoc" and "Indiscriminately from the Skies") and their deadly poisons ("Beyond the Dreams of the Borgias"). Throughout the book, the popular science writer whose studies of the sea had risen to the top of the best-seller lists in the 1950s used poetic language to elicit wonderment at nature and shock at its desecration. Moreover, her carefully chosen words echoed through many of the reviews, challenging her critics. For example, though some criticized her as emotional and unscientific, Carson turned the tables, describing the proponents of pesticides as irrational: "The *crusade* to create a chemically-sterile, insect-free world seems to have engendered a *fanatic zeal* on the part of many specialists and most of the so-called control agencies." She dismissed the enthusiastic suburban embrace of pesticides as "the *fad* of gardening by poisons" dictated by shallow mores prizing a weed-free lawn. She indicated that the average suburbanite was manipulated by slick advertising ("lulled by the soft sell and the hidden persuader") and unaware of the dangers that lurked on his or her pesticide-treated lawn.

In her discussion of the campaign to save elm trees from disease, she exposed the unrealistic assumptions at work: "The illusion that salvation of the elms lies at the end of a spray nozzle is a dangerous will-o'-the-wisp." In addition, those dedicated to pesticides appeared childish in Carson's account: "The chemical weed killers are a bright new toy. . . . They give a giddy sense of power over nature to those who wield them." Finally, she indicated that it was the proponents of pesticides who were unscientific, not their critics:

> The "control of nature" is a phrase conceived in arrogance, born of the Neanderthal age of biology and philosophy, when it was supposed that nature exists for the convenience of man. The concepts and practices of applied entomology for the most part date from that Stone Age of science. It is our alarming misfortune that so primitive a science has armed itself with the most modern and terrible weapons, and that in turning them against the insects it has also turned them against the earth.[78]

Through her language, Carson raised broad philosophical and moral questions about Americans' views of nature and humanity. She questioned whether people could continue to think of themselves as "civilized" when they knowingly inflicted widespread suffering on countless creatures such as birds dying torturous deaths from pesticide poisoning. Moreover, in her insistence on rethinking the human place in the "balance of nature," she challenged the economic system that distorted that balance. She observed, "[This] is . . . an era dominated by industry, in which the right to make a dollar at whatever cost is seldom challenged. When the public protests, confronted with some obvious evidence of damaging results of pesticide applications, it is fed little tranquilizing pills of half-truths."[79]

Carson's critique of the power of marketing both to frame how ordinary people understood the natural world and to mask the possibility of risk was astute. Moreover, it remained relevant as a way to help explain the enduring embrace of pesticides. As discussed in earlier chapters, advertisements and news articles that highlighted the magical power of pesticides helped to make them appealing consumer products that could seemingly give people mastery over nature. Carson understood not only the sense of power that people could feel by buying pesticides but also that they were less likely to feel a sense of risk from such accessible and naturalized commodities. One could argue that despite the warnings of Carson and others, Americans at the start of the twenty-first century were just as susceptible to "the soft sell and the hidden persuader" as were those in 1962. Hence, they continued to blanket their lawns and foods with pesticides—even if the products that they used were different than those used in Carson's day.

Carson ended her study by laying out viable alternatives to chemical pesticides, but, at the same time, she moderated the strong condemnations that characterized most of the book. There was no discussion of organic agriculture, no reference back to her brief mention in chapter 2 of the pitfalls of "single-crop farming." Indeed, the alternatives that she discussed were modern and scientific—sterilization techniques and microbial diseases—to be perfected in the laboratory.[80] Carson seemed so determined to avoid being dismissed as a crackpot organic or natural food advocate that she carefully avoided direct questioning of modern, corporate agriculture.

Thus, there was a puzzling disjuncture between the main thrust of the book and its conclusion as well as the parts of the argument that were highlighted in the favorable articles about it. The reasons for this are not certain, but the evidence indicates that those who supported the book wanted to emphasize that it was not a radical statement by extremists. Whatever the reasons, there were real consequences to this public filter about the meaning of *Silent Spring*. Most importantly, if newspaper articles and columns and Carson herself focused on the misuse, indiscriminate use, irresponsible use, and overuse of pesticides, it followed that there *was* a correct, discriminating, responsible, and prudent use of pesticides. These rhetorical formulations were highly significant in shaping the public and political reception of *Silent Spring*. By carving out a moderate, sober position, Carson, along with her publisher and agent, helped, ironically and unintentionally, to circumscribe the impact of the book.

Yet, there was no denying that the way in which Carson framed her argument was also its strength. She was careful to avoid appearing too extreme and possibly alienating readers, even while she laid some of the philosophical and scientific underpinnings of modern environmentalism. The strategy was necessary, though in the end frustrating: if *Silent Spring* had been perceived as too radical or on the fringe (for example, denouncing all pesticide use and endorsing organic agriculture), it would have been dismissed by the public, the agricultural industry, and politicians. But by holding to a moderate position, Carson ensured a public debate and invited reform of the worst abuses *and* a continuation of an agricultural industry wedded to the use of chemical pesticides.

The concrete results of *Silent Spring* demonstrated this dual effect. Most immediately, John Kennedy's President's Science Advisory Committee (PSAC) was formed and issued its report in May 1963 on the dangers of the misuse of pesticides.[81] The underlying assumptions of the report were that pesticides were a necessity in modern agriculture and that material progress always included hazards. The carefully phrased report laid out both the impressive successes of pesticides in increasing agricultural output and protecting people from diseases and the toxic effects of pesticides in the environment. Although the report stressed the dangers to wildlife and humans from pesticide contamination, it also assured readers that current federal programs regulated the introduction of new pesticides and screened foods to ensure that residues remained low. For the most part, the report failed to challenge assumptions about modern agriculture and the "struggle for survival" in which humans were engaged, though it did in places deliver a clear condemnation of status quo practices. For example, the committee concluded, "Although eradication of a pest population is a laudable goal, it is seldom realistic." Another example was the committee's recommendation that some hazardous compounds should be banned from use if less harmful alternatives were available. Finally, the report recommended that "elimination of the use of persistent toxic chemicals should be the goal."

The most important goals of the report were to recommend how federal policies should change to address the dangers of pesticides. The president's commission called for more study into the effects of pesticides and more regulation of their use. Specifically, the report called for better collaboration between the Departments of Agriculture; Interior; and Health, Education, and Welfare. It emphasized that registrations of pesticides that had an impact on human health should be left to the Department of Health, Education, and Welfare, and registration decisions that affected fish and wildlife should include the secretary of the interior. The report ended with a plea for moderation: "The government should present this information to the public in a way that will make it aware of the dangers while recognizing the value of pesticides."

Many in the press at the time and others subsequently argued that the president's commission report amounted to an official endorsement of Rachel Carson's position.[82] Houghton Mifflin was quick to assert that the advisory commission "vindicates" *Silent Spring*, and to use this assertion in its advertisements, which concluded in the spring of 1963 that if the public was to understand the soon-to-be-proposed legislation on pesticides, "you owe it to yourself" to read the book.[83] Similarly, in summarizing the report, most of articles in the press emphasized that the committee experts endorsed modern pesticides but called for further research into their effects and more curbs on their use; for example, "Pesticides are useful and important to man, judiciously applied, but may be harmful in overuse or misuse."[84] Moreover, almost every article cited Carson and *Silent Spring* as the impetus for the work of the president's commission.

For her part, Rachel Carson gave interviews praising the report, calling it "strong and objective" as well as a "vindication of my principal contentions." Nevertheless, Carson cautioned Americans that the "report is not in itself a solution of the pesticide problem; it is rather a blueprint for a solution."[85] In addition to Carson, others pointed out that for the report to have an impact, it needed to be backed up with strong action. Joseph Alsop observed in his influential column that Americans were addicted to pesticides and that one government report would not cause people to give up their use. He observed, "The something done needs to be considerably sterner than the report of the President's scientific advisers, which had the approximate power of an old lady's moral lecture to a confirmed drunk."[86]

Alsop focused on a different aspect of the PSAC report and *Silent Spring* than did most other commentators—or historians since. The report *did* overlap with Carson's argument in clear ways and helped to bring broad political acceptance for *Silent Spring*, but it also strongly emphasized a theme that Carson had carefully avoided: the benefits of modern agriculture and pesticides. Paul Brooks, though, along with Carson and a number of journalists, recognized the value of a stamp of approval from the PSAC, so they paid attention to one aspect of the report and ignored another. This reframing of *Silent Spring* made it more moderate and less of a challenge to the status quo.

Along with the formation of the presidential commission, others in Washington swung into action. Secretary of the Interior Stewart Udall became a champion of *Silent Spring* and by spring 1963 dedicated a new government laboratory to wildlife pesticide research, invoking Carson's name and work in the dedication ceremony: "A great woman has awakened the Nation by her forceful account of the dangers around us." He observed that the department's Maryland lab "marks the beginnings of a new national awareness of the present and potential danger" of pesticides.[87]

Congressional hearings on pesticides and proposed legislation were scheduled by a number of committees in 1963, including the Natural Resources and Power Subcommittee of the House Committee on Government Operations, the Senate Commerce Committee, and the Reorganization and International Organizations Subcommittee of the Senate Committee on Government Operations. This last subcommittee was chaired by Senator Abraham Ribicoff, a former secretary of health, education, and welfare who became a very public supporter of Carson and critic of government policies regarding pesticides. Indeed, during the week of Carson's testimony, Ribicoff engaged in a public battle with the Department of Agriculture over "protest registrations" of pesticides.[88] This was the practice by which pesticide companies were allowed to sell pesticides even if the USDA had refused to register them for use. Ribicoff blasted the department for refusing to disclose the names of the products that were being sold under protest. The USDA relented, releasing the names of the seven pesticides then currently marketed "under protest" as newspaper stories described the "shocking loophole" that Senator Ribicoff's proposed law sought to plug.[89]

Carson's testimony before the Ribicoff committee on 4 June 1963 was in some ways triumphant, as Linda Lear describes it: "This was the moment she had hoped for; one final chance to translate her vision into policy, to make a difference, to change the way people looked at the natural world, to stop the warfare against it."[90] Carson focused her testimony on several key themes and made recommendations to the committee for government action. She emphasized that although environmental contamination was widespread and remote from points of pesticide applications, the effects of such pollution could not be fully understood until scientists better understood the reactions among different pollutants and chemicals in the environment.

Her two main recommendations were for the strict control of aerial spraying, to be used only when absolutely necessary, and for the great reduction and eventual elimination of persistent pesticides. She made additional recommendations, including protection for property owners against unwanted spraying; more medical research and education about the effects of pesticides; restriction of pesticide sales to those who could understand their hazards; involvement of the Departments of Health, Education, and Welfare and Interior in decisions about pesticide registration; approval only of pesticides that did not duplicate the functions of another chemical; and, finally, support for nonchemical methods of pest control. Thus, Carson reiterated arguments from her book and maintained a moderate tone throughout. One *Newsweek* article observed that her charges against pesticides "seemed toned down, but her substance was the same: 'Before automatically reaching for the spray gun . . . we must begin to take account of the hazards.'"[91] Her two *key* recommendations were strategically chosen; they were ones around which there was already a growing consensus, and one had already been made by the president's commission. They were the most modest and moderate of proposals.

Coverage of Carson's testimony emphasized that she was not calling for the elimination of pesticides: "Restraint is what she preached," summarized one article.[92] The press made it clear that the senators were listening to Carson. The day after her testimony, articles led with the decision of the subcommittee to investigate the possible link between pesticides and leukemia, hepatitis, and cancer in children.

Moreover, articles on Carson's testimony also covered Ribicoff's standoff with the USDA, indicating that senators were on the same side as the author of *Silent Spring*.[93] Other members of Congress jumped on the anti-USDA bandwagon. Representative John Dingell, for example, testified before the Senate Commerce Committee in favor of antipesticide legislation; he criticized the USDA for what he termed its "public-be-damned attitude" on pesticides.[94] The press was also not immune to an anti-USDA tone. One paper took the opportunity to remind readers of an exposé it had published the previous year finding that many government scientists said privately that not enough research had been done on pesticide dangers but were unwilling to publicly criticize the USDA. *Newsday* concluded that only 75 of 250 chemicals in pesticides had been tested for long-term effects on wildlife, and none had been tested for effects on humans, although the agriculture department had "been enthusiastically promoting the use of pesticides for 17 years."[95]

Within two days of her testimony before the Ribicoff committee, Carson testified before the Senate Committee on Commerce on two pending pieces of pesticide legislation; she reiterated some of her points from 4 June with additional recommendations.[96] The bills in question had been introduced by Senator Maurine Neuberger of Oregon, who joined forces with Senator Ribicoff to call for more research into long-term effects of pesticide exposure on humans.[97] Neuberger's legislation would increase the ability of the secretary of the interior to research pesticides and require the USDA to consult with the FWS before any large new spraying programs were approved. In addition, Carson called for the formation of an independent, cabinet-level department, staffed by scientific experts without ties to industry or other governmental agencies, to be the final arbiter when there were conflicts in pesticide-control policy.

Not everyone in Washington was a fan of Carson. In addition to the harsh disagreements from the Department of Agriculture, criticism also came from within Congress, especially the farm bloc. Most outspoken was Representative Jamie Whitten of Mississippi, chair of the House Appropriations Subcommittee on Agriculture.[98] In response to *Silent Spring*, he released "The Whitten Report" from his committee and in 1966 published a book, *That We May Live*, stridently defending the necessity of pesticides. He concluded that Carson had manipulated public fears and did not understand that people had always been engaged in a struggle with nature: pesticides were "new weapons in an ancient war."[99] In addition, he argued that under current rules, the government carefully tested and regulated pesticides for safety. From his powerful position, Whitten had a strong relationship with the agriculture industry; he based his book on research from the USDA, and three pesticide manufacturers subsidized its printing.[100]

While official Washington and the national media paid close attention to the hearings on Capitol Hill, the chemical and agricultural industries assessed the damage. Industry magazine *Farm Chemicals* opined in its July 1963 issue, "There have been few quiet moments for the pesticide industry since the release of the report of the President's Science Advisory Committee. No less than three separate hearings involving pesticides are now being conducted by Congress."[101] The article observed that Secretary of Agriculture Orville Freeman, appearing before the Ribicoff committee, strongly defended pesticides and criticized the report from the president's science advisers. A month earlier, the same trade journal explained to its readers the flaws of the report from the PSAC and asked, "Why so much havoc when no *emergency exists*?"[102] The industry also highlighted the testimony of other defenders, including biochemist William Darby and the chief of toxicology at the Public Health Service, Wayland Hayes.[103] For his part, Hayes belittled the idea that storage of DDT in human bodies was necessarily harmful. Reflecting industry sentiment, he argued that "there is no conclusive evidence that pesticides, old or new, are a cause of any disease except poisoning."

Following Rachel Carson's testimony (and that of other experts) on Capitol Hill, the proposed legislation—albeit of limited impact (for example, requiring consultation between the FWS and state wildlife agencies before any spraying could take place or requiring better labeling on pesticides and the secretary of the interior to evaluate chemicals for use as pesticides)—was passed. The passage of the Ribicoff-Pearson Bill in 1963 was perhaps the strongest initial legislative step taken then; it eliminated protest registrations (under which manufacturers had been able to produce and market chemical pesticides even when the USDA was not willing to grant them a registration).[104] But, following Carson, supporters of actual and proposed legislation hewed to a moderate path, asserting that they were not calling for the abandonment of modern agriculture. Senator Neuberger said that without pesticides, the world's growing population could not be supported. Senator Hubert Humphrey, on Ribicoff's subcommittee, added that "no one in a position of responsibility . . . has suggested that all chemical poisons be taken off the market."[105] Nevertheless, cautious though politicians were, legislation was passed beginning in 1963 to start to address the worst effects of pesticide use. This was only the beginning of years of wrangling and debating on Capitol Hill over the power to control pesticide use. And although the political changes coming from Washington remained limited by the middle of the decade, states were passing their own legislation as well. By the spring of 1963, more than three dozen bills had already been introduced in legislatures around the country.[106]

When Rachel Carson died in April 1964, newspapers wrote of her "vindication" and the "fitting memorial" for her work found in evidence about the dangers of pesticides in the environment and the public reversal in the position of Secretary of Agriculture Freeman. New evidence was published attributing massive fish kills in the Mississippi (10 million fish over the previous four years) and elsewhere to pesticide contamination and uncovering contamination of canned oysters and shrimp. Referring to the ridicule that Carson had faced from chemical companies, agricultural interests, and their allies in government, one paper concluded in the week after her death, "At the highest levels of the federal government, the mockery has ceased altogether."[107] Secretary of Interior Udall told Senator Ribicoff's subcommittee that month that there should be a federal law completely prohibiting the use of DDT, endrin, dieldrin, aldrin, and lindane. Most dramatic was the testimony of Secretary Freeman before the same gathering. Just one day after Rachel Carson's death, Freeman told senators that the nation must quickly find alternatives to toxic pesticides, a "crash program" to control pests.

Freeman affirmed that depending on what the subcommittee uncovered, he was prepared to cancel registrations of various pesticides and implement stricter policing of the industry.

Interestingly, the coverage of Freeman's testimony and the whole pesticide issue remained linked to Carson herself. One article on the secretary's appearance was subtitled "The Rachel Carson Cause."[108] Continued Senate hearings and Carson's "vindication" may have led some to be overly optimistic about progress in solving pesticide pollution, despite evidence to the contrary. Celebration of Rachel Carson's memory and acknowledgment that overuse of poisons was dangerous do not mean that actual practice was changed. Honoring (and circumscribing) the work of a dead pioneer was appealing and certainly easier than changing the direction of American agriculture.

Conclusion

One 1964 editorial observed, "The use of potentially deadly sprays had steadily fallen off, and the birds seem more abundant than ever."[109] Yet there was scant evidence that total pesticides sold had dropped in response to *Silent Spring*. The *Wall Street Journal* observed that in 1962, pesticide sales increased more than 16 percent from 1961 (to $345 million), and in the spring of 1963, sales were up over the same time in 1962.[110] As the trade journal *Farm Chemicals* predicted when federal hearings first began in spring 1963, "The pesticide industry has been plagued with these problems in the past. Concensus [*sic*] is that the industry will ride out the storm."[111] The prediction turned out to be correct because, although massive government programs such as those against the gypsy moth and some insecticides were eventually phased out, routine use of chemical controls continued, sometimes with chemicals dramatically more toxic than DDT.

Although criticisms of *Silent Spring* and its author were enduring (even in 2007, for example, Republican Senator Tom Coburn decried the legacy of "Carson's junk science claims about DDT"), the book resonated throughout the public culture in the early 1960s and contributed to a new way of thinking about pesticides and the environment.[112] It is important to observe that although Rachel Carson's book may have been revolutionary in many ways, it was, nonetheless, a cultural touchstone, awakening anxieties and concerns that had been brewing for several years. As one editorial in the *Shreveport Times* noted, "Pesticides have been controversial at least since 1957. The *Silent Spring* only serves to escalate into a full scale battle what has for years been a running guerilla warfare between conservationists—anglers, hunters and bird watchers—on the one side and the chemicals industry, the Plant Pest Control Division of the U.S. Department of Agriculture, and some farmers on the other."[113] Another article on the pending 1963 report of the president's commission observed that "dangers [of pesticides] had been noted, or suspected, by scientists for many years."[114]

Rachel Carson also noted that criticisms of pesticide use had been spreading in the years before her book was published. She observed that readers' letters in newspapers indicated that many people had begun to notice the impact of pesticides on birds: "Citizens are not only becoming aroused and indignant but . . . often they show a keener understanding of the dangers and inconsistencies of spraying than do the officials who order it done."[115] Carson cited the unpopular campaigns against the gypsy moth and the fire ant as helping to increase criticism of pesticide programs: "A good many people now have misgivings about the aerial distribution of lethal chemicals over millions of acres, and two mass-spraying campaigns undertaken in the late 1950's have done much to increase these doubts."[116] *Silent Spring*, like many cultural documents that crowd our history books as the turning points of an age, drew its power from the simmering debates and changing discourses already widespread throughout the culture.

Carson sought to channel the debate, to prod people into asking skeptical questions instead of avoiding them. As she told a California audience in October 1963 in her last speech, "We behave not like the people guided by scientific knowledge, but more like the proverbial bad housekeeper who sweeps dirt under the rug in the hope of getting it out of sight." Most importantly, her ambitions went beyond pesticides themselves. She sought to change how people viewed nature, to end "the assumption that the rivers, the atmosphere, and the sea are vast enough to contain whatever we pour into them."[117]

After 1962, the lasting impact of Rachel Carson's book was clear. *Silent Spring* and its author became the reference point for a variety of environmental initiatives and discussions. In a very real way, *Silent Spring* inaugurated a different understanding about pesticides and a new consciousness about the environment.

To highlight Carson's careful balance between extreme positions in no way lessens the political and cultural impact of *Silent Spring* nor questions the sincerity of Carson's commitment to educate the public about the human role in the balance of nature. Yet, in the initial responses to *Silent Spring* and the rhetorical strategies used by Carson and others to defend the book, we find insights into the continued American reliance on pesticides. By stressing that she was not attacking all pesticide uses and the modern agricultural system of which they were a part, Carson and her defenders allowed the majority of Americans to embrace the existing system while calling for the elimination of extreme abuses. Meanwhile, as will be discussed in the next chapter, the commitment to a pesticide regime was also strengthened by the contemporary images of Americans using the chemicals abroad to help feed the hungry or to protect American soldiers from attack in Vietnam.

It's possible that in 1962 the only way to begin a dialogue about the overuse of persistent, dangerous pesticides was through the moderate, measured arguments of *Silent Spring* and its supporters. But we are nevertheless left with the uncomfortable conclusion that the status quo remained entrenched, though moderated, and the political and environmental effect of the beautifully written, rigorously argued, pioneering book might not have lived up to the goals of its author.

CHAPTER 4

Foreign Affairs: How Pesticides Could Help Americans Feed the World and Win a War

Americans' embrace of pesticides did not stop at the water's edge. The love affair extended abroad, opening up new possibilities for the chemicals as tools of American foreign policy. At the same time that Rachel Carson was convincing many Americans that the overuse of DDT and its chemical cousins in the United States had to stop, others still believed that pesticides could be a force for good throughout the world by allowing Americans to master nature in the service of two ambitious foreign policy goals: feeding the world's growing population and defeating the enemy in Vietnam.

There was one big difference in the stories that Americans told about domestic and foreign pesticide use. As the preceding three chapters have argued, in the two decades after World War II, synthetic pesticides in the United States were highly visible, both in their early, unproblematic adoption and as they were increasingly a topic of debate. In contrast, pesticide use abroad in these same years, and later, was less visible. Instead, the imperative of fighting the Cold War overshadowed almost everything in the realm of foreign affairs. Providing food to poorer countries or triumphing over independence fighters in Vietnam were both part of broader goals in the service of Cold War imperatives. Moreover, the specific tools to accomplish these goals were less important than the general understanding that superior US technology could master nature in previously unforeseen ways.

Examining the use of pesticides in the Green Revolution and to win the Vietnam War gives us greater understanding about the enduring American embrace of synthetic pesticides. First, it is clear that American confidence in the nation's agricultural technology was strong, whether it was used at home or abroad. Second, many people had a presumption of continuing progress and ever-increasing output. Third, the lack of discussion about specific pesticides in the Green Revolution and the Vietnam War indicated that confidence in American technology was so great that it was naturalized and sometimes unspoken. Fourth, pesticide use abroad was ennobled; it was rich with possibilities, offering the potential to help banish hunger among the world's poor, to demonstrate the superiority of Western technology in the Cold War, and to save people from communist oppression in Vietnam. The apparent altruism of these ambitious goals perhaps helped to keep the embrace of pesticides strong even when the Green Revolution and, especially, Agent Orange faced withering criticism from around the world.

This chapter will explore each of these observations, and the fact that although the disappointments of the Green Revolution or controversies over Agent Orange might have been a turning point and led to a change in attitudes toward pesticides, the cultural and political embrace of these chemicals did not slacken but remained entrenched.

Feeding the World

The agenda of Western scientists and policymakers to bring modern industrial agriculture to the Third World, along with the wealth and political stability that it represented, was written in 1941 when the Rockefeller Foundation sent three scientists to Mexico to study how to improve that nation's production of food. The launch of the Mexican Agricultural Program (MAP) would later be considered by observers as a turning point in international agriculture and the start of what was called by the end of the 1960s "the Green Revolution."[1] Though it sprang from idealism and confidence in the power of modern technology, the Green Revolution took on a broader political meaning within the Cold War paradigm of global politics. The success of modern, industrial agriculture would not only prove the superiority of Western technology but also demonstrate the appeal of the Western political system and win hearts and minds in unstable parts of the world.

Post–World War II international development—of which the Green Revolution was a part—reached its height in the 1950s and 1960s. Though pioneered by private foundations, such as the Rockefeller and Ford Foundations, development policies enjoyed the support of local governments and elites around the world as well as the US government. The marriage of development initiatives with political goals was well illustrated in the technical assistance program, "Point Four," announced by Harry Truman in 1949. By the time Dwight Eisenhower took office, technical and military assistance merged in "New Look" programs, and the American focus on thwarting communism in Asia moved the Green Revolution beyond Latin America. Increasingly, American political leaders understood economic development in the Third World as a key frontier in the Cold War.[2]

If this is the broad arc of American developmentalism and the Green Revolution, it makes sense to go back and look at how support for these policies was built. The United States was in a unique position after World War II. Unscathed in the fighting, its status as the wealthiest, most powerful nation in the world was unassailable. The United States enjoyed advantages not seen elsewhere, and many Americans believed that their country was morally obligated to share its wealth and technology with people around the world. In addition, US policymakers understood that encouraging stability through foreign aid was not just morally right but would benefit the country's strategic interests as well. Support for foreign aid and the export of Western technology came together in the imperative to revolutionize international agriculture and thereby increase food production for growing populations. The need for greater food production appeared straightforward and as an unquestioned good.

Following the devastation of the war, many other parts of the world were unable to supply the food that they needed. President Harry Truman and others foresaw that American farmers would serve an essential role in "the struggle to feed a hungry world."[3] Even two years after the end of the war, the food situation remained desperate in Europe and parts of Asia. Newspaper and magazine editors helped to convince their readers of the seriousness of the crisis through numerous stories, including appeals by international leaders. For example, in late 1947, the first director general of the UN's Food and Agriculture Organization, John Boyd Orr, wrote an article in the *New York Times Magazine* asserting that aside from the prevention of war, the most important international problem was food shortage.[4] The crisis was acute due to the fall of European wheat production from prewar levels, when the continent had been the world's largest producer of wheat. Boyd Orr echoed the views of some commentators, including former President Herbert Hoover, who had been coordinating US food aid to Europe, that there would be political consequences for continued shortages: instability and unrest. "People will not support a government which cannot provide food," he warned readers.

Three years later, after leaving his position at the FAO, Boyd Orr warned that food shortages—especially in the developing world—made many areas vulnerable to spreading communism.[5] Yet, although he and other development leaders may have been worried about pending food crises, they were confident about the promises of technology and the probability of increased outputs. Boyd Orr asserted that there was no limit to what could be produced with the proper application of technologies and knowledge.[6]

Many US government representatives agreed that they had the ability to solve food shortages, and they urged their fellow citizens to support food aid abroad. For example, the chief of the USDA's Bureau of Human Nutrition and Home Economics, Dr. Hazel Stiebeling, told the 1947 annual convention of the American Home Economics Association that there was "a greater disparity in nutrition among countries of the world than before the war."[7] Stiebeling called for a food-sharing plan with international management of food supplies. She asked home economists to help mobilize public opinion for food aid.

A few months later, participants at the annual meeting of the American Farm Bureau Federation were similarly concerned with food shortages around the world and the political impact of such a situation.[8] A group of farmers who had toured Europe in fall 1947 reported back to the delegates that they had a role to play in the international crisis. "We came back more convinced than ever," said one farmer, "that there is a close connection between what happens in the rest of the world and what goes on in our great food-producing areas of the Corn Belt." Another delegate to the conference asserted that farmers had a direct long-term economic interest in these areas because about one-third of US exports and two-thirds of agricultural exports had usually gone to Europe.

On different fronts, then, a multipronged message was reaching average American citizens. In newspapers and magazines, they read about the prodigious output of modern American agriculture, which created surpluses for the present and foreseeable future. Although many of these stories were positive, others self-consciously identified the paradox of Americans juggling unprecedented surpluses as people in other parts of the world were confronted with serious food shortages.[9] Some journalists worried about the moral dilemma presented by surpluses at home amid hunger abroad.[10] The possibility that the miracle of American agriculture could be exported to resolve the dilemma and help others was appealing—and important in understanding one aspect of popular attitudes toward synthetic pesticides.

The feel-good conclusion for many Americans was that with the export of technology and food aid, American benevolence would help their own country and other peoples. Instead of focusing on the wasteful accumulation of surplus commodities, Americans could know that they were putting their technological knowledge and their agricultural surpluses to good use. For example, in early 1950, news stories told about how cheaply purchased surplus dry milk from the USDA would benefit 5.5 million European children.[11]

The American public was also primed to support US foreign aid programs, in part due to the favorable press stories about the Green Revolution, beginning with MAP in the early 1940s. The collaboration between private American foundations and the Mexican government, which would become the model for the agricultural revolution elsewhere, was based on the idea that modernization of agriculture would lead to increased yields and would come through the adoption of hybrid seeds, up-to-date equipment, new methods, and synthetic chemicals. News stories praised MAP as "giv[ing] new life to the nation's economy" or being a "blueprint for Hungry Nations."[12] The pesticides developed during the war became key in Green Revolution programs because those at the Rockefeller Foundation and others involved in agricultural development believed that modern farming necessarily used chemicals.[13]

Increasingly, as the food crisis grew less acute in Europe and Americans foresaw that the region would soon be producing sufficient food, concern over food shortages shifted to the developing world. Journalists shared the concern of policymakers. For example, one 1950 article in *Business Week* observed that although businessmen, farmers, and politicians *at home* might predict that surpluses would be the major agricultural problem of the coming years, probable shortages *abroad* were actually a greater danger. The shift in focus among policymakers and in the press from Europe to the developing world reflected two main concerns: population growth and a lack of productivity. Similar to the predictions made in other press stories, *Business Week* estimated in 1950 that at projected rates of growth, the world population would rise to 3.5 billion by 1990.[14] Stories in the press in 1949 noted with alarm that every day throughout the world, 55,000 babies, with

55,000 new mouths to feed, were born.[15] The stories were often dramatic. *Senior Scholastic*, for example, told teens that at the present moment, there was not enough land to produce sufficient food for the existing population.[16] By 1954, articles in the press were still predicting disaster as population growth would continue to outstrip food supply. For example, one story in the *Saturday Evening Post* asked, "Will Your Grandchildren Go Hungry?"[17]

For many observers in the late 1940s and early 1950s, the problem of inadequate food production to meet the needs of an exploding international population was inextricably tied to the issue of agricultural productivity. And no country was in a better position to demonstrate the promise of agricultural productivity than was the United States. There was a wide gulf between American output and that in the rest of the world even after a great increase occurred worldwide in production and industrialization of agriculture in the second half of the twentieth century. Most farmers throughout the world remained poor and untouched by the agricultural revolution.[18]

In the mid–twentieth century, facing the problems of skyrocketing populations and poor productivity in the developing world, Americans and international leaders, such as John Boyd Orr, increasingly looked to the export of modern agricultural technologies as the best way to address both issues.[19] Boyd Orr's long-term prescription reinforced already widespread faith in the wonders of technology and modern science. He believed, as did many Americans at the time, that greatly increased production was achievable "if modern science were applied to increase food production with the same intensity as it was applied to produce weapons of destruction during the war."

Boyd Orr's successor at the FAO, Norris E. Dodd, also took to the American press to bolster the case for American assistance to the world's needy.[20] Dodd was an Oregon farmer who believed in the benefits of new agricultural technologies. In a *New York Times Magazine* article in 1949, he emphasized that even simple Western technology would go a long way toward alleviating international food shortages.[21] Along with basic tools, the export of "a few chemicals and a little spray equipment" and the drainage of water holes could control malaria in places such as India. Key to any change, Dodd emphasized, was the export and distribution of scientific knowledge.

Like Boyd Orr, Dodd also emphasized that food shortages in the developing world were not just a humanitarian issue but also a political one. He ended his article with the simple question to readers: Was it worthwhile to set up the kind of technology exports that he advocated? His conclusion was an emphatic yes: "If you are satisfied to live in armed camps made necessary by a world torn by strife and discontent, a large part of which springs from empty bellies, then it isn't worth doing."[22] A variety of articles highlighted the views of Dodd and Boyd Orr. For example, *Reader's Digest* in early 1950 (reprinting an article from the *Minneapolis Tribune*) profiled Dodd and his prescriptions.[23]

Observers such as the *Science News Letter* noted with approval that the big suppliers of food in the "post-war emergency," the United States and Canada, had also begun to export improved seed and agricultural know-how to encourage food production abroad.[24] "Total world food supplies are still tragically short of needs," observed one 1949 article in the *New York Times Magazine*, yet "we are making some progress toward closing the gap." The author wrote that the export of hybrid corn as well as technical experts was already improving agricultural prospects abroad.[25]

Press articles calling for the export of agricultural technology took it for granted that there was a political dimension to the issue. Reflecting the views of various political leaders and commentators, the articles contained both implicit and explicit references to the importance of agricultural aid in the Cold War. An article in the *New York Times Magazine* from 1949 illustrated the argument. In this profile, former treasury secretary Henry Morgenthau Jr. called for the US government to simply give away stored agricultural surpluses to needy people abroad: "In our struggle to attain a world of free and peaceful nations capable of withstanding the onslaught of communism and totalitarianism of every kind we have come to recognize that hunger and sickness are our principal enemies."[26] Morgenthau's article summarized what was already explicit in the speeches and writings of other policymakers and journalists: the immediate postwar problem of food shortages and economic devastation in Europe and Japan was under control, and the more urgent need was now in the undeveloped world, where food shortages were described as endemic. In such articles, the mainstream press helped to amplify these views and gain support for the assumptions behind them.

Along with Morgenthau, other policymakers argued that providing agricultural aid was essential in the Cold War. For example, the director of the USDA's Office of Foreign Agricultural Relations told farm cooperative leaders in the summer of 1950 that if the United States did more to support the farm cooperative movement, ordinary people throughout the world would "understand democracy has something for the little man."[27] Such sentiments were echoed outside the government and reported in the press. For example, an article on the 1949 annual meeting of Kiwanis International quoted J. W. P. MacEwan, the keynote speaker, a dean of agriculture and home economics from Winnipeg, as arguing that "the key to world peace may be food."[28]

Business leaders, such as those in the chemical industry responsible for some of the new pesticides, similarly believed that American agricultural innovation would benefit both the United States and the rest of the world. In 1948, for example, the president of the Sherwin-Williams Company, Arthur Steudel, sent a telegram to Harry Truman prior to his company's public announcement regarding the success of chemical weed control.[29] He wrote that DDT and the herbicide 2,4-D could produce hundreds of millions of additional bushels of crops and pounds of meat and milk. In praise of his company, Steudel noted, "It is this industry's method of aiding national prosperity and alleviating world hunger and we are prepared to aid the agricultural program to the limit."

Harry Truman took these views to heart. The significance of agricultural and technical aid in the Cold War was realized in the administration's Point Four initiative, announced in the president's inaugural speech to Congress in January 1949. The initiative—so named because it was the fourth in a list of foreign policy initiatives—reflected a broader belief in "development," which was thought to encompass not just the increase of measurable economic growth but also the transmission of American cultural and political values.[30]

In the detailed Point Four proposal that Truman presented to Congress in June 1949, there were two basic categories of aid: technical and educational assistance, and production goods and financial assistance. He emphasized that the US commitment would complement the existing international programs established through the UN and that, along with the government initiative, private enterprise should be encouraged to invest in the "under-developed areas" with Export-Import Bank guarantees against losses in risky environments. He insisted that peoples in the undeveloped world hungered for this development and integration into "the community of nations."

Secretary of State Dean Acheson laid out similar justifications for Point Four in his 1950 testimony before the Senate Foreign Relations Committee.[31] He asserted that the program was "an essential arm of our foreign policy" because American "military and economic security is vitally dependent on the economic security of other peoples." Acheson made it clear that this was a Cold War imperative because "democracy is on trial for its life." Finally, the secretary asserted that the export of science was the lynchpin for the program: "Here, indeed, is a chance to prove that our civilization which has grown to vigor and maturity with the help of science can bend science to its will—not to destroy but to serve humanity."[32]

Other members of the administration were also deployed in the campaign to gain support for Point Four. Secretary of Agriculture Charles Brannan, for example, told the House Foreign Affairs Committee that such development programs benefited both donors and recipients.[33] The campaign also sought to sway public opinion outside Washington. Truman's foreign affairs assistant W. Averell Harriman encouraged farmers at the 1950 annual meeting of the Farm Bureau that they had a vital role to play in Point Four, increasing production using modern techniques in order to increase the economic well-being of people throughout the world.[34]

Commentators outside the administration also spoke out in favor of Point Four. For example, in her column in the *Chicago Defender* in early 1950, civil rights leader Mary McLeod Bethune told her readers that Point Four would help lead to a genuine peace, reaching people across the world. Echoing the argument made by Truman and others, she further argued that "scientific developments, alone . . . have wiped out forever, the walls of separateness between races and nations."[35] And the FAO's Dodd spoke out to praise Point Four as a program that would greatly expand the work that his organization was already doing.

The political arguments made on behalf of Point Four illustrated the common assumptions about the desirability of international development, the confidence that modern technology—including pesticides—could tame the natural world, and the belief that industrialized agriculture had become essential in the battle to win hearts and minds in the Cold War and to feed the exploding population of the developing world. In this atmosphere, herbicides were a shiny new tool to help achieve these goals.

Miraculous Herbicides

While some policymakers and ordinary Americans anticipated that the export of Western technology would bring an agricultural revolution to the undeveloped world, the chemical tools of industrial agriculture were remaking practices at home and abroad. Just as the chlorinated hydrocarbon insecticides such as DDT developed during World War II were hailed as miraculous weapons in the war against insects, the new synthetic herbicides developed at the same time were seen as having similar potential to industrialize world agriculture.

For American farmers at midcentury, weeds were a serious problem on the grasslands of the Midwest; in the words of one trade publication *Nebraska Farmer*, they were "gangsters in the grass."[36] The enthusiasm that greeted the introduction of 2,4-D in the 1940s, then, was not surprising. 2,4-D and other phenoxy herbicides that had been developed between 1942 and 1944 were revolutionary because of their selectivity and ability to limit toxicity. Companies that manufactured 2,4-D—in 1945, Dow Chemical Company, Sherwin-Williams, and the American Chemical Paint Company—were enthusiastic about the wonders of the widely used herbicide. For example, in a 1948 telegram to Harry Truman, the president of Sherwin-Williams Arthur Steudel predicted that the benefits and increased output from 2,4-D would soon be as impressive as those from DDT.[37] Corporate enthusiasm rubbed off on government officials. For example, an Iowa State University Extension botanist helped to write an educational skit on the benefits of 2,4-D in combating "Weedy the Thief."[38]

Farmers readily adopted the new synthetic herbicides beginning in 1945, which made control of weeds much easier than it had been previously. They soon replaced cultural methods of weed control with chemical applications, even though agricultural experts counseled that they should use a combination of methods for the best results.[39] The enthusiasm of most farmers for 2,4-D—which was inexpensive—led to some problems early on when the herbicides were applied at the wrong time in the growth cycle or when environmental conditions were not optimal.[40]

Not everyone, though, was equally enthusiastic about the new chemical. In 1947, the USDA began receiving complaints from farmers about damage to their crops from 2,4-D dusting done by neighboring farmers to their own fields.[41] With the reports of damage due to drift, aerial regulations were changed to only allow 2,4-D in liquid form to be sprayed from planes. Some crop damage continued after the new regulation, but USDA officials argued that the benefits of 2,4-D were so great that it was important to continue allowing aerial application of the herbicide.[42]

Although some farmers lobbied Washington officials hard about how 2,4-D hurt them, the most important observation regarding these complaints was that they were narrowly focused and came from a small minority of farmers—especially those who cultivated particular crops damaged by 2,4-D, such as grape growers, horticulturists, beekeepers, and occasionally those who raised livestock.[43] The majority of farmers readily embraced the use of chemical herbicides, believing that the easing of weed control was worth any potential problems, including the risk of injury to humans, livestock, and crops.[44] Most farmers, journalists, and extension experts remained optimistic about broad use of synthetic herbicides more than two decades after their introduction.

The widespread adoption of 2,4-D—accounting for half of all herbicide production by 1960—led to the unintended consequence of allowing the growth of those species unaffected by the chemical, especially a variety of grasses.[45] But confidence in chemical methods of control meant that instead of questioning the reliance on 2,4-D, many farmers readily adopted new chemicals introduced to address the problem. At the start of the 1960s, chemicals such as Ambien, Atrazine, and Amitrol came on the market. The new products were more expensive than 2,4-D, so farmers spent a bigger share of production costs on herbicides. By the end of the 1960s, there was a sometimes confusing set of choices available; for example, there were nineteen herbicides for corn and twenty for soybeans. The number of herbicides in use in North America in 1950 was just 25; by 1969, that number was 120, with farmers in the 1960s often using a combination of chemicals to address all types of weeds.[46] Despite the difficulty of juggling a complicated herbicide regimen, famers were not discouraged from using the chemicals.[47] For example, the volume of herbicides used went from 84 million pounds in 1964 to 112 million pounds in 1966 and then to 226 million pounds in 1971.[48] Many of the newer herbicides carried greater apparent risk than did 2,4-D because they were often more persistent in the soil.[49]

Any one of these developments might have weakened support for herbicide use: there was an increase in weed grasses immune to 2,4-D; the cost for farmers of herbicides increased; the complexity of using herbicides increased; and the newer chemicals were riskier than the older 2,4-D. But such a weakening did not happen. Instead, the choice of agricultural herbicides increased, as did the total volume used by farmers. Those outside agriculture followed the farmers' lead.

Nonfarmers—the majority of Americans in the mid–twentieth century—were also enamored with the new herbicides. One area of public concern serves to illustrate these attitudes. As discussed in chapter 1, post–World War II suburbanization encouraged the sense that individuals could have their own little piece of nature to shape; the apparent ability of new chemical products to banish pests from yards and gardens made this goal appear attainable. Herbicides, along with insecticides, were easy-to-use tools to beautify suburban homes, especially lawns.[50] By the mid-1940s, 2,4-D was available to homeowners to use on their lawns for weed control, replacing the arsenical herbicides of the prewar era. The pattern of nonagricultural use of chemical herbicides that began in the mid-1940s accelerated through the early twenty-first century. By the beginning of the new century, a high percentage of the four most widely used herbicides was applied to lawns, not agricultural fields: 23 percent of 2,4-D; 22 percent of glyphosate; 31 percent of chlorpyrifos; and 38 percent of dicamba.[51]

As the inaugural herbicide of this chemical class, 2,4-D was brought to market by American Chemical Paint Company in 1946 under the label "Weedone." Within a year, the company's competitors Dow Chemical Company, Sherwin-Williams, and Swift were marketing their own solutions with names such as "Weed-No-More" and "End-o-Weed." Advertisements for the products emphasized their revolutionary impact: "Kill more weeds—easily—completely—chemically!"[52] Early on, publications such as *House and Garden* followed the lead of such copy, raving about the new products and encouraging their use. 2,4-D removed the broadleaf weeds—such as dandelions, plantains, poison ivy, honeysuckle, ragweed, and wild morning glory—that marred otherwise perfect lawns. Yet, like farmers, suburbanites soon discovered that 2,4-D was ineffective against unwanted grasses, such as crabgrass, which became more noticeable with the elimination of other unsightly weeds. Instead of halting the use of 2,4-D or mowing lawns higher to mask the crabgrass, many homeowners chose to use *more* chemicals in varying combinations.[53] Although suburban homeowners did not banish their weeds with herbicides, and although farmers faced a relatively constant financial loss from weeds even after more than a decade and half of heavy herbicide use, the increasing use of herbicides was not questioned.[54]

Beyond their ubiquity in the domestic landscape, by the beginning of the 1960s, the US military had found a whole new use for herbicides in the jungles of Vietnam. In 1962, the same year that *Silent Spring* was published, the United States began the systematic use of herbicides in Vietnam to defoliate the countryside, eliminating hiding places for guerrilla fighters and destroying their food crops. The US operation in Vietnam employed a variety of herbicides, but the most important ones were 2,4-D and 2,4,5-T. Having observed the success of the phenoxy herbicides in domestic agriculture, army researchers began collaborating with USDA entomologists in the 1950s to explore how the chemicals could be used in warfare.[55] By 1961, the US Military Advisory Group in Vietnam was ready to test herbicides for defoliation operations.

The success of these tests led to the establishment of "Operation Hades" in South Vietnam, soon to be known by the more public-relations-friendly name "Operation Ranch Hand." The operation focused on jungle defoliation, destruction of "enemy" crops, and clearing of US base perimeters. Most of the spraying took place in South Vietnam, with some in Cambodia and Laos and possibly in North Vietnam. Six herbicides were used in the operation: Agent Pink and Agent Green (variations of 2,4,5-T esters, used only from 1961 to 1964); Agent White (a combination of 2,4-D and picloram, the latter extremely persistent, used as a forest defoliant); Agent Blue (arsenic and cacodylic acid, deadly to all life, used in crop destruction); Agent Purple (almost identical to Agent Orange); and Agent Orange (a 50-50 mixture of 2,4-D and 2,4,5-T, the most widely used general defoliant in Vietnam and in forests in the United States). Sixty-two percent of all the spray used in Vietnam was Agent Orange. Putting 2,4-D and 2,4,5-T together was not unique to Vietnam; Dow had marketed such a product to farmers back in the 1940s, promising that it would bring "brush-free brushland."[56]

The main purpose of Operation Ranch Hand was defoliation (86 percent of the missions, whereas only 14 percent were for crop destruction). Although British and American forces had used herbicides in a limited way in the wars in Malaya and Korea, the new American policy was unprecedented in its size and longevity. Overall, 19 million gallons of herbicide were sprayed over 4.5 million acres of south and central Vietnam, equivalent to about 12 percent of the country's total area.[57] While the program remained in effect, political and military leaders continued to assert that the military value of defoliation and crop destruction was great. The strongest case against this rosy view came in two 1967 RAND Corporation studies that asserted that Ranch Hand was not only ineffective but also severely hurt the civilian population of Vietnam.[58]

With such an ambitious spraying program, within a few years, it became clear that the production capacity for both 2,4-D and 2,4,5-T would have to be greatly increased in order to meet domestic and military demand. USDA officials were concerned about protecting the supply to farmers; as one assistant secretary observed in 1966, there were already shortages of 2,4-D in some areas, but it was "essential to agricultural production."[59] USDA officials were worried in particular about the supply of 2,4,5-T because its uses were more limited in the United States (rights of way, rangeland, land reclamation in forestry) and its production capacity therefore smaller. Indeed, since spring 1966, all of the available supply of 2,4,5-T had been diverted to the military program.[60] The director of the President's Office of Emergency Planning complained to Secretary of Agriculture Orville Freeman in mid-1967 that there simply wouldn't be enough supply for both domestic and military needs, leaving Freeman to push back that agricultural needs could not be ignored.[61]

One would assume that such a strain on agricultural supplies in the United States would have garnered more attention outside Washington. Yet what is remarkable in a program of this scale—more than 4 million acres in South Vietnam defoliated and almost half a million acres of food crops destroyed over 9 years, using 12 million gallons of Agent Orange in addition to other chemicals—and novelty is that there was so little public debate about its efficacy and morality. There was a seeming lack of press attention to the widespread use of herbicides in the early to mid-1960s.[62] Although the defoliation and crop-destruction programs were in effect starting in 1961, most articles on the Vietnam War focused on traditional operations, assaults, and firefights.

Instead of talking about herbicides, press articles celebrated technological innovations deployed on the battlefield. For example, a July 1965 article in *Time* magazine described various new military gadgets that were being tested in the "Jungle Proving Ground" but did not mention Agent Orange and other chemical innovations.[63] A similar article from three months before in the *New Republic* also described the innovations of new weapons and tactics in Vietnam, leaving out the use of herbicides.[64] Another article celebrating American technology and firepower that appeared in *Time* a year later made no mention of the use of herbicides.[65] Even after two more years of war and increasing chemical use, a celebratory article in *Popular Mechanics* ("Wild New Weapons for Vietnam") detailed technological advances but left out any mention of chemicals.[66] *Aviation Week*, in one of the few articles before

1969 that discussed defoliation, blended the topics of new weapons and chemicals into a photo essay admiring American innovations. The descriptions explained how C-123 planes had been retrofitted with special spray nozzles to carry out their missions. The herbicide strategy was explained pragmatically as a way to "enhance visibility."[67] Occasionally, articles in the press highlighted the herbicide program. For example, a 1963 editorial in the *New Republic* questioned the safety of the chemicals, likening their potential for harm to that of nuclear weapons.[68] As early as 1964 and 1965, the *New York Times* published a few articles on herbicide use in Vietnam. The early articles were supportive of the policy. For example, an article in 1965 asserted that the chemicals used in defoliation and crop destruction were not poisonous to humans.[69]

Overall, articles in mainstream newspapers and magazines deemphasized the role of herbicides as a weapon in Vietnam, primarily by simply ignoring Operation Ranch Hand in favor of discussing other military technologies and strategies. When journalists did discuss herbicides, they asserted that they were safe. More importantly, they did not associate the chemicals with any uses at home; the military used "defoliation" agents, not the pesticides used by farmers and homeowners in the United States. This wall of separation would end up being significant a decade later, when Operation Ranch Hand and Agent Orange had become discredited, but few associated this failed policy with herbicide use in the United States. In this way, public discussion about Agent Orange use in Vietnam was similar to that about Point Four and the Green Revolution. These were all described as initiatives to export technology for humanitarian or foreign policy goals. Although both the domestic and the foreign realm relied on the pesticides commonly used throughout the United States, they were oddly divorced. The way in which journalists wrote about Agent Orange had two very important effects. First, by making its use largely invisible, the press lessened contemporary controversy about it. Second, by keeping discussion of Agent Orange separate from that of pesticides in general, the press helped to ensure that support for pesticide use overall would not be weakened.

Even while most in the press were ignoring the implications of herbicidal warfare in Vietnam, American scientists sounded the alarm, recognizing the environmental and health impact of Agent Orange. A group of activist scientists lobbied within their own profession, especially in the world's largest scientific organization, the American Association for the Advancement of

Science (AAAS), and urged Washington officials to end Operation Ranch Hand.[70] The scientists were successful due to the fortuitous timing of their efforts, which coincided with both growing environmental consciousness and declining support for anticommunist interventionism.

When scientific criticism of herbicide use began in 1964 with a statement from the Federation of American Scientists on herbicides in Vietnam, officials from the Department of Defense denied that any anticrop agents were still being used but admitted that defoliation of ground cover was taking place. Two years later, scientists' opposition became significant when twenty-nine scientists led by Harvard biochemist John Edsall appealed to Lyndon Johnson to halt the herbicide program, which they labeled "indiscriminate" and therefore "barbarous." Twenty-two of the scientists (including seven Nobel laureates) followed up the letter with a petition calling Operation Ranch Hand a "dangerous precedent in chemical and biological warfare." By the end of the year, 5,000 scientists had cosponsored the petition.[71]

The issue was controversial within the scientific community because some were worried that the campaign against herbicides in Vietnam would politicize their work. More than two years of wrangling within the AAAS led to the establishment of a committee to study the issue at the end of 1968. At the next annual meeting in December 1969, the council of the AAAS passed a resolution calling on the Department of Defense to "immediately cease all use of 2,4-D and 2,4,5-T in Vietnam."[72]

In addition to the increasing scientific criticism of herbicide policies in Vietnam, the second major catalyst for political change was news of a multiyear study of industrial chemicals, including pesticides, commissioned by the National Cancer Institute and carried out by Bionetics Research Lab in Bethesda, Maryland. As early as 1965, preliminary results from the Bionetics study revealed birth defects in mice caused by both 2,4-D and 2,4,5-T. A preliminary report to this effect was completed in 1966, but many agencies within the federal government did not learn of it until 1969. Both the White House and Dow Chemical Company—the largest manufacturer of 2,4-D and 2,4,5-T—worked to suppress the report.

News of the Bionetics study—though not its full contents—finally made it into the public eye through the pressure of scientists such as Yale biologist Arthur Galston, who had learned of its existence and begun calling people he knew in Washington, including the president's science adviser, Dr. Lee DuBridge, to act on the results. The report was, in the words of historian

David Zierler, "a bombshell."[73] The *New York Times* broke the story in October 1969 with an article on the efforts in the government to restrict the use of 2,4,5-T, because of its toxic effects.[74] Thomas Whiteside's articles in the *New Yorker*, beginning in February 1970, were significant in bringing public attention to the issue of herbicide use in Vietnam.

In addition to the news of the Bionetics report, press coverage about chemical use in Vietnam was shaped by the increasing public criticism of the war as a whole. In this climate, the 1969 statement by Dr. DuBridge that civilian and military use of 2,4,5-T should be restricted due to its teratogenic effects found a receptive audience. The statement said that in the United States, the USDA should halt the spraying of 2,4,5-T (a common ingredient in many commercial and household herbicides at the time) on food crops and that the Department of the Interior should not use it near populated areas. The DuBridge announcement—a dramatic departure from earlier government policy—was prompted by two major developments: (1) the mounting criticism of herbicide use from within the scientific community and (2) the release of the Bionetics report.

It's worth pausing to note that the revelations about 2,4,5-T were taking place in the year that the federal Mrak Commission and others outside government were pushing for a ban on DDT and other persistent organochlorine insecticides. Predictably, the debates over 2,4,5-T and DDT reinforced each other, with cultural as well as political results. For example, from 1969 to 1970, there were thirty-one separate proposals in the House Agriculture Committee to ban particular pesticides or to change federal regulations of them. DuBridge recognized the political implications of this synergy when he observed, "Pesticides are straining our image on the whole environmental issue."[75]

The Bionetics study was most definitive on the dangers of 2,4,5-T. Following this lead, political action in Washington was narrowly construed to address this substance instead of challenging Operation Ranch Hand more broadly. In 1970, the US Senate Subcommittee on Energy, Natural Resources, and the Environment held hearings on the effects of 2,4,5-T on humans and on the environment. Also that year, following a study in April 1970 from the National Institute of Health that concluded that 2,4,5-T caused birth defects in mice, the secretaries of agriculture; the interior; and health, education, and welfare suspended registration of 2,4,5-T for use near homes, human habitation, and bodies of water, and the Department of

Defense announced the immediate halt of the use of 2,4,5-T in Vietnam. The herbicide was soon canceled for use on all food crops in the United States.[76]

In response to the momentum that was building for a broader cancellation of 2,4,5-T, Dow Chemical Company began its court challenge to any attempts to restrict the use of 2,4,5-T in the United States. The company fought fiercely throughout the 1970s to defend its herbicide by controlling the terms of scientific assessment and government regulation; thus, Dow stalled actions to eliminate 2,4,5-T.[77] The company worked to derail the criticisms of 2,4,5-T with counterarguments. In one of its pamphlets, "A Closer Look at the Pesticide Question," the company used what one Audubon official from Massachusetts, Ian Nisbet, called "half-truths, selective quotations, innuendos" to defend 2,4,5-T, denying that any deaths or injuries had been caused by the herbicide.[78] Meanwhile, while most of the regulatory proposals remained focused on 2,4,5-T, Dow greatly increased its production and sales of 2,4-D.

USDA officials also responded defensively to the Bionetics report and the DuBridge statement. Fred Tschirley, the pesticides coordinator for the USDA, still argued three years after the DuBridge statement to Congress that both 2,4,5-T and 2,4-D were useful for rangeland weed control and that there was no serious danger from such uses because human exposure was so low in comparison with the amounts of chemicals used in the Bionetics experiments.[79]

A second theme in the USDA defense of the Agent Orange chemicals was to draw a clear distinction between its components. 2,4-D was often described as relatively safe. For example, the USDA director of science and education Ned Bayley took exception to a 1970 report from the President's Science Advisory Committee that implied 2,4-D was carcinogenic, arguing that only one of the three types of 2,4-D tested had shown a statistically adverse result. Similarly, commentary from the Agricultural Research Division criticized the report's conclusions about 2,4-D.[80] In 1973, explaining to one congressman why the EPA would be holding a public hearing on 2,4,5-T but not on 2,4-D, Tschirley argued, "We believe the risk potential to be so low that a hearing is not necessary."[81]

Although USDA officials drew clear distinctions between the dangers of 2,4-D and 2,4,5-T, they nevertheless tried to defend the continued use of 2,4,5-T even in the face of mounting evidence against it. In mid-1970, for example, Secretary of Agriculture Clifford Hardin wrote to Russell Train, chairman of the Council on Environmental Quality (and future administrator of the EPA), that there were no safe substitutes for 2,4,5-T to control brush. He also denied the implications of the Bionetics study because the samples used in it had high dioxin contamination. Thus, he emphasized that the real culprit was dioxin and that "uncontaminated" 2,4,5-T was therefore safe.[82] A year later, Tschirley was even more direct on this point in writing to a geologist in Arizona: "I still feel that 2,4,5-T, with a low dioxin content (0.1 ppm) is one of the safest chemicals that can be used."[83]

Finally, one last argument made by USDA officials as they continued to defend the use of 2,4-D and 2,4,5-T was economic. For example, the administrator of the department's Economic Research Service wrote in 1975 that banning either of the phenoxy herbicides would "have a major impact on agriculture" by greatly increasing production costs for farmers. The chemicals were simply too important to ban.[84]

At the same time that USDA officials were broadly defending 2,4-D and 2,4,5-T, the Bionetics story and the DuBridge statement touched off a series of articles in the press about an issue that had hitherto been almost ignored. Journalists helped to focus public attention on the herbicide program, and Agent Orange, observed historian David Zierler, "achieved its status as a proper noun."[85] The newspaper and magazine articles had a number of common themes. First, the articles followed the lead of scientists whose earliest focus had been on the ecological consequences of herbicide use. Frequent articles on Agent Orange and herbicide use continued through the 1970s and the end of the war. For example, in April 1971, *Look* magazine published "Silent Vietnam: How We Invented Ecocide and Killed a Country."[86] That same year, Paul Erlich wrote an article for *Saturday Review* that criticized the crop destruction program as a "starvation policy" that killed civilians, and *Natural History* worried that the effects of the American "ecocide" might last for "centuries."[87]

After 1969, news stories focused in particular on the duplicity of US officials who had tried to keep using Agent Orange and 2,4,5-T even after their harmful effects were known; the moral and environmental effects of defoliation and crop destruction; the disposition of Agent Orange stores; and the use of herbicides in the United States. But what is also significant about the press coverage is the extent to which it magnified political developments in Washington and increasingly focused on 2,4,5-T as the major danger among herbicides. Thus, journalists helped to shape the story that

Agent Orange was more about politics than about the environment or human health and that the problem of Agent Orange could be solved by eliminating 2,4,5-T. These narratives kept the focus narrow, on one chemical, and did not question the ideas that pesticide use in general might be problematic or that humans could control the environment through chemicals.

Although Dow worked hard to protect 2,4,5-T, the campaign against the herbicide was shaped, ironically, by Dow's first criticism of the Bionetics report: the samples of 2,4,5-T had been highly contaminated with 2,3,7,8-tetrachlorodibenzo-p-dioxin (TCDD, or dioxin). Dow argued that dioxin was a manufacturing byproduct of 2,4,5-T but that 2,4,5-T could be made purer with less contamination. Dioxin, Dow argued, was the real cause of birth defects, not 2,4,5-T.

Many followed the lead of Dow. The power of dioxin, thus, came to dominate the political and public debate over Agent Orange, leaving most people to ignore the other 50 percent of the compound herbicide. As one writer observed, "The spectacular toxicity of the dioxin in 2,4,5-T easily upstaged 2,4-D."[88] 2,4-D and other herbicides appeared benign in comparison with 2,4,5-T. Similar in some ways to the growing movement to ban DDT and soon other persistent chlorinated hydrocarbons, the push to eliminate the use of 2,4,5-T was based on the idea that such a ban would "solve" the problems of herbicide policy and usage. Thus, addressing the worst aspects of Agent Orange had the unintended consequence of reinforcing the status quo for the use of other herbicides. The reaction to Agent Orange and the ensuing political firestorm had the potential to upend popular and political attitudes toward broader herbicide use. But this did not happen. Instead, 2,4,5-T with its dioxin was the villain to be blamed, and pesticides in general escaped untarnished.

Domestic use of herbicides was also reinforced by industry arguments that the chemicals were essential for agricultural productivity. Such arguments were sometimes repeated in the press. One November 1970 article in the *Milwaukee Journal*, for example, argued that complete government bans on 2,4-D and 2,4,5-T would end up costing $290 million a year unless inexpensive substitutes were found.[89] The cost would be felt in reduced income for farmers as well as higher costs for food. The article included the information that pregnant rats injected with the herbicides had deformed babies, but this was overshadowed in the same article by the USDA argument that herbicides helped farmers economically.

Because the 1970 federal ban on 2,4,5-T use was only partial, press coverage of Agent Orange continued and continued to be narrowly focused on only one of its components. For example, in July 1970, *American Forests* advised readers that 2,4,5-T was extremely dangerous but did not mention other herbicides being used in Vietnam.[90] In September 1972, *Newsweek* ran a story about the use of 2,4,5-T in the United States. It described the dangers of the dioxin in 2,4,5-T that had been used in Vietnam but did not mention any other herbicides.[91] An article in *Consumer Reports* giving advice about weed killers singled out 2,4,5-T as unacceptable for use around the home but did not give advice on other Vietnam herbicides.[92]

Meanwhile, local and national activists at home continued to apply pressure to eliminate 2,4,5-T from the environment. For example, one Audubon Society chapter president from Indiana urged the head of the EPA, Russell Train, not to allow the burning of stocks of Agent Orange or its recycling in a "safe" form.[93] At the national level, Audubon continued its vigilance on the 2,4,5-T issue after the war. For example, Executive Vice President Charles Callison wrote to Secretary of Agriculture Earl Butz in 1972 urging that the USDA prepare environmental-impact statements regarding continued use of 2,4-D and 2,4,5-T on grassland in Kansas. Two years later, when he was president of Audubon, Callison urged the EPA in 1974 to go ahead with plans to cancel then allowable 2,4,5-T uses on rice, rangeland, and rights of way.[94] Audubon and the Environmental Defense Fund similarly waged a public campaign in the summer of 1974, issuing press releases outlining the dangers of continued use of 2,4,5-T and its links to birth defects due to the dioxin it contained.[95]

The press coverage of herbicide use in Vietnam had gone through different stages in the 1960s and early 1970s. First, journalists almost ignored the widespread and revolutionary policies of massive defoliation and crop destruction. Second, articles detailed the political wrangling in Washington to change herbicide use in Vietnam and at home. Third, stories focused on the dangers of 2,4,5-T and dioxin and the struggles to ban this chemical and its contaminant. In this last stage, journalists did not just report on the political debates in Washington but helped to keep consideration of herbicide use narrowly focused on one poison and thus avoid the messy scientific, foreign policy, and moral questions raised by Operation Ranch Hand.

The public discussion about Agent Orange can be divided into clear stages. From the mid-1960s to the end of the herbicide program in Vietnam, those mainly concerned were scientific experts lobbying each other and officials in the Nixon administration to end herbicidal warfare, which they considered a threat to the environment and to human health. But long after the war was over and its use was no longer a point of debate, Agent Orange received its greatest publicity in the United States. The image of Agent Orange from this stage has endured to the present day. Agent Orange became best known as the chemical that had poisoned American veterans, reinforcing the narrative that these men were victims and serving as an uncomfortable reminder of a shameful war. The people and landscape of Vietnam were relatively absent from this image.

National press attention to the plight of American veterans suffering health problems after Agent Orange exposure was touched off by the airing of an hour-long documentary, "Agent Orange: Vietnam's Deadly Fog," in March 1979. The report, by a CBS affiliate in Chicago, was produced by journalist Bill Curtis, who had been alerted to the situation by a coordinator of veteran services, Ron de Young. Once the program aired, hundreds of veterans began reporting that they were suffering from many of the symptoms detailed but had not known why. Their illnesses included skin rashes, headaches, swelling, nausea, liver problems, cancers, and difficulty having children. Soon, journalists outside Chicago were investigating Agent Orange and its impact on veterans.[96]

A sampling of television news stories on Agent Orange leads to a number of conclusions about how the topic was perceived in the public culture.[97] Television segments on Agent Orange were infrequent in the late 1970s, with the number of stories peaking in 1981 and in 1984 and quickly tapering off after 1985. The most common focus of the stories was the health effects of Agent Orange on American veterans and the resistance of the US government to acknowledge responsibility or provide treatment through the US Department of Veterans Affairs (VA). "Agent Orange" was the term most frequently used, not "herbicide" or "pesticide." Thus, no connection was made to agricultural uses in the United States. Sometimes Agent Orange was simply described as a "poison." The purpose of Agent Orange was most frequently described as "defoliation," and the crop-destruction aspect of Operation Ranch Hand or the other chemicals used were not mentioned. The repetition of the term "defoliation" further reinforced the idea that the chemical had a military purpose, not an agricultural or land-management one. Finally, though Agent Orange and dioxin were the most common descriptors used, the components of 2,4-D or 2,4,5-T were almost never mentioned, further distinguishing the Vietnamese policy from practices at home. In sum, the television news stories on Agent Orange reinforced the idea that this controversy had little to do with agriculture, land management, other pesticides, or pollution in the United States. Agent Orange appeared as an abstraction that was of little threat to ordinary Americans.

Since many of the stories focused on the health of American veterans and the refusal of the US government to admit any connection of their problems with Agent Orange exposure, the television segments often summarized the conflicting positions in the debate. In so doing, reporters and news anchors seemed to overstate the inconclusiveness of the evidence and the idea that there was "no proof" of a causal link between Agent Orange and ill health. For example, NBC coverage highlighted the findings of a mid-1983 US Air Force study that cast doubt on the idea that veterans exposed to Agent Orange suffered higher death rates, only to follow up with another story that pointed out the methodological flaws of the air force report.[98] In the end, the stories were more about the conflict between veterans and the VA, and the treatment of veterans, than about the chemical itself and its impact.

Also absent from the stories, along with any connection to use in the United States, was discussion of the Vietnamese and their experience with Agent Orange. Television reports on Agent Orange mentioned the devastating health effects on Vietnamese beginning only around 2000, and those stories were rare.

Books detailing Operation Ranch Hand and describing the plight of American veterans who had serious health problems presumably from Agent Orange exposure were published throughout the 1980s.[99] A prominent theme of the books was that the VA and the US government had ignored the needs of the veterans and so forced them to seek legal redress in a class-action suit. After years of litigation, the suit was settled in May 1984 for $180 million. Many veterans felt betrayed because they did not get the corporate or government accountability that they had sought and instead received only minor monetary payouts, with a maximum of $12,000 to a disabled veteran paid out over ten years.[100]

In the years after the settlement, federal policy changed with the passage of the Agent Orange Act of 1991, which obligated the government to treat soldiers whose illnesses had a "presumptive" association with Agent Orange exposure. Under this law, the VA was mandated to monitor and commission continuing research into the health effects of herbicide exposure and to treat veterans accordingly when there was a presumptive correlation between their conditions and exposure. Yet the predictable methodological problems of isolating exposure and determining specific causes of particular conditions left many veterans with a lack of definitive evidence, and few conditions were labeled as having "sufficient evidence of association."[101] Thus, by 2008, the US government had formally acknowledged only thirteen diseases as having been caused by dioxin (only one of which, spina bifida, was a birth defect). Such findings were denounced by many veterans and scientists in both the United States and Vietnam who believed that Agent Orange exposure had multigenerational effects in men, women, and children in both countries.[102] Finally, in 2009, the VA expanded its list of diseases that had a presumed association with Agent Orange exposure, leading to an increase in veterans' claims and the expansion of government medical care for them.[103]

By the early twenty-first century, Vietnamese victims increased pressure on the US government for compensation. In 2004, a new class-action suit on behalf of as many as 4 million Vietnamese claimed that their land and its inhabitants had been so poisoned by Agent Orange that the companies that had supplied it to the US government had committed war crimes. The chemical companies defended themselves against such accusations by saying that they had only supplied what had been directly ordered by the US government. The US District Court agreed with the companies' argument and dismissed the suit in 2005. The court ruled that the companies had not committed war crimes and that the plaintiffs had not proven any causal link between the chemicals and their health conditions.[104]

In addition to the court cases, the legacy of Agent Orange continued to be felt in United States–Vietnam relations four decades after the war. Many thousands of Vietnamese were severely disabled due—their families believed—to Agent Orange exposure.[105] In some areas, the countryside remained denuded, and there was a high rate of fetal and infant mortality.[106] Many Vietnamese were bitter over the issue, and Agent Orange remained a frequent topic in Vietnam's media. Each year on 10 August (the day that the United States began its first test spraying in 1961), victims of Agent Orange were commemorated. Finally, in August 2012, the US government announced a commitment to clean up the still highly contaminated former air base at Da Nang. The $43 million program was to take four years and was called by many Vietnamese "too little . . . and very late."[107]

Conclusion

The use of Agent Orange had an ignominious end, symbolizing the tragic failure of the American war in Vietnam. But the launch of the strategic program began otherwise, born of an idealistic faith that many Americans had in the promise of technology and, in particular, their ability to manipulate nature in faraway countries for the good of all.

Following the devastation of World War II, American policymakers faced two dilemmas: first, how to reconstruct the world economy while at the same time bringing the benefits of modern technology and development to rapidly growing populations of the non-Western world; second, how to secure political loyalty and strategic position in the amorphous, expansive Cold War. One way that US policymakers addressed these two dilemmas was in the export of industrial food surpluses, technical knowledge, and whole agricultural systems through programs such as Point Four and the Green Revolution. Integral to these initiatives was the ubiquitous use of chemicals, particularly pesticides. The enthusiasm of agricultural experts and government officials was conveyed to the public through frequent press stories about a Third World in need and generous Americans willing and able to help. Thus, Point Four, the Green Revolution, and similar foreign policies helped to reinforce generally positive attitudes toward industrial agriculture—and the pesticides that were a part of it—in the three decades after World War II.

In retrospect, the export of industrial agriculture was both a success and a failure. The Green Revolution had a monumental impact on world agriculture, transferring new crops across the oceans. There were, though, downsides to this transformation of world food systems, including the spread of monocultures, excessive chemical use, income inequality, and the decrease of nonexport food production within the Third World. In the short term, export yields nevertheless remained high with the availability of the cheap oil and water on which industrial agriculture depended. But the system was not sustainable, especially due to the high energy costs of industrial agriculture and the spread of pest resistance.[108]

Increasingly, in the 1970s and after, critics would use a different measure to evaluate the Green Revolution, arguing that the unintended economic, health, and environmental consequences were more significant than amassing ever greater yields for export agriculture. Some observers criticized, in particular, the increase of pesticide use associated with the Green Revolution, with global sales of the chemicals going from $8.1 billion in 1972 to $12.8 billion in 1983.[109] The consequences for certain countries were particularly dramatic. India, for example, had become the tenth-largest pesticide market in the world by 1971, with consumption almost quadrupling from 1970 to 1984, when it reached 96,000 tons.[110] Increased pesticide use and heightened demand encouraged excess production capacity, which, as chapter 6 shows, contributed to the tragedy of Bhopal.

Long before the unraveling of the Green Revolution became apparent, though, American political and military officials, convinced that agricultural chemicals were a powerful force for good, had found a new use for herbicides in Vietnam. Military officials embarked on the use of Agent Orange and its cousins for defoliation and crop destruction and, at first, received general if unthinking approval in the press. As public criticisms of the Vietnam War increased, so, too, did criticisms of how it was being waged, including the use of Agent Orange. Nevertheless, for several reasons, criticism of the Agent Orange program had a limited effect on the continued use of herbicides elsewhere. First, those who initially spoke out against Operation Ranch Hand were a relatively small group: scientists and antiwar activists. It was not until the early 1980s that complaints from American veterans about the health effects of their exposure to chemicals made the issue a frequently discussed topic in the mainstream press.

Second, even after the health effects of Agent Orange were widely debated, discussions almost always addressed its use in Vietnam, with little mention of herbicides, pesticides, or agricultural and land management uses in the United States. Third, criticisms of Agent Orange came to rest almost exclusively on one of its two components, 2,4,5-T, and its contaminant, dioxin. Thus, when Agent Orange use was ended in Vietnam and 2,4,5-T was restricted in the United States, there was much less public attention to the issue of ongoing herbicide use because the biggest problems appeared to have been solved.[111] In a pattern similar to that unfolding in the debate over DDT and persistent chlorinated hydrocarbon insecticides, focusing the greatest attention on a chemical with obvious and acutely dangerous environmental effects gave unintended reassurance that other chemicals were safe. Thus, 2,4-D maintained its reputation as the "good" pesticide, with its use increasing until it became the most widely used herbicide in the world even in 2013.[112] The demonization of 2,4,5-T therefore had the unintended consequence of reinforcing widespread herbicide use by making 2,4-D appear benign.

Finally, criticism of Agent Orange policy was directed at the execution of the policy and of the particular chemical selected, not at the underpinnings of the policy itself. In the end, the manipulation of the environment through the massive use of herbicides was not questioned by most Americans.

Criticisms that narrowly focused only on 2,4,5-T exposure of American soldiers during wartime had lasting consequences for herbicide use within the United States. In addition to the growing agricultural application of herbicides, such chemicals also continued to be used in land management (and suburbs) throughout the 1970s. US government use of different combinations of 2,4-D and 2,4,5-T in the American Southwest exposed many citizens, as well as domestic and wild animals, to the chemicals, leading to devastating health consequences for some.[113] Nevertheless, the domestic use of these herbicides received little press attention in comparison with the extensive coverage given to the health of Vietnam veterans in the 1980s.

Many Americans had long known that the export of agricultural technology had not accomplished all of its goals during the Cold War and even that there had been serious unintended consequences of the Green Revolution. The failures of Agent Orange use in Vietnam were even more dramatic and obvious in the public culture. Ironically, though, both of these foreign policies were strangely disassociated from overall pesticide use in the United States. Thus, attitudes toward pesticides remained relatively unchanged by these controversies, and the popular and political embrace of the chemicals continued to be strong.

CHAPTER 5

The Twenty-Year Itch: Activists, Experts, and the Regulatory Era

Surprisingly, the failures of the Green Revolution and Agent Orange did not drastically affect popular and political attitudes toward pesticide use in the United States. One would expect a different result from the new environmental attitudes and the explosion of domestic regulations in the two decades following the publication of *Silent Spring*, but expectations are not always fulfilled. Instead, the pesticide politics of the 1960s and 1970s reveal more examples of continuity than of change, more ways in which the political and scientific embrace of pesticides was reinforced rather than overturned.

The modern environmentalism that Rachel Carson helped to create had very concrete aspirations. Activists outside government started new organizations and strengthened existing ones to channel popular support for the growing movement and to lobby the government to protect the natural world. In the 1960s and 1970s, organizations such as the National Audubon Society were transformed from small, narrow groups into large, broad-based ones that had an outsized impact on the popular and political culture. Importantly, organizations such as Audubon might have ballooned in size, but they adhered to a moderate course, rejecting radical measures and appeals.

Organizational changes were also taking place inside government. When it came to pesticides, the biggest change came from the shifting role of the US Department of Agriculture. For decades, the USDA was the most powerful voice in Washington with respect to pesticides. But, increasingly, the agency faced challenges from activists and from other agencies in the government, especially with the creation of the Environmental Protection Agency in

1970. Many at the USDA saw themselves as fighting a rearguard action to defend not only their own role but also pesticides and how they were used.

Although some at the USDA were anxious to defend the pesticide status quo, others, such as USDA entomologist Edward Knipling, questioned existing policies and sought to change people's views to a more holistic understanding of pesticide impact. Knipling became an apostle of an approach known as integrated pest management (IPM). Within a short time, though, IPM became a broad catchall term, defined differently by Knipling and by environmental activists. Thus, Knipling's work ended up reinforcing dominant attitudes toward pesticides and their use rather than questioning them.

This chapter investigates changes on three fronts in the 1960s and 1970s: expectations for pesticide use and IPM; the diminishing role of the USDA; and the expanding role of the National Audubon Society. All three of these developments had the potential to severely weaken American support for industrial agriculture and pesticide use. Instead, the embrace of pesticides remained strong. Ironically, in what came to be called the regulatory era, when environmentalism flourished and became mainstream, challenges to the pesticide system were co-opted rather than fulfilled.

The National Audubon Society and the Crescendo for Reform

In the 1960s, environmentalism increasingly reshaped American politics, and one of the issues that excited much interest was pesticide regulation. By 1970, the calls to change course were concrete and overwhelming. From 1973 to 1976, there were twenty-four hearings related to pesticides in the House of Representatives and twenty in the Senate.[1] This congressional focus was reflected in the political and legal revolutions of the decade. The most important new environmental laws regarding pesticides were the National Environmental Policy Act (NEPA) of 1969, the 1972 Federal Environmental Pesticide Control Act (FEPCA), and the 1976 Toxic Substances Control Act (TOSCA) as well as the executive order establishing the Environmental Protection Agency in 1970. These acts have been discussed and debated in many histories about this high point of American environmentalism.[2]

NEPA created the President's Council on Environmental Quality and mandated that all federal agencies complete environmental assessments and environmental-impact statements on any proposed actions. FEPCA, revising the Federal Insecticide, Fungicide, and Rodenticide Act of 1947, gave jurisdiction over pesticide regulation to the new EPA and gave its administrator more authority to suspend or cancel registration of certain pesticides; under this new law, pesticide regulation became more focused on the protection of the environment and human health, and manufacturers shouldered a greater burden of proof to demonstrate safety. The passage of TOSCA was significant because it called for premarket testing and, if necessary, banning of chemicals when there was an "unreasonable risk of injury to health or environment."[3] And, finally, the creation of the EPA, whose administrator had cabinet-level rank, was important not just in the enforcement of FEPCA and other specific laws but in unifying environmental policy questions and signaling that this was a priority for the US government.[4]

Against this legal backdrop, environmental organizations such as the National Audubon Society grew dramatically. The organization's rise reflected the spread of environmental criticism from wildlife biologists, beginning in the 1950s, and writers such as Murray Bookchin and Rachel Carson in the early 1960s.[5] In particular, these critics had cited the 1950s USDA campaigns against the fire ant and gypsy moth as examples of misguided pesticide policies. By the 1960s, Audubon and other organizations grew even more as a reflection of the spreading counterculture, which criticized amassing private wealth at the expense of public wealth, focusing on issues such as clean air and water.[6] In many ways, environmentalism was a natural fit with the emerging liberal countercultures from the early 1960s onward, especially their utopian values.[7]

Environmentalism also sprang from the counterculture in its questioning of the production ideal and the assumption that natural resources were unlimited. The overlap of these two cultural trends was most clearly seen in concerns about world population. Paul Ehrlich's 1968 best seller, *The Population Bomb*, argued that the looming population explosion would lead to mass starvation in the 1970s and 1980s unless growth was curbed.[8] These worries showed up in fiction as well, such as in a 1966 book called *Make Room! Make Room!* and the 1973 film based upon it, *Soylent Green*.[9] Closely related to concerns about excessive population growth was the challenge to the idea that growth was both necessary and valuable. In 1972, a team of researchers from the Club of Rome led by Donella Meadows published *The Limits to Growth*, which laid out reasons that the current growth model was unsustainable.[10]

As many Americans questioned the economic assumptions of an industrial system that polluted the earth and harmed wildlife, organizations dedicated to taking care of the environment were remaking themselves to address these broader concerns, including worry about the impact of pesticides. The Audubon Society was one of the most successful in this transformation. It started as the Massachusetts Audubon Society, formed by a group of elite Boston women who began organizing against the use of bird plumage in fashion in 1896.[11] Within a few years, more than thirty state societies incorporated as the National Association of Audubon Societies. Nevertheless, the state societies remained somewhat decentralized in the first half of the twentieth century and primarily concerned with issues related to birds; the umbrella organization did not change its name to National Audubon Society until 1940. But by midcentury, Audubon, along with other groups such as the Sierra Club, began to broaden its agenda to address industrial pollution in the chemical age.

By almost any measure, Audubon was one of the most successful environmental organizations in the second half of the twentieth century and into the twenty-first. It was the second-largest US conservation group in 1950 (when there were few such organizations); after two decades of tremendous growth, it reached 115,000 members and then more than half a million members by the start of the twenty-first century. Audubon had also grown in terms of budget, membership contributions, and total staff. With an operating budget of $70 million in 2002 and more than 500 paid staff, the organization was a powerful national organization.[12]

Audubon turned its attention to pesticides in 1945, even before the end of World War II. It was one of the first conservation organizations to conduct a study of DDT, working with the US Forest Service in Pennsylvania to measure the impact of the chemical on wildlife. Audubon staff member Dick Pough was very direct in his criticism of the possible civilian use of DDT. He described the devastating impact on wildlife that was likely as well as the philosophy that lay behind its adoption. Pough's blunt condemnation was quoted in the *New Yorker* in May 1945:

> A spray like DDT makes people think of a continent arranged like a manicured garden, but you can't kick nature around that way. If DDT should ever be used widely and without care, we would have a country without freshwater fish, serpents, frogs, and most of the birds we have

> now. Mind you, we don't object to its use to save lives now. What we are afraid of is what might happen when peace comes.[13]

Audubon president John Baker's column in the organization's *Audubon* magazine was similarly negative but more tempered in its language, saying that DDT's "unchecked use could endanger bird life."[14]

A decade later, leaders of the National Audubon Society were increasingly worried about the widespread use of chemical pesticides and became more active in trying to change government policies endorsing pesticide use. For example, in 1956, the Washington, DC, office tried to rally affiliates in Florida to lobby the state government to abandon its program of spraying dieldrin and malathion to control the Mediterranean fruit fly. A memo from Audubon headquarters cautioned that not enough was known about the effects of these chemicals, saying, "The division between a safe and a lethal dose may be extremely small."[15]

Audubon activism took a giant leap forward the following year with the organization's opposition to the USDA's fire ant spraying program. Many conservation groups, along with Audubon, protested the program, including the National Wildlife Federation, the Conservation Foundation, and the New York Zoological Society.[16] Other organizations also increased public attention to the issue through studies and meetings. The Garden Club of America, for example, sponsored a panel discussion on aerial spraying in March 1958.[17] Many wild and domestic animals had been killed by the spraying, including fish, wild birds, and poultry as well as shrimp, snakes, frogs, and lizards.[18] The fire ant program had become, Baker observed, "the hottest topic discussed at the sundry wildlife conferences throughout the country."[19]

After the initial furor over the USDA program, more mainstream scientific organizations focused on the issue of pesticide contamination of the environment. The National Academy of Sciences—National Research Council formed a Committee on Pest Control and Wildlife Relationships in mid-1960. The committee was intended to give technical advice to the federal government and encourage cooperation among agencies as well as evaluate pesticide effects and encourage further research. It started with the premise that pesticides had been and would continue to be extremely beneficial, but greater attention had to be paid to "minimizing the danger to wildlife."[20]

In their opposition to the fire ant program, Audubon leaders became increasingly cynical about the justifications for it, especially from the USDA.

For example, USDA statements and a press release from HEW found in National Audubon Society files were annotated with marginal comments about the veracity of the points made. "Nonsense" was scrawled a number of times in response to assertions that the fire ant was harmful; that aerial spraying was used sparingly; and that only minimal, targeted spraying was used in proximity to bodies of water. Audubon files also contained a memo, "False Statements by the USDA before Subcommittee of Agricultural Appropriations Bill," as well as an assessment and list of talking points for Audubon officials to criticize the fire ant program.[21]

The National Audubon Society seized the moment to criticize not only the fire ant program but also the USDA's gypsy moth program in the Northeast and Midwest. Baker sent a letter to Dwight Eisenhower calling for an end to the campaign because no one knew the full effects or the full costs of the program. He focused his criticism on the indiscriminate, broadcast use ofpoisons and made it clear that his organization opposed all aerial spraying of extremely toxic chemicals unless there was a serious danger to people or wildlife.[22] The organization sent a similar telegram to Secretary of Agriculture Benson in December 1957.[23] In its lobbying efforts, Audubon also focused directly on congressional leaders. In March 1959, Baker testified before the House Subcommittee on Agricultural Appropriations. He used an analogy that Rachel Carson would adopt three years later, explaining that pesticide contamination might present an even greater threat to human reproduction than did radioactive fallout.

"The Hazards of Broadcasting Toxic Pesticides, as Illustrated by Experience with the Imported Fire Ant Control Program" was an Audubon booklet based on extensive discussions at the organization's 1958 annual meeting.[24] The booklet reported on findings from Audubon's ten-month study of the program; it was a blunt indictment, charging not only that wildlife and livestock had been killed immediately following the spraying but that "claims of serious damage by the ants [were] false and misleading." In addition, the booklet focused on the need for more study of both target species and of the effects of pesticides before they were used and stated that both acute and chronic effects had to be studied. Much of the report criticized the "broadcast" of toxic chemicals. It is not clear how Audubon would have reacted to a more narrowly defined, nonaerial pesticide program.[25]

In comparison with Audubon's later activism and the legislative and regulatory goals of the environmental movement after the publication of

Silent Spring, the organization's actions in the late 1950s may appear inadequate. But the need for direct action against pesticides that later seemed self-evident to environmentalists was not yet an unquestioned imperative. From this perspective, the National Audubon Society's pesticide policies may have been tempered but nevertheless showed active engagement with the issue as the organization lobbied both executive-branch officials and elected representatives for specific policy changes and legislation.[26] In addition, Audubon annual meetings in 1961, 1962, 1963, and 1964 all had panels on pesticides.[27] Carl Buchheister, Audubon president from 1959 to 1967, made changing national pesticide policies one of his priorities. Members, along with the general public, identified the organization with its support for new pesticide laws and public education on the issue in these years.[28]

In addition to its lobbying on pesticide use generally, there is a record of Audubon's support for Rachel Carson and *Silent Spring* long before the book's publication. Both President John Baker and his successor, Carl Buchheister, wrote to Carson in 1958 expressing their enthusiasm, or "delight," as Buchheister said, for her project. Buchheister added his assessment that the 1958 Audubon convention session on pesticides had garnered good publicity and even the endorsement of the "Society's stand" from the normally critical *Hartford Courant*.[29] Carson proceeded to work with Audubon as she gathered information for her book. In 1959, 1960, and 1961, she and Charles Callison (who became executive vice president in 1960) exchanged information and sources, often with Carson making inquiries and Callison offering referrals and bits of information.[30] Audubon public information officer Robert Burnap in 1959 told Carson he had many files, reports, and publications on pesticide use that he would be happy to share with her.[31]

In the months just prior to the publication of *Silent Spring*, Buchheister assisted in the book's promotion. He responded to a request from Houghton Mifflin editor Paul Brooks with a list of people to whom advance copies and requests for publicity endorsements should be sent. Furthermore, he requested that if Audubon did not object to anything in the book (which he did not anticipate would be the case), it would also consider giving an endorsement for publicity. Finally, he inquired about the possibility of *Audubon* magazine excerpting a chapter prior to publication. Buchheister received a grateful thank-you from Carson's agent, who deemed his work on behalf of the book "magnificent."[32]

Buchheister also played a public role in debating the widespread use of pesticides, such as participating in a panel at Johns Hopkins Medical School to counter the position of a USDA scientist.[33] He used Audubon to actively defend *Silent Spring* against its detractors. In 1962, he reminded all branch and affiliate officers that there was a nationwide campaign to discredit *Silent Spring*, forwarding a copy of a full-page ad in the *New York Times* that "contain[ed] rebuttal material that may come in handy."[34] Similarly, Audubon responded to queries from local organizations (such as the Schenectady Bird Club) about chemical-industry attacks on *Silent Spring*. The form letter urged everyone to pressure their local media outlets into presenting "our side" of the story, making the message of Rachel Carson and Audubon synonymous.[35]

Audubon's increased concern with the use of pesticides can probably be traced to the work of staff biologist Roland Clement more than to anyone else. Clement was an early and strong critic of the chemicals. He had recommended that the society publish Rachel Carson's book and warned as early as 1958 about the bioaccumulation of pesticides, as evidenced in earthworms and birds, that was dangerous to ecosystems.[36] In one talk at the 1961 annual National Audubon Society convention, "The Failure of Common Sense," Clement argued that modern agricultural systems were based on biological ignorance: "Man's attempts at simplifying habitats for his own benefit . . . are bucking nature. . . . Not only is the control efficacy of insecticides so often disappointing, but these poisons, by upsetting nature's built-in mechanisms, often actually lead to an increase in pest numbers."[37] In addition, Clement reiterated other warnings that wildlife biologists had been issuing for years: increased production of crops was unnecessary because the government had to pay to store grain surpluses; insect resistance was a serious problem caused by overuse of pesticides; and the effects of residues of chemicals in the soil were not yet known.

Clement further argued that since their effects were not fully known, synthetic pesticides should be only a "last resort" for "emergency use" and, even then, applied only in small, isolated areas as needed. His caution about pesticide use was also premised on the idea that labeling particular insects as "pests" was based on a misunderstanding of how nature worked: "Pest control is a problem in ecology and population dynamics; today's pest may be tomorrow's friend, and vice versa, so the scientist must avoid this misleading terminology." Clement corresponded with Carson in 1962, viewing himself as an ally in the struggle against the pro-pesticide lobby. By spring 1963, his position had evolved further, and he made the argument that *all* chlorinated hydrocarbons, with the possible exception of methoxychlor, should be barred from general use.[38]

Clement's determination to criticize then-current pesticide practices meant that he as an individual sometimes pushed for more action than the moderate National Audubon Society was willing to support. For example, by 1970, Clement wrote to Callison in frustration that he sometimes felt as if he were taking on the National Agricultural Chemicals Association (NACA) alone. In a plea for Audubon to directly counter a NACA booklet by printing and distributing a rebuttal, he wrote, "I have scientific facts against them, but I don't like butting my head against a wall unless someone will provide a helmet, back-up troops, etc."[39]

Even if Roland Clement led the way in calling for a broad ecological approach to agriculture and pesticide use, the National Audubon Society as an organization, especially after the publication of *Silent Spring*, mainly echoed this message. For example, at a speech in Washington, DC, in October 1962, Audubon president Carl Buchheister told his audience that the "challenge [regarding pesticides] is ecological."[40] He criticized the approach of the USDA, arguing that the agency considered only the short-term economic interests of the farmer and was an "agent for the chemical industry." Following Clement's lead, Buchheister argued that "pest" was an economically relative concept and that policies of eradication were "futile."

To lessen the use of harmful chemicals, Buchheister called for more research into pesticides before they were allowed on the market as well as into more selective chemicals and biological and cultural methods of pest control. In addition, he called for new legal regulations, beginning with the then-proposed Pesticides Coordination Act, an act that he called "modest" but that had nevertheless been killed in the previous Congress when the chair of the Senate Agricultural Committee had prevented hearings or any consideration of the measure. Along with passage of the coordination act, he called for increased federal funding for research into pesticide effects. Charles Callison, similarly, made arguments to increase knowledge about pesticides and to think of their impact more broadly. Months before the publication of *Silent Spring*, for example, Callison told the chairman of the Interdepartmental Committee on Pest Control, Dr. Justus Ward, "The absence of any evidence of detrimental effects on wildlife does not mean there are no such effects but rather, as in so many other cases of the extensive use of chemical insecticides, that little or no research had been done on the wildlife aspects."[41]

Audubon's support for the "modest" Pesticides Coordination Act illustrated the group's strategy not to support overly radical measures that might backfire. Two years earlier, Callison had also supported the then-proposed Pesticides Coordination Act, and the bill's author, Representative Leonard Wolf of Iowa, had consulted with the National Audubon Society. The act would require further study of pesticides prior to use, not only by the federal Fish and Wildlife Service but also by the game and fish departments in the affected states.[42] Audubon submitted a statement on the bill (HR 11502) to the House Subcommittee on Fisheries and Wildlife in May 1960. The Audubon statement criticized not all pesticide use but only overuse and inappropriate use.[43] Examples of incorrect or irresponsible use were included, such as the fields in Illinois that had been sprayed three times since 1954 to "eradicate" the Japanese beetle to no avail or the inexplicable switch in this program from dieldrin to the extremely toxic aldrin simply because the aldrin supplier had submitted a lower bid to the Illinois Department of Agriculture.

With news that the Subcommittee on Fisheries and Wildlife was going to report the bill to the full committee of Merchant Marines and Fisheries, Callison wrote to Wolf that the progress on the bill "proves that our strategy had been sound in not trying to accomplish too much in one piece of legislation."[44] Such a calculation did not mean that this was an ideal bill. Buchheister had written to a scientist with the Department of Conservation at Cornell University in April 1960 that "it does not go nearly as far as we would like, but it does appear to be a sound step in the right direction. Strengthening amendments or legislative 'teeth' can be proposed when hearings are held."[45] Buchheister, representing Audubon, carefully circumscribed a moderate course as the effective route, taking small steps that would be most likely to lead to the long-term goal of changing pesticide use.

Thus, Callison, Buchheister, and Audubon as an organization, following the lead of Roland Clement and Rachel Carson, became champions of a new way of viewing the environment and the human role in it. By the mid-1960s, pesticides had become a major focus of the National Audubon Society. The leaders of Audubon, like Carson, chose a moderate strategy as the one most likely to yield results. This approach can be seen as overly timid or as pragmatic, depending on one's perspective. But whichever of these judgments is made, Audubon could not be accused of challenging industrial agriculture and land management policies as a whole; instead, its leaders—along with other conservationists—sought to prevent the worst effects of chemical overuse.

One strategy for leaders of Audubon was to try to change political attitudes by increasing press coverage of environmental news. In 1964, Callison wrote to state game, fish, and conservation directors, encouraging them to recognize the opportunities at that particular point in time:

> Federal, state, and local pest-control agencies, that in the past have tended to be either apathetic, disbelieving, or stubborn about the pesticides problem, are beginning to have second thoughts. I think we are on the verge of seeing some genuine reforms take place, if we can keep up the pressure. One way to do it is to see that every kill of fish caused by pesticides, every new discovery of damages caused to birds or other wildlife, is reported in the press.[46]

Here is an example of why the 1960s—what speakers at Audubon's 1966 annual meeting referred to as the "environmental decade"—were the beginning of a period of tremendous growth for Audubon and other environmental organizations such as the Sierra Club and the National Wildlife Federation.[47] Audubon worked to transform itself into a mass organization, for instance by changing its flagship magazine, *Audubon*, into a general-interest publication.[48] The goal of broadening the society's base was also reflected in its leaders' efforts to have a moderate voice on issues such as pesticides so as not to alienate potential supporters.

The growing popular and political concern about pesticides in the 1960s and 1970s—and the influence of an environmental organization such as the National Audubon Society—is well illustrated by the fight to ban DDT in the late 1960s and early 1970s. Building upon the political momentum following the publication of *Silent Spring* and the release of the 1963 President's Science Advisory Committee Report, Audubon tried to get state and national governments to lessen DDT use—even simply urging the substitution of less-persistent pesticides. For example, in 1965, Executive Vice President Charles Callison wrote to the secretary of the Department of Forests and Waters in Pennsylvania, urging that malathion or carbamate be used instead of DDT in the upcoming spraying of 100,000 acres of forest: "It distresses me and grieves me to see your otherwise enlightened Department embarking upon a 100,000-acre spraying. . . . I urge you to get your forest entomologists out of their rut. This is 1965, not 1945."[49]

Audubon also worked with people at the grassroots level to encourage the passage of local laws restricting the use of DDT and chlorinated hydrocarbons. For example, in August 1969, the public information director at Audubon responded to a query for organizing information from Queens, New York, by sending back a model bill to establish a Pesticide Control Board that could lessen local pesticide use.[50] Such organizing took place across the country as Audubon worked to get bills calling for pesticide restrictions introduced in a number of states.[51]

Audubon officers lobbied officials at the USDA to reassess their existing pesticide programs and work toward an "orderly reduction in persistent pesticides."[52] By 1969, Audubon president Elvis Stahr was writing to Secretary of Agriculture Clifford Hardin (the two were on a first-name basis, as Stahr had been with Secretary Freeman), pressing him to support a ban on DDT. Stahr appealed to Hardin that "the nation is ready for the change we have urged."[53] Stahr's lobbying in 1969 built on the momentum of the federal commission chaired by microbiologist Emil Mrak, which had recommended the USDA cancel all residential uses of DDT.[54]

Meanwhile, Audubon lobbying continued outside the USDA, encouraging members of Congress to support bills in 1969 banning DDT and other chlorinated hydrocarbons. The arguments made by Audubon officials, in particular, focused on the demonstrated effects of these pesticides on the reproduction of birds at the top of the food chain.[55] Audubon leaders also sought to make sure that ordinary people understood the importance of the DDT ban. For example, Callison sent a letter to the *New York Times Magazine* in 1974, criticizing a cover story that had seemed to minimize "the dire warnings of environmentalists." On the contrary, wrote Callison, birds such as the osprey and brown pelican stood a chance of recovery only because of the ban on DDT.[56]

Audubon had joined forces with other environmental organizations to push for the domestic DDT ban. The Environmental Defense Fund (EDF) took the lead in the fight by filing suit in 1969, first against the USDA and then against the EPA, to cancel registrations for the chemical. The EDF suit was also on behalf of other organizations: the National Audubon Society, the Sierra Club, and the West Michigan Environmental Action Council. After a lengthy cancellation hearing within the EPA, the administrator of the agency, William Ruckelshaus, issued a ruling in June 1972 canceling all uses of DDT in crop production and non-health-related areas, with the exception of allowing some ad hoc emergency uses with EPA approval.

The fight against DDT was an increasingly public issue in the late 1960s, and there were many articles in the mainstream press about it. Articles gave details of the agricultural and chemical industry argument that the banning of DDT would have a significant economic "impact," particularly on some crops and against some pests, and clearly showed that the USDA and environmentalists were antagonists in this debate.[57] The fight to ban DDT not only garnered much public attention but also stoked anger among some farmers and those in the chemical industry, who were furious at what they saw as a government intrusion into their business.[58]

Even after the victory of cancellation in 1972, leaders of Audubon remained vigilant in monitoring any attempts by government agencies or private companies to obtain emergency exceptions to the ban, for example, for use against forest pests or in cotton cultivation, and lobbied the EPA not to grant exemptions in such circumstances.[59]

One case that received much publicity in the press and involvement from Audubon was the US Forest Service's request to use DDT against the tussock moth in the Northwest just one year after the ban had been approved. EPA officials, apparently not eager to grant the exemption, welcomed counterarguments from groups such as Audubon.[60] Callison wrote about the issue in *Audubon* and alerted local chapters in the Northwest that this was a threat in summer 1973, warning, "We may have to fight this battle all over again."[61] Many officials agreed with those at Audubon and the EPA. For example, one 1973 memo from the Department of the Interior's Bureau of Sport Fisheries and Wildlife argued that granting the exemption for DDT use against the tussock moth would "turn back . . . all gains made in recent years."[62]

Audubon officials seem to have developed a good relationship with the EPA, which probably helped to make their lobbying more effective. EPA administrator Russell Train wrote to "Charlie" Callison in January 1976, thanking Audubon for its support of the EPA decision to ban major uses of heptachlor and chlordane; he added, "It is satisfying to know that veteran environmental groups such as yours endorse our decision, for as you know, we at EPA value highly your support."[63] Train also accepted Audubon's suggestions. For example, in early 1976, after Callison complained that state and local mosquito-control programs sometimes overused pesticides and that their operations did not seem to have much supervision, Train said that he would have the EPA's Office of Pesticide Programs investigate the situation and see if any action was needed.[64]

The National Audubon Society, along with other environmental organizations, remained active and vigilant on the pesticides issue throughout the 1970s. Audubon, along with the EDF, jointly employed a "pesticides monitor" (Maureen Hinkle) to work on lobbying and legislative issues in Washington.[65] Both organizations were concerned not only with lobbying politicians in Washington, DC, and officials in various states. They also saw a large part of their role as educating the public about pesticides and other environmental issues—and Hinkle was active in such efforts. For example, at the end of the 1970s, she produced a thirty-two-page "Citizen's Action Guide to the Federal Insecticide, Fungicide, and Rodenticide Act." Audubon continued such efforts of public education, for example, distributing "Getting the Bugs Out: A Guide to Sensible Pest Management in and around the Home" in 1981.[66] This pamphlet began by trying to change people's understanding of "pest," asserting that the concept was a relative one. Even if an insect or plant was an economic problem, "the goal must be controlled management, not eradication."

Although there was clear evidence of Audubon activism in the 1960s and 1970s against pesticide overuse and abuse, it's worth remembering that the organization was careful not to be perceived as "antipesticide." Even when the fight to ban DDT was nearing its successful conclusion, Audubon continued to assert—as summarized in one 1969 memo—that it was not against the use of all pesticides, only the very toxic, persistent chemicals such as DDT, aldrin, dieldrin, endrin, and heptachlor.[67] The same memo endorsed the selective use of other admittedly dangerous chemicals (chlordane, benzene hexachloride [BHC], endosulfan, and toxaphene) when warranted by particular pest problems and included a list of other acceptable agricultural chemicals. Even Roland Clement, with a strong record of action against zealous pesticide use, was careful in 1973 to make sure that Audubon didn't come across as anti-pesticide. For example, he criticized the draft of an editorial for *Audubon* magazine on proposed USDA use of DDT against the tussock moth. He wrote to Vice President Callison and other Audubon leaders, "The barrage of emotion-laden phrases like 'fear-mongering,' 'chemical hucksters,' 'simplistic control entomologists,' 'hooked on DDT,' and 'DDT-addicted' is not only intemperate but makes us look as though we too are hooked on something."[68]

The National Audubon Society was actively engaged in the debate over pesticides and worked closely with others, such as the EDF. Nevertheless, it hewed closely to the parameters set out by Rachel Carson in *Silent Spring* when she asserted, "It is not my contention that chemical insecticides must never be used. I do contend that we have put poisonous and biologically potent chemicals indiscriminately into the hands of persons largely or wholly ignorant of their potentials for harm."[69] Carson's argument of reasonable moderation set the tone that mainstream environmental organizations would strike in the 1960s and 1970s as they sought to establish a regulatory structure for the industry and to ban only the most toxic of the chemicals.

The Shifting Political Role of the USDA

The regulatory decades of the 1960s and 1970s were shaped not only by the activism of environmental organizations such as Audubon but also by changing politics in Washington, DC. Since its founding in the late nineteenth century, the USDA had played an essential role in the industrialization of agriculture, with numerous programs that encouraged farmers to adopt new technologies and approaches.[70] For decades, the USDA controlled pesticide policies and use. Yet, following the highly visible debacles of its fire ant and gypsy moth campaigns of the late 1950s and early 1960s, and especially after the publication of *Silent Spring*, the agency had been fighting a rearguard action to defend widespread pesticide use in the face of mounting criticism.

An examination of USDA actions tells much about the views of many officials who supported the pesticide status quo as well as about the shifting role of the federal government on this issue. In addition, the escalating disagreements between the USDA, HEW, and the Department of the Interior, as well as the creation of the EPA, revealed not only long-standing power conflicts but also how the existing chemical order was adapted to a pro-environmental discourse.

Nineteen sixty-four was a difficult year for many officials at the USDA. If there had been any hope that the controversies over pesticides ushered in by *Silent Spring* two years before would die down, that hope was short-lived. A massive fish kill in the Mississippi River in the spring of that year pushed its way onto the front pages of many newspapers. The papers reported that chemical plants on the river might be the source of the poisoning; the agricultural use of endrin and other pesticides in neighboring states was another possible culprit. The USDA's response to the fish kills (going on for four years but making headlines in 1964) illustrates the department's goals as well as its relationship with the chemical industry and HEW.

In March 1964, the Public Health Service (PHS) of HEW released its report on the previous year's fish kill in the Mississippi, finding that the mud and water in the area were heavily contaminated with endrin. At the same time, news of a massive fish kill in another region of the river broke. USDA officials were anxious that field runoff not be blamed for the kills lest it invite scrutiny of the department's regulatory policies.[71]

In addition to being concerned about the origins of the contamination and the focus on endrin and dieldrin to the exclusion of other chemicals, USDA officials were also upset that the PHS had given them little warning of the impending report. Director of Science Education for the Agricultural Research Service (ARS) Nyle Brady complained to Secretary of Agriculture Orville Freeman in April that the evidence did not show that endrin and dieldrin were the only possible sources of the kills and, moreover, that the actions of HEW showed a lack of coordination among agencies.[72] The secretary's assistant also complained about the conduct of the PHS and the FDA, writing that they had released information to the press before sharing it with the USDA.[73]

The USDA criticized the PHS report in the press as well. For example, USDA official Charles Murphy told the *New York Times* that his department needed more than "probabilities, iffy conjectures, likelihoods or presumptions" such as those in the PHS report to make regulatory decisions about pesticides. At the same time, the USDA faced opposition from other federal agencies; the FWS, for example, had asserted in early 1963 that even minute amounts of pesticides in water could cause fish kills.[74]

From the perspective of USDA officials, interdepartmental differences over how to interpret and manage the fish kills exacerbated the problems of how to control press coverage. For example, staffer Tom Hughes was upset over April articles in the *New Republic*, *Washington Post*, and *New York Times* that he thought made the USDA look bad in comparison with the PHS. He wrote to the secretary that he had wanted to "play the public relations game" by publicly releasing information to the PHS and Senator Abraham Ribicoff that a company had dumped endrin into the river at Nashville. According to Hughes, the information remained stuck in the departmental bureaucracy while the PHS released it to Senator Ribicoff, meaning that "they are in the newspaper and we aren't. . . . We always take a 'responsible' position and get lined up with the chemical industry and look back [*sic*] in the press." Hughes's perception appeared to be fairly accurate. The press articles noted that the PHS was the agency releasing the information, and an editorial in the *Washington Post* implied that Secretary Freeman did not have an appreciation of the dangers in persistent pesticides.[75]

Press coverage of the fish kills illustrated for some USDA officials that they would have to remain on their guard. Jim Ward, special assistant to the undersecretary of agriculture, wrote to his boss in November 1964, warning that the department needed to be prepared for future articles by "trained hatchet m[e]n" in the press as well as for investigative committees in Congress or any person or group that wanted to reintroduce the issue. He added, "This is not to say that we have no defense and that our position is entirely wrong—only that in anticipating some of the accusations, if made, can we hope to minimize them."[76] In one example of anticipating accusations, the secretary's assistant, Rod Leonard, drafted a statement summarizing the department's positions with respect to pesticides.[77] The USDA, the statement said, was concerned primarily with "insur[ing] adequate and safe supplies of food, fiber, and forest products" for the nation as well as people in other parts of the world. This goal rested on the "modern agriculture" practiced in the United States. And although pest control was "not an end in itself," it was one way to achieve "a friendly environment." Clearly, Leonard and Freeman had not adopted Rachel Carson's "balance of nature" views.

Meanwhile, USDA officials were also trying to manage not just the stories told in the press but also those told on Capitol Hill. Following news of the spills, Senator Ribicoff—who had become a leading environmental voice in Congress and had held hearings on pesticide use soon after the publication of *Silent Spring*—announced that his subcommittee of the Committee on Government Operations would hold hearings on the fish kills.[78] The April hearings showed how the federal departments were sometimes at cross-purposes: an assistant secretary from the HEW testified that pesticides were the suspected cause of the kills and that the fish had all been contaminated with endrin; Senator Ribicoff cited the views of Secretary of the Interior Stewart Udall that persistent pesticides should be banned; and Secretary Freeman argued in his testimony that the more than 100 chemical plants on the Mississippi River, not just agricultural runoff, should be investigated as the source of pollution. In private as well as in public, USDA officials seemed more inclined to believe that agricultural runoff was not the culprit in the fish kills. ARS administrator B. T. Shaw, for example, wrote to the secretary that departmental investigations showed that waste-disposal practices of pesticide plants on the Mississippi "are contributing significantly to the contamination" of the river.[79]

At first glance, it might seem that the USDA belief that errant releases from manufacturing plants were the main culprits in fish contamination would be harmful to the interests of chemical companies. But in this, as in so many other issues, the interests of the USDA and the pesticide industry coincided. If the pollution came from chemical plants on the river, manufacturing and disposal practices could have been changed to solve the problem. But if runoff was judged to be the main problem, the solution would have been difficult because it would have involved directly challenging the widespread use of chemicals on surrounding agricultural fields.

Press materials from the chemical industry reflected the close relationship that the manufacturers had with the USDA and highlighted the idea that both the private companies and the USDA were concerned about safety. For example, in April 1964—just one month after fish kills in the Mississippi were making headlines—the NACA sent to radio and television stations recorded news features on the national "safe-use" campaign that included statements from Nyle Brady of the USDA. The spots emphasized that the safety campaign was a joint effort of NACA and the USDA as well as the National Safety Council, HEW, 4-H, and Future Farmers of America and said that "protective spraying" was necessary and perfectly safe when "these government accepted chemical servants . . . [were] used properly."[80] Press releases from individual companies such as Shell also supported the "intensive safety program" and quoted USDA spokesmen to make their point.[81]

In addition to joint releases with chemical companies and NACA, USDA public relations efforts in the safety campaign were broad and included enlisting the help of radio and TV celebrities such as Arthur Godfrey and Eddie Albert to record public service announcements about the importance of pesticide safety.[82] The radio and television spots had a folksy tone, aimed at the home gardener, and often emphasized reading label directions. They discussed commonsense precautions such as not spraying around children and animals or in windy conditions and not using more chemicals than needed.

This type of general bromide offered few specific directions nor a clear sense of danger about chemical pesticides. The safety campaign, overall, was more about endorsing the continued use of chemicals, directly and indirectly arguing that pesticides were necessary, such as when one spot asserted that "pesticides protect our never-ending supply of quality food, as well as our lawns and gardens."[83] The campaign allowed both the USDA and industry to demonstrate that they took the issue of safety seriously but also to defuse criticisms of pesticide use and thus to protect industrial agriculture.

Two years later, USDA officials felt some satisfaction that their safety campaign had paid off. Director of Information Harold Lewis wrote to Assistant Secretary G. L. Mehren that a recent public opinion survey (carried out on behalf of Shell Chemical Company) demonstrated that there had been "a dramatic shift in the attitude of the general public" since the initial alarm following the publication of *Silent Spring*.[84] Lewis cited the "intensive pesticide information-education effort stressing USDA's role in safeguarding the public" as partly responsible for the shift. (Although it is clear from the questions asked that it would have been hard for results unfavorable to the industry to have emerged from the survey, the information officer was oblivious to the manipulations.)

Meanwhile, as the department celebrated the success of its safety campaign, it continued related campaigns to educate Americans about the benefits of pesticides. At the end of 1966, the USDA was sending booklets to elementary and other school teachers titled "The War That Never Ends . . . Facts about Pest Control." The department's deputy director for science and education laid out the purpose of the initiative: "Once our foot is firmly in the classroom door, then the Office of Information, working with ARS and other agencies, plans to further develop the opportunities offered for reaching our young people."[85] With such planning, USDA officials were laying the foundations for continued pesticide use well into the future.

Not surprisingly, as public and political criticisms of pesticides escalated by the early 1970s, the chemical industry and other agricultural interests were increasingly concerned about the trend. Industry officials worked to maintain their close relationship with the USDA in order to, in the words of one lobbyist for the cotton industry, "keep essential pesticides available" by using "scientific evidence," not "emotions and untruths."[86] Shortly before, the president of the NACA had written to Secretary of Agriculture Clifford

Hardin, "There is a feeling that the farmer and his interests are not being given adequate consideration."[87]

Even if the interests of the USDA and the pesticide industry often coincided, there were times when, by the early 1970s, government officials were motivated to assert that they were not antienvironment and to put some distance between themselves and the industry if needed. For example, in November 1972, Parke Brinkley, the outraged head of NACA, complained to Secretary of Agriculture Earl Butz about a recent news release from the department that he felt was an effort to "placate" environmentalists and would further prejudice the public about chemical pest control. Brinkley objected to language in the news release saying that the department sought "to protect the environment and to improve efficiency" as well as "to maximize producer profits and minimize the amount of insecticide needed."[88]

The response from Butz might have surprised Brinkley. Although the secretary agreed that he, too, was concerned about "the reaction of extreme environmentalists," he asserted that part of the USDA mission was to "protect the environment" and that it was good to remind the public of this. In addition, Butz cited the problems of chemical dependency in the cotton industry that had led to resistance; periodic pest outbreaks; and costly, frequent spraying.[89] Before the 1970s, it is unlikely that the secretary of agriculture would have written such a letter. But USDA officials, like other Americans, had seen at least some of the drawbacks of the current system.

In the mid- to late 1960s, USDA officials had begun addressing another issue that reflected the changing pesticide landscape: the growing public and political movement to ban DDT. As the earlier discussion about Audubon's involvement in the DDT issue indicates, this was an important rallying point for environmentalists. But the fight to ban DDT had other political and cultural implications. In *Silent Spring* and in the publicity surrounding the book, DDT came to symbolize the dangers of persistent, organic pesticides for reasons that were predictable and logical. DDT was the first widely used chlorinated hydrocarbon during and after World War II, remained the most widely used of this class of chemicals through the end of the 1950s, was cheap and easily available, and had appeared to have low toxicity for mammals and many other animals. Being the most visible, though, had its consequences. DDT was soon the favorite target for those who took Rachel Carson's message to heart. Unintentionally, as discussed in chapter 3, the relentless focus on DDT would end up giving a backhanded endorsement to other pesticides that appeared to be the safer fallback options because they were less persistent.

The story of DDT and its domestic ban in 1972 has been told in detail elsewhere and won't be repeated here.[90] But a brief look at USDA reactions to this issue and changing public opinion reveals much about cultural attitudes in the late 1960s and 1970s. Concrete, legal steps to ban DDT in the United States were launched when Wisconsin Senator Gaylord Nelson introduced such a bill in the summer of 1966. The USDA response to the senator asserted that all the pesticides the department registered could be used safely but also that its long-range goal was "an orderly reduction in the recommended uses of persistent insecticides," even if this would take a long time due to the thousands of insect pests.[91] Although Nelson's bill languished in the Agriculture Committee, the senator remained active on the DDT issue, in 1969 pressing Secretary of Agriculture Clifford Hardin to ban the pesticide.[92] Cautious officials at the USDA took a month to send responses to the communications from Nelson, not fully answering his April letter and telegram until May.[93]

The USDA sensitivity to Senator Nelson's pressure was perhaps predictable in the face of heavy press coverage of the issue and shifting public opinion. For example, one article in the *New Republic* in June 1967 said that contrary to the arguments of pesticide defenders, the harm caused by DDT was not due to carelessness: "There could be *no* safe application of persistent pesticides outdoors."[94] Importantly, though, such a condemnation of DDT and other persistent pesticides did not mean that the author was casting doubt on chemical agriculture, as he concluded, "Modern agriculture and forestry could not survive without the control of pest populations."

Two years later, some in the press took note of the reported connections between DDT and cancer and then, in 1970, described the USDA's escalating restrictions against DDT with a certain inevitability. News articles in August 1970 explaining bans on DDT for livestock, lumber, and many crops (about one-quarter of remaining uses) were somewhat critical of the USDA, noting that the government could have taken more stringent action by ordering a suspension, not just a cancellation of some uses. An underlying implication of the articles was that the current system did not work.[95] USDA officials continued to monitor press coverage of the DDT controversy, sometimes skeptical about the information reported. One confidential 1969 memo from

T. C. Byerly to Ned Bayley observed, "It is likely that there will be increasing allegations of nerve and brain damage from chlorinated hydrocarbon pesticides."[96] Byerly appeared more concerned about the allegations that might be made than about whether or not they might be true.

The shift in public opinion against DDT was seen in reactions to comments from Norman Borlaug, dubbed the "father of the Green Revolution" for his research into high-yielding hybrid seeds. Borlaug held a news conference in late 1971 at the headquarters of the then-largest manufacturer of DDT, Montrose Corporation, denouncing "privileged environmentalists" who criticized DDT and other pesticides. Many responses to Borlaug were similar to those of the editorial board of the *New York Times*, which called his remarks "intemperate," "careless," and "a display of . . . unrelieved propaganda."[97] Sentiment against DDT remained evident three years after the 1972 domestic ban when the USDA received an exemption for aerial spraying of the chemical against the tussock moth in the Northwest. One *Wall Street Journal* article asked if "DDT's Harm Outweigh[ed] Any Gain?" in the operation with an "army of helicopters" "dumping" 300,000 pounds of the chemical. The article described how cattle and wild animals had become contaminated and thousands of birds had died; it quoted EPA administrator Russell Train's observation that there was a possible connection between DDT and human cancer.[98]

As USDA officials watched the tide of public opinion turn against DDT and worked to blunt the activism of Gaylord Nelson and others, Congressman Jamie Whitten of Mississippi, long-standing chair of the agriculture committee and champion of pesticide use, illustrated the views of many department officials and why sentiment in support of agricultural chemicals remained strong. USDA officials were of course well aware that it was important to stay on the good side of Whitten, who controlled the purse strings funding their agency, but it also seems clear that their common interests were ideological, not just mercenary.[99] Secretary Orville Freeman, for example, praised Whitten's 1966 book, *That We May Live*, which was designed to counter the arguments of *Silent Spring* as "a factual, realistic, and temperate approach to the overall pesticides issue."[100] In his book, Whitten dismissed *Silent Spring* as a "polemic" and asserted that the residues of organic pesticides found on food were harmless.[101]

Not all federal officials shared Whitten's views, including many at the Department of the Interior. Throughout the postwar period, the Departments of

Agriculture and the Interior had different approaches to synthetic pesticide use, based to a large degree on their founding missions. Staffers at the USDA were most concerned with using pesticides to benefit agricultural interests in the United States, whereas those at the Department of the Interior were more concerned with protecting the land and wildlife of the country, or what was most commonly referred to as the nation's "natural resources." Although the shift to an "environmental" sensibility beginning in the 1960s signaled a change in opinion to a view of nature as more than something for humans to exploit, before that, many in Interior were already concerned about the damage inflicted by human exploitation. For example, a pamphlet from the FWS, the Interior agency where Rachel Carson had worked, told citizens in 1966 that although controlled use of chemicals was necessary, it was important not to pollute the world and damage wild animals. Arguing that there had not yet been a "Silent Spring," the pamphlet argued that perhaps the awareness raised by Carson's book would prevent this from happening.[102]

Differences in outlook between officials of the two departments were reflected in their views of whether or not particular pesticides should be banned. Secretary Udall wrote to Secretary Freeman, for example, in May 1964, arguing that his department had acquired enough data on the toxicity of aldrin, dieldrin, and endrin to call for restrictions on their use. He wrote that their respective departments should cooperate in further research in order "to carry out the recommendation in the President's Science Advisory Committee 1963 report calling for the eventual elimination of persistent toxic pesticides." Freeman's response made no such reference to the inevitability of eliminating persistent pesticides and instead emphasized that the two departments should cooperate to ensure their safe use.[103] The two secretaries reflected the differing views of those in their respective departments, one assuming that safe use was a matter of following directions and the other seeing the substances as inherently dangerous.

Sometimes the contrasting approaches of officials from the two departments spilled out in public. For example, in the summer of 1970, Interior issued a press release linking dieldrin to the deaths of growing numbers of bald eagles, based on studies that had found high levels of the insecticide in the brains of dead birds; the department indicated there was evidence that other birds were also affected, including the osprey.[104] The differing outlooks of Interior officials also led to more activist pesticide policies than those from the USDA. For example, in mid-1970, Interior banned the use of sixteen different pesticides, including DDT and other persistent chlorinated hydrocarbons, on the federal lands that it administered.[105]

The contrasting views between the USDA and Interior led not only to policy differences but sometimes to tension. For example, the USDA's Byerly wrote to Congressman John Dingell in July 1970 about the different positions of the USDA and Interior. Byerly explained that the USDA must have clear evidence for all registrations or restrictions and that "this Department does not favor arbitrary banning of pesticides." Although unspoken, the clear implication in the letter, written one month after the announcement by Interior of the ban of sixteen pesticides on public land, was that Interior's actions were arbitrary and not based on sound evidence.[106] Dingell reacted by admonishing Secretary of Agriculture Clifford Hardin that the USDA and Interior should have the same policies "with regard to dangerous pesticide compounds."[107]

The contrasting policies between the two agencies were not just about political turf. They reflected philosophical differences. A typical USDA view was that expressed by N. C. Brady in a department memo to the undersecretary of agriculture, "Economic Importance of Pesticides to the U.S. Consumer." He argued that without pesticides, "production of crops and livestock would be curtailed and the quality of farm products would be lowered," as would "the level of living of U.S. consumers."[108] Five years later, such views remained strong. Shortly before Interior banned use of sixteen different pesticides on federal land, the agriculture secretary clarified his department's policy on pesticides. Secretary Hardin wrote in October 1969, "For the foreseeable future, pesticides will be necessary tools for the protection of the nation's food and fiber supplies, people, and their homes."[109] Enduring belief in the necessity of pesticides sometimes led USDA officials to make hyperbolic claims, such as in a 1974 handout from the ARS asserting that if the United States stopped using pesticides at that point, farm exports would disappear and 40 percent of the population wouldn't get fed.[110]

Meanwhile, the philosophical approach at Interior was often different. For example, in 1971, Deputy Assistant Secretary Curtis Bohlen wrote to Representative Dingell about the use of a poison to prevent damage by blackbirds to corn crops in Midwestern states. He said that the poison, Avitrol, should kill very few birds because those that were poisoned made distress calls that frightened away the rest of the flock before they, too, could be poisoned. More importantly, though, he put this control program in a broader context: "From the mid-1940s through the mid-1960s hundreds of pesticides were cleared for public use with little study or consideration given to possible adverse ecological side effects. With Avitrol, as with other new chemicals intended for use in reducing wild animal damage, we are determined that environmental hazards, if any, be defined and corrected prior to operational use."[111] The outlook reflected here was common among Interior officials. As discussed in chapter 3, the sympathetic response of many within the department to the publication of *Silent Spring* was very different from the reaction of USDA officials.

Fred Tschirley, the pesticides coordinator at the USDA, believed fervently in the necessity of using pesticides and other technologies in agriculture. For example, he responded to one citizen worried about the safety of pesticide residues in foods by reassuring the woman that only residues known to be safe were allowed and that "if pesticides were not used, food quality would deteriorate, and people would starve because we would not be able to supply adequate food."[112] Many others in the USDA agreed with Tschirley about the dangers of starvation if pesticides were not used. In the spring of 1970, Director of Science and Education Ned Bayley, for example, responded to a citizen letter about the dangers of DDT by saying that "pesticides were needed in many countries of the world to prevent human disasters and starvation."[113] As a corollary point, many in the department argued that pesticides—and especially DDT in the middle of the debate to ban that chemical—were *economic* necessities. For example, a representative of the department's Economic Research Service argued in 1971 that if DDT were banned in agriculture, he believed it would double the cost of insect control for crops and livestock.[114]

Although some USDA officials might have been frustrated that those from Interior did not fall in line behind their lead, they could also take comfort in the divided bureaucratic responsibilities for pesticides, especially as debates about the chemicals began to increase starting in the 1960s. Passing off responsibility to another agency was a good way to deflect criticism. For example, in mid-1969, responding to pressure on the USDA from Senator Nelson to take action to ban DDT, a departmental representative answered that specific research on pesticide effects on the environment, animals, and health was actually the responsibility of HEW and Interior. Thus, he took refuge in the position that the USDA was powerless to act on its own against DDT, relying on others for advice and information about its effects.[115] Similarly, in mid-1970, USDA's assistant director of science and education,

T. C. Byerly, told Congressman Dingell that his department's policies were reviewed by the Working Group of the Subcommittee on Pesticides of the President's Committee on the Environment and that the USDA did "not proceed without approval of this Working Group."[116]

USDA officials made similar claims of shared responsibility in answers to citizen complaints. For example, in response to a 1966 citizen letter protesting increased levels of DDT in milk, Secretary Freeman wrote that because food tolerances for pesticides under the federal Food, Drug, and Cosmetic Act were established by the FDA, housed in HEW, he would pass the letter on to that department.[117]

Before 1970, the USDA, Interior, and HEW negotiated pesticide policy based on different areas of legislative responsibility. The USDA had jurisdiction over registration of pesticides, Interior was concerned with pesticide effects on fish and wildlife as well as public lands, and HEW oversaw food tolerances or allowable residues in foods. Although jurisdictions were split, USDA dominance was clear in that government emphasis overall remained on effective agricultural use of the chemicals, not their side effects. Ostensibly, the creation of the EPA in 1970 changed everything about pesticides regulation, centralizing control in a new agency that was supposed to be dedicated to protecting the environment. In this bureaucratic shake-up, the diminution of power for the USDA seemed to be greatest.

There were many indications that a new pesticide regime was in effect. In August 1974, the EPA announced the suspension of aldrin and dieldrin, although USDA pesticides coordinator Tschirley complained that EPA officials had looked only at one side of the story and hadn't investigated potential hazards of alternative pesticides.[118] Another example of the changes brought by the EPA was reflected in a 1975 report on pesticide releases; it criticized the overuse of some chemicals based on erroneous assumptions that more was better; some people's "sterile approach to gardening" meant they wanted to spray preventively and eradicate all insects, whether or not they might be beneficial.[119] Although this type of EPA thinking was clearly different from the USDA approach, it still did not question whether or not pesticide use was necessary and should continue. The report called for making enough information available so that pesticide use would be "environmentally sound." It also endorsed the existing idea of using a cost/benefit paradigm to guide chemical use, calling on "governmental agencies and the pesticide industry" to make users aware of the positive and negative effects of use.

The 1975 EPA report can be read as an example of both change and continuity. At this moment of new government regulations, when the rise of the EPA might have upended American attitudes toward pesticides, some of the bedrock assumptions of the USDA and others remained unchanged, and the embrace of the chemicals did not slacken.

Alternative Entomological Visions?

Despite the strong commitment of many at the USDA to chemical pesticide use, many officials at the same time supported continued research into a broader array of methods. By the end of the decade, amid increasing criticism of chemical agriculture, alternative control systems incorporating a variety of methods—what came to be known as integrated pest management—had gained more support. For example, in Secretary Clifford Hardin's memo broadly laying out pesticides policy in 1969, he wrote, "Integrated control systems utilizing both chemical and nonchemical techniques will be used and recommended in the interest of maximum effectiveness and safety."[120]

The idea of integrating control systems soon became the mainstream position of many not only at the USDA but also at other government agencies. For example, an advisory agency for Congress, the Office of Technology Assessment, issued a paper on pest management strategies in 1979, noting that "IPM is the most promising approach to U.S. crop protection over the next 15 years." The report argued that the biggest obstacle was that people did not yet know enough about this approach and that Congress had to commit the necessary resources to go down this path.[121] Officials at Interior were also supportive of the new emphasis on IPM. In 1972, one assistant secretary wrote to Russell Train at the Council on Environmental Quality that "we are pleased to see the emphasis now being placed on this important topic."[122]

Although IPM increasingly gained supporters inside and outside the government, not everyone agreed on how to define the concept. Ideas about integrated systems could be found along a spectrum of positions that went from a rejection of any use of chemical pesticides to a continuation of existing practices. Most of the time, activists, entomologists, and others assumed that the ideal was to be flexible about pest control. For example, a 1977 pamphlet from the Rachel Carson Center for the Living Environment called on home gardeners to use natural controls as much as possible and to adopt an IPM strategy based on the idea that all living and nonliving parts of an ecosystem were interconnected. The pamphlet was careful not to call for the abolition of all chemical use; instead, it recommended using chemicals only as a last resort.[123]

In his study of changing regulations in this era, historian John Perkins described the clash between two positions on this spectrum, that of IPM and what Perkins dubbed "total population management" (TPM).[124] As a rhetorical category, IPM was triumphant and was later used to describe what previously might have fallen in the TPM category. Nevertheless, in the 1970s, proponents of IPM and TPM both agreed that pest control should be undertaken through a variety of methods, including the use of natural enemies, pathogens, cultural practices, and pesticides. The position that pesticides should be only a last resort was much more important in IPM. But the fundamental disagreement between the two was that they were based on different foundational paradigms about how the world worked and the role of humans in the natural world.

Within the first decade after World War II, when examples of insect resistance to chemicals started to become more common, many entomologists understood the limitations of conventional chemical pest control. Nevertheless, it was not until the 1960s and 1970s that the experiments in biological control undertaken by researchers such as Carl Barton Huffaker began to convince some entomologists that there was an effective alternative to the existing system. Following years of experimentation in biological control and insect entomology, Huffaker became the organizer for a large coordinated undertaking, the "Huffaker Project," which worked with researchers from eighteen universities, the USDA, and private industry and lasted from 1972 to 1978. The project was responsible for solidifying the IPM concept, leading many university entomologists to embrace IPM.

At its heart, IPM was based in classical biological control, which included using field observations and natural history to support such policies as the propagation of insect enemies to keep a pest in check. IPM aimed at using such controls to keep insects or weeds below an economic threshold that might make them pests; its goal was not to eliminate species but to manage them in ways that interfered as little as possible with natural environmental processes. It was, from the perspective of one of its proponents, biologist Robert van den Bosch, "rational pest control."[125] Another biologist who similarly articulated IPM principles soon after Rachel Carson published *Silent*

Spring—but did not label them as such in the first edition of his book—was Robert Rudd, who explained that "the integrated-control concept . . . rests upon the awareness of applied biologists that crop ecosystems, like all others, are complex, living communities. Insecticides intruded into them inevitably cause disturbances."[126] In its respect for the natural functioning of ecosystems, IPM did not call for elimination of species or eradication because this approach would fundamentally and permanently change an ecosystem. As more than one observer has noted, IPM followed comfortably from the balance-of-nature approach that Rachel Carson had articulated a decade earlier in *Silent Spring*.

While the number of scientists, activists, and politicians who supported an IPM approach grew, some entomologists and others held fast to an existing paradigm that was fundamentally at odds with a balance-of-nature outlook: they gravitated more to a TPM approach. Instead of believing that humans should interfere as little as possible in nature's own systems, these people believed that "pests" existed in a fixed category as opponents to human interests. They needed to be controlled, if not eliminated. Not only did people have the economic imperative to eliminate pests, but they had the ability through modern technologies to manipulate nature in a beneficent way while trying to minimize harm or unintended side effects.

Edward Fred Knipling was one of the most influential entomologists of the mid–twentieth century and an exemplar of TPM ideas. Contemporaneous with the Huffaker Project, Knipling designed an ambitious example of a TPM initiative, the Pilot Boll Weevil Eradication Experiment (PBWEE). The multimillion-dollar project was an attempt to use a systemic, interventionist approach to eliminate one of the most persistent threats to commercial cotton farming. The Huffaker Project and the PBWEE were the two most important entomological research initiatives of the 1970s.[127] In contrast to an IPM approach, the PBWEE was aimed at completely eradicating the boll weevil species in areas of cotton cultivation through carefully timed use of chemicals to first lessen numbers of the insects and then defoliate plants that were insect food sources, followed by pheromone traps to lure boll weevils where they would be killed with more insecticides.

The goals of the program highlighted its differences from an IPM approach. Knipling and other USDA entomologists who aimed at eradication of a species assumed that this goal was synonymous with the goal of eliminating an insect as an economic pest. In contrast, the goal of those dedicated to an

IPM approach was to push the number of insects below the level at which they became an economic problem.

Knipling, who was head of entomological research at the USDA from 1953 to 1970, was instrumental in getting the PBWEE off the ground and funded from 1971 to 1973 (and he continued to work as a consultant for the USDA after his official retirement in 1973). He was a fascinating figure, not only for his prominent position within the field of entomology but also for his sincere commitment to researching alternative methods while still embracing the chemically dependent, modern agricultural system. Like many entomologists, Knipling was well aware of the drawbacks of the postwar pesticide regime. At the beginning of June 1962—before the publication of *Silent Spring*—Knipling gave a speech focusing on the problems of then-current insect-control practices, including residues; harming beneficial insects, fish, and wildlife; and insect resistance.[128] These were, of course, three of the most important criticisms offered by Carson that summer. Yet, in the end, Knipling, though thoughtful and more holistic in his understanding of the human role in nature than many of his colleagues, chose the mainstream position, rejecting the full implications of *Silent Spring*.

Knipling started his career with the USDA in 1931, before completion of his graduate degrees. By 1942, he had become director of the department's laboratory in Orlando, Florida, where the first American tests into the viability of DDT use on troops were conducted. Early on, then, he had an opportunity to be impressed by the possibilities of the new organic pesticides. His publications for the rest of the decade reflected this interest. At the same time, he was researching a new technique of insect control: introduction of the sterile male. Following experimentation with radiation to sterilize insects, he and colleagues used the method to eradicate the screwworm from the Caribbean island of Curaçao by 1955. Within a few years, Knipling and fellow researchers had successfully used the technique to eradicate the screwworm from Florida and then used it to do the same in other Southern states.[129] This success was important and remained influential in Knipling's approach to pest control. Over the next two decades, roughly half of the papers that he published concerned eradication.[130] During this time, he wrote to subordinates in laboratories throughout the country about the great potential of using insect self-destruction: "The use of insects themselves to destroy their own kind by interfering with reproduction offers almost unlimited possibilities for control or eradication."[131]

Knipling believed that human intervention in the environment was necessary. But even though this concept was part of his foundational paradigm, he remained a dedicated scientist and counseled others in the department to pursue their research with open minds. For example, in a pair of memos from 1966 about research into use of insect sex attractants and expanding the species for which the sterile male technique should be used, Knipling observed, "I am sure that we are all optimistic about the possibilities for insect control that sex attractants offer. However . . . preconceived ideas in research can be a drawback and can lead to blind alleys."[132] He was also careful to evaluate each method based upon the particular circumstances of a given population.[133] Knipling expressed frustration that his goal of a vigorous research program at ARS that would explore alternative approaches to pest control was sometimes stymied by the biases among entomology faculty at land-grant universities, most of whom worked in the existing categories of chemical control and trained their students in the same vein.[134]

Throughout his career, Knipling remained committed to the idea of integrating different methods. For example, in 1979, he wrote, "No single concept or approach to insect pest management will be the best long-range solution for most problems. . . . Perhaps several techniques appropriately combined may be required in order to achieve satisfactory control."[135] Practical integration for effective control was more important to him than what particular method was to be used. For example, in a 1966 report to colleagues on the sugarcane borer, Knipling observed that this pest "offers unusual opportunities for integrating several systems of insect control" because the current reliance on conventional insecticides by themselves was not working, and all alternatives had to be explored. Yet his emphasis on integration did not mean that he would reject conventional methods if he believed them to be appropriate.[136]

Throughout the 1960s and 1970s, Knipling tried to balance the tensions between challenging the existing system and defending it. At times, one position or the other seemed more dominant in his thinking. For example, in the midst of the debate about the banning of DDT in the early 1970s, Knipling repeated the familiar positions of others at the USDA. He revealed his core assumptions on this issue in his simplified answers to queries from his niece for a school project about the controversy.[137] He told the girl that DDT was "among the safest of insecticides" and that "its value far exceeds its potential harm." In his assertion that DDT was safe for humans, he used one of the explanations that entomologists had been using since the 1950s: more accidental deaths had been caused by the overuse of aspirin than by accidental poisoning by DDT. Nevertheless, he added that because DDT caused some environmental harm, it was a good idea to find an insecticide that did not do so.

Knipling's core beliefs shaped his approach to IPM. In some ways, IPM became a catchall label to describe pest-control approaches; for example, some self-described adherents urged that chemicals should be only a last resort and others gave them more legitimacy. Nevertheless, most agreed that IPM was an approach that included a combination of different control methods such as natural enemies, pathogens, cultural practices, and pesticides. In some ways, Knipling reflected an IPM outlook. He had an appreciation for the complexity of ecosystems and believed that pest-control efforts should try to imitate or work with nature. But, at a fundamental level, he parted company with an IPM view. Historian John Perkins observed that "Knipling did not accept . . . the notion that technological advances were subject to intrinsic limitations."[138]

Knipling's strong convictions led him to defend the pesticide status quo in a variety of ways. By the 1970s, after he and many at the USDA had faced years of attack on their agency's policies, there was a defensive tone in Knipling's writings and speeches. At times, it seemed that he either had a selective memory or was mischaracterizing the USDA record. For example, in a 1973 memo to an official at the General Accounting Office, Knipling asserted that from the mid-1950s on, most of the research coming out of the Entomology Research Division of the ARS had "involved work on methods that would avoid or minimize environmental pollution."[139] While this might have been the case in terms of new research, it left the impression that the USDA was genuinely trying to end the chemical regime, a proposition for which there is little evidence. At the same time, Knipling was sometimes introspective about the blind spots that entomologists might have when it came to technological solutions. In a 1976 speech on alternatives to the modern agricultural system, he observed, "Scientists are prone to emphasize progress but not the short comings of solutions to problems."[140]

In the late 1970s, when John Perkins was writing journal articles and what would become his book *Insects, Experts, and the Insecticide Crisis: The Quest for New Pest Management Strategies*, he had an extensive correspondence with Knipling, as well as other entomologists, to gain more insights into the topic of changing pest control and to get comments on his research. The correspondence revealed much about Knipling's views of pest control in the 1970s as well as how the entomologist looked back on his career. (It also illustrated the delicate balance between historian and living subject.) Perkins, initially trained as a biologist who then moved into the history of science, had great respect for Knipling and presented a more complex picture of USDA entomologists than the caricatures of the USDA created by the agency's critics. In the end, Perkins revised his work following vociferous criticisms from Knipling and his USDA colleagues, though the author's argument remained critical of the entomologist's basic assumptions.

A few examples illustrate the interaction between the two. In November and December 1978, Perkins sent two separate drafts to Knipling for comments, both drawn from Perkins's book, which was nearing completion. They were "Boll Weevil Eradication; Changing Technology and the Roots of a Public Policy Controversy" and "Insights from the History of Pest Control for Public Policy." Knipling's reaction was harsh and detailed, including a twenty-one-page critique of the second essay. Regarding the boll-weevil paper, Knipling wrote, "The comments on the paper do not adequately reflect my disappointments, however, in the manner in which you have treated the subject." Knipling charged that Perkins's paper was based "on the unproven premise that boll weevil eradication is not a justifiable goal."[141]

In his response to the second essay, Knipling began, "It is very unpleasant for me to write the harsh criticisms I am compelled to make."[142] He asserted that Perkins's description made it seem that USDA scientists were too caught up in chemical methods and had not emphasized biological research enough: "This is a gross misrepresentation of facts." He argued that they all knew by the early 1950s that research had to shift to reduce chemical insecticide use because it was unsustainable and that USDA work had changed accordingly.[143]

To his colleagues at the USDA, Knipling was even more blunt and defensive, writing of one of the drafts, "This is the most distorted paper I have ever read. His targets for criticism are the USDA research program and my views on pest management." Furthermore, Knipling was very worried about the impact of Perkins's work if the USDA did not counter by publishing an explanation of its work: "Unless this is done the highly progressive and forward looking program the ARS has had will be completely discredited by distortions, inaccuracies, and misrepresentations."[144] Knipling told colleagues at the USDA as well as industry representatives that Perkins was biased against him and had aligned himself with people at particular academic institutions who were also biased.[145]

In his responses to Perkins, Knipling not only defended his reputation but also carefully explained his broad philosophical approach to pest control. First, on a basic level, Knipling asserted that his approach was "practical," balancing broader goals of lessening interference in the environment with doing what was necessary economically to control pests. Second, Knipling clarified what he meant by "eradication," writing, "I argue for the eradication, if possible, not of a species, but of populations from specified areas where major pests conflict with the welfare of society." Third, he asserted that the goal should be for "preventative suppressive measures" because pest control that was wholly reactive to an extreme situation might prove ineffective when the problem had gotten too big.

Finally, Knipling argued that he was actually trying to restore the natural balance that had existed before human interference, not radically alter the natural world: "The pest species for which I advocate eradication or rigid population management are either alien to our environment or have emerged as major pests, because of ecological imbalances caused by normal agricultural practices and industrialization." Of course, many who favored IPM would have argued with his definition of "normal" and whether or not modern agriculture and industry should be allowed to have such an impact on the environment. But whatever his critics might have said, Knipling was advocating for what he believed was a fair balance between economic and environmental interests.[146] By January 1979, Knipling was satisfied that Perkins intended to revise the draft based upon his comments, even if he remained convinced that Perkins could not truly be objective about the USDA programs.[147]

Even if Knipling praised what he saw as the improvement in Perkins's argument and was cordial toward the author, he remained emphatically opposed to Perkins's work getting wide circulation. In September 1979, Knipling was one of the anonymous reviewers of Perkins's article on boll-weevil eradication for the journal *Science*. In his evaluation, he put Perkins's article in the "mediocre or poor" category that should not be published. In his comments, he elaborated that the analysis was biased, outdated, discussed too many controversial issues, and would "be a discredit to *Science* and could be an obstacle to progress on more effective and more acceptable solutions to insect pest problems."[148]

The other reviewers must have had a different view because the article was published in *Science* in March 1980. Knipling, not surprisingly, gave no indication to Perkins of his negative review, offering praise for the piece when he received offprints from Perkins a few months later.[149] His letter to Perkins asserted that he disagreed more with some supporters of IPM than with Perkins himself: "The major criticism I have, which is not directed at you as a reporter of events, is that those who do not support organized, areawide suppression or eradication programs take a position that is too rigid, and inflexible." Knipling viewed his own position as reasonable and moderate: "I am confident that in time . . . there will be broader recognition that there is an important role for both the IPM and TPM approaches to insect pest management depending on the nature of the pest, the technology available and the economic or ecological advantages of the contrasting approaches."[150]

By the mid-1990s, Edward Knipling was still consulting with researchers in the USDA and a number of other agencies. He was forcefully advocating for a broader approach to pest control. For example, in 1996, he circulated to researchers at different government agencies a report titled "Environmentally Safe and Economically Sound Insect Pest Control Techniques and Strategies for the Future." He wrote, "My primary interests are to discuss the advantages to be gained by the holistic approach to insect pest management and how this might be achieved by the use of mobile biological organisms."[151] Two years later, Knipling sent a new report, also arguing on behalf of what he labeled a holistic approach.[152] Like his earlier work, the report highlighted parasite augmentation, sterile-insect technique, and, most importantly, "area-wide management of insect pests." Knipling's advocacy of an areawide approach reflected the confidence that he and other entomologists had in their ability to remake nature to suit the needs of industrial agriculture.

Knipling had reached the height of his influence in the 1970s when, through his position at the USDA, he signaled that entomologists could endorse parts of an IPM philosophy—without calling it that—and make it their own, broadening the definition of IPM so much that it could include almost any multipronged approach to pest control. Even if entomologists and industrial farmers did not adopt the areawide approach that Knipling favored, they enacted many of the other parts of his views under the umbrella of IPM. Although there is no evidence that his motives were anything but sincere, Knipling's work helped to co-opt the ideas behind IPM and, thus, support the existing system of pesticide use.

Conclusion

The adoption of IPM as a mainstream approach to pest control introduced the possibility of a radical transformation in pesticide use. In the end, that possibility evaporated as IPM was redefined in the service of the existing system. In the 1960s and 1970s, there were other potential openings for radical transformation in pesticide use and regulation. One possibility was in the bureaucratic upheavals of government agencies. Yet even with Interior and HEW pushing for tighter regulations and the USDA losing power to the newly created EPA, pesticide use remained entrenched in both agriculture and land management policies. The pro-pesticide views and policies of USDA officials were remarkably durable, even though the shift away from persistent chlorinated hydrocarbons was clear and the rhetoric used to express pesticide policies adapted to the mainstreaming of IPM.

The meteoric rise in both influence of and membership in mainstream environmental organizations in the 1960s and 1970s had also held out the possibility of radical change in pesticide policies. There were many indications that the growth of groups such as the National Audubon Society was based on a clear proenvironment shift in public opinion. But environmental leaders, such as the officials at the EPA and elsewhere, ended up focusing more on how to *monitor* the widespread use of pesticides rather than fundamentally challenging the assumptions on which such use was based.

The 1960s and 1970s, then, were a time of tremendous regulatory change with regard to pesticides as well as a transformation in public attitudes. But the debates unleashed by the publication of *Silent Spring* in 1962 did not lead to the immediate transformations that some might have expected. The director of science and education at the USDA, Ned Bayley, for example, observed in 1968 that "the issue of pesticides [had] cooled off so much" since the beginning of the decade, and he confidently predicted that more evidence was accumulating "to show that the pesticide hazard problem is not as alarming as the picture painted by Rachel Carson."[153] Bayley's observation to the pro-pesticide congressman Jamie Whitten might have been in part wishful thinking, and his belief that pesticides were not a great hazard was certainly premature. Nevertheless, his confidence that the reliance on pesticides was not about to disappear was borne out in the subsequent decades.

The persistence of the existing order does not, of course, mean that there were no challenges to the status quo. The 1970s were, as many scholars have described, the height of political and popular support for environmentalism, heralded by the prominence of popular scientists such as Barry Commoner, the passage of significant new environmental regulations, and the launch of Earth Day.[154] Commoner's popular book, *The Closing Circle*, built on the legacy of Earth Day and also took up Carson's mantle in articulating the principle of interconnectedness between humans and nature, pointing to "the foibles of unchecked technological progress."[155]

Changes in the 1970s were clear not just in popular culture and politics outside the government but also within the federal bureaucracy led by officials such as Russell Train, head of the Council on Environmental Quality and then the EPA; congressional leaders such as Senator Gaylord Nelson; and researchers such as Edward Knipling. There is no denying the sincerity of such leaders and the concrete impact of laws such as NEPA, the revised FIFRA, and TOSCA. But the political mainstreaming of environmentalism was also an exercise in compromise and, sometimes, co-optation.[156] On a popular level, for example, Earth Day was a turning point of increasing commitment to environmentalism, but it represented a moderate, feel-good celebration of the environment rather than a radical critique of industrial society.[157]

The mainstreaming of environmentalism in the 1960s and 1970s was also clear in attitudes toward pesticides. On one hand, the lessening of calls for radical change might have been due to mistaken assumptions about the regulatory system, even among environmentalists. For example, an article in *Audubon* magazine in mid-1967 observed, "Today each product must undergo longer and more costly tests, first by the manufacturer and later by USDA scientists."[158] The implication of the article was that a rigorous system of examination already existed. If this was the belief expressed in an environmental organization's publication, it is not difficult to imagine that those outside the environmental community would have even less occasion to doubt the comprehensiveness of government regulations and testing. With the creation of the EPA and passage of FEPCA and TOSCA, confidence that federal regulations were adequate to the task only increased. Even news that particular chemicals caused both genetic damage and cancer seemed to be simply a problem that could be managed by a methodical EPA. For example, far from panicking over 1979 National Cancer Institute (NCI) reports on the dangers of toxaphene (which amounted to 20 percent of pesticides used in the United States annually), the EPA noted that the matter would need to be discussed further because the NCI data was not yet conclusive.[159]

The spirit of compromise and accommodation with respect to pesticides was, ironically, bolstered by the important victories in the 1970s of banning persistent chlorinated hydrocarbons such as DDT and heptachlor and the revelations about 2,4,5-T and dioxin. This contradictory development was well understood by the editors of *Chemical Week* in 1969 when they recognized that the tide of public opinion was irretrievably shifting against DDT (as it later would against 2,4,5-T).[160] The editors predicted that although "the pesticide industry emerged with few serious scars from the 'Silent Spring' controversy of the early '60s," the same would not be true of DDT in 1970. The editors in essence recommended that DDT and other persistents be sacrificed to the greater pesticide system: "A rigorous defense of persistent chlorinated hydrocarbons might win a skirmish here and there, but the longer the fight lasts, the more these [chemical] companies may lose in the end. If they lose badly, they may invite unnecessarily restrictive new controls on all pesticides, as well as problems of public relations and of relations with consumers and stockholders that could last a long time." The recommendations were not only clever and cynical but prescient because they outlined the future direction of public opinion about pesticides, with the abandonment of chlorinated hydrocarbons amid the strengthening of the chemical order. In some respects, the backlash against environmentalism that would take hold in the 1980s and after was not surprising.

CHAPTER 6

Love Is Blind: Chemical Disasters at Home and Abroad

It's a cliché to observe that love can be blind, that we do not always see the flaws in the object of our affection. As the previous chapters indicate, this cliché might provide some insight into popular and political attitudes toward pesticides. In the years after 1945, there were many opportunities to observe the downsides of synthetic pesticides and the way they were used in industrial agriculture, land management, and warfare. The most obvious drawbacks were decreasing effectiveness, pest resistance, contaminated food, chemical dependency, animal die-offs, and human illness. And, from the perspective of a burgeoning environmental sensibility, we might add the illusion that technology would allow humans to control nature and a failure to appreciate the balance of nature.

Thus, in the three decades following World War II, Americans had numerous opportunities to marvel at the benefits of pesticides as well as to contemplate their negative impact. But, as I have argued, such contemplation did not lead the majority of Americans to weaken their embrace of synthetic pesticides or to question the assumptions on which their use was based. Instead, the most common cultural and political responses to bad news were to address the worst cases (e.g., banning DDT and dioxin), to press for incremental reform (e.g., enacting weak environmental legislation and strengthening moderate environmental organizations), and to avoid labeling pesticides as the main problem (e.g., describing Agent Orange as a flawed military weapon and as an example of government exploitation of GIs, not as a dangerous pesticide).

In the late 1970s and 1980s, Americans had yet another opportunity to appreciate the flaws of synthetic pesticides both at home and abroad.

Following extensive press coverage of the environmental dangers of chemical leaks at Love Canal, New York, and radiation leaks at Three Mile Island, Pennsylvania, citizens also read about how the pesticides ethylene dibromide (EDB) and dibromochloropropane (DBCP) had contaminated drinking water and made workers ill. But amid these publicized episodes of chemical and environmental disasters, officials of the Reagan administration came into office pledging to roll back what they argued were intrusive environmental regulations. Although public opinion polls indicated that most Americans disagreed with these policy goals, they nevertheless seemed to acquiesce in the weakening of environmental regulations once the most extreme members of the Reagan administration were forced out.

Even if the publicized stories of chemical contamination and the anti-environmentalist rhetoric of the Reagan administration had not changed public opinion about pesticides, one might have expected that the story of Bhopal would have done so. In December 1984, a pesticide manufacturing plant in the Indian city spewed out toxic gas, killing and injuring thousands. Yet despite this tragedy, which came on the heels of news stories about chemical contamination in different regions of the United States, public and political attitudes toward pesticide use seemed unaffected. Assumptions about the necessity of pesticides and their pattern of use continued as before. In fact, although many Americans adopted an environmental outlook and asserted that they cared about the human impact on nature, the rightward shift of American politics during the Reagan administration further strengthened faith in industrial agriculture and technological mastery over the environment and, thus, the continued embrace of widespread pesticide use.

The reaction to the Bhopal disaster provided dramatic illustration of another blind spot that many Americans had: how synthetic pesticides and industrial agriculture were connected to globalization and its consequences. As discussed in chapter 4, the promises of the Green Revolution were celebrated by most as a demonstration of technical mastery and American altruism in feeding hungry people. By the 1970s and 1980s, some observers criticized the economic and political impact of the Green Revolution and the spread of industrial agriculture. Two effects of this agricultural globalization were the increase of food contaminated by pesticides and the increase of pesticide production across the globe in places such as Bhopal. Nevertheless, many Americans remained unaware of the connection between the globalization of industrial agriculture and a disaster such as that in India.

This chapter examines these possible turning points in the late 1970s and 1980s, when domestic and foreign disasters might have led to a rejection of industrial business as usual—but did not. It offers some answers as to why these possible changes never came to pass and why there was more continuity than change in popular and political attitudes toward pesticide use.

Deregulation and Ideology in the Reagan Era

As discussed in chapter 5, the 1970s had been a decade of unprecedented expansion of federal regulatory authority in many areas, including the environment, health, and safety. Public support for the activist trend in government policy appeared strong, especially with respect to the environment. More than 70 percent of Americans polled favored better environmental protection even if it meant higher taxes or personal sacrifice. Many of the assumptions symbolized by the start of Earth Day in 1970 had apparently taken hold.[1] For many Americans, the polluted air and water around them were visible reminders of environmental problems in the United States. Some took inspiration from the countercultural values that had challenged mainstream ideas about development and how progress was measured. Moreover, many people had been listening to and absorbing detailed exposés in the press about the health hazards of pollution and chemical contamination.

Pro-environmentalist feeling remained strong into the 1980s, illustrating one of the many political ironies of the Reagan administration: the president was personally very popular even when many Americans disagreed with his political values and policies.[2] Given the years of stagflation, high unemployment, and relative economic decline beginning in the 1970s, one might have predicted that a majority of Americans would be willing to sacrifice environmental standards, at least temporarily. But this was not the case. A Gallup poll for *Newsweek* in June 1981, for example, reported that a large majority of respondents was willing to pay the extra cost in goods and services of environmental regulations and requirements; three-quarters asserted that you could have strong economic growth and high environmental standards at the same time. Five months later, a national poll for the US Chamber of Commerce found that only 22 percent of respondents said that environmental standards should be relaxed for economic or job growth. Such sentiments held a year and a half later in an ABC News/*Washington Post* poll in which a majority of respondents said that the cost of environmental regulations was worthwhile, and government standards should not be relaxed.[3]

Although indications in public opinion polls and discussion in the mainstream media showed strong support for an environmental outlook among the majority of Americans, on another part of the political spectrum, broad opposition to postwar liberalism had been growing. This backlash was seen in different areas of American politics, including environmental, health, and safety regulations. Historians have long debated the key turning points that blossomed into the new conservative consensus of the late twentieth century. As the discussion of environmental politics in the 1970s revealed, there was considerable push-back in Washington against increased strictures on businesses. Opposition was also brewing outside Washington in both industry and politics.[4] The way that companies such as chemical manufacturers perceived their economic interests and tried to protect them was predictable. The emergence, though, of a political ideology that challenged environmentalism and undermined it in more subtle ways was less so. In the long run, this ideological response can help us understand a lot about environmental attitudes, including those toward pesticides.

When Ronald Reagan ascended to the presidency in 1980, many of his domestic goals stemmed from his antigovernment views, including his rejection of most government regulations as unnecessary at best and a hindrance to economic growth at worst. He trusted market forces to ensure that products were safe and effective. Although it's clear that the broad ideological direction of policies came from the top, Reagan became famously known as one who was apt to delegate implementation and detailed formulation to others. He brought into office with him many officials who shared his values and fervor. Most visible in the realm of environmental policy were Secretary of the Interior James Watt and Anne Gorsuch (whose surname changed to Burford during her term in office following her marriage), administrator of the Environmental Protection Agency. These two abrasive warriors, determined to dismantle the structure of federal environmental protection, became lightning rods for political criticism and were forced out, along with a number of their deputies, just two years after they arrived in Washington. At first glance, this might appear to be an instructive tale of the affirmation of environmental values, but the narrative is not so straightforward. Their resignations illustrated the rejection of extremism, but left in their wake was a decided shift against environmental regulation in the guise of moderation and compromise, offered up as an alternative to the so-called extremes of pro- and anti-environmentalists.

James Watt and Anne Gorsuch both came from Colorado, where two decades of dramatic state growth had led to tension between the imperatives of development and the demands to protect the environment from abuse. Watt and Gorsuch had both been in the Colorado legislature in the 1970s, where they had honed their resentment of interfering federal regulators with Eastern values. Helping to lead the "sagebrush rebellion" of the 1970s and 1980s, these two Western legislators became symbols of the anti-Washington values of the new administration. They spoke to the political core of the newly formed conservative coalition.[5]

Along with Watt and Gorsuch were other key figures who helped to shape the pesticide policies of the Reagan administration. John Hernandez was deputy administrator of the EPA and was seen by Gorsuch, in the words of another EPA staffer, as her "chief scientific adviser" in the agency despite his background as a civil engineer.[6] Rita Lavelle, chief of toxic waste cleanup, and John Todhunter, head of the Office of Toxic Substances and Pesticides, became, along with Hernandez, spokespeople for an ideal they and conservative think tanks at the time referred to as "Good Science."

Rhetorically, the concept of Good Science was hard to criticize (who would counter that they favored "bad science"?) and articulated an argument that pesticides, chemicals, and other substances should be restricted or banned only when there was conclusive scientific proof that they seriously harmed humans and that such harm outweighed the benefits they might bring. Asserting the practical value of this ideology, Hernandez argued, "Good science makes good economics." Hernandez, Lavelle, and Todhunter were true believers in the value of Good Science and made it their goal, argued one observer, "to change the basis for the EPA's assessment of cancer risks."[7]

Good Science was posited as objective and rational, in contrast to environmentalism, which was politicized and characterized by emotional elites who rejected modernity and progress, seeking to return to a pre-industrial time. One of the Good Science proponents outside politics was biochemist Bruce Ames. Ames's research on carcinogens and his assertion that lifestyle choices and natural carcinogens were a bigger hazard than was industrial pollution were widely cited by anti-environmental activists as well as in the media. For example, in 1987, the *New York Times*'s Jane Brody reprinted his arguments, and the following year, ABC's *20/20* broadcast a report on whether pesticide residues were carcinogenic. The host of the show, Hugh Downs, clearly revealed his views in his introduction: "All the concern about this toxin, that pesticide, was much ado about nothing."[8]

Of all of the figures at the EPA, John Todhunter had the most responsibility for day-to-day pesticide policy. His strong belief that pesticides had been too heavily regulated on the basis of flimsy evidence (or "bad science") indicated the radical policy shift planned by the new administration. His goal to deemphasize the hazards of pesticides was clear in his speeches to industry members. For example, in March 1982, he told his audience at the Ohio Pesticide and Fertilizer Association that the Reagan administration wanted pesticide registration to be sped up and streamlined, based on better science and with industry involvement in the process. In a speech to the Aviation Trades Association (crop dusters), he focused on the importance of language in changing people's opinions of pesticides. He complained that the media too often used the words "hazardous" and "toxic." Instead, he proposed that pesticides should be referred to as "crop protection chemicals." He gave the same message to nonindustry audiences. In October 1982, he told an audience at the University of Massachusetts, Amherst, that use of terms such as "hazardous" and "toxic" to describe pesticides "conveys a lack of trust in the producers of the chemicals, the government which regulates the industry and the applicators who apply those chemicals."[9]

Such rhetoric was manifest in a number of concrete changes at the EPA. If the agency intended to rely more on voluntary compliance by industry, it certainly didn't need as many regulators on staff; personnel in the pesticide division fell from 760 in 1980 to 540 by 1983. Meanwhile, the number of "emergency" exemptions issued by the EPA went from 180 in 1978 to 750 in 1982. Emergency exemptions were designed to circumvent the lengthy process of regular approvals when there was a public health emergency, when farmers faced sudden losses (or even stood to gain) on a particular crop, or when a newly imported pest needed to be quarantined.[10] Another way to circumvent the regular process was with the "special local needs registration." Moreover, a pesticide that had won approval on a certain crop in a particular area might then be approved for additional crops in the same area if growers asserted the need for such a chemical. By the end of 1982, the EPA had used this exemption for 8,650 different pest-crop combinations.[11] Other administration figures outside the EPA also had a big impact on pesticide regulation. Thorne Auchter was assistant secretary of labor for the Occupational, Safety, and Health Administration (OSHA) and thus helped shape policy on worker exposure to pesticides, encouraging businesses to do more voluntary self-inspections. Not surprisingly, OSHA issued no new health standards during his term, and existing ones were weakened.[12]

One more administration figure who had a significant effect on pesticide regulation was the director of the Office of Management and Budget (OMB), David Stockman. Stockman was committed to cutting government regulations and was particularly hostile toward the EPA as a regulatory agency, calling its rules on hazardous waste "a monument to mindless excess."[13] At the start of the Reagan term in early 1981, Stockman called for dramatic budget cuts in all four major areas of EPA regulation (water, air, hazardous wastes, and pesticides). By October 1982, more than half of the EPA policies planned at the end of the Carter administration had been canceled or were behind schedule, reflecting the 30 percent EPA budget reductions in 1981 and 1982. Stockman even proposed an additional 19 percent reduction in 1982, which was blocked by Congress.[14]

Stockman's influence was further increased by the new president's Executive Order 12291 in February 1981. The order had two main purposes: first, to establish that only regulations with a greater benefit than cost would be approved and that the lowest-cost choice must be selected, and second, to centralize regulatory power in the White House and OMB because the deciding factor in regulations was economic, not technical or scientific. Ironically, of course, a policy meant to establish objective criteria such as cost/benefit comparisons was far from neutral: it was supposed to rely on detailed analyses just when agency budgets were being slashed, and it was implemented by people with no technical expertise in the policies they considered.[15] Stockman and two of his OMB subordinates also worked to implement the deregulation ideology of the administration through the Task Force on Regulatory Reform, led by Vice President George H. W. Bush. The task force was intended to review government regulations, finding areas to cut, to streamline, and in which to improve efficiency. Within five months, it had selected the EPA and pesticide regulations as a particular area of cumbersome bureaucracy in need of reform.[16]

The policies of the task force and officials at other agencies, including the OMB, the EPA, OSHA, and the Department of the Interior, had a concrete and an immediate impact on pesticide regulation in the United States.

Environmentalists and historians have written about numerous ways in which pro-business ideals of streamlining and deregulation were realized. Three episodes concerning pesticides will be sufficient to illustrate the policy shift and explain the political consequences within the administration: reactions to the Industrial Bio-Test Laboratory (IBT) scandal and policies toward the pesticides EDB and DBCP.

Industrial Bio-Test Laboratory was the largest independent laboratory testing chemicals under contract for industry, including the pesticides industry. By the start of the Reagan administration, the EPA had registered more than 200 pesticides on the basis of IBT data.[17] In 1976, EPA scientist M. Adrian Gross uncovered problems with IBT testing. Investigations followed, and in May 1981, four officers of the company were indicted by a federal grand jury for fraud and falsification of reports; at their trial in 1983, three were convicted.[18]

The seriousness of the IBT scandal was due not only to the number of chemicals involved but also to the fact that many chronic toxicity tests had to be thrown out; according to one estimate, this set back the pesticide registration process by a decade.[19] Revelations about the fraud led to some key reforms in pesticide and toxics regulation, but the actual changes that took place were disappointing. First, the EPA was already overburdened by the cumbersome registration process put in place under FIFRA and its amendments in 1978; it lagged far behind targets for reviewing pesticides and was now given the job of redoing registrations that had previously been deemed completed. Second, the EPA was expected to take on this work just as its budget and personnel were being slashed. By 1983, there was only one full-time staff member working in the lab-inspection program. Third, the scale of the IBT scandal led many Americans to lose faith in the whole system of pesticide testing and registration.[20] There was evidence to support the conviction of many that the system was broken. As of 1984, 140 pesticides that had been registered on the basis of fraudulent data remained on the market. Of these, the EPA announced that manufacturers of 35 had agreed to gather new data on the pesticides but that they would remain on the market pending such information.[21] The IBT scandal illustrated how many of the structural problems of the regulatory system established in the 1970s remained unresolved even after a crisis had put the system under scrutiny.

If the overall system of pesticide testing and registration was tainted by the IBT scandal, the policies of Reagan officials toward particular pesticides confirmed their lack of interest in protecting citizens from widely used toxic substances. EDB had been in industrial use since the 1950s. It was used as an additive in leaded gasoline as well as a fumigant for grain, citrus, and other fruits and was injected into the soil to kill nematodes before they attacked the roots of plants. Its residues could be found on raw foods as well as in processed foods made from treated crops. Despite its many uses, EDB turned out to be a potent carcinogen, an effect first identified by the National Cancer Institute (NCI) in 1974. In subsequent years, it was found to affect reproduction in both men and women, cause sterility in men, and cause birth defects. Evidence of its potency mounted when experimental rats fell ill and died at low doses. Following a three-year review of the chemical, the EPA reported in December 1980 on the dangers of EDB. It proposed ending use of EDB as a fumigant of fruit and monitoring its use in soil fumigation to make sure that it wasn't contaminating groundwater.[22]

Meanwhile, EDB presented a special danger to those exposed to it on the job. Two publicized stories in 1983 illustrated the risks. The first involved a worker fumigating grain in a Minneapolis flour mill. After getting some EDB on his hands, he fell acutely ill, was hospitalized for several days, and nearly died. Two other workers in a California chemical plant came in contact with less than an ounce of EDB in a container that they were cleaning; one died immediately and the other within seventy-two hours.[23] Food handlers, truckers, and dock workers were already aware of the risk they faced from fumigated foods. Two years earlier, in September 1981, the AFL-CIO, the Teamsters, and the Longshoremen's Union had petitioned OSHA for temporary emergency action to lower the allowable workplace exposure from its level at that time of 20 ppm. An EPA study had shown that at exposures of 20 ppm, it was a virtual certainty that workers would get cancer. Another researcher at Northeastern University found that even at 10 ppm, 270 out of 1,000 would get cancer. A study by the NCI found that at 10 ppm, 40 percent of rats got cancer.[24] One EPA scientist reported that the danger of cancer from EDB was "among the highest the agency has ever confronted."[25]

The apparent consensus about the danger of EDB among scientists, labor unions, and government officials raised the question of why it continued to be widely used until 1984. The first answer to this question was found in the determination of John Todhunter to block what he saw as unnecessary restrictions on business. Todhunter directly stopped EPA action on at least three occasions, stalling for time until his own departure from the EPA in spring 1983. Todhunter was joined in his determination to block action by Thorne Auchter of OSHA, who didn't want to reset the exposure levels. Meanwhile, the continued use of EDB to fumigate fruit seemed to be urgent in the summer of 1981, when there was a panic over the possible spread of the Mediterranean fruit fly in California. Government and business officials worried that customers would refuse California shipments without fumigation—as was the case with Japan, a heavy importer of California citrus. When EDB fumigation of fruit in California got under way that August, the press quoted a "senior EPA scientist" who called the risk from EDB "negligible" and likened it to that of smoking one cigarette over a lifetime. The source of the information was Todhunter, whose conclusions were ridiculed by others at the EPA.[26]

In fall 1981, Todhunter rejected the report of EPA scientists that EDB was carcinogenic and their recommendation that it should be banned or phased out. While EPA staff reiterated their original recommendations, Todhunter confidentially contacted Florida citrus growers, assuring them that the EPA was not in a hurry to act on EDB. He publicly announced that the EPA couldn't issue any new policy on EDB until OSHA had decided on new workplace standards so that there would be "coordination" between the agencies.[27]

With evidence that groundwater in Florida, California, Georgia, and Hawaii was contaminated, the new administrator of the EPA, William Ruckelshaus, who replaced Anne Gorsuch in May 1983, issued an emergency suspension of EDB as a soil fumigant six months after Todhunter had resigned. This was only the second time in EPA history that such an action had been taken. Ruckelshaus announced that bans on other uses were to be phased in, with fumigation of fruit not ending until September 1984. The agency announced recommended safe residue levels in processed and raw foods in February 1984.[28]

Press coverage of the EDB controversy was especially heavy in early 1984 and highlighted a few different themes. A number of articles described the differences among state policies, revealing what one *New York Times* article called a "pattern of confusion."[29] Florida, for example, had banned seventy-six processed foods made with grain in December 1983, only to relax its regulations in reaction to new, more lenient federal guidelines in February 1984. California and Illinois also accepted the new EPA standards, and the New York governor threatened stricter rules within his state unless the federal government tightened its standards. By March, New York (and then other states in the Northeast) set allowable EDB levels in foods lower than the federal standard, illustrating what one article referred to as a "regulatory patchwork."[30] News articles clearly referred to EDB as cancer-causing but also gave thorough coverage to the administrator of the EPA, William Ruckelshaus, calling for people to "calm down." Highlighting that there was only a threat from a lifetime of exposure, Ruckelshaus was quoted as saying that EDB was "not a public health emergency" and was being slowly taken out of the nation's food supply.[31] Press stories did not seem to challenge Ruckelshaus's message of reassurance, especially in articles that noted disagreement among scientific experts about the danger of EDB, and those that emphasized the risks implied that only a buildup of chronic exposures was dangerous.[32] Overall, then, the press stories helped to publicize the EDB problem, but their underlying tone of reassurance conveyed the message that the issue could be solved with decisive but measured federal action.

Editorial and op-ed essays ranged from those critical of any exposure to EDB to those more critical of the strong measures taken against EDB. For example, in January, the *New York Times* charged that Americans faced a "needless cancer crisis" because, although the dangers of EDB had been known for a decade, the government had failed to take any action. The editorial cited the EPA estimate that a lifetime of exposure to EDB would lead to cancer in 3 of every 1,000 people. Two months later, the *Times* again criticized the neglect of former EPA administrator Anne Gorsuch and the continued lack of uniformity in EDB regulations. In between the editorials, an op-ed in the *Times* also criticized the inconsistent regulations among states. Meanwhile, the *Wall Street Journal* ran an essay by Keith Barrons, formerly of Dow Chemical Company, asserting that the danger from EDB had been overblown and that using it was better than having worms or other insect contamination in grains. Two months later, a *Journal* editorial echoed the idea that the cancer danger had been exaggerated and a "crisis" manufactured. It also asserted that there weren't good or safe substitutes for EDB.[33] The opinion pieces in these two papers illustrate the polarity of opinion on EDB.

Controversies over DBCP also received a lot of publicity in the early 1980s and presented another clear example of Reagan administration attempts to "streamline" the pesticide regulation process and to serve the reported interests of business. Like EDB, DBCP had been around since the 1950s; by the 1970s, it was widely used by farmers and orchardists as well as home gardeners. It was also a nematocide that turned out to cause sterility in male workers in a plant where the chemical was produced. Although as far back as the 1950s, scientists had found that DBCP caused the atrophy of testes in lab animals, it was not until 1977 that casual conversations among workers at a plant where the chemical was made publicly revealed the danger of human sterility. Testing led to the conclusion that some of the workers were completely sterile and others had very low sperm counts. Testing of pesticide applicators also revealed sterility, including among workers in Standard Fruit Company banana plantations in Costa Rica. Meanwhile, the NCI announced that DBCP was an animal carcinogen and was strongly suspected to be a human carcinogen. By 1977, DBCP was shown to have contaminated many of the wells in California's Central Valley.[34]

With clear evidence in 1977 of toxicity, the state of California banned DBCP. The EPA followed the state's lead but first embarked on two years of investigation and hearings. Sociologist Angus Wright pointed to the case of DBCP as an illustration of the common pattern of ignoring dangers to farm workers because it was not until groundwater contamination was demonstrated—even though threats to workers were already clear—that the EPA moved to ban the chemical.[35] Manufacturers of the chemical and the EPA came to an agreement that within fifteen months it would be withdrawn from the American market except for use on pineapples in Hawaii, where two major growers petitioned for an exemption, arguing that it was necessary for their crop.[36]

Meanwhile, farmers in at least one other state were determined not to lose DBCP. Peach growers in South Carolina were supported by researchers at Clemson University who argued that if DBCP was used on trees before fruit appeared, there would be no danger of residue; researchers there also completed a study showing the damage done by nematodes to the peach crop. These studies, though, were hardly objective. The residue study was funded by Amvac Chemical Company, the only remaining manufacturer of DBCP. And officials from Clemson University, which acted as the state's regulatory body under FIFRA, had previously met with representatives from the EPA to determine what kinds of studies would be needed to overturn the ban on the chemical.[37] In August 1982, Todhunter of the EPA issued an emergency exemption for use of DBCP on South Carolina peach orchards. The exemption, though, was blocked by a court injunction after the group Grass Roots Organizing Workshop sued to stop the use of DBCP as a threat to public health.[38] Although many fruit growers predicted disaster with the banning of DBCP, peach yields in both South Carolina and California went up after DBCP use was discontinued.[39]

The first stage of the Reagan administration's environmental policy came to a close in spring 1983 with the resignation of Anne Gorsuch and her deputies John Hernandez and John Todhunter. The resignations were followed later in the year by that of James Watt, who had similarly antagonized critics and faced removal by a Republican-controlled Congress.[40] The abrasive style and outspoken determination of these policymakers to dismantle regulations and deny that environmentalism had popular support were rejected by public opinion and many in Congress.[41]

As a political decision for Reagan policymakers anxious to repair the damage done in the first two years of the administration, the selection of Ruckelshaus as Gorsuch's replacement at the EPA was astute. Ruckelshaus had been the original administrator of the EPA and enjoyed a reputation for incorruptibility (he was the deputy attorney general who had defied Richard Nixon's order to fire independent special prosecutor Archibald Cox during the Watergate scandal) and dedication to the environment. Nevertheless, even Ruckelshaus admitted that he had changed since his first term as EPA administrator. In the interim, he had been a consultant to the vinyl chloride industry, seeking to weaken government regulations of it, and an executive of Weyerhauser, a timber company with a poor environmental record. Although his style and commitment to law and transparency were very different from Gorsuch's approach, he reflected the political shift rightward when he explained that the EPA should be an "educator," not an "advocate" for a cleaner environment. He also bemoaned Americans becoming too emotional about toxic chemicals and suggested that they should be more rational. Other signs of continuity in the administration of the EPA included initial support for the continuation of budget cuts proposed by the OMB, opposition to stricter control of hazardous-waste disposal in landfills, and the assertion that there was no need for a federal groundwater policy.[42]

The drama over personnel in the Reagan administration illustrated a pattern that can be seen elsewhere in environmental history. People with extreme views, such as the antiscientific apostle John Todhunter, were pushed out and replaced by those who appeared to be moderate simply because they were less extreme. Thus, the idea of stepping back from the brink masked the rightward shift under the Reagan administration. An anti-environmental tilt appeared as a moderate relief from the extreme views of the early administration. As I have argued in these pages, such a dynamic was a familiar pattern that helped to maintain support for widespread pesticide use. Pesticides that were seen to be dangerous—such as DDT or 2,4,5-T—were banned while alternative, safer chemicals—such as less-persistent insecticides or 2,4-D—took their place. Thus, the dangerous substance was replaced by the safer one; the extreme solution gave way to a more moderate one. And all the while, pesticides and the industrialized agricultural system of which they were a part were not fundamentally challenged.

The Underside of Agricultural Globalization

The rightward shift of environmental policies under the Reagan administration was also clearly in evidence when it came to foreign policies. By the late 1970s, many policymakers had grown more concerned that recent efforts to lessen chemical pollution in the United States had not addressed the issue of Americans continuing to export toxic chemicals, including as part of the global agricultural system. Immediately before he left office, President Jimmy Carter tried to rectify the situation with Executive Order 12264, which stopped the export of banned or restricted substances from the United States to other countries. Carter's eleventh-hour initiative was an attempt to address what had become an entrenched but hitherto ignored aspect of the globalization of an industrial food economy. Although efforts to regulate pesticides and other chemical pollutants in the United States had been growing since the publication of *Silent Spring*, the export of these chemicals had continued largely unimpeded. Moreover, the threat to workers and residents in developing countries had increased because the use of more acutely toxic organophosphates had gone up while use of the more persistent organochlorines had gone down. Meanwhile, American consumers ate growing amounts of imported fruits and vegetables with pesticide residues. Journalists David Weir and Mark Schapiro described this pattern as a "circle of poison."[43] But this pattern was of little concern to Ronald Reagan and others in his administration. Just one month after taking office, the new president rescinded Carter's order, explaining that the United States shouldn't tell other countries what to do if they wanted to import particular chemicals.

Reagan's decision, of course, did not cause the disaster at Bhopal, but it provides insights into the cavalier American attitude about which toxic chemicals were exported, used, or produced abroad. Moreover, his views illustrate a broad American refusal to understand the consequences of the globalization of industrial agriculture, for better or for worse. Events at Bhopal were one example of the dangers people faced from the mass production of pesticides.

The massive chemical leak at the Union Carbide plant in Bhopal on 2–3 December 1984 taught different lessons to different groups of people. This shifting interpretive lens was reflected in the variety of in-depth stories about the disaster. Books on Bhopal fell into particular categories. There were some dramatic and detailed journalistic accounts of the events, their immediate causes, and their human impact; most of these were written within a few years of the tragedy.[44] There were also accounts whose main purpose was to call for justice for the victims. Many of these advocacy books were published in India by organized victims' or workers' groups; the bulk of them was also published shortly after the leak.[45] Other authors probed the meaning of Bhopal in a larger context of environmental pollution and man-made disasters.[46] Finally, another group of studies focused on questions of legality and business ethics as a framework for understanding Bhopal.[47]

Most ordinary Americans, of course, learned about Bhopal not from books but from a variety of news stories on the leak and its aftermath. These stories revealed much about the impact of Bhopal in the United States and help us better understand contemporary attitudes toward pesticides. Before examining the news coverage and its themes, it makes sense to review some of the facts about the events in India.

In 1984, Union Carbide was the thirty-fifth-largest industrial firm and the seventh-largest chemical company in the United States, with sales of almost $10 billion that year. It had operations in thirty-eight different countries, including India since 1905.[48] Since 1969, Union Carbide of India Ltd. (UCIL), a subsidiary, had been making the carbamate pesticides Temik (extremely toxic) and Sevin (its most important pesticide) at a plant in Bhopal, India, a city of roughly 900,000 in 1984. UCIL was a large company in India, with fourteen factories, and about half of its income came from the manufacture of Eveready batteries.[49] The Indian government had welcomed the Bhopal plant, built at the height of the Green Revolution, when high-yield seeds, fertilizers, pesticides, and irrigation combined to increase output and commodity exports, thus bringing many areas of the developing world into the industrial food system. Reflecting the goals of the Green Revolution, pesticide use tripled in India between 1956 and 1970.[50] Unfortunately for Union Carbide, though, the company expanded its facilities and production capacity at Bhopal following a famine and financial crisis in India, which meant lower incomes in the country and less ability to spend on high-priced pesticides. In addition, a new class of less-toxic pesticides, synthetic pyrethoids, was introduced around this time, further shrinking the market for Sevin.[51]

In 1978, Union Carbide changed its manufacturing process to use the highly toxic and volatile methyl isocyanate (MIC) as a component in the production of Sevin; by 1980, the Bhopal plant began on-site production of MIC. Yet the MIC and Sevin units at Bhopal never worked at full capacity; built to make 5,000 tons of pesticides a year, the Bhopal facility produced 2,308 tons in 1982, 1,647 tons in 1983, and probably less than 1,000 tons in 1984, when the unit was $4 million in debt. It was, according to the words of one observer, a "white elephant" in the middle of Bhopal.[52] By the early 1980s, the parent company was anxious to reduce costs at the factory. Staff was cut dramatically, with the total number of employees going from 850 to 642 in 1982, and the number of people per shift was also cut; with morale plummeting, many of the most skilled engineers soon left the MIC unit. Routine maintenance was postponed, and safety systems were not kept in functioning order.[53]

Some critics argued that even before this, there were fundamental problems with the factory itself. Environmental and worker safety were not priorities in either the design or the running of the plant, reflecting a double standard between how multinational corporations ran their US and Third World factories.[54] Just one example of the design flaws of the plant was the decision to have large holding tanks for MIC instead of small individual containers. Officials at the parent company overrode the objections of managers in India, choosing what they believed to be a more cost-effective plan. When operations were changed to include MIC production, objections from municipal officials at the location of a now very hazardous plant close to population centers were also overridden, this time by the state government of Madya Pradesh, which was reluctant to restrict the activities of the regionally powerful UCIL.[55]

There are several examples of differences between the Bhopal facility and the only other Union Carbide factory that produced MIC in Institute, West Virginia. For one, the former had no gas detectors for leaks and only manual safety systems, not automatic ones, in contrast to the factory on American soil. Another difference was that at the Institute plant, there was a scrubber to neutralize "ordinary" leaks as well as a much larger one for emergency leaks; Bhopal had no scrubber that could handle large-volume, high-pressure leaks. The flare tower at Institute was more sophisticated, as were the instrument and control devices, and the plant had an extensive computer system. Institute also had much larger dump tanks and a self-contained dump system to handle a runaway reaction in MIC.[56]

Union Carbide officials were well aware that there were many safety problems at the Bhopal plant, as the company's own 1982 inspection report had detailed, focusing on poor instrumentation and controls and manual safety systems. In addition, the report described an inadequate water-spray system that could not properly reach an emergency gas leak coming through the flare tower, a relief valve for the MIC tank that did not function properly, failing pressure gauges, and a work force untrained for emergencies. The May 1982 inspection found sixty-one hazards at the Bhopal plant, thirty of which were classified as major and eleven of which were in the MIC unit.[57] The parent company received regular updates from UCIL about how it was addressing the issues in the report as well as monthly reports on all operation issues; in addition, Union Carbide retained control of UCIL's budget.[58] The poor design and safety record of the plant were more than theoretical. In the six years before the Bhopal disaster, there were six major accidents at the plant.[59]

On the evening of 2 December 1984, water flowed into one of three holding tanks for MIC at the Bhopal plant. Witnesses and almost all who scrutinized the situation, including international inspection teams brought in after the disaster, explained that the water was introduced inadvertently when a worker was flushing sediment out of pipes near the MIC storage tanks. The worker, new at his job and working without a maintenance supervisor, was supposed to insert a slip bind as a backup safety system to ensure no leakage of water into the MIC tanks. He neglected to do so. Moreover, the system was notoriously leaky and in poor repair, and the piping had been jerry-rigged with a jumper line to make water flushing easier and cheaper, but the change also made the system more apt to leak into the MIC tanks.

Even before the flushing operation began, there were other problems that night. The refrigeration system for the MIC tanks had been previously shut down to save money, so the MIC was at ambient temperature and thus more difficult to control if there was a chain reaction. In addition, the reserve tank, which was supposed to be kept empty so that reactive MIC could be dumped to reduce pressure from the first tank, already had some MIC in it, so it could not be used as a relief container. The MIC that would spiral out of control in a chain reaction had an excess of chloroform, which reacted with the metal in the tank and caused the chemical to further break down, leading to a buildup of heat and pressure in the tank—even before water was introduced to set off its own unstable reaction. Other inadequacies of the safety system worsened the disaster once the water had been introduced. The alarm system to warn of a leak, both inside and outside the plant, was not functioning.[60] The flare tower to burn off escaping gas was improperly positioned to catch any release, and the scrubber for neutralizing escaping gas with caustic acid was empty. Finally, the structural and functional problems that had been detailed in the 1982 safety inspection report had not been addressed and thus made the situation worse.

The water set off a chain reaction in the highly reactive MIC, leading to a buildup of pressure within the tank that hours later burst out, spewing forty tons of the chemical and other breakdown components into the atmosphere. Due to the faulty equipment and inadequate staffing, workers at the plant did not realize what was going on until it was too late. The gas fog was heavier than air and so clung close to the ground, where people were sleeping on the floors of their houses in ramshackle neighborhoods that abutted the plant. Many were awakened by coughing, burning eyes, and vomiting. At least 3,000 people died almost immediately (some estimates were higher), another 15,000 died within a few years, and 500,000 more were injured or suffered permanent damage to their health.

The chaos was horrific as people tried to flee. Workers at the plant failed to sound an alarm in the surrounding neighborhoods, but even had they done so, there had been no emergency evacuation drills, and most did not have access to transportation to escape. Some made their way to the overwhelmed hospital, where medical personnel had no emergency information about the chemicals released and which antidotes to give. In the days following, information, including chemical and medical details, was slow in coming from Union Carbide, which tended to minimize the toxicity of MIC, referring to it as similar to a strong tear gas. Local doctors were sure, based on their observation of symptoms, that cyanide had also been part of the poisoned cloud; this last question was very important because a cyanide antidote, sodium thiosulphate, was readily available. These issues remained controversial for years to come, with some scientists arguing that cyanide was a breakdown product of MIC under the right conditions and Union Carbide continuing to deny that any cyanide had been released.

The shock of the events lingered for weeks. Union Carbide and UCIL soon moved to damage control, each tending to blame the other or the Indian government. There followed four years of legal wrangling among the parties, culminating in a $470 million out-of-court settlement in January 1989 from Union Carbide to the government of India, representing the victims. The money was deposited into a court-administered account while claims were sorted out, but three years later, monies had still not been paid to victims.[61] The amount of the settlement was surprisingly small to many, even taking into account the Indian standard of living.[62] No clearer evidence of the benefit that accrued to Union Carbide from the settlement could be seen than the immediate increase of company stock by $2 per share (7 percent) on the day the settlement was announced.[63]

In response to petitions by victims' groups in 1991, the Supreme Court of India withdrew the criminal immunity that the company had been granted in the initial settlement. Senior officials from the Indian subsidiary were brought to trial, and American officials of Union Carbide, including former CEO Warren Anderson, were charged with culpable homicide. The government of India did not pursue Anderson's extradition until 2003, when activists pressed for action—although the US government refused the request.[64] Back in the United States, another attempt for legal redress came in 1999 with the filing of a new lawsuit against Union Carbide. Four years later, the US District Court dismissed the suit on the grounds that the American corporation had already paid adequate compensation by funding the construction of a hospital in Bhopal. Moreover, the judge added that Union Carbide had long before sold its shares in UCIL and that the tragedy was too far in the past to litigate in 2003.

Despite the findings of the US District Court, many victims had yet to receive compensation or adequate health care two and a half decades after the tragedy. Meanwhile, Union Carbide had been acquired in 2001 by Dow Chemical Company, which denied any responsibility for past or future liabilities in the Bhopal tragedy.[65] The site of the former plant remained contaminated, with chemicals seeping into the soil and groundwater. News reports on the twenty-fifth anniversary of the disaster cited continuing physical maladies for the people around the plant, including lung and eye damage, high rates of birth defects, cancer, neurological damage, abnormal menstrual cycles, and mental illness.[66]

News coverage of the disaster and its legacy highlighted particular themes and changed over time. The first and most obvious observation was that news accounts in the initial six months after the leak were focused upon repeated descriptions of the incident and the immediate casualties.[67] Surveying stories from the first two months, communications scholar Lee Wilkins observed that 62.2 percent of the more than 700 stories made no mention of any of the long-term effects of the disaster.[68] Nevertheless, news coverage in the initial aftermath was heavy, and the story was ranked by Associated Press editors as the most significant of the year.[69] Typical of news accounts in the early days of the tragedy, one *New York Times* story on 7 December 1984 focused on the number of dead (2,000 at that point by unofficial count), the financial health of Union Carbide in light of the tragedy, the unanswered questions as to how and why the accident had occurred, and the arrest of Union Carbide chair Anderson when he had stepped off a plane in India.[70] Reflecting the tendency of early press coverage to focus on the immediate devastation and casualty numbers, none of the media stories made much connection to broader agricultural or international issues. There was also little assignment of blame.[71]

Following the predictable emphasis on the suddenness of the tragedy and the number of casualties that dominated the earliest coverage, within three months, the media coverage focused more upon the causes of the disaster and its impact on Union Carbide as a company. This change had consequences for how Americans related to the events. "The media's attention to the fate of Union Carbide shifted focus," according to one observer, "from the tragedy in Bhopal to the preservation of U.S. capitalist interests."[72] In part, this coverage reflected the public relations offensive in March and April 1985 from Union Carbide to absolve itself of responsibility for the disaster. Although the United States–based multinational owned 50.9 percent of the Indian subsidiary UCIL, it released detailed information about the failures of the management and staff of the Indian company to uphold Union Carbide standards of safety. Press stories reprinted the charges from company headquarters, thus helping to create the picture of an incompetent Third World subsidiary. Warren Anderson was quoted as referring to a "whole litany of non-standard operating procedures, omissions and commissions" on the part of the Indian subsidiary.[73] Meanwhile, at the time of the public relations initiative, many press stories helpfully mentioned the $5 million in emergency aid that Union Carbide would provide to victims while lawsuits made their way through the courts.[74]

Anderson, in particular, was viewed with sympathy in some of the press stories as trying to protect his company, which was, *Business Week* said, "fighting for its life." Anderson found that hearing the news from Bhopal was "a shattering experience." *Fortune* noted that he was "home in bed with a bad cold" at the time. In May 1985, the *New York Times* ran a three-page article on the "personal ordeal" of Warren Anderson.[75]

Articles included defensive responses from managers of UCIL, although they were not covered as prominently as were the accusations by Anderson and Union Carbide. In one article, the former managing director of UCIL said that major decisions about plant operations were made in Union Carbide headquarters in Danbury, Connecticut, as well as in Bhopal. He added that local officials had objected to the design of the MIC unit with its large storage tanks of the dangerous chemical. Newspaper coverage did note that the parent companies of overseas chemical plants, such as Union Carbide, DuPont, and American Cyanamid, all had schedules to inspect operations and safety of subsidiary facilities but that there was no industry standard for the frequency of such inspections.[76]

In subtle and obvious ways, media coverage reflected the Union Carbide argument that the backwardness of Third World peoples was a key explanation for events in Bhopal. The contention was found not only in early press releases, which disavowed responsibility for day-to-day factory management around the world ("You can't run a $9 or $10 billion corporation all out of Danbury," according to Anderson), but also in corporate statements for years after. For example, the 1984 annual report for Union Carbide criticized the sophistication of Third World staff as well as their nationalistic interest in providing native jobs.[77] The media reinforced these ideas and thus privileged Union Carbide's perspective. For example, an article in the *Wall Street Journal* observed, "We are thrusting 20th century technology into countries that aren't ready," and another column in the *Journal* observed that regulations about local sourcing might have lessened Union Carbide's ability to have a hands-on role in environmental and safety regulations. Meanwhile, a series in the *New York Times* in January and February 1985 failed to answer the question about the extent of Union Carbide control over UCIL but instead highlighted the procedural violations at the Bhopal plant and lax environmental regulations in the state as well as low educational and technical levels in India. Stories such as these implied that although disasters might be tragic, they could usually be avoided when proper Western safety standards were followed; if this was not always possible in areas of the developing world, accidents were the inevitable price of technological progress.[78]

Bhopal faded from the American media after a few months, but the one-year anniversary in December 1985 brought a spate of news stories. There were common themes in these stories that reflected the unresolved situation of the victims as well as the public relations efforts of Union Carbide.[79] These stories highlighted the plight of Bhopal residents, many thousands of whom continued to suffer debilitating health effects, most frequently breathing and eye problems, gastrointestinal problems, and general weakness. The number of injured varied in the stories, though 200,000 was the most frequently cited figure. The articles noted that many were effectively disabled and unable to return to their previous jobs. Nevertheless, the Bhopal residents as a group appeared somewhat irrational as they burned effigies of Warren Anderson in widespread protests on the one-year anniversary of the disaster. The stories were sympathetic to the plight of victims, although one *New York Times* story surprisingly challenged the provenance of injuries: "Questions persist, however, about the causes of the widespread illnesses in Bhopal: which were caused or aggravated by the leak? Which had other causes?"[80]

In summer 1986, with the lawsuits against Union Carbide unresolved and the compensation for victims minimal and ill organized, the multinational company launched a new effort to shift blame away from itself. The company announced that its own exhaustive investigation into the accident revealed that the leak had been deliberately caused by sabotage from a disgruntled worker. Although the ignorant worker had not intended for the leak to occur (he had only wanted to ruin a batch of MIC), he was nevertheless angry at a demotion and had taken revenge on the company. The company argued that because litigation was pending, it could not name the alleged saboteur. American press stories paid a lot of attention to the contention from Union Carbide, thus giving it legitimacy.[81] Farther down in the stories, authors observed that Union Carbide's allegations were controversial, for example: "No independent inquiry . . . had endorsed the theory, which in India is widely seen as an attempt to escape liability." The countercharge from the Indian government, also buried in press stories, was more general and therefore less potent than the position of Union Carbide: the government blamed "faulty plant design, poor maintenance, and inadequate safety features" for the leak.[82] Some detailed critiques of the Union Carbide position made it into the press. For example, an Indian journalist based in Chicago wrote a lengthy article in the *Chicago Tribune* explaining why the company's assertions of sabotage were illogical and not logistically possible.[83]

In 1988, two years after Union Carbide first asserted its theory of sabotage and as the legal case against the company continued to languish, a detailed article in the *Wall Street Journal* captured the dominant impression left in the American press about the cause of the leak.[84] Although the article carefully explained the criticisms of Union Carbide's position and the company's public relations campaign, it included a detailed account of the company's sabotage theory and left the overall impression that this was indeed a possible explanation for the disaster. In addition, the article highlighted the pitiable status of a Third World India peopled with "multitudes" and having "outdated employee records and poor telephone service," not to mention a "flea-infested [railway] station" where "a cow roamed." Thus, the article, and others, encouraged readers to have reasonable doubt regarding the culpability of the multinational company.

The next spate of news stories came in early 1989, when the Indian government and Union Carbide finally reached the $470 million settlement. Stories noted that it was "the largest award for an industrial accident" and argued that it was "generous by Indian standards."[85] Once the settlement was finally concluded, the tragedy and victimhood of the Bhopal residents became more of the focus of American news articles. The press described the continued daily deaths of residents five years after the disaster and the feelings of betrayal among those affected. Also, once the money from Union Carbide was decided upon, descriptions of the Indian government implied that it was incompetent and to blame for the ongoing problems of the victims.[86] The incompetence of the government appeared even worse with reports of administrative problems in classifying victims and distributing monies.

Predictably, the tenth anniversary of the tragedy brought some attention in the US press, although the issue had otherwise largely disappeared from the media. One *New York Times* article repeated the positions of Union Carbide, highlighting the ideas that the Indian subsidiary was run independent of the parent company, that its officials had not allowed Union Carbide to help in the early days of the accident by granting access to the plant, and that the Indian government was responsible for letting people move into houses that were too close to the plant. In addition, the author observed that Union Carbide had "never been able to argue its case in an Indian court," implying—mistakenly—that the company had been opposed to an out-of-court settlement. Although the article clearly had pity for the victims, its overall message was to exonerate Union Carbide, adding that in addition to the settlement, the company had contributed $40 million to build a medical center for those affected.[87] The tenth-anniversary stories noted that people continued to suffer physically and that few individual claims had been settled.[88]

Scattered articles appeared near the twentieth anniversary of the tragedy and then again on the twenty-fifth anniversary.[89] The common theme in both sets of stories was that the horrific effects on the people of Bhopal continued with elevated cancer rates, neurological damage, birth defects, and mental illness. The articles emphasized that the groundwater was contaminated with chemicals and pesticides and that the site itself was abandoned and contaminated. Blame seemed to go to Dow Chemical Company, owner of Union Carbide since 2001, which had refused any responsibility for the cleanup or aftereffects of the disaster, and to the Indian government, which continued to deny that the site itself had become a hazard to the surrounding residents and had failed to distribute half the monies to the victims who were due to get them. As for the causes of the tragedy, most of these later articles gave little credence to the Union Carbide explanation.[90]

Surveying a selection of press stories over a period of twenty-five years reveals common themes, some predictable. The earliest stories were descriptive and highlighted the immediate plight of the victims. The basic mechanics of events were given, including an identification of the escaped gas as methyl isocyanate, a chemical used in—usually unspecified—pesticide production. Later stories continued to describe the events and the impact on Bhopal residents, adding details about the lawsuits against Union Carbide. The descriptions of Union Carbide's sabotage theory tended to give the company's version of events more credibility than it warranted. As a number of critics later pointed out, this deference was illustrated in the press failure to discuss that other toxic ingredients, including cyanide, had been released along with MIC.[91] Before 3 December 1984, very little was understood about MIC, but cyanide was well known as a poison that would kill people instantly. Union Carbide had a strong interest in making sure there was no association between cyanide and MIC. There was little press attention to the issue of cyanide being present or to the point that Union Carbide had knowingly withheld the widely available treatment, sodium thiosulfate.[92]

The words used to describe the events at Bhopal were most often "disaster" or "tragedy." The choice of these words seems obvious as a way to convey the scope of the events. Less often, "gas leak" or "accident" were used in the press, but these words seemed to minimize the event or erase responsibility for its occurrence.[93] Avoiding these descriptions reflected the views of both Union Carbide officials, arguing passionately for the theory of sabotage, and critics of the company who believed corporate negligence to have been responsible.

If the descriptive words used in the press conveyed some neutrality in laying blame for the disaster, there was nevertheless a clear villain in the majority of stories in the American press, especially in the early coverage: the Indian government. The incompetence and corruption of the Indian government was a recurring theme. Whereas stories that included negative charges against Union Carbide almost always included a company defense and explanation for its decisions, charges against the government included no such justifications. The other Indian entity of the story, UCIL, appeared in a more negative light than did the parent company because the conduct of its workers and managers appeared bumbling and incompetent at best and insensitive and negligent at worst. With the distance that comes from the passage of time in later stories, the condemnation of Indian authorities and business managers lessened while the cynical references to Union Carbide's failure to adequately help the victims increased.

Another observation that can be made of the press coverage is that from the first days of the tragedy to the stories a quarter of a century later, there was no clear consensus on the number of people killed and injured in Bhopal. Initially, the most commonly used number of dead was 2,000. By early 1985, some in the press cited the official death toll from the Indian government of 1,700, with 200,000 injured; stories, nevertheless, often continued to use the figure 2,000. Within five years of the tragedy, press stories revised the numbers further because more of the injured had died; the official death toll cited in 1989 was 3,598, with the number of injured fluctuating widely, from 30,000 to 60,000 to 100,000; the number of death and injury claims submitted was sometimes included (7,100 and 650,00 respectively). By the twenty-fifth anniversary of the disaster, the numbers had been increased further. Most commonly, press stories said that about 4,000 had been killed on the first night and another 15,000 had since died, with about 500,000 suffering illness and injury after December 1984.[94]

What was missing in many of the stories was context about pesticides and the industrial agriculture system of which they were a part. There was not much detail about the chemical MIC and how it was used, the pesticide carbaryl (Sevin), the impact of the Green Revolution, or the role of multinational corporations in the developing world. Indeed, after initial identification of MIC, there was not much emphasis on the fact that it was a pesticide ingredient. As I discussed earlier, the ideals of agricultural modernity and technological solutions of the Green Revolution had helped spread pesticide use to diverse parts of the developing world, first through research foundations and then through multinational corporations and government programs. The impact on India accelerated in the 1960s, especially following serious grain shortages in the country in 1966 and the launch of a new US program to provide agricultural assistance to other countries using technological and chemical approaches. The Food for Freedom effort launched by Lyndon Johnson helped to increase the number of acres in India that used Green Revolution technologies from 200 acres in 1965 to 38 million acres in 1968. Thus, government agencies such as the US Agency for International Development worked with private companies to increase the use of chemical fertilizers and pesticides in India and elsewhere.[95]

Union Carbide was one of the multinational corporations active in this endeavor. Back in 1962, the company had run a full-page advertisement in *National Geographic* depicting the "new science" that was transforming India.[96] The ad signaled the role that Union Carbide and other companies would play in bringing the Green Revolution to India. In 1966, Union Carbide sent one of its agronomists, Eduardo Munoz, to India to sell the wonders of Sevin. India signed a contract to import 1,200 tons of the pesticide, and Union Carbide announced that it would build a factory to produce Sevin there.[97] Thus, the roots of the 1984 disaster were sown years earlier.

Such background information might have given American readers of newspapers and magazines a different way of understanding the events at Bhopal. Focusing on the profit motivations of private multinational corporations might have also reframed the meaning of the Green Revolution, making Bhopal seem less like a natural disaster and more like a tragic but calculated risk of doing business. Years after the disaster, activists in India strongly criticized Union Carbide on these grounds. One former worker at

Bhopal observed that the motivations behind the Green Revolution were not altruistic: "Carbide's initiative to market pesticides in India was not a benevolent gesture to aid the Third World. The primary motivation was to make money for the American company, not to serve the interests of the Indian people."[98]

Decisions made at the Bhopal plant lent credence to this cynicism. For example, until 1978, Union Carbide had manufactured Sevin without MIC, reversing the steps in which chemicals were combined and thus eliminating the need for MIC. The process was changed in 1978 because the use of MIC was less expensive and created less waste. Yet news stories after 1984 failed to question the use of MIC in the production process. The press could also have investigated the Union Carbide manufacturing process before 1978, which did not use MIC but still included dangerous chemical components. In contrast to Union Carbide, the German firm Bayer, another manufacturer of carbaryl, used less-toxic chemicals in its production process, but its process was considered less economical and efficient.[99]

There was also not much discussion in the press about why so many people had lived crowded around a dangerous chemical plant and why the Indian government had worked hard to encourage the presence of multinational corporations and thus put few restrictions on their operations. This was especially true for the government of a poor state such as Madya Pradesh. For example, there were no air or water pollution laws in India before Bhopal, and restrictions such as zoning laws were routinely ignored by multinational corporations such as Union Carbide.[100]

Other background information that was missing from the American press coverage was a discussion of the market demand for Sevin and the economic condition of the Bhopal plant, which had led Union Carbide to cut corners when it came to safety and personnel. An understanding of the relationship between their own industrial food system and the factory half a world away in Bhopal would have provided a crucial context for American readers. No articles discussed on which crops Sevin was used, its purpose, or its effects.

Press articles that injected some international context into the events in Bhopal most often pointed back to chemical plants in the United States. A few stories in the media raised the question of whether such a catastrophic accident could happen on American soil, specifically at the only other Union Carbide plant that manufactured MIC in Institute, West Virginia.[101] Union Carbide was, not surprisingly, anxious to lessen any fears that the operations in Institute and Bhopal were equivalent. The American press inadvertently cooperated by publishing few articles on Institute, and those that were published highlighted the differences between the First and Third World operations.[102]

Despite the benign stories from Union Carbide or in the American press, the safety record at Institute was uneven. The Union Carbide plant was one of many chemical facilities in the Kanawha Valley of West Virginia. Pollutants and toxic chemicals were released frequently and hung in the valley.[103] Even so, safety systems at a plant such as Union Carbide's MIC unit were better than those in Bhopal. Nevertheless, right after the accident, Union Carbide immediately suspended operations in Institute and invested another $5 million to further improve safety there.[104] Previously, there had been leaks at the plant. In the five years before Bhopal, there had been twenty-eight leaks at the Institute plant big enough that they were required to be reported to the EPA; following Bhopal, another thirty-three leaks that had gone unreported were investigated by the EPA.[105]

Under the glare of increased scrutiny, the Institute plant experienced two notable accidents in 1985. A leak of mestityl oxide on 28 March 1985 received much publicity, sickening eight people in a local mall.[106] Several months later, on 11 August, a more dangerous leak occurred. Steam introduced into a tank of aldicarb oxime and methyl chloride created a buildup of temperature and pressure. Faulty venting and spray neutralization systems then led to a cloud of toxic gas wafting over the city of Institute, injuring 135 people, 31 of whom were sent to the hospital.[107] The focus on these acute episodes in Institute was relatively short-lived, even though the news stories and local activism made it clear that the accidents were unacceptable lapses in US industrial safety. A few years before the focus on Institute, alarm over news of another episode of chemical contamination more dramatically illustrated the different expectations for environmental safety in the United States and in the Third World.

The disaster that unfolded at Love Canal, a neighborhood of Niagara Falls, New York, was years in the making but received extensive publicity in the late 1970s and early 1980s and was one of the watersheds of modern environmental history.[108] Legally, it led to the 1980 passage of the Comprehensive Environmental Response, Compensation, and Liability Act, or "Superfund," which provided the EPA with authority to force private polluters to clean up hazardous-waste sites. In environmental history and activism, it provided greater understanding of what historian Michelle Murphy called "popular epidemiology," empowering ordinary people with a role in building the science of environmental contamination.[109] And, culturally, news of Love Canal heightened people's awareness of the dangers that lurked in the unseen wastes of industrialization.

In brief, the Love Canal neighborhood got its name from William Love, who began but never completed the building of a canal in 1890. Half a century later, the land was owned by Hooker Chemical Company, which used the partially excavated canal as a chemical-waste dumping ground from 1942 to 1954. Although aware of the danger of the 25,000 tons of waste it had put there, Hooker deeded the land to the Niagara Falls Board of Education, later asserting that it warned the city about the waste at the time, clearly indicating that the land would not be suitable for housing and that the soil should not be disturbed or excavated. By the mid-1970s, the land contained not only a school and park but also a number of homes, both single-family houses and apartment buildings, whose residents were increasingly complaining about chemical odors and seepage in their basements and on their properties. In 1978, the local paper published investigative articles on the issue, and residents begin forming activist groups shortly thereafter. The story made it into the national press in the summer of 1978, especially following an hour-long 1979 program on ABC, *The Killing Ground*.[110] Although the state of New York and the federal government announced in 1978 that the homeowners closest to the canal would be bought out, over the next few years, controversies raged about whether homeowners who lived slightly farther away from the canal would also be compensated for their houses and whether renters deserved payments for relocation.

The controversy about how to compensate victims was not the only similarity between the cases of Love Canal and Bhopal. The legal cases in both were lengthy and complex. By the end of 1983, one suit on behalf of 1,300 Love Canal residents was settled with Occidental Chemical Company (the parent company of Hooker) for a $20 million payout; within two years, a medical fund was established to pay for illnesses as they arose. Figuring payments for environmental cleanup took longer. It was not until 1994 that Occidental agreed to pay $98 million to New York State for cleanup; one year later, the New York State Supreme Court found that Occidental was negligent and had to pay another $129 million to the federal government for environmental costs.[111] Although activists, scientists, and the government disagreed on whether the neighborhood had been fully remediated and was safe for residences, all would agree that the worst contamination had been removed by the 1990s; residents soon moved into new houses there.

In contrast, the Union Carbide site in Bhopal remained highly contaminated decades later, and victims were inadequately compensated even after legal settlements had been won. Many more people in Bhopal had suffered much more catastrophic consequences than those in Love Canal, but they received much less compensation and care for their suffering. There are different reasons for this: the legal system changed in the United States with the passage of Superfund, the state and federal governments were determined to enforce cleanup, and public opinion in the wealthier United States exacted retribution.

Although there were clear differences in the fate of those who lived in Bhopal and those who lived in Love Canal, there were some similarities between these highly publicized episodes. Both were examples of the chemical contamination that was ubiquitous in industrial societies, even if it was, sometimes, seemingly invisible. Both episodes also involved pesticides. The MIC that was released in Bhopal was an ingredient in the manufacture of Sevin. The wastes dumped at Love Canal were varied, though the biggest component by weight (25 percent) was benzene hexachloride, or spent cake, waste from production of the insecticide lindane. In addition, government investigation about the Love Canal site actually began in 1976 with the discovery of elevated levels of the insecticide Mirex in Lake Ontario, whose source was traced back to another Hooker dump site a few blocks from the Love Canal one.[112] Nevertheless, in the ensuing public controversies about contamination in both countries, specific discussion of pesticides was almost nonexistent. So although many Americans were clearly concerned about the impact of chemical wastes in 1980 and in 1984, few connected this concern with pesticides.

Conclusion

Public opinion at the start of the 1980s had been shaped by a decade of new regulations and a new understanding about the human relationship to the natural world. For some, such as the leaders of the sagebrush rebellion, this led to a backlash against the changes of the 1970s. Others remained convinced that these developments had been basically sound, and they rejected what they perceived to be extreme voices trying to turn their backs on an environmental consciousness. It is easy to reject extreme positions, but such rejection often leads to the political embrace of a compromise or moderate position. James Watt, Anne Gorsuch, and others may have left the Reagan administration, but the cost/benefit litmus test for environmental regulations remained. What also remained was a regulatory system inadequate to address the complex issues of pesticide use. The Federal Insecticide, Fungicide, and Rodenticide Act, even as amended in 1972 by the Federal Environmental Pesticide Control Act, was ineffective. By 1986, only 6 of the 600 active ingredients in pesticides had been tested for health and safety.[113] The drawn-out controversies over EDB and DBCP illustrated the weaknesses of the system. In addition, FIFRA did not cover chemicals exported for use in other countries. Thus, pesticides were routinely exported to other countries, and their residues remained on food imported back into the United States, sometimes endangering workers as well as US consumers.

The 1980s was a potential turning point in American attitudes toward pesticide use. Many Americans embraced the nascent environmentalism of the previous decade and rejected extremist efforts to eliminate new regulations. But once extremist voices were quieted, people could settle back into a comfortable confidence that environmental issues were being addressed; in a way, the new laws of the 1970s gave many false confidence and obscured the systemic and philosophical impact of industrialization on the environment. In this way, many remained blind to the widespread environmental effects of pesticides.

Similarly, it is easy to react with horror to a large environmental disaster of dramatic proportions. People expressed their outrage that thousands of innocent Indians in Bhopal had died in one night and others remained seriously ill afterward. The initial shock at the disaster—which many called "the Hiroshima of the chemical industry"—was both understandable and predictable.[114] But with time, that reaction wore off. The ebb and flow of publicity was true of chemical contamination in the United States as well—even if the victims fared better. Thus, residents of Love Canal were compensated and the area cleaned up, but there was little lasting attention to the causes of the pollution or to the particular chemicals involved, including pesticides. Love Canal might have been a watershed in environmental legal history and in waste disposal regulations, but it did not lead to deeper questioning about the overall industrial system or the human relationship to the environment. Similarly, Bhopal could have been a turning point, a moment to raise fundamental questions about the production of food and the impact of industrialized agriculture on ordinary people. Instead, the moment passed, the opportunity was lost, and the embrace of pesticides remained strong.

CHAPTER 7

Recommitment: Endocrine Disruptors, GMOs, and Organic Food

Risk is relative and, usually, situational. Why do some states, for example, allow the purchase and use of fireworks by amateurs whereas others do not? States with easy access to fireworks have made a legislative judgment that the risk of a few individuals getting injured or maimed is outweighed by the cultural tradition and joy that will be experienced by the users, and the predictable number of annual injuries is not enough to change the laws in particular states. When the negative consequences of some risks reach a tipping point so that they are no longer perceived as acceptable, legal or policy restrictions may follow. But finding the tipping point is not always easy. In *Nature's Nation*, historian John Opie wrote that Americans were often confused about environmental risk. Opie cited answers to a national poll to illustrate his point: Whereas respondents believed that botulism killed 500 Americans a year, it actually killed 5. Similarly, those polled were worried about radiation from dental X-rays when they should have been more concerned about radon in their basements. They also had a poor appreciation of the danger of automobiles because driving was ubiquitous, although 1 in 5,000 died in a car accident each year.[1]

Maybe the real lesson from this survey was not that Americans had a poor understanding of risk and statistics but that risk was defined by individuals and societies and was therefore about perception more than absolute standards. Thus, the question of how to define risk was contested by people, groups, states, and nations. Moreover, some scholars have emphasized that response to risk was shaped not just by awareness of its existence but also by the belief that opportunities to lessen particular hazards existed.[2] Natural disasters, presumably divorced from human action, were placed in a different category from human-caused events.

Nevertheless, in a modern industrial society, individuals might feel powerless to avoid certain human-created risks, such as pollution and chemical contamination of the environment. In addition, the risks of a technological society might be difficult for a layperson to understand if the consequences were not fully manifested for decades or even generations. This opaqueness encouraged uncertainty and doubt, which was sometimes willfully and often easily encouraged by those who wanted to mask risk. Risk evaluations by experts often ended up encouraging ordinary people to accept risk.[3] Politically, one way to reinforce the uncertainty of risk is to assert that the burden of proving danger should rest with those who want to restrict a substance or chemical unless there is incontrovertible proof of danger. Finally, risk in a modern capitalist economy has always been measured through a cost/benefit lens, a yardstick that might be wholly incompatible with nonquantifiable values such as human health and a clean environment.

By the late 1950s, many Americans had begun to question the environmental risks that surrounded them. Rising concerns about the effects of atomic testing—specifically contamination of milk by radioactive elements—alarmed many Americans and was widely covered in the press.[4] Debates about the risk of chemical pesticides soon followed, especially after the publication of Rachel Carson's *Silent Spring* in 1962. In her book, Carson was well aware that the public had been primed for this discussion by concern about the risks of radiation and referred to the topic as she introduced questions about the effects of chemical pesticides. Growing worry about the risk of chemical pollution led to concrete political action within a decade. By 1972, the health and aesthetic consequences of heavily polluted air and water led to the passage of the Clean Air and Water Acts, and DDT use in the United States was banned.

But, as we have seen, the shifting perceptions of pesticide risk were haphazard and did not lead to a clear consensus about pesticide use. For decades after World War II, the perceived benefits of synthetic pesticides—in plentiful, cheap food; in lowered labor costs for land management; in international development; and in the ability to manipulate the environment—outweighed the risks they might pose to human health or the environment. If Rachel Carson, growing environmentalism, a backlash from the Vietnam War, and disasters abroad started to change that calculus, there was still not a groundswell at the popular, political, or industry level to abandon industrial agriculture or the conviction that humans could successfully manipulate the environment.

At the end of the twentieth century and start of the twenty-first, the enduring commitment to industrial agriculture and chemical manipulation of the environment could be understood in different ways. First, most at a popular and political level remained convinced that the status quo was more efficient and cheaper than any alternative system; the former was practical, the latter a luxury. Second, confidence that technology and capitalism could be used to resolve the problems of environmental risk remained widespread. Third, many Americans seemed to rely more on their own individual actions rather than on a collective solution for pollution and health risks.

This chapter examines three areas in which Americans attempted to address the risks of pesticide exposure: debates about endocrine disruptors, introduction of genetically modified organisms (GMOs) in foods, and the embrace of organic food. Policies and public opinion about each of these areas illustrated that there were widespread fears about the effects of pesticides but that, in the end, there was limited questioning of the existing industrial system.

Understanding the Risks of Endocrine Disruptors

Before turning our attention to popular attitudes about the class of chemicals known as "endocrine disruptors," it makes sense to start with the conception of risk. Since risk is relative, one logical way that societies have always framed it is through a cost/benefit paradigm. Although a cost/benefit paradigm may be fairly useful for weighing business options, it is less so for environmental choices as people try to decide the worth of a clean environment, a healthier population, or a thriving ecosystem. Some business leaders might argue that ordinary Americans don't always understand the importance of using a cost/benefit analysis. For example, one speaker at a General Motors symposium on risk analysis concluded that "most people do not think in terms of comparative analysis of alternatives; they do not think in terms of value tradeoffs."[5] But when we actually look at the record of how people come to terms with risk, a cost/benefit paradigm seems dominant even when it is interpreted differently than a General Motors executive might wish.

One way of calculating costs and benefits sometimes comes down to what happens in the short term and what in the long term. In modern American culture, there is an enduring bias in favor of short-term gains over possible or projected long-term losses. Issues of environmental pollution and risk don't fit neatly into this framework, yet the trade-off of short-term gains for long-term consequences shaped how Americans approached environmental risks, including those of synthetic pesticides. As previous chapters have emphasized, the unforeseen impact of pesticides—such as resistance or harm to nontarget species—appeared much less important to many people than the immediate benefits that the chemicals brought.

Starting in the late twentieth century, research increasingly showed the negative effects of the long-term impact of pollutants. But long-term impacts were harder to visualize and harder to measure. With respect to chemicals and pesticides, one consequence of this bias has been a focus on the acute consequence and less emphasis on the chronic one. Discussion about the risks of chemical pollutants has also been shaped by the "dose-response curve," which was an effort to quantify and rationalize the human consequences of industrial workers and others exposed to such elements as lead and radium.[6] Moreover, this type of rational risk/benefit equation relies on the idea that the side effects of dangerous chemicals could be readily observed and that, aside from death, cancer was the chief danger against which regulators should be guarding.

Understanding the risk factors of cancer was a drawn-out and contentious process over the second half of the twentieth century. In part, this was because the lines between environmental, genetic, and lifestyle causes were blurry and became politicized, especially as cancer rates continued to rise (for example, from 1950 to 1988, the age-adjusted incidence rate of cancer went up 44 percent, whereas the age-adjusted death rate from cancer went up 3 percent). Ideas about cancer risk became especially politicized in the 1980s as the backlash against environmentalism gained strength, and many environmental critics and people in the media came to rely on the widely cited work of biochemist Bruce Ames, who argued that natural carcinogens and lifestyle choices were much more significant than industrial pollutants in causing disease.[7]

Unfortunately, assessing risk became even more complex as people debated health consequences in addition to cancer, including endocrine disruption. When an awareness of endocrine disruptors burst into the media and public culture in the mid-1990s, ordinary Americans, as well as scientists and business leaders, had to shift their way of thinking. Understanding endocrine disruptors meant looking at chronic, not acute, effects, upending a decades-long cultural and legal emphasis on cancer, overturning a linear cause-and-effect idea that the poison was in the dose, and wrestling with the risk of less-than-deadly consequences. So coming to terms with endocrine disruptors seemed to challenge long-standing views of risk in general and of pesticides in particular. Situations, though, are not always what they appear. Although it's true that endocrine disruptors were unique, with effects more subtle than those of other toxins, for many decades Americans had had trouble understanding the impact of pesticides for anything short of immediate death. Thus, one of the reasons that the embrace of pesticides remained entrenched despite various health or environmental crises was that long-term consequences seemed remote, and a linear cause-and-effect relationship was elusive. In many respects, the debates over endocrine disruptors—some of which were pesticides—fell into a familiar paradigm of how risk was understood.

In the 1990s and after, scientists and historians who wrote about endocrine disruptors highlighted some of the difficulties of this framework. Zoologist Theo Colburn was one of the conveners in 1991 of a gathering of twenty-one scientists that first labeled a class of chemicals "endocrine disruptors"; she wrote in 1996 with coauthors Dianne Dumanoski and John Peterson Myers the widely read and controversial *Our Stolen Future: Are We Threatening Our Fertility, Intelligence, and Survival?* Colburn argued that endocrine disruptors would be misunderstood as long as people were trapped in a "cancer paradigm" in which risk and concern about that disease became the measure of toxicity and shaped cultural attitudes and government regulations.[8] She asserted that until the United States moved beyond this paradigm, it wouldn't really be able to understand the implications of endocrine disruptors whose effects were "manifest . . . in many shades of gray rather than in the black-and-white distinctions made between illness and health."[9] By the early twenty-first century, many researchers were exploring links between endocrine disruptors and disturbing health statistics, such as a 191 percent rise in learning disabilities from 1977 to 1994, a 210 percent increase in California autism rates after the mid-1990s, and a 30 percent increase in premature births since 1981.[10]

If endocrine disruptors were manifest in shades of gray, one reason was the inherent flexibility of the endocrine system. In this biological communication network, glands secrete minute amounts of hormones that bond with receptor cells in various parts of the body, bringing instructions to grow or produce proteins at particular times. Some of the receptor sites are highly specific about which molecules they will accept; others are more flexible and will bind with a variety of substances, including synthetic chemicals, which will thus mimic the effects of estrogen and other hormones. Endocrine disruptors, found in many synthetic chemicals—among them petroleum products, polychlorinated biphenyls (PCBs), and pesticides—intrude on this finely balanced system. Many pesticides fall into the category of endocrine disruptors; about half of the chemicals identified as endocrine disruptors are organochlorines, including what was once the most heavily used insecticide in the United States (though banned in 1982), toxaphene, and the still widely used endosulfan. The most widely used herbicide, 2,4-D, was listed as a suspected endocrine disruptor by the National Institutes of Health in 2011.[11]

Serious attention to the health effects of synthetic chemicals with estrogenic responses emerged in the 1970s when the effects of diethylstilbestrol (DES), a synthetic estrogen given to pregnant women in the 1950s and 1960s, became apparent in the daughters of those who had taken the medicine.[12] By the beginning of the twenty-first century, scientists agreed that groups of synthetic chemicals mimicked sex hormones in wildlife and lab studies and that these chemicals built up in human tissues and could affect a developing fetus.[13] But there was less consensus about the implications for human health overall or the seriousness of the chemical threat. So, in addition to the accepted wisdom that evaluated toxic chemicals based on their cancer threat, there were other reasons for resistance to the endocrine disruptor theory.

One barrier to understanding endocrine disruptors and other pesticides was that it was hard to isolate chemicals and paths of exposure to create a cause-and-effect story.[14] Such isolation of particular factors was especially difficult with endocrine disruptors due to a time delay before their effects were known, and those effects were sometimes subtle or hard to discern. Even when studies found clear correlations between exposure and health effects, many scientists resisted such findings unless causation was proven.[15]

In their writings on endocrine disruptors, biologist Sandra Steingrabber and historians Linda Nash and Nancy Langston have emphasized that the barrier between human bodies and the environment in which they lived was not as impenetrable as some might have supposed. Thus, the three authors echoed one of the revolutionary ideas of Rachel Carson and all environmentalists after her: humans were part of the balance of nature, not apart from it.

Accepting the endocrine disruptor thesis shattered the illusion that humans can divorce themselves from nature.

Analyzing the recent historical and media coverage of endocrine disruptors, one could draw the conclusion that many scientists and nonscientists believed that the long-term health impact of endocrine disruptors would prove more serious and difficult to address than minimizing exposures to carcinogens. Endocrine disruptors were both more widespread and more subtle than demonstrably deadly chemicals that caused cancer. Given the seriousness and scope of the threat from these chemicals, one would expect a huge amount of coverage of the issue in the media. After the 1991 meeting of scientists convened by Theo Colburn and others, the attendees issued in 1992 the "Wingspread Statement on the Precautionary Principle," which, in its effort to address the impact of endocrine disruptors, articulated a new way of understanding risk. The statement asserted that the inability to demonstrate cause and effect was no excuse for inaction: "When an activity raises threats to the environment or human health, precautionary measures should be taken, even if some cause-and-effect relationships are not fully established scientifically. In this context, the proponent of an activity, rather than the public, should bear the burden of proof."[16] The general principle became the bedrock ideal of environmentalists responding to antiregulation arguments of some in industry, government, and the general public.

The scientists who issued the Wingspread Statement were concerned particularly about endocrine disruptors and the widespread threat that they posed.[17] Strong as it was, the message took a while to filter into the mainstream public discourse. A survey of the national press since 1990 showed that "endocrine disruption" was an infrequent topic, not appearing as a subject heading in the *New York Times* until 1994 and not as a story on national television news until 2009.[18] In the print media, stories in the general-interest, mass-market press that specifically focused on endocrine disruption totaled about sixty-five in almost two decades; on television, there was just one story on NBC those years.[19]

The first observation that we can make from these surveys is that there was a paucity of coverage, which might indicate a lack of interest in the topic or a difficulty in understanding a complex collection of scientific concepts. It certainly leads to the conclusion that there was a low level of awareness among the public as a whole regarding endocrine disruptors. But beyond the numbers, other interesting observations can be made about what was said in the articles, the biases reflected therein, the publications in which they appeared, and when they were published. Media articles on the topic of endocrine disruptors did not appear with any predictable regularity in the eighteen years from 1994 to 2012. In nine of those eighteen years, there were no more than two articles during the year (sometimes zero), with news coverage peaking from 2008 to 2010, when more than one-third of the total articles were published. One could speculate that consciousness on the topic built over time except that the number of articles fell sharply again in 2011 and 2012.

Another sign that general public knowledge about endocrine disruptors was probably quite low was seen in the types of publications that ran most of the articles. The two greatest sources of articles on the topic were *E: The Environmental Magazine*, a publication written for environmentalists or those already likely to be concerned about issues of chemical pollution and its health effects, and the *New York Times* (the latter having such high numbers due to five columns by Nicholas Kristof). The *E: The Environmental Magazine* articles were spread out from 1996 to 2011, showing an ongoing concern with this issue in the publication. Other environmentally focused publications with articles about endocrine disruptors were *Mother Earth News*, *On Earth*, *Women and Environments International Magazine*, and *World Watch*. Some science magazines also published articles about the impact of these synthetic chemicals, ranging from publications such as *Popular Science* to *Discover* to *Scientific American Earth*, as did health magazines including *Men's Health*, *Better Nutrition*, and *Total Health*. From the general press, the publisher of the largest number of articles (including opinion essays) was the *New York Times*; fewer articles appeared in other general news outlets, including the *Los Angeles Times*, *Newsweek*, *U.S. News & World Report*, and the *New Republic*. Finally, the list of magazines and newspapers was rounded out with titles such as *Forbes*, *Vegetarian Times*, *Farmer's Weekly*, and *Psychology Today*. All in all, about thirty mainstream magazines or newspapers carried articles on endocrine disruptors in eighteen years, and just one television network did.

Among this variety of publications, the majority of the articles were sympathetic to the new scientific research being done on endocrine disruptors and critical about the impact that these synthetic chemicals seemed to be having on humans and wildlife. A few articles—found in the *Washington Post*, *Popular Science*, *Chemical Week*, and *Farmer's Weekly*—were decidedly noncommittal regarding the reliability of the new research on endocrine disruptors. *Chemical Week* and *Farmer's Weekly* also contained two articles that were clearly hostile to endocrine disruptor theories, as was an article in *Forbes*.[20]

One 1996 article by *New York Times* science correspondent Gina Kolata used what purported to be balanced language but strongly cast doubt on the veracity of endocrine disruptor theory.[21] Kolata noted at the outset that celebrity environmentalists Robert Redford and Vice President Al Gore were warning about the danger of endocrine-disrupting chemicals that could impair fertility and fetal development and which environmentalists also linked to breast and prostate cancers, attention deficit/hyperactivity disorder (ADHD), and lower intelligence. The article introduced the 1996 book *Our Stolen Future* but undermined its argument by describing the disagreement between "environmentalists" and "scientists." Thus, although she identified two of the three authors as "Dr.," in one stroke she undercut their legitimacy by framing the book as one opposed by "scientists": "That is where environmentalists like Dr. Colburn part company with many scientists." She wrote that some biologists acknowledged that the chemicals in question might be a problem with respect to fish and birds, but "many others say there is no factual basis for the book's alarms, several of which have been refuted by careful studies." Thus, she left readers with the implication that the studies on which the book was based might not have been "careful." The article quoted several scientists who explained that the authors had made an unfounded leap between "hypothesis and convincing evidence."

Stronger and more direct criticism of endocrine disruptor theory came two years later in *Forbes*. The 1998 article was by Michael Fumento, a conservative journalist already well known for criticizing what he labeled alarmist publicity about scientific developments such as global warming, AIDS among heterosexuals, increases in obesity, and avian flu in humans.[22] In the *Forbes* article, Fumento denounced the whole concept of endocrine disruptors and charged that the EPA testing of chemicals for hormonal effects was a "witch-hunt" that would hurt industry. He blamed *Our Stolen Future* for what he felt was erroneous coverage on the issue in the press.

The far more numerous articles that gave credence to theories about endocrine disruptors primarily emphasized the harmful effects of the chemicals on human health. According to many of the news articles, the impact on human health was so great because endocrine disruptors were ubiquitous.[23]

Foremost, the articles brought up the endocrine-disrupting properties of commonly used plastics, especially those in close contact with food, such as bisphenol A (BPA), and of cosmetics.[24] Articles that emphasized the ubiquity of endocrine disruptors were closely related to those that turned into primers for readers wanting to avoid contact with the chemicals. These how-to articles not only implied that consumers should get their packaged goods at Whole Foods after 2011 (when the food chain announced that its brands would have only BPA-free packaging) but also instructed readers to make basic changes to dietary practices (such as microwaving in glass instead of plastic), avoid certain cosmetics, peel root vegetables, and buy organic foods.[25]

The articles that focused on the dangers of endocrine disruptors addressed, in particular, the effects on sexual development. They described the effects on sperm counts and fertility of humans, echoing the language in one 2002 full-page ad from Mount Sinai Hospital in the *New York Times*: "Pesticides Could Become the Ultimate Male Contraceptive."[26] Most of the articles that commented on the damage to sexual development focused on the fact that fetuses and children would be most affected, arguing that the priority should be for parents as well as society to protect their children.[27] One effect on children that was frequently discussed was that endocrine disruptors brought on early puberty, a highly visual and dramatic sign of harm.[28]

It was a short leap from worrying about sexual development of children and infertility to describing already visible and obvious effects of endocrine disruptors on wildlife populations, especially those shown to be highly vulnerable, such as amphibians. Most dramatically, journalists in the popular press described recent scientific studies, writing of "intersex fish" and, especially, "hermaphrodite frogs." One chemical specifically mentioned for its impact in this regard was the herbicide atrazine, especially after the release of a report in the *Proceedings of the National Academy of Sciences* in 2002 that had looked at the chemical's effects on tadpoles.[29] The report was published by University of California biologist Tyrone Hayes, who had previously completed a study for the Swiss manufacturer Novartis (now Syngenta) about its popular weed killer atrazine. As one journalist wrote in a lengthy article in *Harper's* on the endocrine-disrupting effects of atrazine, the herbicide was among the oldest and most effective and extremely common, "the aspirin of weedkillers."[30] The herbicide was particularly widespread on certain crops; for example, it was used on two-thirds of all cornfields in the United States (and 81 percent of the cornfields in Illinois), and it was a common contaminant of

Midwestern drinking water.[31] More than one magazine article mentioned the demonstrable impact on sexual development of frogs but also that the manufacturer was casting doubt on the data, arguing that more study should be done and that the reregistration of the herbicide by the EPA was on track and unlikely to be derailed. In 2003, the EPA approved the continued use of atrazine, while in the same month the European Union (EU) banned its use. Despite Syngenta's ongoing energetic defense of atrazine, consensus was clearly shifting as many scientists concluded that the herbicide definitely disrupted male reproduction and had other health consequences.[32]

The issue of how endocrine disruptors affected sexual development of animals and humans received more attention due to the columns of Nicholas Kristof in the *New York Times*.[33] Unlike many journalists, Kristof was alarmed at the research about hermaphrodite frogs and links between endocrine disruptors and genital malformations in humans as well as obesity, insulin resistance, diabetes, and autism. He wrote about the whole class of chemicals, which could be found in pesticides, plastics, and common household products, and cited the pronouncements of the Endocrine Society and the studies published in scientific and medical journals indicating that endocrine disruptors were a serious health threat. He compared the obfuscation tactics of "Big Chem" to those used for decades by "Big Tobacco."

Another theme of endocrine disruptor science that came through in the news articles was that the old model of the dose determining the poison did not work for this category of chemicals. The more-detailed articles explained that unlike the dominant model used to understand the effects of chemicals on diseases, dose became irrelevant when talking about endocrine disruptors. As one article phrased it, the classic "linear" dose-response association did not apply to endocrine disruptors, which were often nonlinear in their effects on the hormonal system.[34] Instead, the new paradigm was that *timing* of exposure rather than dose determined toxic effects.

It is interesting to note that overall, the articles on endocrine disruptors de-emphasized pesticides. Most of the literature focused on the category of the chemicals, as opposed to their origins, and those that did specify the source of endocrine disruptors mentioned plastics more often than other chemicals such as pesticides. This type of obfuscation is familiar in earlier media coverage of pesticides. For example, coverage of the dangers of DDT and Agent Orange came to focus on those particular chemicals, often not discussing pesticides in general or the industrial system of which they were a part. Thus, emphasis was placed on specific dangers without questioning the underpinnings of the whole chemical system. Similarly, newspaper and magazine articles on endocrine disruptors left out a broader discussion of the health and environmental impact of widespread chemical contamination and did not question the ubiquity of pesticides in farming and land management.

The impact of media coverage of endocrine disruptors, then, was as conservative as the earlier articles about DDT, Agent Orange, and other pesticides had been. For example, an article in the *New York Times* in August 1997 described how Tulane University researchers had withdrawn a paper from the previous summer that had warned about the synergistic effects of combinations of pesticides to disrupt human hormones because they couldn't reproduce the results.[35] The article at the time noted that the whole idea that some chemicals were endocrine disruptors remained in dispute. Over the next decade and a half, the doubts reported upon in the 1997 article evaporated for most scientists working in the field, but not perhaps for the majority of the public, which remained relatively unconcerned about the issue. What the 1997 article observed held true fifteen years later: "The concern and fear [over endocrine disruptors] that rose so quickly has quietly died."

When the issue of endocrine disruptors first appeared in the mainstream press around 1994, an article in the *New York Times* quoted the biologists working on the issue and noted that some of the scientists involved sometimes used "apocalyptic tones" in this debate, which was "in some ways a replay of *Silent Spring*."[36] More than ten years later, there were still articles in the paper that referred to "so-called 'endocrine disruptors.'" By 2012, media coverage of the issue remained sporadic, although less doubtful about the science of the issue. A lengthy article in an unlikely source, *Psychology Today*, summarized for readers not only the danger of pesticides for human health—tied to such conditions as ADHD and possibly Parkinson's disease—but also for bees because they were neurotoxins causing colony-collapse disorder.[37]

The main conclusion that can be drawn about the public discourse on this issue is that the number of articles and their tone did not match the alarm of many scientific researchers. Public attention to endocrine disruptors remained sporadic and low key. Apparently, the risk of these chemicals was too distant and hypothetical to merit more attention in the press, whereas the benefits that they brought in consumer products and modern industry and agriculture were too great to sacrifice. Similarly, at the political level, concern about endocrine disruptors flared up and then seemed to fade away. In 1996,

Congress passed the Food Quality Protection Act with the provision that the EPA begin screening chemicals and pesticides for endocrine-disrupting properties by 1999. Initially, environmental and research communities were enthusiastic, and the EPA announced plans to proceed quickly with testing. But the program was plagued by delays, calls from industry for more scientific research, and dubious testing protocols. After more than a decade of debates about protocols, not a single chemical had been screened by 2009.[38] Even then, the trade association CropLife America was still petitioning the EPA to make the pesticide-screening tests less rigorous; for its part, the EPA responded that it was open to concerns about cost and might allow computer modeling as a substitute for laboratory animal testing.[39] Endocrine disruptors, apparently, were too distant a threat to concern legislators at the start of the twenty-first century.

GMOs: Safer Than Pesticides or Risky Gamble?

As entomologists and other scientists had realized in the 1950s, overreliance on pesticides in agriculture was unsustainable due to insect and plant resistance. And, since the 1960s, growing numbers of scientists had realized that the environmental effects of persistent, broad-spectrum pesticides such as organochlorines were harmful. Meanwhile, some scientists and environmentalists were increasingly worried about the health effects of widespread pesticide use. At least some entomologists looked ahead to what would become a paradigm shift, moving from a chemical to a biological approach to pest control by the end of the twentieth century. The philosophy that would lead to advances in genetic engineering was summarized by USDA officials in a 1970 report describing the goals of the department: "The most effective method of pest control is the development of crop varieties that have acceptable agronomic qualities in addition to resistance to or tolerance for a pest or group of pests."[40] From the 1970s on, numerous scientists and many in agricultural-industrial corporations took this dictum to heart, shifting to a biological approach for pest control, specifically through the manipulation of DNA.[41]

The building blocks of the biotech revolution of the 1970s and 1980s were found in government-funded research in molecular biology and biochemistry departments throughout the country. These public roots quickly gave way to the commercialization of biotech through contractual relationships between academic researchers at universities and corporations. Commercialization could not proceed until the issue of intellectual property was clarified, which it was in a 1980 5–4 Supreme Court decision. The ruling in *Diamond v. Chakrabarty* said that a genetically modified organism (an oil-eating microbe) could be patented because it had not previously existed in nature and had been changed by a human. This ruling provided the legal basis for the subsequent genetically modified organism industry by allowing living organisms to be patented. Soon critics began to decry the privatization of public science, or what then-congressman Albert Gore of Tennessee wryly called the "selling of the tree of knowledge to Wall Street."[42]

New start-ups were born of the marriage between venture capital and university professors, leading to attention-grabbing growth, such as when Genentech's initial public offering in 1980 set a New York Stock Exchange record for the fastest increase of per-share price, moving from $35 to $89 in just twenty minutes. Large multinational chemical companies proceeded to snatch up the new biotech start-ups as well as traditional seed companies so that within two decades, the field had narrowed dramatically and in 2003 was dominated by five large companies: Syngenta, Monsanto, Bayer, DuPont, and Dow.[43]

If biotech's scientific roots were found in land-grant universities and its financial roots among venture capitalists and multinational corporations, its philosophical roots could be found in the Green Revolution. The post–World War II program of crop improvement for Latin America and Asia that reached its heyday in the 1960s and 1970s was based on an industrial-agricultural prescription to be imposed on the developing world as the best way to increase food output—and to integrate far-flung regions of the world into the global capitalist economy. The biotech revolution had similar characteristics, to be implemented both in American agriculture and abroad, but its proponents sought to correct the flaws of the Green Revolution, which was based on heavy use of chemical and petrochemical inputs and thus resulted in extensive environmental pollution.[44] The increase in pesticide use due to Green Revolution policies was dramatic. By the middle of the 1980s, for example, one-fifth of world pesticide use was found in Asia, and the number of acres sprayed in India went from 15 million in 1960 to 200 million by the mid-1980s.[45]

Reflecting the same confidence that underlay the Green Revolution that agricultural technology could improve food production—combined with the new research and investments of the 1970s and 1980s—a quick return on genetic engineering through commercial applications was eagerly anticipated by scientists and those in the agricultural industry. But it was not until 1994 that the first food application of genetic engineering (GE) arrived: Calgene's Flavr Savr tomato, with a gene to delay ripening, promising to make the tomato more flavorful than its industrially produced cousins, which were picked early and then ripened with ethylene gas. The launch fizzled. Despite the company's promises, the tomato was soon withdrawn from the market because its flavor did not improve on that of existing tomato varieties.[46] More important than the Flavr Savr in terms of lasting impact and as an indication of the direction in which GE technology would go was the marketing two years later of corn seeds engineered with the natural toxin *Bacillus thuringiensis* (Bt), thus killing insects that ate any part of the corn plant. Soon thereafter, soy, cotton, and canola seeds resistant to the herbicide glyphosate (Monsanto's Roundup) were launched. Growth of GMOs was nothing short of astronomical from there. Acres planted with these crops went from less than 2 million in 1996 to 167 million worldwide by 2003. GMO foods were found in 70 percent of processed foods in the United States by 2003 (especially through high-fructose corn syrup, soy, and cotton and canola oils).[47]

Despite the success revealed in such a growth of market share, the statistics were not as straightforward as they at first appeared. By 2003, 98 percent of the millions of GMO acres planted were in just five countries: the United States (63 percent), Argentina (21 percent), Canada (6 percent), China (4 percent), and Brazil (4 percent). Moreover, 100 percent of the GMOs planted were in four crops: soybeans (62 percent), corn (21 percent), cotton (12 percent), and canola (5 percent), and they were divided among just two GM traits: herbicide tolerance (73 percent) and Bt insecticide (18 percent) plus a combination of herbicide tolerance and Bt action (8 percent). Thus, the ambitions of the early days of biotech research—when a Ciba-Geigy spokeswoman said in 1984, "We'll be able to do anything [with gene manipulations] that our imaginations will get us to"—were far from being fulfilled.[48]

There were a number of reasons that GMOs were not living up to their expectations, both for the manufacturers as well as for citizens who had thought this technology would usher in an agriculture revolution. Corporate manufacturers launched GMO crops based on two main promises: better yields and less chemical use. Neither was fulfilled. The promise of increased yields had an economic as well as humanitarian appeal. Farmers would presumably make more money or expand operations as yields increased. The multinational corporations would also presumably make more money as farmers eagerly sought to plant GMO seeds and use the accompanying herbicides on which they were dependent. For other Americans not directly involved in farming or the industry, GMOs would be appealing because who would be against growing more food, especially if they thought it would benefit people with nutritional deficiencies in developing countries? But yields did not always act as expected. Although corn yields increased, GMO soybeans apparently had a "yield drag" over conventional ones. At the same time, farmers had to pay a premium for the new seeds, and overall herbicide use increased with GMO crops (with one estimate, for example, putting increases of herbicide sprayed at 2 to 5 times per pound per acre with Roundup Ready soybeans). Thus, for farmers, the first promise of increased yields was modestly achieved at the expense of the second promise of lessened chemical use (and decreased cost). In his assessment of GMOs, author Peter Pringle concluded, "Overall, it would appear the gains have been marginal."[49]

The financial impact of GMOs for the seed/chemical companies, though, was different. The sale of high-priced GMO seeds increased rapidly after their introduction, with Roundup Ready varieties in 2003 accounting for 70 percent of soybeans, 65 percent of cotton, 55 percent of canola, and 10 percent of corn grown in the United States. Five years later, GMO soybeans reached 90 percent, and corn was up to 61 percent. With such figures, glyphosate became increasingly profitable, its use doubling from 1996 to 2003 as it became the world's largest-selling herbicide by 2004. By 1994, Monsanto had come to rely on agricultural biological and chemical products for 48 percent of its operating income and 27 percent of its revenue.[50]

Despite the short-term gains of seed and herbicide sales, though, the introduction of GMO crops was accompanied by controversy—both in the United States and abroad. In Europe (and Japan), hostility to the concept of GM foods was strong from their introduction. There were a few reasons for this. First, the food culture in these countries was more likely to treat foods as part of the essence of identity and national character and less as a science experiment or a means to improve production efficiencies. Second, Europeans were unnerved by the outbreak of mad cow disease in 1996 and worried about possibly dangerous food contaminations. Third, most Europeans had a different attitude toward environmental risk than did Americans; thus, the "precautionary principle" was integrated into many EU regulatory systems. In one survey of Europeans, for example, 85 percent reported that they would not purchase GMOs if they had a choice. In 1997, the EU imposed mandatory labeling for any foods with GMOs; in 1998, the union placed a moratorium on any GMO crops and increased the testing of imported foods. In 2002, the European Union adopted stringent labeling requirements for all foods containing more than 0.5 percent GMOs and the rule that all GM ingredients had to be able to be traced back to their source.[51]

The European rejection of GMOs had real economic consequences for American agriculture, which raised questions about the long-term viability of this economic sector. In 1996, the United States exported 3.15 million metric tons of corn to the European Union, equaling 82 percent of corn imported by Europe. By 2005, the figure was down to 33,000 metric tons. So, over one decade, there was a 90 percent fall in one of the strongest US export markets. Not surprisingly, the price of corn fell rapidly in the United States, and other countries began selling non-GMO corn to Europe and elsewhere. Due to the trade cutoff, Commodity Credit Corporation compensatory payments to US farmers for loss of income came to $35 billion from 1996 to 2005. The price of corn started to rise again with the new (subsidized) US market of ethanol in 2006 and 2007.[52] Meanwhile, by 2002, the United States protested European exclusions and labeling requirements to the World Trade Organization (WTO). Although the European Union ended its total ban on GMOs in 2004 (allowing limited amounts of Bt corn to be imported), the restrictive terms were still unsatisfying to American officials and farmers.[53] By 2006, the WTO ruled that the Europeans' blanket ban had indeed been a barrier to trade. But, at the time of the ruling, the European Union had already answered the charge by eliminating its total ban on GMOs and had instituted case-by-case scientific evaluations of particular GMO products for environmental and health impacts.[54]

Opposition to GMOs was also widespread in the United States and was varied. One reason that some people opposed GMOs can be described as philosophical. Many rejected the assertion of biotech advocates that genetic engineering was just what farmers had always done with species selection and crossbreeding; they argued that this was different because it involved transplanting genes across species.[55] It was tampering with the very nature of life forms, and the effects of such interference were not yet known, possibly including the introduction of new allergens or toxic substances into foods.[56]

Such critics called for adoption of the precautionary principle regarding GMOs: they should not be allowed until they were proven to be safe.

Critics' call for the adoption of the precautionary principle when it came to GMOs was not surprising, nor was its rejection by supporters of GMOs. Reflecting the paradigm that shaped how most Americans viewed environmental risk, the material benefits of a technology needed to be weighed against its costs. Without definitive evidence that a given technology caused serious harm, it should not be banned from use. Such a calculus had been used for decades to justify widespread use of pesticides even in the face of mounting criticisms.

Thus, absent clear proof to the contrary, GMO defenders and the US government rejected the argument that genetic engineering created completely new life forms. The FDA ruled in 1992 that GMO foods had "substantial equivalence" with existing foods unless proven otherwise in specific circumstances (e.g., a peanut allergen was introduced into a plant that had not previously contained such an allergen). Since they were substantially equivalent, the agency argued, GMOs did not have to be labeled as such. This designation of substantial equivalence was accepted in 1993 by the Organization for Economic Cooperation and Development (a group with representatives from industrial nations that formed economic and social policies). Critics countered that this vague formulation did not define "substantial" nor recognize that subtle changes in plants might have a big impact on health or the environment.[57]

The arguments against substantial equivalence gained ground with stories about adverse health and environmental effects of GMO crops. In 1997, in the face of inconclusive evidence as to whether a particular Bt corn (marketed by Aventis under the name Starlink) might contain a human allergen, the EPA ruled that the corn was approved only as animal feed. The ruling made little sense to farmers and environmentalists who knew that there was always extensive cross-contamination at grain elevators. The issue made headlines when taco shells bought at a grocery store were found to contain Starlink and when seventeen people over six months' time had allergic reactions to taco shells. The Centers for Disease Control and Prevention and the FDA said there was no conclusive evidence that the reactions were due to Starlink, though some rejected their findings. Following the public relations disaster, Aventis withdrew its registration for Starlink in 2000.[58]

In 1998, a researcher at the Rowett Institute, Arpad Pusztai, announced that GM potatoes containing lectin, a toxin for some insects, changed the stomach linings of rats as compared with those fed non-GM potatoes and said that these foods shouldn't be eaten until there was further testing. In the controversy that erupted, supporters and opponents debated the methodology used in the experiment, and Pusztai was fired from his job. Although neither side of the argument was publicly demonstrated to be negligent nor 100 percent correct, the episode helped to fuel public worry about GMOs.[59] Two years later, another study published in the *Lancet* found that rats who ate potatoes with Bt had impaired organ development, body metabolism, and immune function. This study was also attacked by the biotech companies, but they did not produce any new research to counter it.[60]

Another health concern raised by critics of GMOs was that the spread of GM foods would encourage antibiotic resistance because almost all GMOs were made with an antibiotic marker gene. Since the process of GE was rather haphazard, the antibiotic marker genes were put into host cells along with the DNA that was supposed to be transferred. The host would then be flooded with bacteria, and if the antibiotic reacted, then technicians would know that the gene transfer was successfully completed. Over several years, FDA scientists, as well as others outside the US government, warned that this technique would soon lead to antibiotic resistance.[61]

Along with health concerns, critics also had environmental concerns. They argued that although biotech companies had initially promised that GMOs would lessen pesticide use, the spread of herbicide-resistant plants had actually encouraged the use of chemicals, as demonstrated in numerous measures of increased herbicide use.[62]

Fears about the environmental impact of GMOs increased with news in 1999 of research by Cornell biologist Joseph Losey, who reported in *Nature* that monarch butterflies were endangered by Bt corn.[63] Although monarchs did not eat corn, they ate milkweed that grew at the edges of cornfields and became contaminated with corn pollen; Losey found that half of the larvae exposed to the contaminated milkweed died and that the surviving ones were half the weight of those in the control group. Monarchs were a popular insect, and the story quickly spread in the general press. Numerous studies attempted to replicate Losey's results, some supported by the biotech industry and some independent. Although the multinational corporations tried to contain the public relations disaster by criticizing Losey's methodology, in the end, scientists at an international symposium on the issue in November 1999 remained concerned about the threat to monarchs and other pollinators. They cited, in particular, GM Bt corns, Novartis's Knockout and Event 176, which were particularly toxic and therefore more of a threat to the pollinators. By 2001, six different papers on Bt corn and monarchs concluded that the most common Bt corn strains were not likely to harm monarchs but that Knockout and Event 176 were harmful to larvae at very low concentrations. Novartis then announced that it would phase out those two corns by 2003. The anxiety elicited by the work of Losey and others filtered into the mainstream press and increasingly became a topic of debate.

Another argument made against GMOs in the United States as well as in other countries was that the technology enriched multinational corporations at the expense of ordinary people and granted the companies too much power over individuals, a state that some critics labeled "bioserfdom."[64] Not only did farmers have to sign restrictive agreements with seed companies pledging that they would not save seeds from year to year but they also became less able to get off the "pesticide treadmill." As their Roundup use went up with the new seeds, they had to confront weeds resistant to glyphosate and then had to find additional herbicides to control these invaders. Reaction from activists and farmers to this power relationship turned to fury against what critics named "Terminator" seeds. Newly engineered plants produced infertile seeds so that farmers did not just have to pledge not to save seeds, they were also prevented from doing so. The reaction against the new GMO was so great that Monsanto issued a statement in 1999 that it would not market this new technology.[65] Criticisms of these seeds were a prominent theme of protests at the 1999 meeting of the WTO in Seattle, where GMOs became a hated symbol of globalization and the manipulation of ordinary people by multinational corporations.[66]

American and international activists also charged that multinational corporations not only controlled people economically but were hurting them nutritionally. The activist Vandana Shiva, among others, argued that GMO crops were made and marketed with the promise of nutritional benefits but without any appeal to local food cultures. Golden Rice, for example, designed to supply people with the beta-carotene they were lacking, might not appeal to people in particular regions who habitually ate, for example, white rice or long-grain rice. Meanwhile, the push to get farmers in the developing world to adopt Western monocultures, including GMO crops, for an export market crowded out alternative grains and vegetables that supplied a greater percentage of vitamins and other nutritional needs in farming communities.[67]

From the launch of GMOs, the largest manufacturers worked to gain favorable public opinion for the foods. Elaborate and sophisticated public relations campaigns were, in part, a reaction to growing environmentalism of the 1970s and to debates about environmental issues in the 1980s. Monsanto's campaign, for instance, included several educational films on biotech; pamphlets; funding of a national survey on attitudes of scientific, environmental, and policy leaders toward biotech; a traveling museum exhibit on the topic; advertising on television and in newspapers; exhibits in shopping malls; meetings with business and community leaders; and speeches by Monsanto executives.[68] The theme that reverberated throughout was summarized in the title of one of the company pamphlets: "Genetic Engineering: A Natural Science." If GE was "natural," it was by extension "familiar and safe." Another prominent theme in the materials was that GMOs would help to alleviate world hunger.[69]

Despite the best efforts of multinational executives, controversies over GMOs nevertheless erupted but were met with a swift response. For example, following the controversy over monarch butterflies, the multinational companies formed a trade organization, the Council for Biotechnology Information (CBI), to lead its counteroffensive, including a $50 million advertising campaign. Formal ads were placed in traditional venues such as the *New York Times*, and the CBI also placed advertorials in *National Geographic*, *Natural History*, and *Gourmet*. The campaign emphasized the beneficial side of GMOs and their potential to alleviate world hunger. A GMO such as Golden Rice was highlighted; as one critic observed, it was the "poster product that the biotech industry trots out over and over as evidence that the industry is altruistic in its intentions." In its cover story on Golden Rice in July 2000, *Time* argued that the new crop could save 1 million children a year who suffered from severe consequences of vitamin A deficiency. The public relations campaign in 2000 was aided by the fascination with all things genetic in conjunction with the announcement in June that the human genome had been sequenced.[70]

Even with very good marketing, products did not always live up to their promise. Take, for example, Golden Rice, which had 33.3 micrograms of vitamin A per 100 grams of rice. At that rate, a single serving of rice would give someone 1.32 percent of the RDA for vitamin A, so a person would have to eat 20 pounds of rice per day to get the desired amount of beta-carotene. Moreover, for the body to use and convert the vitamin in the rice, the addition of fat to the diet was needed, which many poor people could not afford. Critics also argued that the vitamin might degrade when the rice was stored or cooked by certain methods (such as boiling or sautéing).[71]

More broadly, the marketing campaigns of the biotech companies had a fundamental weakness beyond the qualities of any particular food or product. On one hand, the campaigns argued that GMOs had "substantial equivalence" and therefore didn't need to be regulated or labeled; on the other hand, GMOs were put forward as revolutionary foods that would miraculously transform food production and feed the hungry. Writer Michael Pollan described the self-serving logic thus: "The new plants are novel enough to be patented, yet not so novel as to warrant a label telling us what it is we're eating. It would seem they are chimeras: 'revolutionary' in the patent office and on the farm, 'nothing new' in the supermarket and the environment."[72]

Despite a sophisticated public relations campaign and diligent efforts by the biotech companies to discredit the various criticisms of GMOs, there were some clear indications of a backlash against GMOs. Most significant for the agricultural industry as a whole was the European cutoff of American imported and home-grown GMOs. Other examples of victories among the critics included Monsanto's pledge not to market "Terminator" seeds; Gerber, Heinz, and other companies announcing that they wouldn't use any GMO foods in their products; and McDonald's telling potato suppliers that it did not want GM potatoes. Numerous articles about and public awareness of GMOs remained high a decade after the first marketing of a GMO food. Respondents to a public opinion poll in 2004, for example, overwhelmingly reported that they wanted GM foods to be labeled as such. By 2012, a poll found that nine in ten respondents wanted GM food clearly labeled.[73]

Yet, by 2012, most Americans had long acquiesced to the ubiquity of GMOs in their diet: GMOs were found in 70 percent of processed food with no evidence of revolts in the supermarket aisles. But the issue remained a topic in the press, especially around political initiatives. In 2012, a proposed California initiative to require labeling of GMO foods came before voters in November. Along with popular support (65 percent for, 20 percent against, and 15 percent undecided in September 2012), the campaign to pass the initiative was led by people in the organic food industry such as Gary Hershberg, chair of Stonyfield Farms, who raised more than $1 million for the Just Label It campaign, and supported by writers such as Pollan and Mark Bittman of the *New York Times*. With the measure favored to win in

September, the biotech and multinational food companies poured millions into the campaign to defeat it. Opponents, such as Monsanto and Hershey, eventually spent $44 million in comparison with the $7.3 million spent by supporters; nevertheless, the initiative was defeated by only a relatively small margin, 51 percent to 47 percent.[74]

Despite the defeat, the labeling issue did not go away. In June 2013, Connecticut became the first state to pass a GMO food labeling law. Although the groundbreaking law passed by a vote of 134 to 3, it would not go into effect unless four other states (at least one of which bordered Connecticut) also passed mandatory labeling. Maine passed a similar law, also dependent on what its neighbors chose to do. But in April 2014, Vermont passed a law requiring labeling by July 2016, no matter what other New England states did.[75]

Although American consumers who wanted to know what was in their food were gaining some ground in 2013, the complaints of another constituency continued to fall on deaf ears. For years, organic farmers complained that the spread of GMOs endangered their livelihood for two primary reasons. First, the widespread growth of Bt crops would lead to more and more insects resistant to that natural insecticide. Bt was one of the few acute interventions available to organic farmers for occasional use to control a pest outbreak; the toxin was considered to be benign for the environment and for human health. But if insects were resistant to Bt, it would no longer be available as a tool for organic farmers. As early as 2001, Monsanto scientists (who wanted to protect their customers as opposed to organic farmers) realized that resistance was inevitable. They proposed various plans to postpone it, such as asking farmers to leave some of their land planted with non-Bt crops as "refuges" for target pest species.[76]

The second threat to organic farmers was that GMO crops could very easily cross-pollinate with, and thus contaminate, neighboring non-GMO crops. For a nonorganic farmer, this could result in court action from a seed company such as Monsanto. For an organic farmer, the potential consequences were even worse. An organic farmer could lose his or her organic certification (which might have taken years to earn) and have his or her livelihood threatened. This was not just a hypothetical threat. There were many examples of farmers whose crops were ruined, such as one from Iowa who lost her certification when her fields were contaminated with a neighbor's Bt corn. When the Union of Concerned Scientists conducted tests on seed corn in 2004, it found evidence of GMOs in 50 percent of the samples. Organic farmers and food companies such as Nature's Path, Eden Foods, and Lundberg Family Farms continued to try to raise awareness about the contamination issue, but they received a big setback in 2011 when the USDA announced that it was deregulating a new GMO alfalfa created by Monsanto. Alfalfa was one of the most plentiful crops grown in the United States because it was used as feed for dairy cows, but it was also a plant whose pollen had a strong tendency to drift from one field to another. A 2012 news story on the issue reflected acquiescence to the presence of GMOs, noting, "Organic and transgenic seeds are coexisting on American farmland."[77]

By the beginning of the twenty-first century, one problem for all farmers, whether organic or not, was the spread of herbicide-resistant weeds. Although the issue predated GMOs, it was exacerbated due to the increased planting of Roundup Ready crops, which encouraged greater use of herbicides. By 2013, there were 217 different weeds that were resistant to at least one herbicide. As more farmers came to rely almost exclusively on glyphosate, weeds more quickly adapted to that particular chemical. Resistance to glyphosate was widespread, with 24 different weeds immune that could be found on half of American farms by 2012. One year earlier, only 34 percent of US farms had had glyphosate-resistant weeds.[78]

After almost twenty years on the market, GMO foods were entrenched in the American diet and agricultural economy by 2014, despite the steady criticism of organic farmers and some environmental activists. GMOs were clearly in the short-term financial interests of large chemical-seed companies; corporate farmers who continued to expand; and food processors that desired cheap, predictable inputs. The long-term economic impact was not as clear if GMOs continued to erode foreign markets as well as contribute to high chemical use and genetic uniformity, which even industry scientists knew was not sustainable.[79] Moreover, the future of GMOs was unclear if public opinion against them grew.

Indications from the public culture were that many Americans were ambivalent about GMOs. On one hand, people ate them with increasing frequency, and press coverage about them was sporadic at best. On the other hand, when asked, large majorities of people said that they wanted GMO foods to be labeled. Perhaps one way to think about this ambivalence is to focus on a contemporaneous parallel development in American food. While there was spectacular growth in GMOs, there was a similar dramatic growth in organic food produced and sold in the United States. Were the growth of biotech and the strengthening of industrial food that it represented offset by a return to authentic, natural food in the organic sector?

The Embrace of Organics

Beginning in the 1970s, a small but growing number of Americans began to embrace organic food. Thirty years later, this was a multimillion-dollar sector of the economy. USDA-certified organic cropland for grains, fruits, and vegetables more than doubled from 1992 to 1997 and then doubled again from 1997 to 2003. In the early 2000s, the sales of organic food was rising faster than were the sales of conventionally produced food, and many big supermarket chains had growing sections for organic produce and processed foods. In addition, the number of farm markets in the United States—which usually sold much organic produce—doubled from 1994 to 2004, reaching 3,700, while the number of community-supported agriculture (CSA) subscription farms (usually organic) tripled in this period. Even many land-grant universities, the research engines of conventional industrial agriculture, started sustainable agriculture programs.[80]

There were many explanations for this trend, including modern environmentalism, the flowering of the counterculture, highly publicized examples of environmental contamination, and the decision of large food companies to enter the organic market.[81] How were Americans who were not committed environmentalists, or who came of age after the counterculture was a distant memory, convinced to buy organic, making this the fastest-growing part of the food economy in the early twenty-first century? Back when Rachel Carson published *Silent Spring* in 1962, organic food was considered a radical fad, and Carson went out of her way to make sure that her message about pesticide use would not be confused with the message of those who advocated such foods. But once environmentalism and the counterculture had taken root, organic food began its migration to the mainstream, albeit minority, position that it enjoyed by 2014. Once it made it to the mainstream, what was the public image of organic food? Some answers were revealed in press stories over more than four decades, which showed the evolution of organics from a fringe market to a multimillion-dollar business. What did these images and the messages they conveyed tell us about why more and more people were buying organic? Hint: it had less to do with environmental commitments than with individual consumerism.

The many articles that appeared in the press from the 1970s to the 2010s on organic food (though much less frequent in the 1970s and 1980s than they would become in subsequent decades, especially after 2000) highlighted particular themes from which we can draw some conclusions about attitudes toward organic foods and at least some of the reasons that their consumption grew in these years.

At the most basic level, many of the stories defined organic food, a concept that was probably unfamiliar to most readers, and explained that consumers did not have clear information at their disposal. One 1989 story in the *Los Angeles Times* observed that anxiety about dietary health hazards sent many people scurrying for organic food, but they could not always be certain of what they were getting because many terms were used interchangeably at California markets, including "organically grown, organic, naturally grown, wild, ecologically grown and biologically grown." Articles observed that anxiety had been triggered by stories in 1989 about the side effects of the growth regulator alar sprayed on apples, as well as stories about pesticide residues including cyanide on Chilean grapes.[82] Definitions were not yet familiar by 1993 when another story in the *Los Angeles Times* put "organic milk" in quotations and explained to readers that the milk in question came from cows "unexposed to artificial pesticides and antibiotics."[83]

Many articles detailed the process to establish a US government definition for organic food. The codification of "organic" began with efforts from Rodale Press's *Organic Gardening* magazine and became more systematized in 1973 with the formation of the California Certified Organic Farmers Organization. A revision of the California Health and Safety Code in 1979 established a government definition of organic with no enforcement mechanism, and, finally, the California Organic Foods Act was passed in 1990. This California law required registration of organic farmers with the state and the prohibition of chemical pesticides and fertilizers for at least one year in order to be considered organic.[84]

The formulation of national standards and the establishment of the USDA label certifying organic products evolved from California law but was long in the making and the subject of much debate, including a period of public comment on the first draft of the law; the 275,000 letters, postcards, and E-mail comments were the second-highest number of responses ever sent on any one issue to the USDA.[85] Many articles in the press described the protracted debates over the new USDA standards and provided explanations of what the completed new rules, announced in 2000 and set to go into effect by 2002, would mean for individual citizens.[86] After the establishment of USDA rules, the press continued to follow controversies about their meaning. For example, one article in an environmental magazine in 2003 observed that consumers were confronted with a confusing array of names for various types of "specialty" eggs, including free range, cage free, organic, natural, fortified with omega-3s, and from hens fed natural grains.[87] In another article in 2005, the *Los Angeles Times* asked, "So what does organic really mean? Government standards are arbitrary and incomplete, critics say, and, ironically, the standards support big producers over smaller ones."[88]

As the amount of organic food continued to grow, interest in it did as well, and new people became introduced to the concept. In 2006, the *Wall Street Journal* was still defining "organic food, which is produced without using conventional pesticides, artificial fertilizers, sewage sludge, antibiotics or growth hormones." In its definition the same year, *Consumer Reports* added that animals cannot be given feed made from animal by-products, that animals had to have "access" to the outdoors, and that no genetic modification or irradiation was permitted. Even in 2010, an article in the *Chicago Tribune* about the "value" of organic food defined its meaning as it applied to meat, dairy, produce, and cosmetics.[89] Most news stories assumed a greater knowledge about organic food by this point, but there were still some descriptions of continuing confusion among consumers.

As many Americans became more familiar with and knowledgeable about organics, press attention went beyond basic definitions, for example, covering industry efforts to get the new USDA standards watered down in 2003 and 2004. In those years, President George W. Bush and the USDA approved two separate measures that would have allowed limited use of nonorganic feed, pesticides, and antibiotics in foods that still carried the organic label. Swift, strong grassroots reaction led the government to back down both times and scrap the new rules.[90] There was also some press attention to the inadequacies of the USDA regulations. For example, an article in the *Los Angeles Times* noted that a committee called the National Organic Standards Board could approve nonorganic ingredients that could compose up to 5 percent of a product that still received an organic certification. Although the original goal had been to shrink this list of exceptions (granted after petitions from industry), it had grown from 77 substances in 2002 to 245 by 2009.[91]

In addition to explaining the meaning of organic, including its governmental and legal permutations, a third theme of the press stories was the origins of the organic idea. Invariably, these stories connected the concept to the "rebellious '60s" and the counterculture. This image was not just imagined by journalists but reflected the emergence of a "countercuisine" that embodied the cultural and social criticisms of the 1960s and 1970s. Many who embraced organic food in these early years saw the establishment, the military-industrial complex, and the modern food industry all as a part of the same corporate life. Publications such as *Mother Earth News* and *Whole Earth Catalogue* expressed this yearning for a new way of living. A vision of countercultural food also included vegetarian foods as well as those that were locally raised and distributed, outside the mass-production network.[92]

The countercultural roots of organic food—questioning as they did mass industrial society—came to be expressed in an environmental philosophy rooted in respect for the balance of nature instead of attempting to control nature. Such an approach was familiar from the rise of twentieth-century environmentalism and the earlier work of such writers as Aldo Leopold and Rachel Carson. The organic philosophy that emerged in the late twentieth century emphasized the ideal that human food production should be based on nature's own rhythms rather than upon a human schedule and imperative. Food production needed to be understood holistically, not as a collection of separate inputs. On a popular level, the portrait of organic farmer Joel Salatin found in Michael Pollan's *Omnivore's Dilemma* and Robert Kenner's film *Food Inc.* illustrated this ideal of being at one with nature's rotation of species, time, and space.[93]

Back in the 1970s, media stereotypes about organic food were common, assuming either that it was a type of gardening practiced by "little old ladies in tennis shoes" or by the "lunatic fringe." In addition, magazines published articles from critics of organic farming such as nutritionist Dr. Frederick Stare, who charged that the new health-food industry and its advocates were perpetuating a "fraud," wasting money on organic food instead of feeding hungry people. Negative images of organic food softened within a few years but did not disappear.[94]

Later news stories often contrasted the roots of organic hippies with the modern face of the food industry in the 1990s and after. A 1993 story in the *Los Angeles Times* labeled the typical 1968 consumer of the natural food company Erewhon "a stereotype: a sandal-wearing, long-haired, turquoise-bedecked flower child"; the article contrasted the modern Erewhon consumer of 1993 as "well-educated, tends to have a higher income and is environmentally conscious." In a 2001 article focusing on the mainstreaming of organic gardening, a *Chicago Tribune* journalist observed, "Mention 'organic gardening,' and many people still think of back-to-the-land folks in tie-dyed T-shirts and overalls planting tomatoes in old tires." An article in *Newsweek* made the contrast between old and new organic explicit as it described the growth in the amount of organic food sold to more than $11 billion in 2002: "Could dusty neighborhood co-ops sell that many wormy little apples? Well, no. That was the old organic. The new organic is all about bigger farms, heartier crops, better distribution and slicker packaging and promotion. Conglomerates as big as Heinz and General Mills are now launching or buying organic lines and selling them in mainstream supermarkets."[95]

Developing the contrast between old and new organic, some articles indicated that the embrace of organics was shallow, a fashion for "fad-conscious consumers." Inevitably, such descriptions implied that those who wanted to consume organic food did so for emotional or irrational reasons. One article in 1989 echoed the sentiments of a USDA official who said that for some, organic farming was "a cause, a movement, almost a religion." Similarly, a 1998 *Newsweek* article quoting a food writer who called eating organic food her "religion" observed that organic shoppers have an "emotional investment in their choice." One *Newsweek* article in 2002 noted the roots of these feelings: "When the counterculture embraced organic food and farming in the early '70s, the motivation was more philosophical than practical."[96] But if the early organic adherents were motivated more by philosophy, religion, or emotion, that was not as true, press stories explained, of modern organic consumers. The nature of the food consumed changed ("Organic food isn't just about sprouts and wheat germ anymore"), as did the motivation of those who bought it.[97]

Demonstrating the evolution from the old organic to the new was Rodale Press, publisher of *Organic Gardening* magazine. The press illustrated the mainstreaming of organic ideals, not only discussed in the media but as part of the media itself. The press's founder, J. I. Rodale, was held up as a true believer in organics, predating the counterculture. One 1998 article in the *Chicago Tribune* dubbed him a "pioneering evangelist for organic gardening methods." When Rodale founded his magazine in 1942, he was far outside the norm and focused solely on growing vegetables. Demonstrating the mainstream aspirations of the magazine, vice chair Maria Rodale (granddaughter of the founder) announced that the publication's focus would move beyond vegetables in 1999 to all types of home gardening. The *Chicago Tribune* explained that organic gardening was "no longer a countercultural choice but . . . a mainstream way for all sorts of gardeners to manage the land around their homes." By 2001, Rodale introduced a spin-off magazine, *Organic Style*, reflecting the broadening of organic ideals—and the fact that many readers of the original were not actually gardeners: "These people—educated, affluent people who shop at Whole Foods Market and Smith and Hawken—are concerned about the safety of what they eat, and like the idea of trying to live a life of beauty and abundance without the fear of hidden hazards. And they have money to spend to do it." Organic, then, was a *culture*, not just a gardening method, embraced by a self-defined group within the US population.[98]

Whereas some press stories carefully distinguished between old and new organic consumers, others contained more than a hint of nostalgia for small family farmers who benefited from the growth in the organic industry. One story shortly before the USDA standards went into effect noted, "Spurred by a swelling demand for natural foods and the growth of chains such as Whole Foods and Wild Oats, the organic movement had become a savior for a number of family farmers nationwide."[99] Such messages were related to broader images of organics harkening back to a preindustrial ideal and became incorporated into the marketing of organic food, visually represented by bucolic pictures of grazing cows and farmers on the side of packages. More than one commentator remarked on these images, which Michael Pollan dubbed "Supermarket Pastoral."[100] The nostalgic images of the new organic also drew upon, ironically, increased consumer expectations for lush food appearance and year-round access to varied fruits and vegetables, whether organic or not, that were ingrained as part of the globalization of food.[101]

Nostalgia for a preglobalization era was, of course, not created by the media or marketers, even if it was celebrated by them. Small-scale local farming was inherent in the ideals articulated by environmental activists such as Wendell Berry and J. I. Rodale. The Jeffersonian ideal of the small farmer was then reshaped in the counterculture, which celebrated the possibility of communal farms and cooperative groceries outside the industrial system.[102]

Periodic efforts to romanticize the family farm were dwarfed by two other themes in the press stories about organic food: the economics of organic food and its "healthfulness," the most frequently cited motivation to buy organic. Articles on the economics of organic food were almost always positive, describing an ever-upward trajectory of organic market share and the number of large corporations that were investing in the sector. Beginning in the early 1990s, the success of new chains such as Whole Foods was a focus in the news. One 1993 story, for example, observed that "selling organic produce is big business" as it described the $56 million acquisition of Mrs. Gooch's stores by Whole Foods.[103]

Along with the growth of specialty chains such as Whole Foods, newspapers in 1995 also described how mainstream supermarkets were stocking more and more organic foods. A decade and a half later, organic and natural specialty stores had expanded outlets throughout the country, not just in large urban or coastal markets. By the time the new USDA standards were announced in 2000, articles predicted that they would boost the $6 billion a year organic food industry even more.[104] Whole Foods remained the symbol of organic success and growth, continuing to gain new customers, pleasing Wall Street investors, and being celebrated in press stories. For example, at the end of 2012, the company reported an increase in sales of 7.5 percent and a jump in earnings per share from 65 cents to 78 cents between 2011 and 2012. In comparison with traditional supermarket chains, Whole Foods continued to have operating margins of 4.75 percent, 3 percent higher than its competitors.[105]

Even though organic food remained a small sector of the overall US food market (2 percent of the nation's food supply in 2002 and less than 1 percent of cropland, though 4 percent of the food supply, by 2012), articles usually emphasized its relative growth. One 2002 *Newsweek* article, for example, noted that sales of organic food had been going up 15 percent to 20 percent per year for the previous decade, five times faster than food sales overall. The 20 percent growth rate was still being cited in 2005, when a survey also observed that more than 25 percent of Americans ate fresh organic produce at least once a week, and an article in 2009 called the $23-billion-a-year organic business "the fastest growing segment of the food industry."[106] With sales projected to reach $15.5 billion in 2006, major supermarket chains were trying to reap profits by creating their own, less expensive store-brand organic lines. In addition, major food manufacturers had been acquiring organic brands since the USDA regulations had been put into effect.[107] Large retailers, of course, also capitalized on these trends, not just by creating their own organic brands but by selling established ones, such as Walmart selling Stonyfield Yogurt.[108] Even when the country was in the midst of a severe recession, press articles observed that organic purchases and growth of the industry remained high.[109]

The triumphalist theme that ran through many press stories about the growth in organic food elided the debate between what some believed to be original, authentic organic and industrial organic food systems. For some involved in organic food—as farmers, sellers, producers, or consumers—this choice and the threat to the philosophical values of "organic" was wrenching. Many producers who went the corporate route, such as the chair of Stonyfield Farms, Gary Hershberg, argued that the increased sale of organic food—even if mass produced—was an absolute good because it lessened the amount of pesticides released into the environment. For most in the mainstream media, the victory of Big Organic was clear in both market share and the government imprimatur represented in the 1990 Organic Food and Production Act and its subsequent implementation through the National Organic Standards Board.[110]

Many observers answered the question of whether a factory farm could be organic with a resounding no. Sociologist Raj Patel, for example, wrote that "the social difference between industrially produced organic and non-organic food at the supermarket is vanishingly small. We already have a colloquialism to describe the kind of choice that's no choice at all, the kind of choice that supermarkets are geared to provide—'Coke or Pepsi?'"[111]

Although press stories celebrated the success of the organic food industry, they also pondered the reasons for its success. Specifically, stories looked at why increasing numbers of average Americans were buying organic food. The most frequent answer was health, which said something not only about the motivations of individuals but also about the perspective of the mainstream press. Stories in 1989 cited alar and cyanide contamination on fruit as the reason for new interest in organic food, implying that such a motivation was bound to be short-lived as consumers forgot about the scandals.[112] Such cynicism was not borne out, as the embrace of organic foods continued to grow, and concern for health continued to be the prime motivator reported by consumers. In one survey in 2000, for example, 66 percent of respondents said that they bought organic food because it was healthier.[113] By 2011, one health-care survey found that the majority of Americans (58 percent) chose organic over conventional foods when possible, with 63 percent of those under age 35 making that choice.[114]

Periodic articles described the ubiquity of pesticides sprayed on foods as well as the growing evidence that their residues on food and in contaminated drinking water endangered health. Media discussions of health concerns, in particular, focused on children, who scientists understood to be more vulnerable to the impact of chemicals and whose image of innocence and purity made the motivation behind organics more justifiable. Articles, of course, also included quotations from government experts who assured readers that the safety of the general food supply was no danger to the health of any children. By 2012, news stories included opinions from mainstream organizations such as the American Academy of Pediatrics (AAP) asserting that there were many studies finding adverse impacts from pesticide exposure for children; the AAP therefore supported buying organic produce and meats for children.[115]

More than one article indicated that the individual's concern about his or her health was reinforced by a growing belief that organic food tasted better.[116] Despite increasing support for these opinions, the debate over nutritional value and superior taste of organics was ongoing. For instance, one article in 2005 observed, "The jury is still out on whether organic produce is healthier or tastier."[117] There was little debate over the conclusion that if consumers were motivated to buy organic because they wanted to avoid consuming pesticide residues, their choice was a good one.[118] Occasionally, press stories focused on scientific studies attesting to the increased nutritional content of organic foods. For example, one 2007 study found increased levels of flavonoids in organic tomatoes as compared with conventionally grown ones.[119]

Back in 1972, when organic food was first taking hold in a limited way, some asked whether it was more nutritious than food grown with pesticides and other chemicals.[120] Forty years later, that same question was still being asked as observers tried to fathom objective or rational reasons for choosing organic food. In fall 2012, publication of a study from Stanford University scientists added to this debate in the media. At first, the study was announced in headlines blaring that organic foods were *not* nutritionally superior to nonorganic foods, as measured in content of specific vitamins.[121] But, despite the initial attention the press paid to it, the study was soon widely criticized as providing misleading data about the value of organic foods and asking the wrong questions about why people chose to eat them. The study was a meta-analysis, examining many earlier studies about the nutritional content of organic and nonorganic foods, and was criticized for its methodology (averaging out variables that should not have been averaged) and for confusing two categories of nutrients (flavanols and flavonoids).[122] The study, though, was soon criticized more broadly for not understanding other values of organics. For example, opinion pieces and blogs noted that many people bought organic food to cut down on the amount of chemical pollution of the environment; to create more-sustainable food systems; and to lessen exposure to chemicals that caused cancer and other illnesses, disrupted endocrine systems, and increased global warming. In addition, critics soon pointed out that other studies had come to opposing conclusions.[123]

Over decades, many news stories focused on individual health as the most important reason that a person decided to buy organic food; very few people, it seems, were motivated by environmental health. For example, a 1998 story in *Newsweek* about the value of organics included only brief mention of an Environmental Working Group study on drinking-water contamination by pesticides following a lengthy consideration of concern for individual health. A 2000 opinion survey bore out the implications. Only 25 percent of respondents cited concern for the environment as the reason that they bought organic food.[124]

Another topic of debate in the media was whether organic methods produced enough food to provide sufficient amounts for global needs. When the Green Revolution was at its height and before the spread of organic food, the conventional wisdom was that modern industrial agriculture was necessary to produce the amount of food needed for the planet's ever-growing population and to stave off starvation for some. For example, one agricultural scientist at the University of California–Davis observed bluntly in 1972, "It would not be possible to produce the 300 billion pounds of food that are produced in the United States annually" by organic methods.[125] A more prominent voice in the early 1970s who criticized organic food as a recipe for disaster belonged to USDA Secretary Earl Butz. Butz famously declared, "Without the modern input of chemicals, of pesticides, of antibiotics, we simply could not do the job. Before we go back to organic agriculture in this country, somebody must decide which 50 million Americans we are going to let starve or go hungry."[126]

Such extreme rhetoric was gone by the early twenty-first century, but some continued to measure the success of organics by output per acre. By the 2000s, when the organic industry had grown substantially, there were articles that refuted the "long-standing assumption that organic farming methods cannot produce enough food to feed the global population."[127] Even if some continued to argue that organic agriculture could not provide for all of the world's food needs, it was no longer a common topic of debate. Thus, an op-ed article making this argument in late 2012 in the *Wall Street Journal* seemed anachronistic and elicited strong criticism.[128] In addition, some put forward the compromise proposition that different types of agriculture would together provide the food needed. One 2014 article in *National Geographic* asserted that "it needn't be an either-or proposition. . . . We would be wise to explore all good ideas, whether from organic and local farms or from high-tech and conventional farms, and blend the best of both."[129]

Even though many press stories included various justifications for individual consumers to choose organic foods, the dominant question that often re-emerged was the economics of making that choice. The question of eating organic food was framed as a rational economic choice more than a philosophical one to protect the environment, challenge industrial food systems, or improve health overall. A corollary assumption was that buying organic should not radically change the amount of money that people spent on food. Compared with people in many other countries, Americans spent relatively little of their take-home pay on food (in the early 2000s, an average of 13 percent), and news stories assumed that people wanted it to stay that way.[130]

Many articles read as economic primers, offering advice about how to purchase organic foods without spending too much. *Consumer Reports*—a publication devoted to helping consumers get the best value in all areas—had more than one article of this genre. For example, a 2006 story observed, "We found many ways to add more organic products to your shopping list without busting your budget. . . . You don't have to buy organic across the board." Such articles included specific lists of which foods were found to have more pesticide residues and which less, so people could make an informed choice about which organic products to buy, and acknowledged directly that most people who bought organics did so to lower their own exposure to chemicals, not to protect the environment or agricultural workers.[131] An article the following year in the *Wall Street Journal* illustrated the sometimes unspoken cynicism that "pricey organic" foods "may not always be worth their higher price tags." Some mainstream press articles such as this one included the fact that even fruits and vegetables with greater residues were "still within levels permitted by the government," and there was no proof that those levels were harmful. Nevertheless, the article—and others like it—provided a list of what foods were probably worth paying more for *if* one were "interested in organic food."[132] The number of articles that functioned as how-to manuals in this vein increased as the economy slid into recession in 2008.[133]

Related to the articles that advised readers about which organic foods were worth buying were observations about how organic foods had changed as they had been integrated into the mainstream food industry. Some news stories echoed the criticisms that industrial food systems, by definition, did not reflect an organic ethos. Processed food, some charged, could not really be organic. Just as the new USDA standards were taking effect, *Good Housekeeping* questioned the value of organic macaroni and cheese or vanilla wafers. The organic industry now promoted "sugary and fatty processed foods," the *Wall Street Journal* cautioned, that its "Birkenstock-clad founders once shunned."[134] Thus, while most articles admired the economic success represented by the mainstreaming and corporatization of organics, some contained a cynical tone about unhealthy processed foods being counter to organic values.

A survey of press articles at the end of the twentieth and beginning of the twenty-first centuries tells us much about the attitudes toward organic food and about the values on which they were based. The most prominent theme was to assess organic food through an economic framework, celebrating its success as seen in growing sales and the creation of a new industry. A related sign of organic success was the extent to which it was mainstreamed into the existing food industry. The growth of organic food was described as a result of individuals making choices about what to buy. Some articles observed that individuals were often motivated by concerns for their own health, but there was no reference to the health of society as a whole or to the specific health dangers inherent in food produced with pesticides or chemicals. There was also almost no reference to the health of the environment and its relationship to organic foods. Concern for workers—the people who planted, picked, and processed food—was almost absent from articles on organic foods. Thus, press coverage did not depict organic foods as an environmental issue, a public health issue, a labor issue, or a philosophical issue. Rather, organic foods could be understood mainly in terms of dollars and cents, a new industry fueled by individual consumerism. In this way, the press articles were fundamentally conservative: the success of organic food was celebrated, but the system of industrial agriculture and the pesticides essential to its success were not challenged.

Conclusion

Endocrine disruptors, GMOs, and organic food all raised questions about how the risk of pesticides affected individuals. Developments in each of these three areas sent a different message about risk, and about the control that people had over their own lives.

When it came to endocrine disruptors and GMOs, political debates and their coverage in the media conveyed the message that individuals might be powerless to avoid chemicals or organisms spread throughout the environment by large corporations and sanctioned by government. But in the end, this situation elicited acquiescence more than rebellion. The rhetoric about endocrine disruptors was both alarming (hermaphrodite frogs!) and confusing (Which chemicals were endocrine disruptors? How much exposure would hurt humans?). Moreover, those who spoke out against the dangers of endocrine disruptors and in favor of the precautionary principle were effectively painted as unscientific, willing to stop progress without enough evidence of harm. In the end, taking simple steps to protect individuals (avoiding BPA in baby bottles) masked the larger issue of endocrine disruptors spread throughout the environment.

If Americans could choose what type of baby bottle to buy, they also wanted the option of whether or not to buy GM food (hence the strong support for labeling GMOs). But, as with endocrine disruptors, focus on the individual's ability to make choices in the store distracted from the ubiquity of GMOs by the beginning of the twenty-first century. Also similar to the discussion about endocrine disruptors, evidence about the environmental and health effects of GMOs was incomplete and confusing in the popular press (How was GE different from plant breeding? Weren't GMOs substantially equivalent to other foods after all?). In response to the related issue of GMOs encouraging increased herbicide use, many news stories and industry spokespeople cited the relative safety of glyphosate. And, after all, most suburban homeowners squirted Roundup all around their property, seemingly with no ill effects. Thus, familiarity seemed to trump ill-publicized studies that glyphosate increased risks for non-Hodgkins lymphoma or was an endocrine disruptor.[135]

The growth of organic foods in the 1990s and after demonstrated both a growing awareness of pesticide risk in the public culture and the desire of many people to control the risks they faced. But this growth was paradoxical. The spread of organic food made many more people aware of pesticide risk and empowered them to make decisions about their exposure, which, in turn, further encouraged the spread of organic food. But the flourishing organic sector was increasingly integrated into the existing industrial food system, which ran counter to the environmental and cultural precepts of organic food. Consumers who felt they could control their own risk felt less need to question the overall system of industrial monoculture, which rested on extensive human manipulation of nature and, usually, heavy use of pesticides.

The growth of organic food was not just a matter of consumers making decisions about what they bought; it was also due to a government-supported regulatory system. The passage of the 1990 Organic Food and Production Act and the USDA food standards announced in 2000 were revolutionary in many ways, but these developments should also be considered next to the 1996 Food Quality Protection Act. This law replaced the long-standing Delaney Clause, the 1958 amendment to the Food, Drugs, and Cosmetic Act of 1938, which had established a zero tolerance for any cancer-causing ingredients in processed foods. With the 1996 law, carcinogens in processed foods, particularly pesticides, were allowed if there was "reasonable certainty that no harm will result from aggregate exposure to pesticide residue." So if residues had a "negligible risk" of causing cancer, they were allowable. Proponents of the law argued that it was needed in order to standardize the health criteria by which pesticides were evaluated; moreover, they emphasized that the act gave special attention to the health of infants and children in determining safety.[136]

This little-publicized redefinition of what risks were acceptable in food occurred just as more people were buying organics. And, although the new law rested on the assumption that scientists could establish what constituted a "negligible" risk, the complications of such a measurement were numerous. The new law, then, ended up allowing the use of some pesticides that might previously have been banned under the Delaney Clause. Whether or not the new law increased food "protection" was a relative question with no clear answer. Moreover, it's hard to escape the paradox that government regulations changed to permit previously banned chemicals into foods just at the time when more individual consumers had the option to avoid chemicals by buying organic foods.

At the end of the twentieth century and beginning of the twenty-first century, discussion of risks from pesticides was most often personalized in the public culture, not considered as a political or an environmental issue. As countercultural activists and political critics of the 1960s and beyond learned, there was great value in "making the political personal" in terms of motivating action and a realization about the relevance of politics in all aspects of life.

But the downside of this personalization was well illustrated in the twenty-first-century growth of environmentalism. Writer Marcy Darnovsky observed, "Everyday environmentalism is simultaneously a private response to a social problem, a product of corporate marketers eager to tame the environmental imagination, and a remarkable achievement of green activism."[137] Everyday environmentalism, or choosing a "green lifestyle," was often a consumerist simplification of complex problems. Many books—as well as articles in the press—presented how-to guides to lifestyle choices.[138] The flowering of everyday environmentalism was demonstrated in the growth of organic food, which became for many merely a lifestyle choice instead of a challenge to the environmental status quo. In this era of personalization, even popular cultural exposés about the industrial food system such as *Fast Food Nation* and *Super Size Me* failed to elicit any concerted efforts for political reform. There was a sharp contrast between the impact of these works and the regulatory reforms that had followed in the wake of Upton Sinclair's *The Jungle* 100 years earlier.[139] The choice of a green lifestyle was made all the easier as the corporatization of organic food seamlessly integrated produce and products on the shelves of favorite supermarkets. Instead of worrying about transgendered amphibians or the increased use of Roundup blanketing the countryside, Americans could buy organic apples or organic potato chips and believe that they were improving their own health and the environment around them.

Conclusion

One of the inescapable conclusions of this book is that popular and political attitudes toward pesticides have shifted over time. But those shifts have not always been as significant as they might at first have appeared. An example of this contention is seen in the response to Rachel Carson's *Silent Spring*. On one hand, the 1962 book was rightly described as a seminal turning point, giving voice to modern environmentalism and leading to the ban of DDT and other pesticides as well as to concrete changes in the federal regulatory role. On the other hand, overall pesticide use went up tenfold in the decade after *Silent Spring* was published. By the end of the twentieth century, American farmers were using an average of 3 pounds of pesticides per acre annually, while suburban homeowners dispensed the chemicals at the rate of 8 pounds per acre.[1] Clearly, the commitment to pesticides remained strong.

Though some pesticides were banned in the wake of Carson's book, it might not have been just because environmentalist sentiment was flourishing. Use of DDT and related chlorinated hydrocarbons had already been falling in the United States due to growing insect resistance to those chemicals. For example, DDT use had fallen 50 percent in the 1960s, and by the time it was banned for most domestic uses in 1970, 79 percent of the supply produced in the United States was for the export market.[2]

As we consider the complicated legacy of *Silent Spring*, it leads back to the paradox laid out at the start of this book: Why did pesticide use remain entrenched in modern America even in the face of philosophical challenges, not to mention declining efficacy, rising costs, evidence of harm to the environment and to humans, catastrophic disasters, and numerous opportunities to change directions?

There is no simple answer to this question. Certainly, some might argue that the material benefits of industrial agriculture with its seemingly inexpensive food make the embrace of pesticides logical. A more critical economic interpretation might cite the power and influence of the chemical-industrial complex and big agriculture as an explanation for the ubiquity of pesticides. Alternatively, an explanation for widespread pesticide use might cite the liberal imperative to lead modernization efforts throughout the developing world for humanitarian and political reasons. Looking at domestic politics, one might focus upon the power of entrenched economic, bureaucratic, and scientific interests as an explanation for the commitment to pesticides.

Rather than providing a single answer to the question of why Americans continued to use pesticides heavily for more than half a century, this book has argued that the economic, political, and scientific justifications for pesticides relied on an enduring cultural embrace of or at least acquiescence to the chemicals at a popular and political level. Furthermore, in the preceding pages I have argued that this cultural discourse has been surprisingly favorable and stable, even in the face of numerous challenges. Although environmental rhetoric may have been modified or particular pesticides banned, there was no paradigm shift, no wholesale rejection of pesticides and what they represented.

The story has been told both chronologically and thematically. The cultural attitudes toward pesticide use can be divided into three main periods. The years 1945 to 1962 were a time of remarkable consensus about the chemicals, which were just one example of the modern technologies celebrated as fundamental to American identity. Unbridled enthusiasm for synthetic pesticides began with their wartime use against typhus and malaria and quickly proliferated in civilian products as pesticides were domesticated. They were easy to use, cheap, and soon ubiquitous. Adoption of these chemicals reflected trends of US history at the time, a period of a great increase in per capita wealth, and rising expectations about quality of life and material comforts, including inexpensive and plentiful food.

In addition to reaping the benefits of the agricultural use of pesticides, Americans who had joined the great wave flowing to the suburbs experienced pesticides directly as a way to master and control their very own piece of nature. Most prominently, the American marriage to a manicured, monocropped lawn—which depended on an array of pesticides, fertilizers, and fuel-powered equipment—was cemented during post–World War II suburbanization, and the aesthetic remained deeply ingrained into the early twenty-first century. By one estimate, the number of American households using pesticides by then was 82 percent. Many Americans were convinced that such use was necessary, either out of habit, social pressure, or because they agreed with lawn-care advertisements such as one in 2012 that warned, "Weeds and pests aren't just ugly. They're a threat."[3]

Amid postwar celebrations of the new chemicals, there were also increasing criticisms of their effects—even before the publication of Carson's book. By the late 1950s, wildlife biologists, conservationists, and others had become alarmed at the environmental consequences of heavy use of persistent chlorinated hydrocarbon insecticides. Such critical discussions, though, were a minority position, not known to the general public.

The publication of *Silent Spring*, then, began a new phase of cultural and political attitudes toward pesticides. The 1960s and the 1970s were a period of upheaval in many ways, when some became more critical of their government, questioned the economic and political establishment at all levels of American life, and proposed a counterculture alternative to mainstream mores. Environmentalism flourished in this atmosphere, criticism of pesticides grew, and new legislation and regulations were enacted to protect the natural world from human folly. Despite the concrete changes of these two decades, especially the latter, the growth in pesticide use even while the chemicals were being more carefully regulated was clear.[4]

Environmentalism, although part of a new regulatory and legal framework, faced a powerful backlash in the 1980s from regional coalitions as well as a new administration in Washington. Government officials' failure to enforce environmental regulations was bolstered by a growing cultural cynicism about environmental risk—or at least the expectation that it was unavoidable in modern, industrial society.[5] Initial public revulsion at the tragedy in Bhopal and the health crisis faced by Vietnam veterans exposed to Agent Orange fizzled. In many ways, the 1960s, 1970s, and 1980s were a time of great environmental advances but also of roads not taken and of possibilities not explored as pesticide use continued to rise.

The first two stages of the pesticide era can be characterized first by unqualified use, and then by questioning and reform. The third stage, from the 1990s into the 2010s, incorporates these opposing trends into a compromise between reform and a recommitment to a technological, chemical order. Beginning in 1990, there were what might appear to be contradictory developments in attitudes toward pesticides. Some celebrated the ban on DDT and other persistent chlorinated hydrocarbons, whereas others blamed this policy for the resurgence in malaria and the deaths that resulted. Environmental regulations continued to elicit—simultaneously—both strong support and criticism. New technological interventions in agriculture, such as genetically modified organisms, had both their supporters and their detractors, who instead embraced the growth of organic foods. Thus, in the last decade of the twentieth century and the first of the twenty-first, both GMOs and organic foods grew dramatically.

I have argued in the preceding pages that the simultaneous growth of GMOs and organics was not as contradictory as it might at first have appeared. Though the discourse about pesticides in the early twenty-first century was more sophisticated and complex than it was in 1950, the commitment to an industrial, agricultural order and chemical interference in the environment was no less strong. In essence, there was no indication that most Americans had given up four bedrock assumptions of their cultural outlook: modern human society could, to some degree, manipulate or control the environment; short-term interests were more important than long-term ones; individual and human concerns trumped collective and environmental ones; and environmental decisions should be made on the basis of clear evidence of what had happened, not out of fear for what might happen. Each of these assumptions presumed that a certain amount of risk must be accepted as part of modern life. If risk was unavoidable, it could be managed and merely factored into a cost-benefit calculation. Moreover, one way to manage risk was to treat it as a problem for individual consumers, who could be protected by giving them enough information to make choices in the marketplace. Thus were the environmental and health risks of pesticides rationalized.

Confidence that modernity brought technological mastery over the environment was a deeply held belief throughout the twentieth century. One clear example of this conviction was the commitment to monoculture that came with the industrialization of agriculture. As a method to make agriculture ever more efficient, monocultures encouraged many farmers and others to believe that they could continually increase production, decreasing the cost of food as well as providing nourishment for a growing world population. Although the focus on output was predictable and natural, this criterion rose in importance in the postwar period, skewing how agricultural success was measured. Biologist Robert Rudd criticized this expectation in 1958: "Not only must there be increase in quantity but there must be increase in the rate of increase. This is the production fetish of which I speak. It is a false god to which are sacrificed a host of other secondary values."[6] Many—from those in the USDA to environmentalists in the 1970s—focused on production issues because they worried about how to feed a ballooning world population. Thus, Secretary of Agriculture Earl Butz encouraged farmers in the 1970s to "plant fence row to fence row" in order to increase output (and exports).[7] In 1992, more than two decades after he left office, another USDA secretary, Orville Freeman, was still writing about the coming crisis of feeding the 11 billion people expected to be living in 2050.[8] In the first decades of the twenty-first century, anxiety about feeding the growing world population remained a potent agricultural and political issue. For example, a 2014 cover story in *National Geographic* argued that food production would need to double by 2050.[9]

The commitment to monoculture, then, grew out of the industrialization of agriculture beginning in the nineteenth century, as well as what many perceived as the imperative to continually increase output. But such a commitment was not without its costs. Monoculture was designed to foster simplicity, efficiency, and predictability—none of which were inherent in nature. Where nature's diversity created complementary systems and protections, monoculture led to plants (and animals) vulnerable to numerous types of pests, both predictable and not. Such inescapable developments led writer Michael Pollan to forcefully assert that "monoculture is the root of virtually every problem that bedevils the modern farmer, and from which virtually every agricultural product is designed to deliver him."[10]

Over several decades, mainstream agriculture remained wedded to a technological solution to pest problems, getting on what more than one critic called "the pesticide treadmill." Ostensibly, the motivation for steady pesticide use would have been that such practices effectively solved pest problems. The fact that this was not the case is one of the most powerful indications that the commitment to pesticides was complex, not just a rational decision based on effectiveness. Being on the "treadmill" meant increasing pest resistance to the chemicals (the number of resistant insects went up sixteenfold from 1955 to 1980, and the number of resistant species in the first decade of the twenty-first century was more than 1,000) as well as a resulting pressure to use chemicals in greater volume or ones that were more potent. This pattern applied to herbicide use as much as to insecticide use.[11] Meanwhile, the percentage of crops lost to pests remained roughly the same even as pesticide use—and the cost to farmers—mounted. Crop loss to pests in 2005 (including insects, diseases, and weeds) was 30 to 40 percent, slightly *higher* than it was before the age of "chemical dependence." Total crop yields, though, were slightly higher because there were other ways to boost productivity. Nevertheless, some writers have cited numerous examples of per acre production from *non*industrial farms exceeding the output of conventional ones.[12]

In addition to insect resistance and crop loss, the dominance of monoculture also meant increased vulnerability of the world's food supply due to the narrow band of crops cultivated. By the end of the twentieth century, three-quarters of all food came from only seven crops (wheat, rice, corn, potatoes, barley, cassava, and sorghum), and, among these, the varieties grown shrank drastically in the second half of the century.[13]

Although the costs of the pesticide treadmill seemed to rise by the end of the twentieth century with increased resistance, a decline in soil fertility due to overuse of chemicals and less organic matter, and concern about the health effects of agricultural chemicals, the commitment to industrialized agriculture did not slacken. Entomologists and those in the agricultural industry sought a solution to these problems in GMOs. But, as discussed in chapter 7, no matter how they were marketed, GMOs were neither a "silver bullet" nor a departure from a technological approach to the environment. They did not offer a new paradigm or an alternative to the industrial monoculture system.[14]

For those who remained wedded to the paradigm of chemical solutions for environmental problems and dismissive of risks that might be associated with those chemicals, stories about increases in malaria were a dramatic illustration of what happened when societies rejected available technologies. Media coverage of the malaria issue illustrated the backlash against environmental precautions and regulations as well as the strength of the technological paradigm as a way to frame pest problems. Beginning in the 1990s, a number of commentators and organizations began praising DDT as relatively safe and effective against mosquitoes that carried malaria (one scholar, for example, asserted that "the hazards posed by DDT were exaggerated") and condemned Rachel Carson as responsible for its ban.[15] The organization Competitive Enterprise Institute operated the website Rachel

Was Wrong, which charged that millions of people around the world had malaria because of Carson. Author Michael Crichton added that Carson was responsible for more deaths than was Adolph Hitler. In 2007, Oklahoma senator Tom Coburn—citing the spread of malaria through the developing world—blocked legislation that would have honored Carson.[16]

Understanding the post–World War II decline of malaria was more complicated than indicated by the media frenzy. All of the credit could not go to DDT and other insecticides. In the United States, for example, migration from the rural areas of the South to cities, as well as increased government spending on projects such as marsh drainage, was responsible for some of the dramatic decline.[17] Moreover, heavy agricultural use of DDT resulted in mosquito resistance, thus leading many to question the chemical's continued effectiveness for malaria control even before the chemical was banned by many countries in the 1970s and after.[18]

By the beginning of the twenty-first century, world health officials and environmentalists came to believe that indoor, targeted use of DDT on bed nets and walls for malaria outbreaks was effective and should be supported.[19] Such policies were very different from the broadcast, outdoor spraying of DDT that had taken place in earlier decades and had had widespread environmental consequences. Despite the consensus that only targeted indoor use of DDT should be sanctioned and that more general spraying of DDT was not only dangerous but ineffective, the charges against Carson were kept alive in some parts of the press and political culture, thus, also nurturing the idea that pesticides were safe and effective.[20]

Along with the basic cultural assumption that technology could be used to control the environment with minimal risk was a second assumption that supported continued pesticide use: short-term interests were more important than were long-term ones. This assumption applied when considering the effectiveness of pesticides as well as the environmental and health impact of the chemicals. In the short term, the new synthetic pesticides appeared wildly effective from 1945 on, dramatically increasing yields for little cost. As discussed in chapter 1, this remained the dominant perception in the public culture until *Silent Spring* shattered many people's illusions. Although it was clear to many entomologists in the 1950s that reliance on a simple chemical regimen was a dead-end solution due to insect resistance, the idea that modern agriculture necessitated increasing use of chemicals was unquestioned by many in the public culture.

Although the subtleties of insect control may have been absent from public debates, there was some attention to the health impact of pesticides. Occasional press stories focused on acute effects such as accidental poisonings resulting in death. But, in general, stories about the effect of pesticides on farmworkers were hard to find. One memorable scene from Alfred Hitchcock's 1959 film *North by Northwest* illustrated the idea that the danger from pesticides came more from being choked by a foreign substance than from long-term, internal effects of the chemicals themselves. Cary Grant's character, who was being pursued by an assassin in a crop-dusting plane through a cornfield, had trouble breathing due to the sheer amount of a granular substance showered over him and was endangered by the threat that the low-flying plane would hit him. After escaping from his attacker onto a passing bus, Grant merely brushed off the pesticide powder covering him. His casual response, and his lack of any ill effects, reflected and reinforced the popular notion that pesticides were harmless.

Looking beyond the acute dangers of pesticides, popular and political stories sometimes highlighted one chronic danger: cancer. Years before *Silent Spring* was published, Washington officials had made efforts to protect citizens from the danger of cancer. The 1958 Delaney Clause of the Food Additives Amendment to the Food, Drug, and Cosmetic Act of 1938 banned food additives (including pesticides and other chemicals) known to be carcinogenic. But even such a strong policy of zero tolerance for carcinogens masked the difficulty of proving causality for chronic conditions. Because cancer usually took many years to develop, it was hard to isolate definitively particular causes. Moreover, most industrial chemicals, including pesticides, had not been tested for their carcinogenicity when the law went into effect. This remained a problem decades later, when cancers attributable to pesticides were still widespread. Entomologist David Pimentel estimated that at the start of the twenty-first century, the health of 110,000 people was adversely affected every year from pesticide exposure, with maybe 10,000 of those cases being cancer. Nevertheless, the Delaney Clause was eviscerated by the Food Quality Protection Act in 1996, which allowed residues of carcinogenic pesticides on foods as long as amounts were regulated.[21]

Proving causality for long-term (or even short-term) health consequences was one of the issues used to criticize Rachel Carson in the early 1960s. Three important sources for Carson were medical doctors who had looked at the link between chronic diseases and pesticide exposure: Morton Biskind,

Malcolm Hargreaves, and William Hueper. Each had used clinical medicine and case histories to make this connection, though critics treated the evidence as invalid or even illegitimate when compared with laboratory testing.[22]

Thus, understanding the health risks of pesticides was difficult for a number of reasons. First, the bias of focusing on acute poisoning made pesticides seem safer than they were. Second, when chronic illnesses, such as cancer, were a concern, it was difficult to isolate definitive causes. And third, the focus on clearly observable diseases, such as cancer or physical birth defects such as deformed limbs, masked harder-to-understand, more-subtle health effects such as those from endocrine disruption. As discussed in chapter 7, public understanding of endocrine disruptors remained confused and controversial at the start of the twenty-first century. The concept was an abstract, elusive risk, with no consensus to sharply limit exposure. In a pattern familiar from earlier public responses to pesticide dangers, a specific, concrete threat was eliminated while use of seemingly less-harmful substances continued. A ban on DDT and its more-toxic persistent, chlorinated hydrocarbon cousins in the 1970s reassured the public that the worst pesticides had been eliminated; meanwhile, overall use of the chemicals increased. Similarly, for example, manufacturers taking BPA out of plastic baby bottles reassured parents that endocrine disruptors wouldn't harm their children, yet BPA continued to coat retail store receipts, and other endocrine disruptors, such as 2,4-D, remained widely used throughout the world.

A third cultural assumption that appeared to support the continued widespread use of synthetic pesticides was the belief that risk was best measured individually and with respect to human health, not collectively or in terms of environmental health. Signs of this assumption can be found throughout the public and political culture in the nearly six decades of synthetic pesticide use. Before *Silent Spring*, very little public attention was paid to the environment or to the environmental consequences of pesticides. When press stories critical of pesticides appeared, they were almost always about the impact for individual Americans, such as the dangers of eating contaminated cranberries in 1959, the risk of cancer discussed by Rachel Carson, the situation of army veterans exposed to Agent Orange, or the health benefits of eating organic foods. Occasional attention to the environmental impact of pesticides was narrowly focused (weakened shells of bald eagle eggs or contamination by dioxin) and had specific solutions (ban DDT or stop spraying 2,4,5-T near people). Thus, as measured by individual interests (such as plentiful, cheap food or weed-free lawns) and human health (a lack of acute, catastrophic consequences), widespread pesticide use seemed to be a reasonable choice.[23]

With the common assumption that pesticides should be assessed based on their impact on individuals—especially readers of the national press and those involved in politics—groups of people who faced greater risks from pesticides tended to be ignored. The problem was most serious for agricultural workers. In the American press and in government policies, the impact of chemical pesticides on these laborers—in the United States and around the globe—was often invisible. In addition, poor wages and safety conditions made the price of produce apparently low and encouraged the growth of the global market.[24] There were periodic attempts to address the welfare of farmworkers. This was one of the prime factors in the organizing work of Cesar Chavez, the formation of the United Farm Workers (UFW), and the UFW-led boycott of table grapes in the late 1960s and 1970s. But throughout the campaign, public support for the farmworkers was weak, as was support from mainstream environmental organizations such as the Sierra Club.[25] The dangers to workers and residents of developing countries increased by the early twenty-first century as the share of pesticides used and manufactured in the Southern Hemisphere grew to about 50 percent of the world's total.[26]

If the value of pesticides was assessed based on how they affected individuals, particularly individual consumers, so, too, was the idea of lessening pesticide use. As discussed in the preceding pages, the marketing of organic food was presented as a lifestyle choice, seamlessly integrated into industrial food systems. Individual consumers, especially middle-class and affluent ones, could make the choice not to consume products with as many pesticides, but they need not go outside or challenge the industrial food system as a whole.

Finally, one more-entrenched cultural assumption bolstered the ubiquitous use of chemical pesticides: rejection of the precautionary principle. The precautionary principle was an effort by environmentalists and others to change people's attitudes about risk in an industrial society. But, in their actions or their acquiescence, the majority of Americans rejected this reconceptualization. Had this principle been applied to pesticides, it would have directly challenged existing government regulations because the majority of the chemicals had never been fully tested for toxicity. Moreover, under the precautionary principle, the burden of proof would have shifted to manufacturers, who would have had to demonstrate the safety of pesticides before they could market their wares.[27]

Instead, generations of Americans held opposing ideas. Industrialization and economic growth in the United States were based on the adoption of ever-new innovations, which were judged more on the basis of whether or not they were effective and profitable than whether or not they were safe. Similarly, the idea that governments had a role to play in regulating the safety of chemicals or other innovations was relatively recent and contested. For the most part, judgment about the risk of pesticides and other innovations was made on a cost/benefit scale. Thus, a cost was assumed, but what was important was its ratio to a benefit. At different turning points in recent history, the defense of pesticides was often made on these terms. For example, one USDA official speaking in 1974 against the ban on 2,4,5-T uses noted, "We believe that some risk is unavoidable when man utilizes modern technology, and feel that the degree of risk must be carefully assessed and balanced against the anticipated benefits when making judgments about the use of such technology. We have identified this principle as the 'rule of reason.'"[28] Another USDA official elaborated on why a "rule of reason" was essential: "There are some who hold the extreme position that no risk can be permitted, particularly as it applies in a toxicological sense. We will develop the rule-of-reason approach because we feel strongly that both risk and benefit result from a single action. And because of an especially strong feeling that the no risk philosophy is inimical to the interest of society."[29] It was clear that most Americans agreed with the proposition that not all environmental risks could be eliminated from their lives. This was true when it came to air pollution, to automobile accidents, and to possible diseases caused by exposure to pesticides.

By the beginning of the twenty-first century, people in other developed countries were increasingly coming to different conclusions about environmental risk than were Americans. For example, there was a growing consensus in a number of countries on the dangers of 2,4-D as both an endocrine disruptor and a carcinogen. Starting in 2003, Canada gradually began banning all lawn chemicals, including 2,4-D. By 2011, Denmark, Sweden, and Norway had all banned 2,4-D. In early 2009, the European Union banned twenty-two different chemicals that were endocrine disruptors or carcinogens and, in 2011, began restricting pesticide use near public spaces such as schools, parks, and hospitals.[30]

In contrast, most Americans continued to accept the idea that lawn chemicals were just one of the compromises in modern life between risks and benefits. Moreover, use of 2,4-D and other chemicals was so widespread by the early twenty-first century that it was naturalized and, thus, often invisible, even when, for example, in 2011, 97 percent of rivers in the United States were contaminated with at least one pesticide.[31] Instead, as the preceding chapters have argued, the dangers of pesticides became visible and loomed as alarming threats only at particular points in history—such as when milk might have been contaminated with DDT or when fish became too toxic to eat or when a community had to be evacuated due to dioxin contamination. Responses to such crises followed familiar patterns as a short-lived controversy addressed the worst hazards while leaving the environmental use of pesticides, overall, unchallenged. Moreover, by focusing on the risks of the most dangerous chemicals, those that seemed to be less dangerous could be rationalized and accepted as the more moderate alternative. Appealing to moderation and compromise was a tried-and-true way that Americans accepted risk and the trade-offs of modern life.

It was not clear at the beginning of the twenty-first century—when 83 percent of Americans polled by Gallup reported that they were sympathetic to the environmental movement—whether appeals to moderation would lead in a different direction.[32] Environmentalist sympathies as well as the growth in organic foods might encourage renewed support for actual moderation, including cultural methods of pest control and more-limited pesticide use. For example, in 2013, *Consumer Reports*—a publication not known for its environmentalism—told readers that citizens should expect the US government to use a version of the precautionary principle when it regulated chemicals. The editorial harshly criticized existing laws that required the EPA to prove that a chemical was unsafe instead of a manufacturer having to prove that it was safe. Under such a system, complained *Consumer Reports*, only 5 chemicals of the 83,000 listed in the EPA's inventory had been banned, limited, or restricted, and there was no indication that the rest had been adequately tested for safety.[33]

Such opinions may start to shift attitudes about the ubiquitous use of pesticides in the United States. But it will take a groundswell of opinion and a sustained consensus to end the American love affair with pesticides.

Acknowledgments

At the outset of this book, I observed that, like love, the attachment to pesticides was not necessarily rational. Similarly, when a scholar focuses on one topic over several years, her devotion might appear irrational to others. Nevertheless, if she is lucky, she enjoys the support of colleagues who share insights and of institutions that extend material support to facilitate the work. I have been fortunate on both counts.

Among the institutions that provided support for this project, the Rachel Carson Center (RCC) for Environment and Society in Munich stands out. For nine months in 2012–2013 and in 2014, I worked on this project at the RCC as a Carson Fellow. I benefited from the generous financial support of the center and the work of its directors, Christof Mauch and Helmuth Trischler, and that of the hardworking staff, including Rob Emmett and Arielle Helmick. In addition, I benefited from the intellectual generosity and creativity of other fellows. Along with the insights I gleaned from workshops, colloquiums, and informal conversations, some colleagues provided valuable critiques of my draft work, including Matthew Booker, Amy Hay, Mike Hulme, Sherilyn MacGregor, Kathleen McAfee, Heather McCrea, Emily O'Gorman, Cindy Ott, Jenny Price, Tom Princen, Sainath Suryanarayanan, and Markus Wilczek. In addition, conversations with numerous fellows, including Ellen Arnold, John Meyer, Ed Russell, Hanna Schösler, Frank Zelko, and Tom Zeller, stimulated my vision and clarified my arguments. I am especially grateful to the seven supportive and inspiring colleagues with whom I shared an office at different times over nine months; they helped to make the Carson Center feel like home.

Outside the Carson Center, I have benefited from the wisdom of many colleagues in their comments and critiques on parts of this book. While working on the project, I received thoughtful criticisms and good recommendations when I presented research at different scholarly venues, including meetings of the American Society for Environmental History, the Society for Historians of American Foreign Relations, the Agricultural History Society, the German Association for American Studies, and the American Historical Association. Among other scholars, I thank the following for their comments: Pete Daniel, Fritz Davis, Tom Dunlap, Sterling Evans, Nancy Langston, Ed Martini, James McWilliams, Cameron Muir, Jody Roberts, and Kendra Smith-Howard.

I am particularly grateful for the comments of one colleague, David Kinkela. Dave read the manuscript more than once and provided incisive and insightful recommendations, making this a better book. (Of course, neither he nor any other colleague who offered advice bears any responsibility for the weaknesses that may remain.)

I have appreciated consistent support from Michael Briggs of the University Press of Kansas and the work of the rest of the press staff, as well as that of acquisitions editor Ranjit Arab, formerly of the press.

This book has benefited from professional and helpful archivists at the Beinecke Library, the Chemical Heritage Foundation, the Harry Truman Library, the National Agricultural Research Library, the National Archives, and the New York Public Library—Manuscript Division as well as librarians at Penn State University Libraries.

Penn State University has been generous in its financial support for work on this book, including Research Development Grants and sabbatical and travel support. In addition, many colleagues at Penn State have offered consistent support for the completion of this project.

Finally, from my perspective, professional achievements mean little if they cannot be shared with friends and family. I am most grateful to have had David, Hannah, and Tobias Walker put up with what might have seemed at times my irrational devotion to this project and provide me with joyful reminders of a world apart from pesticides.

Notes

Introduction

1. Henry Lee, "New Bug Killers for Home and Garden," *Coronet*, April 1955, 171–174. See also Gordon Morrison, "Chemical Aids to Gardening Streamlined," *Chicago Daily Tribune*, 7 April 1957, A9. Dow advertisement, *Saturday Evening Post*, 1952, box 7, Advertisements, Dow Collection, Othmer Library, Chemical Heritage Foundation.

2. Jack Ralph Kloppenberg Jr., *First the Seed: The Political Economy of Plant Biotechnology, 1492–2000*, 2nd ed. (Madison: University of Wisconsin Press, 2004), 316; Mark Schapiro, *Exposed: The Toxic Chemistry of Everyday Products and What's at Stake for American Power* (White River Junction, VT: Chelsea Green Publishing, 2007), 91; *Food, Inc.* (documentary), directed by Robert Kenner, 2008–2009, 91 minutes.

3. Dow advertisement, 1946, box 7, Advertisements, Dow Collection, Othmer Library, Chemical Heritage Foundation.

4. Craig Waddell, ed., *And No Birds Sing: Rhetorical Analyses of Rachel Carson's* Silent Spring (Carbondale: Southern Illinois University Press, 2000), 8; US Environmental Protection Agency, "Pesticides Industry Sales and Usage," http://www.epa.gov/opp00001/pestsales, 2006–2007 market estimates. See also US Geological Survey, "Estimation of Annual Agricultural Pesticide Use for Counties of the Conterminous United States, 1992–2009," http://pubs.usgs.gov/sir/2013/5009/.

5. Waldemar Kaempffert, "DDT, the Army's Insect Powder, Strikes a Blow against Typhus and for Pest Control," *New York Times*, 4 June 1944, E9; "Typhus in Naples Checked by Allies," *New York Times*, 22 February 1944, 11. See also "Army to Use DDT Powder on Malaria Mosquitos," *New York Times*, 1 August 1944; "Malaria and the War," *New York Times*, 2 October 1944, 18.

6. Bruce Gardner, *American Agriculture in the Twentieth Century: How It Flourished and What It Cost* (Cambridge MA: Harvard University Press, 2002), 14. From 1930 to 1950, the use of mechanical harvesters increased ninefold. Peter Pringle, *Food, Inc.: Mendel to Monsanto—the Promises and Perils of the Biotech Harvest* (New York: Simon and Schuster, 2003), 47. American farmers had been using natural and chemical pesticides since the late eighteenth century, though the field had been

transformed by the professionalization of entomology and the spread of industrial agriculture in the late nineteenth century. For discussion of this pre-1945 history, see James Whorton, *Before* Silent Spring*: Pesticides and Public Health in Pre-DDT America* (Princeton, NJ: Princeton University Press, 1974); James McWilliams, *American Pests: The Losing War on Insects from Colonial Times to DDT* (New York: Columbia University Press, 2008); and Edmund Russell, *War and Nature: Fighting Humans and Insects with Chemicals from World War I to* Silent Spring (Cambridge: Cambridge University Press, 2001).

7. Ralph Martin, "How Much Poison Are We Eating?" *Harper's Magazine*, April 1955, 63; Jack Denton Scott, "Those 'New Foods' Can KILL You," *American Mercury*, June 1956, 5–10.

8. Gardner, *American Agriculture in the Twentieth Century*, 24.

9. Throughout this book, "pesticide" will be the general term used to refer to these various types of biocides; particular types of pesticides will be specified as needed.

10. In 2008, 90 percent of soybeans and 61 percent of corn planted in the United States was Roundup Ready. Schapiro, *Exposed*, 91; *Food, Inc.* (documentary); Jack Doyle, *Altered Harvest: Agriculture, Genetics, and the Fate of the World's Food Supply* (New York: Penguin Books, 1995), 214, 215–216; Kloppenberg, *First the Seed*, 247, 316; Alfred D. Chandler Jr., *Shaping the Industrial Century: The Remarkable Story of the Evolution of the Modern Chemical and Pharmaceutical Industries* (Cambridge, MA: Harvard University Press, 2005), 67.

11. Kloppenberg, *First the Seed*, 308; Debi Barker, "Globalization and Industrial Agriculture," in *The Fatal Harvest Reader: The Tragedy of Industrial Agriculture*, ed. Andrew Kimbrell (Washington, DC: Island Press, 2005), 262.

12. Centers for Disease Control and Prevention, "Elimination of Malaria in the United States (1947–1951)," http://www.cdc.gov/malaria/about/history/elimination_us.html.

13. John Soluri, *Banana Cultures: Agriculture, Consumption, and Environmental Change in Honduras and the United States* (Austin: University of Texas Press, 2005), 214, 215. For a good example of the discussion regarding migrant workers in Mexico and the United States, see Angus Wright, *The Death of Ramón Gonzalez: The Modern Agricultural Dilemma*, rev. ed. (Austin: University of Texas Press, 1990), and discussion of Bhopal in chapter 5.

Chapter 1. Falling in Love: The Golden Age of Synthetic Pesticides

1. For more on Truman's prodevelopment attitudes, see Karl Brooks, "A Legacy Cast in Concrete: The Truman Presidency's Transformation of America's Natural

Environment, 1945–1953" (unpublished paper presented at A Conference on the Historical Significance of the Truman Presidency, Harry S. Truman Presidential Library, July 2003). While Truman and other officials ignored evidence about environmental damage from projects of the New Deal and World War II, the Democratic Congress elected with Truman in 1948 passed legislation to authorize almost all of the dam and river projects sought by the president, more than 150 new water projects. Ibid., 7.

2. Brooks, "A Legacy Cast in Concrete," 10.

3. Moreover, increased output was coupled with an increased stabilization of prices throughout the twentieth century but especially after World War II. Bruce Gardner, *American Agriculture in the Twentieth Century: How It Flourished and What It Cost* (Cambridge, MA: Harvard University Press, 2002), 147–148.

4. In the decade and a half after World War II, forage harvesting machinery and the mechanical cotton picker became standard equipment. Gardner, *American Agriculture in the Twentieth Century*, 14, 24. From 1930 to 1950, the use of mechanical harvesters increased ninefold. Peter Pringle, *Food, Inc.: Mendel to Monsanto—The Promises and Perils of the Biotech Harvest* (New York: Simon and Schuster, 2003), 47.

5. Gardner, *American Agriculture in the Twentieth Century*, 19. Sales of hybrid corn seeds went up another 60 percent between 1950 and 1980; by 1970, the farmer who produced his own seed corn had virtually disappeared. Pringle, *Food, Inc.*, 46.

6. See Deborah Fitzgerald, *Every Farm a Factory: The Industrial Ideal in American Agriculture* (New Haven, CT: Yale University Press, 2003). There was a long history of pesticide use in the United States before the age of synthetics; for a discussion of pest control in the pre-1945 period, see James McWilliams, *American Pests: The Losing War on Insects from Colonial Times to DDT* (New York: Columbia University Press, 2008); James Whorton, *Before* Silent Spring*: Pesticides and Public Health in Pre-DDT America* (Princeton, NJ: Princeton University Press, 1974).

7. Robert Spear, *The Great Gypsy Moth War: The History of the First Campaign in Massachusetts to Eradicate the Gypsy Moth, 1890–1901* (Amherst, MA: University of Massachusetts Press, 2005), 254.

8. Jack Ryan, "Farmers Reaping Bumper Crop of Chemicals," *New York Times*, 20 March 1955, F1.

9. Nick Cullather, *The Hungry World: America's Cold War Battle against Poverty in Asia* (Cambridge, MA: Harvard University Press, 2010), 103; Gardner, *American Agriculture in the Twentieth Century*, 51.

10. James Reston, "Iowa Celebrates Its 100th Birthday," *New York Times*, 5 July 1946, 6.

11. "Another Bumper Harvest," *New York Times Magazine*, 26 June 1949, 8–9.

12. "Bigger: Crops and Farm Problem," *U.S. News & World Report*, 19 August 1949, 16.

13. "The Hybrid Onion Appears on a Farm," *New York Times*, 5 July 1946, 10.

14. Joseph Sherman, "Cotton Mechanization Goes to Work on the South," *Barron's National Business and Financial Weekly* 27, no. 8 (24 February 1947): 11. See also "Cotton—Salvation for an Old Sinner?" *Kiplinger Magazine* 1, no. 7 (July 1947): 40.

15. Gilbert Bailey, "Boom Days on the Farm," *New York Times Magazine*, 1 June 1947, 12; Richard Seelye Jones, "The Small Town Hits the Jack Pot," *Nation's Business* 37, no. 6 (June 1949): 34.

16. J. Bird, "Will Our Grandchildren Go Hungry?" *Saturday Evening Post*, 23 October 1954, 30.

17. "U.S. Food Supply Should Meet the Stresses of War," *Saturday Evening Post*, 22 September 1950, 10.

18. Ibid.

19. For more on the political and cultural role of mainstream media, especially as they communicate about the environment, see Timothy E. Cook, *Governing with the News: The News Media as a Political Institution*, 2nd ed. (Chicago: University of Chicago Press, 2005); Libby Lester, *Media and Environment* (Cambridge: Polity Press, 2010); Julia B. Corbett, *Communicating Nature: How We Create and Understand Environmental Messages* (Washington, DC: Island Press, 2006); Stuart Allan, Barbara Adam, and Cynthia Carter, eds., *Environmental Risks and the Media* (London and New York: Routledge, 2000); and Priscilla Coit Murphy, *What a Book Can Do: The Publication and Reception of* Silent Spring (Amherst: University of Massachusetts Press, 2005).

20. Cook, *Governing with the News*, 3, 12.

21. M. Mark Miller and Bonnie Parnell Riechert, "Interest Group Strategies and Journalistic Norms: News Media Framing and Environmental Issues," in *Environmental Risks and the Media*, 50–51; Cook, *Governing with the News*, 5.

22. Corbett, *Communicating Nature*, 223, also 244–245.

23. Ibid., 224.

24. Lester, *Media and Environment*, 108.

25. Ibid., 65; Murphy, *What a Book Can Do*, 35, 120–121.

26. Barbara Adam, "The Media Timescapes of BSE News," in *Environmental Risks and the Media*, 121–122, also 4; Corbett, *Communicating Nature*, 217.

27. Cook, *Governing with the News*, 6; Corbett, *Communicating Nature*, 224, 227.

28. Advertisements 1 and 8 and see four pages of advertisements in box 7, Advertisements, Post Street Archives, Dow Collection, Othmer Library, Chemical Heritage Foundation.

29. Jay Richter, "Our Lazy Acres Can Yield Far More Food," *New York Times Magazine*, 9 October 1949, 24.

30. "Growing Surplus," *Time*, 24 August 1953, 72.

31. "Our Food Surpluses," *Commonweal*, 1 September 1950, 501–502; "U.S. Food Supply Should Meet the Stresses of War," *Saturday Evening Post*, 2 September 1950,

10. Any possible shortages in the future could be remedied if surpluses continued to be stored. "Editorial," *The Country Gentleman*, August 1953, 104.

32. Cullather, *The Hungry World*, 5.

33. Raymond Moley, "The Tyranny of Plenty," *Newsweek*, 30 August 1954, 80; "The Golden Glut," *Time*, 10 August 1953, 20.

34. "Bigger: Crops and Farm Problem," *U.S. News & World Report*, 19 August 1949, 16.

35. Harry Truman, "Agricultural Prosperity: Production Payment Plan," 5 September 1949, *Vital Speeches of the Day*, 711–713. See also Charles Brannan, "Agricultural Abundance: For Better or Worse?" 23 August 1949, *Vital Speeches of the Day*, 764.

36. "Food," *Fortune*, November 1949, 17; Allan B. Kline, "Cheaper Food—Promise or Political Lure?" *Collier's*, 13 May 1950, 13; Ernest Havermann, "The Great Glut," *Reader's Digest*, July 1950, 105–109; "Bumper Crop: Signal of Trouble," *U.S. News & World Report*, 24 February 1950, 54–55.

37. From the late 1940s to the 1950s, a number of articles described charges from both the left and the right that the then current farm programs and price supports were folly. Criticisms included charges that production controls were evil, that they were merely the continuation of discredited New Deal programs, that it cost too much to warehouse surpluses, that there was fallout from dumping commodities on the world market, and that the programs hurt the economic welfare of farmers. "Growing Surplus," *Time*, 24 August 1953, 72; "Hunger and Surpluses," *The Commonweal*, 11 December 1953, 248–249. See also Moley, "The Tyranny of Plenty," 80; "Land of Plenty," *New Republic*, n.d. 1950, 7–8; "Our Food Surpluses," *The Commonweal*, 1 September 1950, 501–502; Kline, "Cheaper Food—Promise or Political Lure?" 13; and "Bumper Crop," 54–55.

38. For the perspective of Secretary of Agriculture Ezra Taft Benson on the controversy over price supports, see "Government and Prices: The ABC's of What Makes Prices," 15 October 1954, *Vital Speeches of the Day*, 784–787.

39. "Farmers—Everyone's Headache Again," *Business Week*, 18 July 1953, 29; "Farm Controls Here to Stay," *U.S. News & World Report*, 28 August 1953, 37; "No End Is in Sight for Farm Problem," *U.S. News & World Report*, 25 December 1953, 57–59. See also "Farm Plans for the Future," *Time*, 7 December 1953, 92–94; Theodore Schulz, "A Guide to Better Policy for Agriculture," *Consumer Reports*, April 1954, 185–189.

Another debate highlighted in 1950s press stories was the welfare of individual farmers. As in earlier coverage, some articles painted a dire picture while others argued that poverty was relatively isolated among particular farmers' groups and that most farmers were middle income or higher. "Is Worst Over for the Farmer?" *U.S. News & World Report*, 29 October 1954, 55–58; Theodore Schulz, "A Guide to Better Policy for Agriculture," *Consumer Reports*, April 1954, 185–189.

40. *Statistical Abstracts, 1951–1994*, accessed 22 August 2012, www.census.gov/prod/www/abs/statab1951–1994.htm.

41. “High Costs, Low Prices,” *Newsweek*, 22 June 1953, 68; “Why Food Bills Keep Going Up,” *U.S. News & World Report*, 21 August 1953, 32; “Food: Prices up, but—Where Do Dollars Go?” *U.S. News & World Report*, 23 October 1953, 100–102; “Why Food Prices Stay High,” *U.S. News & World Report*, 15 October 1954, 81–82.

42. Angus Wright, *The Death of Ramón Gonzalez: The Modern Agricultural Dilemma*, rev. ed. (Austin: University of Texas Press, 2005), 17. In the 1950s, another category of pesticides was synthesized, carbamates, which (like organochlorines) were less toxic to mammals and (like organophosphates) acted as nerve agents. The first of this group was carbaryl in 1956, which soon became widely used in the United States, especially on lawns and gardens.

43. For example, Display Literature 2, 3, Agricultural Chemicals Division, box 12, Series VI—Division Files, and Hercules bound volumes of advertisements, 1945–1952, box 1, Series 1, Hercules Inc., Othmer Library, Chemical Heritage Foundation.

44. “DDT Increased Potato Crop,” *New York Times*, 5 December 1945, 22; “New Insecticides to Aid Housewives,” *New York Times*, 11 March 1946, 28.

45. “New Paper Contains DDT,” *New York Times*, 12 February 1946, 22.

46. “DDT Sprayed Over Rockford Ill., in Test of Power to Halt Polio,” *New York Times*, 20 August 1945, 21; “Use of Big Guns Urged to Kill Jersey ‘Skeeters,’” *New York Times*, 31 March 1945, 21; “Long Island Beaches Rid of Insects by DDT,” *New York Times*, 25 July 1945, 23; “Entire Town Sprayed with DDT,” *New York Times*, 21 August 1946, 22; “DDT Sent to Texas,” *New York Times*, 20 May 1946, 37.

47. “Chemists Say DDT Could Save 1 to 3 Million Lives Each Year,” *New York Times*, 29 August 1945, 25; Louis Pyenson, “New Weapons Against Insects,” *New York Times*, 12 January 1947, X24. See also “Another Peak Year Seen for Insecticide,” *New York Times*, 25 December 1946, 45; “New Insecticide Is Found,” *New York Times*, 23 February 1947, 12.

48. This observation has been discussed by a number of historians; it was most clearly articulated by Edmund Russell in *War and Nature: Fighting Humans and Insects with Chemicals from World War I to* Silent Spring (Cambridge: Cambridge University Press, 2001).

49. “Warns about Insects,” *New York Times*, 9 February 1946, 27.

50. “How the Battle Is Going,” *Business Week*, 14 July 1951, 64.

51. Cynthia Westcott, “Modern Insecticides and Fungicides Hold Plant Enemies in Check,” *New York Times*, 22 May 1960, X21.

52. See Hercules instructional materials and advertisements, 1945–1956, Files Display Literature 1, 2, 3, Agricultural Chemicals Division, box 12, Series VI—Division Files, and bound volumes of advertisements, 1945–1952, box 1, Hercules Inc., Othmer Library, Chemical Heritage Foundation.

53. Examples include Dow advertisements from 1946 to 1948. See box 7, Advertisements, Dow Collection, Post Street Archives, Othmer Library, Chemical Heritage Foundation.

54. "Mosquitoes versus Thanite," Display Literature 1, and "Man against Insect," Display Literature 2, Agricultural Chemicals Division, box 12, Series VI—Division Files, Hercules Inc., Othmer Library, Chemical Heritage Foundation.

55. Examples include Dow advertisements from 1946–1948. See box 7, Dow Advertisements, Dow Collection, Post Street Archives; Display Literature 1, 2, 3, Agricultural Chemicals Division, box 12, Series VI—Division Files; bound Hercules advertisements, 1945–1952, box 1, Series I—Publications, Hercules Inc., Othmer Library, Chemical Heritage Foundation.

56. Advertisement, May 1947, in *Soap and Sanitary Chemicals*, bound volume advertisements 1947, also advertisements in volumes 1945–1947, box 1, Series I—Publications, Hercules Inc., Othmer Library, Chemical Heritage Foundation.

57. Brooks, "A Legacy Cast in Concrete," 20. For more on this period of suburbanization in the United States, see Kenneth Jackson, *Crabgrass Frontier: The Suburbanization of the United States* (New York: Oxford University Press, 1985); Adam Rome, *The Bulldozer in the Countryside: Suburban Sprawl and the Rise of American Environmentalism* (Cambridge: Cambridge University Press, 2001).

58. Sellers argues that contrary to the common assumption that suburbia and the culture it spawned tried to escape from nature, suburbanites were really trying to embrace and manage nature on their own terms; thus, he draws a direct line from postwar suburbanization to the birth of environmentalism. Christopher C. Sellers, *Crabgrass Crucible: Suburban Nature and the Rise of Environmentalism in Twentieth-Century America* (Chapel Hill: University of North Carolina Press, 2012), 42 (emphasis in original), also 11, 44, 65, 95, 284.

59. Bound volume Hercules advertisements, 1946, Series I—Publications, box 1, Hercules Inc., Othmer Library, Chemical Heritage Foundation.

60. For thoughtful meditations on lawn history and culture, see Paul Robbins, *Lawn People: How Grasses, Weeds, and Chemicals Make Us Who We Are* (Philadelphia, PA: Temple University Press, 2007); Ted Steinberg, *American Green: The Obsessive Quest for the Perfect Lawn* (New York and London: W. W. Norton & Company, 2006); Virginia Scott Jenkins, *The Lawn: A History of an American Obsession* (Washington and London: Smithsonian Institution Press, 1994). Also, for the lawn and an environmental sensibility, see Sellers, *Crabgrass Crucible*, 76–80.

61. Henry Lee, "New Bug Killers for Home and Garden," *Coronet*, April 1955, 174.

62. Neely Turner, "Chemical Weapons," *New York Times*, 30 June 1946, X17. See also Louis Pyenson, "New Insecticides," *New York Times*, 27 January 1946, X11; Louis Pyenson, "Controlling Pests," *New York Times*, 1 September 1946, 51.

63. "Block Those Bugs," *American Home*, 1958, 60, 68–69; "Reminder: Check the Arsenal," *Sunset*, March 1954, 197–198. See also George Runge Jr., "War against Black Vine Beetles," *New York Times*, 12 June 1960, 133; Paul Wooley, "The Peach Tree Borer," *New York Times*, 3 July 1960, X29.

64. Dr. Joseph E. Howland, "Save Your Spruces and Hollyhocks," *Better Homes & Gardens*, June 1947, 117; "Deadly as DDT, Harmless to Man," *Better Homes & Gardens*, April 1947, 4.

65. For example, "How to Use Modern Chemicals to Keep Your Plants Healthy," *House & Garden*, June 1953, 174–175; "New Insecticide with Promise," *Better Homes & Gardens*, March 1951, 31.

66. Dr. Joseph E. Howland, "When DDT Will Do the Job—and What to Use When It Won't," *Better Homes & Gardens*, May 1948, 264–265; Cynthia Wescott, "What's Best in Garden Pesticides?" *House & Garden*, March 1954, 160–163; Dr. Joseph E. Howland, "Chemicals Worth Using in Your 1955 Garden," *House Beautiful*, January 1955, 84; "Block Those Bugs," *American Home*, 1958, 60, 68–69; "H&G's Basic Garden Spray Chart," *House & Garden*, 1956, 109, 218–219; "H&G's 1960 Guide to Plant Protection," *House & Garden*, April 1960, 224–227.

67. Howland, "When DDT Will Do the Job"; "Complete Pesticide Shelf," *Better Homes & Gardens*, July 1955, 137–138; "Basic Pest Control," *The American Home*, May 1957, 148; "Beat the Bugs in the Garden," *The American Home*, August 1958, 18–22; Ralph E. Engel, "Important Chores," *New York Times*, 28 August 1960, X37; "New Warfare on Old Bugs," *Life*, 25 May 1953, 156–158.

68. "Poisons for Plant Pests: The June Gardener," *Consumer Reports*, June 1949, 265–266; "Household Insecticides and Control of Common Pests," *Consumer Reports*, July 1956, 347–351.

69. Lee, "New Bug Killers for Home and Garden," 171–174; Gordon Morrison, "Chemical Aids to Gardening Streamlined," *Chicago Daily Tribune*, 7 April 1957, A9.

70. Dr. Louis Pyenson, "Timing: Secret of Garden Insect Control," *House & Garden*, May 1955, 220–221. See also Art Kozelka, "Patience with Spade, Gardeners," *Chicago Daily Tribune*, 9 February 1958, SB.

71. "Beat the Bugs in the Garden," 18–19; "Give Your Plants Health Insurance," *House & Garden*, 1951, 100. See also "Basic Pest Control," *The American Home*, May 1957, 148; Robert Brewster, "Dormant Spray Time," *New York Times*, 13 March 1960, X23; Joan Lee Faust, "Around the Garden," *New York Times*, 24 April 1960, G10.

72. Victor Ries, "Planned Ahead," *New York Times*, 24 May 1959, X19. See also Cynthia Westcott, "Modern Insecticides and Fungicides Hold Plant Enemies in Check," *New York Times*, 22 May 1960, X21.

73. Advertisement in *Better Homes & Gardens*, June 1947, 177.

74. Advertisement in *House & Garden*, May 1955, 220.

75. Advertisement in *The American Home*, May 1957, 148.

76. Advertisements in *House & Garden*, 1956, 109, 218; *House & Garden*, June 1953, 175.

77. Wescott, "What's Best in Garden Pesticides?" 160–161; "Safety Tips for Using Pesticides," *The American Home*, June 1955, 124.

78. "How to Use Modern Chemicals to Keep your Plants Healthy," *House & Garden*, June 1953, 174–175; Wescott, "What's Best in Garden Pesticides," 160–161.

79. "Insecticide Vaporizers—They Should Not Be Used in Homes," *Consumers' Research Bulletin*, March 1953, 29.

80. "Dangerous Friends," *The American Home*, 1956, 55, 35.

81. "More Potent Insect Killers Ready for Market," *Science News Letter*, 4 February 1950, 78.

82. "DDT, Too Much Spraying, Too Little Government Action," *Consumer Reports*, June 1949, 275–277.

83. "Poisons for Plant Pests: The June Gardener."

84. "How the Battle Is Going," 64; "Insecticides: Production Zooms, but the Bugs Are Eating It Up," *Business Week*, 14 February 1953, 54–56.

85. "Bugaboo," *Business Week*, 8 April 1950, 25; "$2 Billion Meal for Bugs," *Life*, 7 August 1950, 48–50.

86. "$2 Billion Meal for Bugs"; "Friend or Foe of the Gardener?" *House & Garden*, August 1949, 60.

87. "Bugaboo," 25.

88. Bound volumes of Hercules advertisements, 1945–1952, box 1, Series I—Publications, Hercules Inc., Othmer Library, Chemical Heritage Foundation.

89. Ryan, "Farmers Reaping Bumper Crop of Chemicals," F1.

Chapter 2. Trouble in Paradise: The USDA and the Rise of Critical Voices

1. Letter from Robert McCaskey to Sen. H. M. Kilgore, 16 August 1945, box 1093, RG 16, US Department of Agriculture (USDA), National Archives II (hereafter NARA). Other examples of letters from the same location include Allen Postel to Sen. Wayland Brooks, 10 July 1945; John Bubb to Rep. John Anderson, 6 July 1945; Dillard Munford to Sen. Richard Russell, 26 June 1945.

2. Examples of responses are Asst. Sec. Charles Brannan to Sen. H. M. Kilgore, 1 September 1945; Clinton Anderson to Sen. Wayland Brooks, 30 July 1945; and Clinton Anderson to Rep. John Anderson, 30 July 1945, box 1093, RG 16, USDA, NARA.

3. P. N. Annaud address summarized in B. T. Shaw, acting research administrator, to secretary of agriculture, 15 May 1947, box 1459, RG 16, USDA, NARA.

4. E. Tomlinson, Special Services, *Newsweek*, to undersecretary of agriculture, 19 July 1946, box 1093, RG 16, USDA, NARA (emphasis in original).

5. Clinton Anderson to Robert Wagner, 11 December 1946, box 1093, RG 16, USDA. See also Clinton Anderson to Sen. Richard Russell, 16 July 1945.

6. "More Light on DDT," *New York Times*, 16 September 1945, X9.

7. M. C. James, acting director FWS, to Sec. Harold Ickes, 14 September 1945, box 3370, RG 48, Department of the Interior (Interior), NARA.

8. For example, Brannan to Sen. Edward Martin, 21 August 1947, box 1459; P. N. Annaud, chief of Bureau of Entomology and Plant Quarantine, to Frances Coffin, 9 April 1948, box 1592; Sen. James Kem to Sec. Charles Brannan, 13 July 1949, box 1725; Acting Sec. A. J. Lowland to Sen. James Kem, 28 July 1949, box 1725, RG 16, USDA, NARA.

9. Oscar Chapman to Charles Brannan, 14 August 1950, box 3370, RG 48, Interior, NARA.

10. P. N. Annaud, chief of Bureau of Entomology and Plant Quarantine, to Frances Coffin, 9 April 1948, box 1592, RG 16, USDA, NARA.

11. "DDT and the Balance of Nature," USDA, Agriculture Research Administration, 2 January 1946, with newspaper clipping attached, box 1459, RG 16, USDA, NARA. The secretary was alarmed enough about the news stories on the balance of nature that he made inquiries within the department; Research Admin. W. V. Lambert was instructed in May 1947: "Secretary wants to know how [DDT] destroys the balance in our animal life and to give him a brief resume of the situation." Note L. Diamond to Dr. Lambert, 8 May 1947, with newspaper clipping, and Shaw to secretary of agriculture, 15 May 1947, box 1459, RG 16, USDA, NARA.

12. He did, though, note that farmers had been told to cease such practices. A. J. Lowland to Sen. Irving Ives, 25 April 1949, and A. J. Lowland to Sen. Irving Ives, 23 May 1949, box 1725, RG 16, USDA, NARA.

13. Sec.-Treas. V. G. Milum, National Federation of State Beekeepers Associations, to secretary of agriculture, 26 March 1945, and Carol Hamilton, assistant to the secretary to Dr. Milum, 30 April 1945, box 1093, RG 16, USDA, NARA; Christopher Bosso, *Pesticides and Politics: The Life Cycle of a Public Issue* (Pittsburgh, PA: University of Pittsburgh Press, 1987), 31.

14. Bureau of Entomology and Plant Quarantine to Rep. Charles Cannon, 26 August 1948, box 1592; and Undersec. A. J. Lowland to Sen. Scott Lucas, 23 January 1950, box 1860, RG 16, USDA, NARA; see also Asst. Sec. Charles Brannan to Sen. Edward Martin, 21 August 1947, RG 16, USDA, NARA.

15. Acting Sec. True Morse to Sen. Thomas Kuchel, 9 September 1954, box 2428, RG 16, USDA, NARA; see also Undersec. C. J. McCormick to Acting Admin. John Thurston, Food Safety Administration (FSA), 10 April 1951, box 1990; Asst. Sec. J. Earl Coke to Sen. Edwin Johnson, 21 June 1954, box 2428; Asst. Sec. E. L. Peterson to Rep. Dewitt Hyde, 24 January 1955, box 2587; and Asst. Sec. Earl Butz to Sen. Wayne Morse, 17 December 1956, box 2776, RG 16, USDA, NARA.

16. B. T. Hutchinson to Rep. Frank Smith, 22 October 1952, box 2083, RG 16, USDA, NARA; see also Undersec. True Morse to Rep. Douglas Stringfellow, 3 March 1953, box 2246, RG 16, USDA, NARA.

17. Acting Sec. True Morse to Sen. Thomas Kuchel, 9 September 1954, box 2428, RG 16, USDA, NARA.

18. Three years later, an editorial in the same publication advised that manufacturers should be honest about all risks and have clear instructions to prevent any problems. The effect of such honesty and even mildly critical self-observations, wrote one historian, allowed companies such as DuPont to portray themselves as the farmer's friend. David D. Vail, "Guardians of Abundance: Aerial Application, Agricultural Chemicals, and Toxicity in the Postwar Prairie West" (PhD diss., Department of History, Kansas State University, 2012), 144–145, 148.

19. For example, pamphlets in Display Literature 2, Agricultural Chemicals Division, box 12, Series VI—Division Files, Hercules Inc., Othmer Library, Chemical Heritage Foundation.

20. For example, B. T. Hutchinson to Sen. Arthur Watkins, 11 September 1952, box 2083; True Morse to Sen. Thomas Kuchel, 9 September 1954, box 2428; Asst. Sec. E. L. Peterson to Rep. Paul Kilday, 20 October 1955, box 2587; and E. L. Peterson to Rep. Dewitt Hyde, 24 January 1955, box 2587, RG 16, USDA, NARA.

21. For example, Asst. Sec. J. Earl Coke to Sen. Lyndon Johnson, 5 August 1954, box 2428, and Asst. Sec. E. L. Peterson to Sen. Richard Neuberger, 24 February 1955, box 2587, RG 16, USDA, NARA.

22. True Morse to Sen. Thomas Kuchel, 9 September 1954, box 2428, RG 16, USDA, NARA.

23. True Morse to Rep. William Hill, chairman, Select Committee on Small Business, 8 June 1953; see also Asst. Sec. J. Earle Coke to Sen. William Langer, 15 September 1954, box 2246, RG 16, USDA, NARA.

24. Undersec. C. J. McCormick to Rep. N. M. Mason, 2 November 1951, box 1990, RG 16, USDA, NARA.

25. For example, from RG 16, USDA, NARA: Undersec. C. J. McCormick to Rep. N. M. Mason, 2 November 1951, box 1990; Acting Admin. John Thurston, FSA, to secretary of agriculture, 22 March 1951, box 1990; True Morse to Rep. William Hill, chairman, Select Committee on Small Business, 8 June 1953, box 2246; Asst. Sec. J. Earle Coke to Rep. Cecil R. King, 29 April 1954, box 2428. The FSA administrator, interestingly, was concerned in 1951 when there was news of a possible shortage of some pesticides because his agency was obligated to seize as "adulterated" any food that was contaminated with insects or rodent filth. Thurston to secretary of agriculture.

26. The evolution of regulations is discussed in a variety of sources, including Bosso, *Pesticides and Politics*.

27. John Wargo, *Our Children's Toxic Legacy: How Science and Law Fail to Protect Us from Pesticides* (New Haven, CT: Yale University Press, 1996), 75–76; Bosso, *Pesticides and Politics*, 73–77; Thomas Dunlap, *DDT: Scientists, Citizens, and Public Policy* (Princeton, NJ: Princeton University Press, 1981), 71–74.

28. Asst. Sec. E. L. Peterson to Rep. Dewitt Hyde, 24 January 1955, box 2587, and Sec. M. Bl. Folsom, HEW, to Sen. Wayne Morse, 5 December 1956, box 2776, RG 16, USDA, NARA; Wargo, *Our Children's Toxic Legacy*, 74–76; Dunlap, *DDT*, 71–74; Bosso, *Pesticides and Politics*, 73–77.

29. Dean William Myers, New York State College of Agriculture, Cornell University, to Undersec. True Morse, 26 May 1955; True Morse to William Myers, 2 August 1955; Director Crops Regulatory Programs Avery Hoyt to Deputy Admin. M. R. Clarkson, Agricultural Research Service, 30 September 1955; B. T. Shaw, administrator to Asst. Sec. E. L. Peterson, 6 October 1955, box 2587, RG 16, USDA, NARA.

30. True Morse to Rep. Douglas Stringfellow, 3 March 1953, box 2246, RG 16, USDA, NARA.

31. J. Earl Coke to Rep. Cecil R. King, 29 April 1954, box 2428, RG 16, USDA, NARA.

32. J. Earl Coke to Sen. Edwin Johnson, 21 June 1954, and John Kollminzer to Sen. Edwin Johnson, 26 May 1954, box 2428, RG 16, USDA, NARA.

33. "Doctors to Study DDT as Food Poison," *New York Times*, 3 April 1949, 53.

34. "Doctors Warn against Drugs in Insecticides," *Chicago Daily Tribune*, 9 September 1950, B5.

35. "Public Warned on DDT," *New York Times*, 10 March 1951, 11.

36. James Wilson, "Are Pesticides Making Your Food Unsafe?" *Hygia*, January 1949, 44–45.

37. Harry Fox, "Insecticide Report," *New York Times*, 4 September 1949, 59.

38. David Kinkela, *DDT and the American Century: Global Health, Environmental Politics, and the Pesticide That Changed the World* (Chapel Hill: University of North Carolina Press, 2011), 31.

39. For example, articles in the *New York Times*: "They Still Buzz In," 10 August 1945, 10; "Mosquitos Survive Raids," 22 August 1945, 25; "Report on DDT Results," 30 September 1945, 4; "Fish Killed by DDT in Mosquito Tests," 9 August 1945, 23; "Care Urged in DDT Use," 20 September 1945, 23; "Calls DDT Not Harmful to Bees," 27 October 1945, 19.

40. "Save Your Spruces and Hollyhocks," *Better Homes & Gardens*, June 1947, 177.

41. Albert Worrell, "Pests, Pesticides and People," *American Forests* 66 (July 1960): 39–81.

42. Two of the groups that he singled out were the National Wildlife Federation, which had strongly opposed pesticides, especially aerial spraying, and the National Audubon Society. He wrote that the National Audubon Society had been one of the

leaders in the campaign against aerial spraying and had called for an immediate end to all large-scale spraying programs. Ibid., 71.

43. William Stevens Jr., "Bad Year for Bugs," *Saturday Evening Post*, 23 June 1956, 30.

44. For example, see "Poisons in Your Home," *Changing Times*, July 1957, 17.

45. Ralph Martin, "How Much Poison Are We Eating?" *Harper's Magazine*, April 1955, 63.

46. Jack Denton Scott, "Those 'New Foods' Can KILL You," *American Mercury*, June 1956, 5–10.

47. Ibid.

48. Such a measure was ineffective because it was still used on cotton, whose fields were rotated with peanuts; thus, it continued to contaminate peanuts.

49. William Longgood, "Pesticides Poison Us," *American Mercury*, July 1958, 33–54.

50. Harold Titus, "Conservation: Pesticides a Menace?" *Field & Stream*, August 1957, 32.

51. Harold Titus, "Conservation: Pesticides: Doom in Small Doses," *Field & Stream*, June 1959, 52.

52. Robert J. Spear, *The Great Gypsy Moth War: The History of the First Campaign in Massachusetts to Eradicate the Gypsy Moth, 1890–1901* (Amherst: University of Massachusetts Press, 2005), 2–3, 245, 256–257. See also, Bosso, *Pesticides and Politics*, 82–95; Dunlap, *DDT*, 85–89; Edmund Russell, *War and Nature: Fighting Humans and Insects with Chemicals from World War I to* Silent Spring (Cambridge: Cambridge University Press, 2001), 214–215.

53. Historians have discussed this reaction to the gypsy moth campaign in many places. For an overview, see Christopher C. Sellers, *Crabgrass Crucible: Suburban Nature and the Rise of Environmentalism in Twentieth-Century America* (Chapel Hill: University of North Carolina Press, 2012), 126–136.

54. CAMP bulletin, 2 October 1957, folder 6/1, box 2940, RG 16, USDA, NARA.

55. "Scientists Argue Harm of L.I. Spray," *New York Times*, 7 July 1957, 33; Dr. Robert C. Murphy, "The Hick Mind in Action?" *American Forests*, February 1958, 4.

56. Robert Cushman Murphy, "DDT Dousing to Date," CAMP bulletin, 28 June 1957, folder 6/1, box 2940, RG 16, USDA, NARA.

57. Paper from E. E. Pfeiffer on the gypsy moth program; E. E. Pfeiffer to Rep. Katharine St. George, 10 May 1957; and E. L. Peterson to Rep. Katharine St. George, 24 May 1957, folder 1/1–5/30/57, box 2940, RG 16, USDA, NARA.

58. A ringing dissent by Justice William O. Douglas called on the court to hear the case and weigh in on the legality of the government spraying poisons. Spear, *The Great Gypsy Moth War*, 257; "DDT Fight Is Lost in Supreme Court," *New York Times*, 29 March 1960, 39.

59. John Oakes, "Conservation: Nature's Balance," *New York Times*, 2 June 1957, 147.

60. See for example, William Blair, "New Drive Aimed at Gypsy Moth," *New York Times*, 29 March 1959, 38.

61. Arthur Grahame, "Will Spraying Boomerang?" *Outdoor Life*, June 1958, 20–21. See also Arthur Grahame, "Big Spray Trouble," *Outdoor Life*, March 1958, 24–25.

62. "A Poisonous Subject, an Editorial," *Nature Magazine*, April 1958, 201.

63. David Cort, "The Pesticide That Came to Dinner," *Nation*, 12 April 1958, 316–319.

64. Spraying for the ant continued into the 1990s, although the range of the insect increased throughout that period. Dr. John George, *The Program to Eradicate the Imported Fire Ant, Preliminary Observations: A Report to the Conservation Foundations and the New York Zoological Society* (New York: The Conservation Foundation, 1958); Pete Daniel, *Lost Revolutions: The South in the 1950s* (Chapel Hill and London: University of North Carolina Press for Smithsonian National Museum of American History, 2000), 78–85; Bosso, *Pesticides and Politics*, 86–90.

65. Asst. Sec. Ross Leffler to Ezra Taft Benson, 2 December 1957, box 3370, RG 48, Interior, NARA.

66. Asst. Sec. Ross Leffler to Rep. John Dingell, 19 August 1959. In a letter from Leffler to Sec. Benson, he complained that the Agricultural Research Service was denying the data and reports from the Department of the Interior showing the loss to wildlife caused by the fire ant program. Leffler concluded, "I must formally protest against these remarks." Leffler to Benson, 27 May 1960, folder Control Part 1, 1/9/59–4/27/60, box 560, RG 48, Interior, NARA.

67. Sec. of interior to Sen. Paul Douglas, 9 March 1961, folder, Control Part 2, box 560, RG 48, Interior, NARA.

68. Clarence Cottam to Exec Asst. to the Sec. Miller Shurtleff, USDA, 15 February 1960, folder 6/29, box 3455, RG 16, USDA, NARA; Russell, *War and Nature*, 214–216; Daniel, *Lost Revolutions*, 81–83.

69. E. L. Peterson to Rep. Katharine St. George, 29 May 1957; E. L. Peterson to Sen. Jacob Javitz, 28 May 1957; Averell Harriman to Sec. Benson, 23 May 1957; E. L. Peterson to Gov. Harriman, 24 May 1957; E. L. Peterson to Rep. Katharine St. George, 24 May 1957; and E. L. Peterson to Edwin Dooley, 1 July 1957, folder 1/1–5/30/57, box 2940, RG 16, USDA, NARA.

70. True Morse to Sen. Alexander Wiley, 5 August 1957, folder 6/1, box 2940, RG 16, USDA, NARA. For more on the Dutch elm campaign, see Dunlap, *DDT*, 79–84.

71. Examples include E. L. Peterson to George Hendrix, Myrtle Beach Chamber of Commerce, 17 April 1958; E. L. Peterson to Sen. Olin Johnston, 15 April 1958; E. L. Peterson to Sen. Jacob Javits, 12 March 1958; and E. L. Peterson to Sen. Hubert Humphrey, 6 March 1958, folder 1/1–4/30, box 3127, RG 16, USDA, NARA.

72. E. L. Peterson to Sen. Jacob Javits, 5 March 1958, folder 1/1–4/30, box 3127, RG 16, USDA, NARA.

73. Examples include True Morse to Rep. Armistead Selden Jr., 1 April 1959; E. L. Peterson to Sen. John Carroll, 3 April 1959; E. L. Peterson to Rep. Clement Zablocki, 17 June 1959; E. L. Peterson to Rep. Frank Karsten, 19 June 1959; True Morse to Sen. Lyndon Johnson, 24 July 1959; True Morse to Sen. Joseph Clark, 15 July 1959; and True Morse to Rep. Tom Murray, 24 July 1959, folder 1/9–6/19, box 3306, RG 16, USDA, NARA.

74. Historian Kendra Smith-Howard wrote that not only was milk "culturally important to American life," but because it was seen "as a staple for children [it] had been considered sacrosanct. Any degree of taint to milk's purity raised alarm." Kendra Smith-Howard, "Perfecting Nature's Food: A Cultural and Environmental History of Milk in the United States, 1900–1975" (PhD diss., Department of History, University of Wisconsin–Madison, 2007), 3, 272.

75. "Antibiotics, Pesticides in Milk Eyed by Federal Agency," *Business Week*, 1 October 1955, 146.

76. Smith-Howard, "Perfecting Nature's Food," 264; "U.S. Puts Curb on Pesticides for Cattle; Rules Milk Top Food in Need for Purity," *New York Times*, 18 January 1958, 17.

77. Murray Illson, "Penicillin Trace Is Found in Milk," *New York Times*, 20 February 1959, 18.

78. Richard Orr, "Farmers Told to Safeguard Chemical Use," *Chicago Daily Tribune*, 15 December 1959, 16; "U.S. Agents Check Milk for Residue," *New York Times*, 3 December 1959, 23.

79. Dunlap, *DDT*, 107–108; Bosso, *Pesticides and Politics*, 96–99.

80. Peter Bart, "Pesticide Scare Worries Makers," *New York Times*, 22 November 1959, F1; William Blair, "Pesticides Both Boon and Threat," *New York Times*, 22 November 1959, E8.

81. "Food Additive Risk Justified, Chemist Says," *Chicago Daily Tribune*, 9 December 1960, B4.

82. Quoted in Karl Brooks, "A Legacy Cast in Concrete: The Truman Presidency's Transformation of America's Natural Environment, 1945–1953" (unpublished paper presented at A Conference on the Historical Significance of the Truman Presidency, Harry S. Truman Presidential Library, July 2003), 12.

83. For example, just after the Seventy-Ninth Congress passed new water project authorizations in 1946, the executive director of the Izaak Walton League, Kenneth Reid, criticized the US Army Corps of Engineers and US Bureau of Reclamation, charging that environmental destruction would be great, including the end of salmon runs on the Pacific coast. The FWS office in Portland, Oregon, and the Oregon Fish

Commission agreed that new dams on Northwestern rivers would destroy the salmon fishery on the Columbia River. Brooks, "A Legacy Cast in Concrete," 15.

84. "To Discuss DDT Perils," *New York Times*, 22 October 1945, 19; "DDT Spray Called Injurious to Birds," *New York Times*, 23 October 1945, 10.

85. Bosso, *Pesticides and Politics*, 34.

86. "Are the New Insecticides Dangerous to Other Wildlife?" *Audubon*, March–April 1949, 114–115.

87. Springer never ended up answering that question, but he did describe both "the enormous good wrought by insecticides" and the widespread damage to wildlife that sometimes occurred. Paul Springer, "Insecticides, Boon or Bane?" *Audubon*, May–June 1956, 128–130.

88. "Insecticide Study for Perils Urged," *New York Times*, 12 November 1957, 39.

89. "Insecticides Are Threat to Humans and Wildlife," *Audubon*, March–April 1958, 75; Audubon press release, "Insecticides Are a Threat to Humans and Wildlife," (n.d.), folder 1/1–4/30, box 3127, RG 16, USDA, NARA.

90. Christopher Bosso wrote that the government's campaign against the moth "transformed the organizational goals and priorities" of the organization. Bosso, *Pesticides and Politics*, 83, 95.

91. "The Cure Worse Than the Disease," *Audubon*, July–August 1958, 151.

92. "The Greatest Killing Program of All?" *Audubon*, November 1958, 254–256.

93. "Pesticides Held Wildlife Hazard," *New York Times*, 11 November 1958, 31. Garden clubs across the United States were early critics of chemical pesticides; see, for example, Asst. Sec. Leffler to Dorothy Zoulek, Organic Farm and Garden Club, Orchard Lake, MI, 12 February 1960, folder Control Part 1, 1/9/59–4/27/60, box 560, RG 48, Interior, NARA.

94. Harold Peters, "Late News from the Fire Ant Front," *Audubon*, March–April 1960, 54–56.

95. John Devlin, "U.S. Is Losing Its Bald Eagles; Sterility Suspected, DDT Cited," *New York Times*, 13 September 1958, 21.

96. "A Protest against Spraying," *Audubon*, July–August 1959, 153.

97. George Wallace, "Another Year of Robin Losses on a University Campus," *Audubon*, March–April 1960, 66–68; John Terres, "Conservation: The Menace of DDT," *New York Times*, 1 March 1959, X29.

98. Carl Buchheister, "Our Work on the Pesticide Problem," *Audubon*, March–April 1960, 65; "Needed: A 'Coordination Act for Pesticides,'" *Audubon*, May–June 1960, 126.

99. Robert L. Rudd, "The Irresponsible Poisoners," *Nation*, 30 May 1959, 496–497; Robert L. Rudd, "Pesticides: The *Real* Peril," *Nation*, 28 November 1959, 399–401.

100. Bosso, *Pesticides and Politics*, 103; "Warn Poisons Used by Man Peril Waters," *Chicago Daily Tribune*, 14 December 1960, 16.

101. Bosso, *Pesticides and Politics*, 103.

102. Robert Strother, "Backfire in the War against Insects," *Reader's Digest*, June 1959, 64–69.

103. "War on Mosquito Begun in Queens," *New York Times*, 16 April 1959, 35; "Essex County Is Hit by Mosquito Plague," *New York Times*, 5 September 1959, 11; "Greenwich Plans War on Mosquito," *New York Times*, 24 January 1960, 77.

104. John Devlin, "Suburbs Invaded by Caterpillars," *New York Times*, 15 May 1960, 120.

105. Robert Plumb, "Pesticide Danger in Foods Doubted," *New York Times*, 2 November 1960, 80.

106. Bosso, *Pesticides and Politics*, 80.

107. William LaTourette, "DDT to 2,4-D: The Outlook Is Promising for the Makers of Pesticides," *Barron's National Business and Financial Weekly*, 23 February 1959, 11.

108. Don Paarlberg, special assistant to the president, Memo for General Persons, 10 October 1959, folder 8/5, box 3306, RG 16, USDA, NARA.

Chapter 3. Breakup? The Cultural Impact of Rachel Carson's *Silent Spring*

1. Linda Lear, *Rachel Carson: Witness for Nature* (New York: Henry Holt and Company, 1997), 454; H. Patricia Hynes, *The Recurring* Silent Spring (New York: Pergamon Press, 1989), 1–2. Such comparisons were also made in the press. For example, see "CBS Reports: The *Silent Spring* of Rachel Carson," broadcast 3 April 1963, folder 1330, box 75, Series I, Rachel Carson Papers YCAL 46, Beinecke Library, Yale University (Carson Papers). See also Elmer Roessner, "Rachel Carson's New Book Already Affecting Business," *News*, Patterson, NJ, 3 October 1962, folder 1147, box 64, and Erwin Knoll, "*Silent Spring* Spurs Proposals for Chemical Curbs," *Advance*, Staten Island, NY, 12 April 1963, folder 1152, box 65, Series I, Carson Papers.

2. Along with Lear, *Rachel Carson*, and Hynes, *The Recurring* Silent Spring, see Mark Hamilton Lytle, *The Gentle Subversive: Rachel Carson,* Silent Spring, *and the Rise of the Environmental Movement* (New York: Oxford University Press, 2007); Craig Waddell, ed., *And No Birds Sing: Rhetorical Analyses of Rachel Carson's* Silent Spring (Carbondale and Edwardsville: Southern Illinois University Press, 2000); Gary Kroll, "The 'Silent Springs' of Rachel Carson: Mass Media and the Origins of Modern Environmentalism," *Public Understanding of Science* 10 (2001): 403–420; Priscilla Coit Murphy, *What a Book Can Do: The Publication and Reception of* Silent Spring (Amherst: University of Massachusetts Press, 2005); Peter McCord, "Divergences on the Left: The Environmentalisms of Rachel Carson and Murray Bookchin," *Left History* 13, no. 1 (Spring/Summer 2008): 14–34; Paul Brooks, *The House of Life: Rachel Carson at*

Work (Boston: Houghton Mifflin Company, 1972); Mary McCay, *Rachel Carson* (New York: Twayne Publishers, 1993); Carol Gartner, *Rachel Carson* (New York: Frederick Unger Publishing Co., 1983); Michael B. Smith, "'Silence, Miss Carson!' Science, Gender, and the Reception of *Silent Spring,*" *Feminist Studies* 27, no. 3 (Fall 2001): 733–752; Maril Hazlett, "Voices from the *Spring: Silent Spring* and the Ecological Turn in American Health," in *Seeing Nature Through Gender*, ed. Virginia Scharff (Lawrence: University Press of Kansas, 2003).

3. Craig Waddell, "The Reception of *Silent Spring,*" in Waddell, ed., *And No Birds Sing*, 8.

4. Carson's call to better understand the balance of nature builds on the work of others such as Aldo Leopold, who earlier had asked his readers to view "land as a community to which we belong" rather than as "a commodity belonging to us." Aldo Leopold, *A Sand County Almanac, with Essays on Conservation from Round River* (New York: Ballantine Books, 1949, 1966), xviii–xix. Historian Bron Taylor argued that Carson's work was also an expression of a spiritual relationship with nature, or a "dark green religion." Bron Taylor, *Dark Green Religion: Nature, Spirituality, and the Planetary Future* (Berkeley: University of California Press, 2010), 149–150. On Carson's focus on the beauty of nature, see Vera Norwood, "How to Value a Flower: Locating Beauty in Toxic Landscapes," in *Rachel Carson: Legacy and Challenge*, ed. Lisa Sideris and Kathleen Dean Moore (Albany: State University of New York Press, 2008), 251.

5. See for example, Samuel P. Hays, *A History of Environmental Politics since 1945* (Pittsburgh, PA: University of Pittsburgh Press, 2000); Robert van den Bosch, *The Pesticide Conspiracy* (Garden City, NY: Doubleday & Company, 1978); John Perkins, *Insects, Experts, and the Insecticide Crisis: The Quest for New Pest Management Strategies* (New York: Plenum Press, 1982); Thomas Dunlap, *DDT: Scientists, Citizens, and Public Policy* (Princeton, NJ: Princeton University Press, 1981).

6. Waddell, "The Reception of *Silent Spring*"; Kroll, "The 'Silent Springs' of Rachel Carson"; Murphy, *What a Book Can Do.*

7. Memoranda from Marie Rodell, 17 August 1962 and 27 September 1962, folder 1075, List of Newspaper and Magazine Reviews 1962, box 61, Series I, Carson Papers.

8. Folders of best-seller lists, 1283–1287, boxes 72 and 73, Series I, Carson Papers.

9. Hynes, *The Recurring* Silent Spring, 2.

10. Brooks Atkinson, "Rachel Carson's Articles on the Danger of Chemical Sprays Prove Effective," *New York Times*, 11 September 1962, folder 1076; Miles Smith, "Strong Indictment," *News-Sun*, Waukegan, IL, 17 November 1962, folder 1077; Irston Barnes, "No Repeal for Law of Gravity," *Post and Times Herald*, 30 September 1962, folder 1078; and Katherine Cushman, "How War on Insects Endangers Human Life," *Detroit News*, 23 September 1962, folder 1080, box 61, Series I, Carson Papers.

11. Atkinson, "Rachel Carson's Articles"; Cushman, "How War on Insects Endangers Human Life."

12. Roy Attaway, "An Unpleasant Thought," *News-Courier*, Charleston, SC, 28 October 1962, folder 1076, Series I, Carson Papers.

13. Paul Brooks, *Speaking for Nature* (San Francisco: Sierra Club Books, 1980), 284, 285.

14. C. Roy Boutard, "A World Where No Birds Sing," *Berkshire Eagle*, Pittsfield, MA, 29 September 62, folder 1078, box 61; Whitney Bolton, "New York Today," *Reporter*, Washington, PA, 28 November 1962, folder 1078, box 61; and Joseph Ator, "Scientist Disputes Pesticide Danger: Blames Furor on Chemical Users' Neglect of Instructions," *Daily Tribune*, Chicago, IL, 20 December 1962, folder 1115, box 63, Series I, Carson Papers.

15. I. L. Baldwin, "Chemicals and Pests," *Science*, 28 September 1962, folder 1078; and William B. Bean, MD, "The Noise of *Silent Spring*," *Archives of Internal Medicine*, September 1963, folder 1079, box 61, Series I, Carson Papers.

16. See letters in folder 1255, Responses (Letters to the Editor), box 71, Series I, Carson Papers.

17. Leland DuVall, "Biological Bug War Comes into Its Own," *Gazette*, Little Rock, AR, 10 April 1963, folder 1129, box 64, Series I, Carson Papers.

18. Barnes, "No Repeal for Law of Gravity."

19. Quoted in Rachel Carson (RC) to Dorothy Freeman (DF), 12 June 1958, in Martha Freeman, ed., *Always Rachel: The Letters of Rachel Carson and Dorothy Freeman, 1952–1964* (Boston: Beacon Press, 1995), 257.

20. Charles Callison, asst. to the president, National Audubon Society, to RC, 14 March 1963, folder 1493, National Audubon Society 1962–1963, box 85, Series I, Carson Papers.

21. Linda Lear, "Afterword: Searching for Rachel Carson," in Waddell, ed., *And No Birds Sing*, 205–218.

22. Lear, *Rachel Carson*, 400.

23. Full-page advertisement, back section of *New York Times*, late November 1962, folder 1324, Publicity, box 75, Series I, Carson Papers.

24. John Barkham, "Among Books and Authors," *Saturday Review*, 29 September 1962, folder 1078, box 61, Series I, Carson Papers.

25. Linda Lear, ed., *Lost Woods: The Discovered Writings of Rachel Carson* (Boston: Beacon Press, 1998), 213.

26. McCord, "Divergences on the Left," 19.

27. Carson's background is taken from Lear, *Rachel Carson*; Brooks, *The House of Life*; McCay, *Rachel Carson*; Gartner, *Rachel Carson.*

28. Lear, *Rachel Carson*, 206.

29. See Brooks, *The House of Life*, 230–231; Lear, *Rachel Carson*, 118–120; Gartner, *Rachel Carson*, 19.

30. Joshua Blu Buhs, *The Fire Ant Wars: Nature, Science, and Public Policy in Twentieth-Century America* (Chicago: University of Chicago Press, 2004), 114.

31. David Wade Chambers, *Worm in the Bud: Case Study of the Pesticide Controversy* (Victoria, Australia: Deakin University, 1984), 42.

32. Lear, *Rachel Carson*, 313; McCay, *Rachel Carson*, 65.

33. "Pesticides: Attack and Counterattack," *Consumer Reports*, January 1963, folder 1305, box 74, Series I, Carson Papers.

34. See, for example, Smith, "'Silence, Miss Carson!'" See also Hynes, *The Recurring* Silent Spring; Lear, "Afterword"; and Hazlett, "Voices from the *Spring*."

35. Smith, "'Silence, Miss Carson!'" 739–740.

36. Cyrene Dear, "Author Questions Pesticide Programs," *Advance*, Elizabeth City, NC, 18 February 1963, folder 1129, box 64, Series I, Carson Papers. Other examples are "Critic of Pesticides: Rachel Louise Carson," *New York Times*, 5 June 1963, folder 1291, box 73; and Frances Lewine, "Rachel Carson, 'No Crusader,' *Observer*, Charlotte, NC, 6 June 1963, folder 1290, box 73, Series I, Carson Papers.

37. "Rachel Carson's Book on Use of Killer Chemicals as Pesticides Stirs Argument," *Gazette and Daily*, York, PA, 30 March 1963, folder 1116, box 63, Series I, Carson Papers.

38. Boutard, "A World Where No Birds Sing."

39. RC to DF, 13 June 1962, in Freeman, ed., *Always Rachel*, 407.

40. Atkinson, "Rachel Carson's Articles."

41. Barkham, "Among Books and Authors"; Boutard, "A World Where No Birds Sing"; Robert Cowen, "Miss Carson's 'Silent Spring'—What the Battle Is About," *Christian Science Monitor*, 27 September 1962, folder 1080, box 61, Series I, Carson Papers.

42. See sample letters in folder 1251, Responses (Letters to Editors), box 71, Series I, Carson Papers.

43. For example, Joseph Alsop, "After Rachel Carson," *New York Herald Tribune*, May 1963, folder 1113, box 63; Atkinson, "Rachel Carson's Articles"; Barkham, "Among Books and Authors"; Hank Andrews, "Outdoors: Insecticide Use Threatens to Close Hunting Areas," *Press and News*, Cleveland, OH, 24 May 1963, folder 1114, box 63, Series I, Carson Papers.

44. Uncle Dudley, "The Poison Sprays," *Evening Globe*, Boston, MA, 4 April 1963, folder 1129, box 64, Series I, Carson Papers.

45. "Rachel Carson's Book on Use of Killer Chemicals as Pesticides Stirs Argument."

46. Rachel Carson, *Silent Spring* (New York: Houghton Mifflin Harcourt, 1962), 22.

47. Atkinson, "Rachel Carson's Articles."

48. William O. Dobler, "Spring Storm in Fall," *Star*, Lincoln, NE, 1 October 1962, folder 1129, box 64, Series I, Carson Papers.

49. Press Release Remarks by Secretary of the Interior Stewart L. Udall at

Dedication of the Department's Wildlife Research Laboratory, Patuxent Wildlife Research Center, Patuxent, MD, 25 April 1963, folder 1516, box 86, Series I, Carson Papers.

50. "Chemical Weed Killers Insure against Starvation," *Tribune*, South Bend, IN, 28 August 1963, folder 1116, box 63, Series I, Carson Papers.

51. Ovid Martin, "Expert Gives Assurance on Test of Pesticides," *Union-Bulletin*, Walla Walla, WA, 4 August 1963, folder 1116, box 63, Series I, Carson Papers.

52. "Silent Spring—Turbulent Fall," *Times*, Shreveport, LA, 26 September 1962, folder 1147, Box 64, Series I, Carson Papers.

53. For example, see Watson Davie, "Be Thankful for Chemicals," *World Telegram & Sun*, New York, 17 November 1962, folder 1129, box 64, Series I, Carson Papers.

54. Linda Nash, *Inescapable Ecologies: A History of Environment, Disease, and Knowledge* (Berkeley: University of California Press, 2006), 158–159.

55. See, for example, Linda Lear, "Bombshell in Beltsville: The USDA and the Challenge of 'Silent Spring,'" *Agricultural History* 66, no. 2 (Spring 1992): 151–170; and Christopher Bosso, *Pesticides and Politics: The Life Cycle of a Public Issue* (Pittsburgh, PA: University of Pittsburgh Press, 1987). See also Lear, *Rachel Carson;* Hynes, *The Recurring* Silent Spring; Hazlett, "Voices from the *Spring*"; Brooks, *The House of Life*; and Chambers, *Worm in the Bud.* It is worth noting that perhaps not all USDA opinions condemned *Silent Spring.* At least one internal department memorandum written when the *New Yorker* articles appeared observed, "Miss Carson presents a lucid description of the real and potential dangers of misusing chemical pesticides." The memo went on to praise Carson for identifying that more public support was needed for the development of biological and nonchemical means of pest control. John Perkins to Edward Knipling, 22 July 1977, with attachment, USDA Memorandum, August 1962, and Knipling to Perkins, 18 August 1977, folder 509, Correspondence with John H. Perkins, 1977, box 11, Series IV, Correspondence, Collection 210, Edward Fred Knipling Papers, National Agricultural Library.

56. "Chemists of Pesticide Firms Dispute Author," *Gazette*, Cedar Rapids, IA, 14 September 1962, folder 1077, box 61, Series I, Carson Papers. Many officials voiced this opinion, including those at the state level. For example, "Pesticides Defended by State Commissioner," *Post Standard*, Syracuse, NY, 24 September 1963, folder 1116, box 63, Series I, Carson Papers.

57. W. H. Anthony, PhD, "An Answer to *Silent Spring*: Consumers Have the Right to Ask about Food Safety," *Atlanta Journal*, 1 December 1962, folder 1115, box 63, Series I, Carson Papers.

58. Dr. William J. Darby, "A Scientist Looks at 'Silent Spring,'" publication of the American Chemical Society, folder 1129, box 64, Series I, Carson Papers.

59. Virginia Kraft, "The Life-Giving Spray," *Sports Illustrated*, 18 November 1963, folder 1152, box 65, Series I, Carson Papers.

60. Television adaptation, "CBS Reports: The *Silent Spring* of Rachel Carson," broadcast 3 April 1963, folder 1330, box 75, Series I, Carson Papers.

61. "Rachel Carson May Debate with Pesticide Expert," *News*, Ann Arbor, MI, 12 December 1962, folder 1116, box 63, Series I, Carson Papers.

62. Television adaptation, "CBS Reports," and footage from the broadcast can be seen in *The American Experience: Rachel Carson's* Silent Spring (PBS); see also Lear, *Rachel Carson*, 449–450; Kroll, "The 'Silent Springs' of Rachel Carson."

63. An example of these criticisms that appeared in the press is I. L. Baldwin, "Chemicals and Pests," *Science*, 28 September 1962, folder 1078, box 61, Series I, Carson Papers.

64. Bean, "The Noise of *Silent Spring*."

65. Pat Fields, "UT Professor Calls New Book 'One-Sided,'" *Journal*, Knoxville, TN, 2 February 1963; Sidney Eaton Boyle, "County Wellesley Club Told 'Silent Spring' Is in Error," *Times*, Mt. Kisco, NY, 20 June 1963, folder 1319, box 74, Series I, Carson Papers.

66. For examples, see folder 1317 and 1318, box 74, Series I, Carson Papers.

67. Lear, *Rachel Carson*, 440.

68. For examples, see folder 1312, box 74, Series I, Carson Papers. For more on how gendered discourse helped shape the debate over *Silent Spring*, see Hazlett, "Voices from the *Spring*."

69. Historian Adam Rome has argued that women's organizations were essential in the success of *Silent Spring*—a relationship of which Carson was aware. Rome writes that "Carson cultivated a network of women supporters, and women eagerly championed her work." Adam Rome, "'Give Earth a Chance': The Environmental Movement and the Sixties," *Journal of American History* 90, no. 2 (September 2003): 525–554.

70. Charles H. Stoddard to secretary of the interior, 4 December 1962, folder Control Part 2, box 560, RG 48, Department of the Interior, National Archives II.

71. Carson, *Silent Spring*, 22.

72. Ibid., 13, 14.

73. Ibid., 157, 159.

74. Lear, *Rachel Carson*, 357.

75. Kendra Smith-Howard, "Perfecting Nature's Food: A Cultural and Environmental History of Milk in the United States, 1900–1975," PhD diss., Department of History, University of Wisconsin–Madison, 2007, 226–227. Historian Ralph Lutts observed, "It is no accident . . . that the first pollutant mentioned by name in *Silent Spring* was not a pesticide, but Strontium-90." Ralph H. Lutts, "Chemical Fallout: Rachel Carson's *Silent Spring*, Radioactive Fallout, and the Environmental Movement," *Environmental Review* 9, no. 3 (Autumn 1985): 221.

76. Smith-Howard argued that Carson strengthened her indictment of

indiscriminate pesticide use "by publicizing the chemicals' ubiquitous presence on the dinner table." Kendra Smith-Howard, "Antibiotics and Agricultural Change: Purifying Milk and Protecting Health in the Postwar Era," *Agricultural History* 84, no. 3 (June 2010): 330.

77. Carson, *Silent Spring*, 186, 206.

78. Ibid., 22, 160, 161, 157, 107, 69, 260–261.

79. Quoted in Smith, "'Silence, Miss Carson!'" 748.

80. John Perkins discusses how in the 1970s, entomologists who embraced such technological solutions were really going in a different direction from the bulk of Rachel Carson's work; those who took up her mantle in the 1970s, he argues, articulated a vision of working in harmony with nature through "Integrated Pest Management." Perkins, *Insects, Experts, and the Insecticide Crisis*, 184–195.

81. President's Science Advisory Committee, Life Sciences Panel, "The Use of Pesticides," 15 May 1963, folder 1322, box 74, Series I, Carson Papers.

82. Brooks, *The House of Life*, 308.

83. Houghton Mifflin advertisement, May 1963, and in *New York Times Book Review*, 14 July 1963, folder 1324, box 75, Series I, Carson Papers.

84. Josephine Ripley, "U.S. Pesticide Report," *Christian Science Monitor*, 16 May 1963, folder 1293, box 73, Series I, Carson Papers.

85. Rachel Carson, "Public Should Awaken to Danger of Widespread Use of Pesticides" (Herald Tribune News Service), *Vindicator*, Youngstown, OH, 20 May 1963, folder 1288, box 73, Series I, Carson Papers.

86. Joseph Alsop, "After Rachel Carson," *New York Herald-Tribune*, 24 May 1963, folder 1113, box 63; and Joseph Alsop, "Giving Up Bug Poisons Is Like Quitting Rum," *Virginia Pilot*, Norfolk, VA, 26 May 1963, folder 1292, box 73, Series I, Carson Papers.

87. Rachel Carson to Stewart Udall, 3 May 1963, folder 1516 Udall, Stewart 1963, box 86; also "Pesticides Harm While Helping US, Udall Says," *Star*, Orlando, FL, 25 April 1963, folder 1296, box 73, Series I, Carson Papers.

88. Statement by Sen. Abraham Ribicoff on the Senate floor, 6 June 1963, and insertion on page 2 of statement, folder 1298, box 73, Series I, Carson Papers.

89. For example, see Neal Sanford, "Pesticide Hearings Crowded," *Christian Science Monitor*, 7 June 1963; "Sen. Ribicoff Denounces Pesticide Secrecy Deal," *Caller*, Corpus Christi, TX, 7 June 1963; John Troan, "Pest-Killers on Market without Okay of U.S.," *Pittsburgh Press*, Pittsburgh, PA, 7 June 1963, folder 1289, box 73, Series I, Carson Papers.

90. Lear, *Rachel Carson*, 3–4; statement of Rachel Carson before the Subcommittee on Reorganization and International Organizations of the Committee on Government Operations, 4 June 1963, folder 1294, box 73, Series I, Carson Papers.

91. "Pests and Poisons," *Newsweek*, 17 June 1963, folder 1288, box 73, Series I, Carson Papers.

92. "Curb Asked on Chemicals," *Pittsburgh Press*, Pittsburgh, PA, 7 June 1963; see also "Senators Order Pesticide Probe," *Courier Journal*, Louisville, KY, 5 June 1963, folder 1289, box 73, Series I, Carson Papers.

93. For example, "Senators Order Pesticide Probe"; "Ribicoff Raps Silence on Pesticides," *Chicago Sun-Times*, Chicago, IL, 5 June 1963, folder 1290, box 73, Series I, Carson Papers.

94. "No One's Come Up with a Cure for Bureaucratic Blight Disease," *New York Herald Tribune*, 7 June 1963, folder 1288, box 73, Series I, Carson Papers.

95. "Senator Backs Author's Fight on Pesticides," *Newsday*, Garden City, NY, 7 June 1963, folder 1290, box 73, Series I, Carson Papers.

96. Statement of Rachel Carson before the Senate Committee on Commerce, 6 June 1963, folder 1301, box 74, Series I, Carson Papers.

97. "Senator Backs Author's Fight on Pesticides."

98. Whitten's power in agricultural appropriations was so great from the 1940s to the 1980s that political scientist Christopher Bosso referred to him as the "seemingly permanent chair of the subcommittee." Bosso, *Pesticides and Politics*, 67.

99. Quoted in Hynes, *The Recurring* Silent Spring, 120–122.

100. Chambers, *Worm in the Bud*, 214.

101. "Aerial Applicators under Attack," *Farm Chemicals*, July 1963, folder 1297, box 73, Series I, Carson Papers.

102. "Pesticide Industry Braces Itself as Public Hearings Begin," *Farm Chemicals*, June 1963, folder 1297, box 73, Series I, Carson Papers.

103. "Proposed Ban on Persistent Pesticides," *Chemical and Engineering News*, 29 July 1963, folder 1308, box 74, Series I, Carson Papers.

104. Bosso, *Pesticides and Politics*, 125; Dunlap, *DDT*, 124.

105. "'Silent Spring' Spurs Proposals for Chemical Curbs," *Advance*, Staten Island, NY, 12 April 1963, folder 1288, box 73, Series I, Carson Papers.

106. Bosso, *Pesticides and Politics*, 132; "'Silent Spring' Spurs Proposals for Chemical Curbs."

107. "Miss Carson, Vindicated," *Richmond News Leader*, 25 April 1964, folder 1304, box 74, Series I, Carson Papers. Examples of other celebrations of Carson are "Fitting Memorial," *Daily Banner*, Cambridge, MD, 25 April 1964; and "Monument for Rachel," *Record*, Troy, NY, 17 April 1964, folder 1304, box 74, Series I, Carson Papers.

108. "Freeman on Pesticides: Time for Crash Program," *New York Herald Tribune*, 16 April 1964, folder 1297, box 73, Series I, Carson Papers.

109. "Singing Spring," *Telegram*, Herkimer, NY, 28 April 1964, folder 1310, box 74, Series I, Carson Papers.

110. Roger May, "Charge That Chemicals Harm Humans, Nature Fails to Hamper Sales," *Wall Street Journal*, 3 April 1963, folder 1296, box 73, Series I, Carson Papers.

111. "Pesticide Industry Braces Itself."

112. Carl Pope, "Trashing Rachel Carson: The Pesticide Lobby Still Wants Revenge," *Sierra*, September/October 2007, 6. Meanwhile, in 2004, some public health activists charged that *Silent Spring* and the consequent ban on DDT were responsible for the deaths of African children due to malaria. Lytle, *The Gentle Subversive*, 222–223.

113. "Silent Spring—Turbulent Fall."

114. William G. Wing, "Report to President on Effects of Poison Use May Be a Real Bombshell." *Gazette*, Janesville, WI, 2 May 1963, folder 1288, box 73, Series I, Carson Papers.

115. Carson, *Silent Spring*, 106.

116. Ibid., 141.

117. Lear, ed., *Lost Woods*, 231, 232.

Chapter 4. Foreign Affairs: How Pesticides Could Help Americans Feed the World and Win a War

1. The Green Revolution has been written about by a number of historians as well as by observers who have criticized its social and economic impact in Third World countries. For an introduction to the topic and a sample of criticism, see Nick Cullather, *The Hungry World: America's Cold War Battle against Poverty in Asia* (Cambridge, MA: Harvard University Press, 2010); David Kinkela, *DDT and the American Century: Global Health, Environmental Politics, and the Pesticide That Changed the World* (Chapel Hill: University of North Carolina Press, 2011); Vandana Shiva, *The Violence of the Green Revolution: Third World Agriculture, Ecology and Politics* (London and New Jersey: Zed Books, and Penang, Malaysia: Third World Network, 1991); John H. Perkins, *Geopolitics and the Green Revolution: Wheat, Genes, and the Cold War* (New York: Oxford University Press, 1997).

2. Cullather, *The Hungry World*, 134.

3. Harry Truman, "Agricultural Prosperity: Production Payment Plan," delivered 5 September 1949, *Vital Speeches of the Day*, 713.

4. John Boyd Orr, "Program to Meet the World's Food Crisis," *New York Times Magazine*, 9 November 1947, 10.

5. Ibid., 11. For a detailed discussion on the establishment of a development infrastructure, see Amy Staples, *The Birth of Development: How the World Bank, Food and Agriculture Organization, and World Health Organization Changed the World, 1945–1965* (Kent, OH: Kent State University Press, 2006). For more on the connection between an infrastructure and political goals, see Perkins, *Geopolitics and the Green Revolution*, 156.

6. John Boyd Orr, "The Food Problem," *Scientific American*, August 1950, 11, 13. Another who argued that modernization of world agriculture and the preservation of resources would ensure the end of world hunger was agricultural researcher and conservationist Starr Chester. A 1954 article in the *Saturday Evening Post* on Chester described his expectation of continued innovation and his call for the better allocation of current resources. John Bird, "Will Your Grandchildren Go Hungry?" *Saturday Evening Post*, 23 October 1954, 30.

7. "Food-Sharing Plan for World Urged," *New York Times*, 27 June 1947, 18.

8. William Blair, "Food as 'Weapon' for Peace Urged," *New York Times*, 16 December 1947, 8.

9. John Boyd Orr, for example, argued that Americans and Canadians enjoyed plentiful food, but their governments spent huge sums to keep surpluses off the market, and many throughout the world did not have enough to eat. Orr, "The Food Problem," 11.

10. In 1953, editors of the *Commonweal* looked to the FAO meeting in Rome to find an "effective relationship between surpluses and impending famines." "Hunger and Surpluses," *Commonweal*, 11 December 1953, 248–249.

11. Readers also learned of generous New York teenagers who had helped to raise money for UN International Children's Emergency Fund to purchase the discounted dry milk to be sent to the Far East. "Dried Milk Put to Use," *New York Times*, 15 February 1950, 4; "Children Who Helped U.N. Agency Buy Milk for Shipment Abroad See It Put on Vessel," *New York Times*, 16 March 1950, 4.

12. "Rockefeller Fund Help to Mexico Greatly Increases Nation's Food," *New York Times*, 16 March 1950, 38; George Gray, "Blueprint for Hungry Nations," *New York Times Magazine*, 93. See also J. K. Galbraith, "Hybrid Corn for Backward Areas," *New York Times Book Review*, 14 May 1950, 232.

13. For a discussion of the origins of the Green Revolution and how it contributed to international pesticide use, see Kinkela, *DDT and the American Century*. For the status of the MAP by the early 1950s, see Peter Pringle, *Food, Inc.: Mendel to Monsanto—the Promises and Perils of the Biotech Harvest* (New York: Simon and Schuster, 2003), 48–49. For discussion of the false assumption that the Mexican population could not be fed from existing agricultural systems, see Cullather, *The Hungry World*, 43–44, 54–55. For discussion of the connection between the Green Revolution's introduction to India and the tragedy of Bhopal, see, for example, Larry Everest, *Behind the Poison Cloud: Union Carbide's Bhopal Massacre* (Chicago: Banner Press, 1985); David Weir, *The Bhopal Syndrome: Pesticides, Environment, and Health* (San Francisco, CA: Sierra Club Books, 1987); William Bogard, *The Bhopal Tragedy: Language, Logic, and Politics in the Production of a Hazard* (Boulder, CO: Westview Press, 1989); Shiva, *The Violence of the Green Revolution*. For further discussion on the Green Revolution and Bhopal, see chapter 6. For a comment on

the political failures of American development policies, see Perkins, *Geopolitics and the Green Revolution*, 260.

14. "Future Food: Too Much or Too Little?" *Business Week*, 21 January 1950, 120–122. Concerns about overpopulation and food shortages were also fueled by the increase in population in the United States, especially with the start of the baby boom. Samuel P. Hays, *A History of Environmental Politics since 1945* (Pittsburgh, PA: University of Pittsburgh Press, 2000), 16. Irrespective of positive feelings toward population increases at home, a real sense of crisis descended on Americans looking at population growth abroad. John Sharpless, "Population Science, Private Foundations, and Development Aid: The Transformation of Demographic Knowledge in the United States, 1945–1965," in *International Development and the Social Sciences: Essays on the History and Politics of Knowledge*, ed. Frederick Cooper and Randall Packard (Berkeley: University of California Press, 1997), 178.

15. "American Know-How to Help Other Countries Grow Food," *Science News Letter*, 2 April 1949, 214; citing the figure of 55,000: "Can the World Feed Three Billion Mouths?" *Senior Scholastic*, 14 October 1949, 9.

16. "Can the World Feed Three Billion Mouths?" 9–10.

17. Bird, "Will Your Grandchildren Go Hungry?"

18. Pringle, *Food, Inc.*, 14–15.

19. It's worth pausing to note that the inconsistent terminologies used to describe the parts of the world thought to need development were revealing about some of the confusions and biases that attended these policy prescriptions. In the press and among policymakers, the following were used: "underdeveloped"; "nondeveloped"; "regions of Asia, Middle East, Far East"; and occasionally, such as in a *Chicago Daily Tribune* article, "backward areas." Chesly Manly, "Bare U.N. Plan for Backward Areas of World," *Chicago Daily Tribune*, 3 June 1949, 3.

20. N. E. Dodd, "Hoes and 'Show-How' Come First," *New York Times Magazine*, 2 October 1949, 20.

21. Dodd highlighted such technologies as small gasoline pumps to aid individual farmers in moving water from one location to another, well-built hoes, and hand cultivators. Ibid.

22. Ibid.

23. Edwin Miller, "A Way to Lessen World Hunger," *Reader's Digest*, March 1950, 131–135.

24. "American Know-How to Help Other Countries Grow Food," *Science News Letter*, 214.

25. Jay Richter, "Our Lazy Acres Can Yield Far More Food," *New York Times Magazine*, 9 October 1949, 87–88.

26. Henry Morgenthau Jr., "Let Us *Give* Food to the World's Hungry," *New York Times Magazine*, 30 October 1949, 13.

27. William Blair, "U.S. Urged to Spur Farm Co-op Plan," *New York Times*, 25 August 1950, 14.

28. "Food Called Basic to Peace of the World," *New York Times*, 22 June 1949, 33.

29. Telegram, Arthur Steudel to Harry Truman, 12 February 1948, file 227—Misc. (1948), Box 830, Papers of Harry S. Truman Official File, Harry S. Truman Library (Truman Papers).

30. From Truman's perspective, the program was a way to bring his Fair Deal to the rest of the world. See Nils Gilman, *Mandarins of the Future: Modernization Theory in Cold War America* (Baltimore, MD: Johns Hopkins University Press, 2003), 71. Point Four encapsulated the more self-interested as well as benevolent aspects of Cold War policy. Amanda Kay McVety, "Pursuing Progress: Point Four in Ethiopia," *Diplomatic History* 32, no. 3 (June 2008): 373, 371–380, for overviews of development and Point Four.

There is an extensive body of literature on issues of modernization and development in postwar American foreign policy. For further discussion and quotations as noted, see Robert Packenham, *Liberal America and the Third World: Political Development Ideas in Foreign Aid and Social Science* (Princeton, NJ: Princeton University Press, 1973), esp. 43–48; David Ekbladh, *The Great American Mission: Modernization and the Construction of an American World Order* (Princeton, NJ: Princeton University Press, 2010), 4, 9, 98–99; Gilman, *Mandarins of the Future*, esp. 3–4, 70–71; Michael Adas, "Modernization Theory and the American Revival of the Scientific and Technological Standards of Social Achievement and Human Worth," in *Staging Growth: Modernization, Development, and the Global Cold War*, ed. David Engerman, Nils Gilman, Mark Haefele, and Michael Latham (Amherst and Boston: University of Massachusetts Press, 2003), 35, 37, and "Introduction"; Frederick Cooper and Randall Packard, eds., *International Development and the Social Sciences: Essays on the History and Politics of Knowledge* (Berkeley: University of California Press, 1997); Perkins, *Geopolitics and the Green Revolution*, 145. For more on ideas of development from international nongovernmental organizations, see Staples, *The Birth of Development*. By liberalism's heyday in the 1960s, development policies had many guises. The Green Revolution being launched in India at that time was joined by the US-supported White Revolution in Iran and the Alliance for Progress in Latin America. Observer Larry Everest noted that even though these latter policies were broader than the Green Revolution, they were all motivated by the belief that development could be used for political ends: "All of these had the same goal of stabilizing certain strategically important countries or regions and creating new investment opportunities for Western capital through stimulating Third World growth in agriculture." Everest, *Behind the Poison Cloud*, 108.

31. "Text of Acheson Statement on Legislation for Point Four Program," *New York Times*, 31 March 1950, 4.

32. Ibid.

33. Clayton Knowles, "Brannan Defends Point 4 Program," *New York Times*, 29 September 1949, 17. Speaking a few months later to American and international participants in a joint meeting of the Inter-American Conference on Agriculture and a regional meeting of the FAO, Brannan contrasted American and communist development policies because communism did not "stand for the private ownership of farm land." Milton Bracker, "Brannan Sees Reds False on Land Aid," *New York Times*, 5 December 1950, 19.

34. William Blair, "Time Very Short, Harriman Warns," *New York Times*, 13 December 1950, 18.

35. Mary McLeod Bethune, "'Point Four': This Is a 'Must' for These Days of International Living," *Chicago Defender*, 14 January 1950, 6.

36. David Vail, "Guardians of Abundance: Aerial Application, Agricultural Chemicals, and Toxicity in the Postwar Prairie West" (PhD diss., Department of History, Kansas State University, 2012), 41.

37. Telegram, Arthur Steudel to Harry Truman, 12 February 1948, file 227—Misc. (1948), Box 830, Truman Papers.

38. J. L. Anderson, *Industrializing the Corn Belt: Agriculture, Technology, and Environment, 1945–1972* (DeKalb: Northern Illinois University Press, 2009), 33–34.

39. One extension official, Dutch Sylwester, observed in 1958, "Too many folks are expecting chemical weed killers to perform the entire control job." J. L. Anderson, "War on Weeds: Iowa Farmers and Growth-Regulator Herbicides," *Technology and Culture* 46, no. 4 (2005): 721, 734–735. Anderson's discussion provides additional information for this paragraph.

40. Farmers across the border in Canada also embraced 2,4-D, disregarding the advice of agricultural scientists preaching an integration of weed-control methods. Clinton L. Evans, *The War on Weeds in the Prairie West: An Environmental History* (Calgary, Alberta: University of Calgary Press, 2002), 160, 165; see also Anderson, *Industrializing the Corn Belt*, 34–41.

41. Two letters from Asst. Sec. Charles Brannan to Rep. Wilbur Mills and Sen. John McClellan, 18 December 1947, and W. V. Lambert, research administrator, to Kanesteaster Hodges, attorney, 17 December 1947, Box 1459, RG 16, USDA, National Archives II (hereafter NARA).

42. Moreover, explained USDA undersecretary A. J. Lowland in 1949, damage had often been due to carelessness or ignorant plane operators, which federal and state officials were seeking to remedy through flight school programs. A. J. Lowland to Sen. William Langer, 24 May 1949, Box 1725, RG 16, USDA, NARA. Spray applicators agreed with the USDA that pilot training was important in solving this problem. See Vail, "Guardians of Abundance," 132. The problem of drift was not solved for all farmers, either because regulations about dusting were not always enforced or because liquids also were subject to drift. See W. A. Whitehill, county

office manager, Harris County Production and Marketing Administration Committee, TX, to Sec. Benson, USDA, 13 July 1953, with enclosed petition from farmers, Box 2246, RG 16, USDA, NARA; Pete Daniel, *Toxic Drift: Pesticides and Health in the Post–World War II South* (Baton Rouge: Louisiana State University Press, 2005), 50; and Pete Daniel, *Lost Revolutions: The South in the 1950s* (Chapel Hill and London: University of North Carolina Press for Smithsonian National Museum of American History, 2000), 65–68.

For their part, chemical manufacturers labeled drift a problem of careless sprayers, not their products. See Vail, "Guardians of Abundance," 92, 144.

43. Linda Nash, *Inescapable Ecologies: A History of Environment, Disease, and Knowledge* (Berkeley: University of California Press, 2006), 135.

44. Anderson, "War on Weeds," 732–733.

45. Sandra Steingrabber, *Living Downstream: A Scientist's Personal Investigation of Cancer and the Environment* (New York: Vintage Books, 1997), 95.

46. Evans, *The War on Weeds in the Prairie West*, 165.

47. Anderson, "War on Weeds," 736–737, 740.

48. Daniel, *Toxic Drift*, 111.

49. Anderson, *Industrializing the Corn Belt*, 50.

50. Three historians who have focused on the evolution of the lawn in American culture include sections on the adoption of various herbicides: Paul Robbins, *Lawn People: How Grasses, Weeds, and Chemicals Make Us Who We Are* (Philadelphia, PA: Temple University Press, 2007); Virginia Scott Jenkins, *The Lawn: A History of an American Obsession* (Washington, DC, and London: Smithsonian Institution Press, 1994); Ted Steinberg, *American Green: The Obsessive Quest for the Perfect Lawn* (New York: W. W. Norton & Company, 2006).

51. Robbins, *Lawn People*, xiii.

52. Dow advertisement in *Country Gentleman*, 1947, box 7, Advertisements, Dow Collection, Post Street Archives, Othmer Library, Chemical Heritage Foundation.

53. Steinberg, *American Green*, 51.

54. David Zierler, *The Invention of Ecocide: Agent Orange, Vietnam, and the Scientists Who Changed the Way We Think about the Environment* (Athens: University of Georgia Press, 2011), 47.

55. Background information about the development of these chemicals and their use in Vietnam can be found in Zierler, *Invention of Ecocide*; Thomas Whiteside, *Defoliation: What Are Our Herbicides Doing to Us?* (New York: Ballantine Books, 1970); Thomas Whiteside, *The Withering Rain: America's Herbicidal Folly* (New York: Dutton, 1971); Arthur Westing, ed., *Herbicides in War: The Long-Term Ecological and Human Consequences* (London: Taylor and Francis, 1984); J. B. Neilands, G. H. Orians, E. W. Pfeiffer, A. Vennema, and A. H. Westing, *Harvest of Death: Chemical Warfare in Vietnam and Cambodia* (New York: Free Press, 1972); Richard D. McCarthy, *The*

Ultimate Folly: War by Pestilence, Asphyxiation, and Defoliation (New York: Knopf, 1969); Carol Van Strum, *A Bitter Fog: Herbicides and Human Rights* (San Francisco: Random House, 1983). See also Paul Frederick Cecil, *Herbicidal Warfare: The Ranch Hand Project in Vietnam* (New York: Praeger, 1986); John Dux and P. J. Young, *Agent Orange: The Bitter Harvest* (Sydney: Hodder & Stoughton, 1980); and Seymour M. Hersh, *Chemical and Biological Warfare: America's Hidden Arsenal* (Indianapolis, IN: Bobbs-Merrill, 1968). The most up-to-date study of Agent Orange use in Vietnam and its implications is Edwin A. Martini, *Agent Orange: History, Science, and the Politics of Uncertainty* (Amherst and Boston: University of Massachusetts Press, 2012).

56. Various advertisements, box 7, Dow Advertisements, Post Street Archives, Dow Collection, Othmer Library, Chemical Heritage Foundation; Jenkins, *The Lawn*, 150–151.

57. In comparison with the price tag for other weapons in the Vietnam War, the cost of Operation Ranch Hand was relatively modest (about $120 million over ten years, with the greatest expenditures in 1967 and 1968), even if the volume of chemicals used and their impact were great. Martini, *Agent Orange*, 2, 23; Arthur Westing, "Herbicides in War: Past and Present," in Westing, ed., *Herbicides in War*, 4–6; Dux and Young, *Agent Orange*, 38; David Zierler, "Against Protocol: Ecocide, Détente, and the Question of Chemical Warfare in Vietnam, 1969–1975," in *Environmental Histories of the Cold War*, ed. J. R. McNeill and Corinna Unger (Washington and Cambridge: German Historical Institute, 2010), 234–235.

58. Martini, *Agent Orange*, 53–54, 86.

59. Robert Reed, assistant secretary to the secretary for defense mobilization planning, to Robert Cliff, chief of the US Forest Service, 22 December 1966, folder 12/66, box 4542, RG 16, USDA, NARA. The scramble over available chemicals in early 1967 led a number of USDA officials to worry that there would be agricultural shortages for the 1967 season, especially since the Department of Defense's acquisition of Agent Orange tripled from fiscal year 1966 to 1967. Alec Olson to the secretary, 23 March 1967, with attachment, "Defoliation Reported Tripled," folder 1/1–3/31/67, box 4713, RG 16, USDA, NARA. Also Sec. of Commerce John Connor to Orville Freeman, 28 November 1966; Freeman to Connor, 26 October 1966; and Rodney Borum, administrator, Business and Defense Services Administration, US Department of Commerce, to Robert Reed, assistant to the secretary for defense mobilization planning, 12 October 1966, folder 10–11/1966, box 4543, RG 16, USDA, NARA.

60. Rodney Borum, administrator, Business and Defense Services Administration, US Department of Commerce, to Robert Reed, assistant to the secretary for defense mobilization planning, 12 October 1966, folder 10–11/1966, box 4543; secretary of defense to Freeman, 16 February 1967, folder 1/1–3/31/1967, box 4713; and Freeman to Rep. E. C. Gathings, 19 November 1967, folder 11/1–12/27/1967, box 4713, RG 16, USDA, NARA.

61. Freeman argued that the military's estimated needs would lead to a 20 percent shortage for farmers in 1968, costing an additional $70 to $75 million in production expenses as well as leading to unrest among farmers, ranchers, and consumers. Farris Bryant, director, Office of Emergency Planning, Executive Office of the President, to Secretary of Defense McNamara, 24 July 1967; and Freeman to Farris Bryant, 4 August 1967, 8/1–10/31/67, box 4713; also Freeman to George Mehren, 29 February 1968 with attachment, "Background Information on Pesticides," folder F Pesticides, 1/1–2/28/1968, box 4851, RG 16, USDA, NARA.

62. Observations are made from a survey of *The Reader's Guide to Periodical Literature* from the Vietnam War years and a selection of articles from publications such as *Aviation Week*, *Bulletin of Atomic Scientists*, *Business Week*, *Life*, *New Republic*, *New York Times*, *Science*, and *Time*.

63. "Jungle Proving Ground," *Time*, 9 July 1965, 47.

64. "New Weapons, New Experience," *New Republic*, 17 April 1965, 7–8.

65. "Arsenal in Action," *Time*, 18 November 1966, 34–39.

66. Mort Schultz, "Wild New Weapons for Vietnam," *Popular Mechanics*, January 1967, 95–98.

67. "C123s Defoliate Jungle Stronghold," *Aviation Week*, 8 May 1967, 82–85.

68. Cited in Zierler, *Invention of Ecocide*, 96.

69. Charles Mohr, "Defoliation Unit Lives Perilously," *New York Times*, 20 December 1965, 3.

70. Zierler, *Invention of Ecocide*, e.g., 4, 96, 102.

71. Whiteside, *The Withering Rain*, 31; Neilands et al., *Harvest of Death*, 118.

72. "Resolution Passed by the Council of the American Association for the Advancement of Science," in Whiteside, *The Withering Rain*, appendix; Neilands et al., *Harvest of Death*, xii, 142.

73. Zierler, *Invention of Ecocide*, 121–122.

74. Neilands et al., *Harvest of Death*, 171–172.

75. J. Brooks Flippen, *Nixon and the Environment* (Albuquerque: University of New Mexico Press, 2000), 101, also 31, 44; Christopher J. Bosso, *Pesticides and Politics: The Life Cycle of a Public Issue* (Pittsburgh, PA: University of Pittsburgh Press, 1987), 137. In 1971, Secretary of State William Rogers argued to President Nixon that the controversy over Agent Orange use had become much more important than any possible military benefit from it. Martini, *Agent Orange*, 102.

76. Press Release, Department of the Interior, 15 April 1970, "Home Use of 2,4,5-T Suspended," file—USDA, 1967–1972, box B-226, Papers of the National Audubon Society, New York Public Library (Audubon Papers).

77. Amy Hay, "Dow Chemical vs. 'Coercive Utopians': Constructing the Contested Ground of Science and Government Regulation in 1970s America," *Business*

and Economic History, On-Line, Vol. 9, 2011, 1–15, http://www.thebhc.org/publications/BEHonline/2011/hay.pdf.

78. Ian Nisbet, MA Audubon Society, to Elvis Stahr and Richard Cutler, n.d., file—Pesticides, 1976–1978, box B-211, Audubon Papers.

79. A focus on the idea that the experimental results were "dose related" was repeated frequently. Fred Tschirley to Rep. William Maillard, 9 June 1972, and Fred Tschirley to Rep. Victor Veysey, 8 June 1972, folder 6–7/1972, box 5604; also Hubert Heffner, Office of Science and Technology, Executive Office of the President, to secretaries of interior, defense, commerce, HEW, and agriculture and chairman, Council on Environmental Quality, 16 September 1970, folder 9/10–10/19/1970, box 5268, RG 16, USDA, NARA.

80. Ned Bayley to Dr. Edward Burger, staff technical assistant, Office of Science and Technology, Executive Office of the President, 21 September 1970, folder 8/1–9/22 [1 of 2], box 5269; and Ned Bayley to Dr. Hubert Heffner, acting director, Office of Science and Technology, Executive Office of the President, 13 October 1970, with attachment of comments from ARS, Crop Research Division, folder 10/9–10/19/70, box 5268, RG 16, USDA, NARA.

81. Fred Tschirley, assistant coordinator, Environmental Quality Activities, to Rep. Bob Wilson, 22 May 1973, folder 1/1–6/11/1973, box 5755, RG 16, USDA, NARA.

82. Clifford Hardin to Russell Train, 6 June 1970, folder 6/1–6/16 [1 of 2], box 5269, RG 16, USDA, NARA.

83. Fred Tschirley to Dr. Paul Martin, Department of Geosciences, University of Arizona, 18 November 1971, folder 11/3–12/31/1971, box 5459, RG 16, USDA, NARA. The defense of 2,4,5-T that had little or no dioxin continued to be made a decade later by Reagan administration officials such as Rita Lavelle of the EPA, who argued that danger from the herbicide was determined solely by its dioxin level. Martini, *Agent Orange*, 132.

84. Quentin West to Robert Long, assistant secretary, 3 October 1975, folder 9/1/75–10/7/75, box 6012, RG 16, USDA, NARA.

85. Zierler, *Invention of Ecocide*, 10.

86. "Silent Vietnam: How We Invented Ecocide and Killed a Country," *Look*, 6 April 1971, 55.

87. "Starvation as a Policy," *Saturday Review*, 4 December 1971, 91; "Ecocide in Indochina," *Natural History*, March 1971, 56–61.

For more on the political discussion in Washington throughout the 1960s about whether or not Agent Orange was a chemical weapon—and therefore in violation of international agreements—see Zierler, "Against Protocol," 231, 240, 250, 237, and Zierler, *Invention of Ecocide*, 24, 96, 103.

88. Van Strum, *A Bitter Fog*, 13. For discussion critical of another corporation's role in defending 2,4,5-T, see Marie-Monique Robin, *The World According to Monsanto: Pollution, Corruption, and the Control of Our Food Supply, an Investigation into the World's Most Controversial Company* (New York: New Press, 2008), 36–70.

89. "Weed Killer Bans Could Cost Millions," *Milwaukee Journal*, 23 November 1970.

90. "2,4,5-T," *American Forests*, July 1970, 11.

91. "Defoliation U.S. Style," *Newsweek*, 25 September 1972, 75.

92. "Weed Killers," *Consumer Reports*, June 1970, 359–363.

93. Mrs. R. L. Schroeder, president of Know and Valley Audubon Society of Southern Indiana, to Russell Train, 25 February 1975, and Press Release, Food and Wildlife Service, Department of the Interior, Great Lakes region news, 12 March 1975, file—Herbicides, box B-181, Audubon Papers.

94. Callison wrote to John Quarles of the EPA that they should not wait to act until the damage from the chemical got worse. Charles Callison to Earl Butz, 8 May 1972, folder 5/1972, box 5460, RG 16, USDA, NARA; Callison to Quarles, 22 August 1974, file—Herbicides, box B-181, Audubon Papers.

95. National Audubon Society Release, 26 August 1974, and Environmental Defense Fund Release, 28 June 1974, file—Herbicides, box B-181, Audubon Papers.

96. Dux and Young, *Agent Orange*, 101–105; Martini, *Agent Orange*, 155–157.

97. Stories were sampled through the Vanderbilt Television News Archive, Nashville, TN, by accessing the index of stories on this topic and then by viewing segments online.

98. NBC News, 30 June 1983 and 1 July 1983, Vanderbilt Television News Archive.

99. For example, see Dux and Young, *Agent Orange*; Peter H. Schuck, *Agent Orange on Trial: Mass Toxic Disasters in the Courts* (Cambridge, MA: Belknap Press of Harvard University Press, 1986), 7; Fred A. Wilcox, *Waiting for an Army to Die: The Tragedy of Agent Orange* (Cabin John, MD: Seven Locks Press, 1989).

100. A widow who could prove that her husband died of Agent Orange could get $3,700, but there were no other payments to wives or children of veterans. Wilcox, *Waiting for an Army to Die*, xiv–xvii, 81–92.

101. See, for example, periodic publications from the National Academy of Sciences mandated by the law: Institute of Medicine of the National Academies, *Veterans and Agent Orange, Update 2006* (Washington, DC: National Academy of Sciences, 2007), ix–x, 1, 5, 11–15.

102. Robin, *The World According to Monsanto*, 47–68. On the effects of dioxin in different parts of the world, see Thomas Whiteside, *The Pendulum and the Toxic Cloud: The Course of Dioxin Contamination* (New Haven, CT: Yale University Press, 1977, 9).

103. Clyde Haberman, "Agent Orange's Long Legacy for Vietnam and American

Veterans," *New York Times*, 11 May 2014; "Agent Orange and Veterans: A Forty Year Wait," 30 August 2010, www.whitehouse.gov/blog/2010/08/30/agent-orange-and-veterans-a-40-year-wait. Government acknowledgment of "association" between Agent Orange and certain diseases—limited though it was—probably encouraged some Americans and Vietnamese to return to the courts for redress in the early 2000s. Some American veterans sued the government for payments because the last of the money from the 1984 settlement had been paid out in 1997 (291,000 people had received benefits), but they had only recently found out about their serious health problems that they said had been caused by Agent Orange. See Martini, *Agent Orange*, 162, 222–225.

104. William Glaberson, "Agent Orange, the Next Generation; in Vietnam and America, Some See a Wrong Still Not Righted," *New York Times*, 8 August 2004; Thomas Fuller, "4 Decades on, U.S. Starts Cleanup of Agent Orange in Vietnam," *New York Times*, 9 August 2012.

105. Years after the war, the scientific and political debates about the relationship between Agent Orange and disease and deformity remain. Martini, *Agent Orange*, grapples with this uncertainty, for example, 4, 14, 227–246.

106. The Vietnamese government had established "peace villages" to care for some of these people but did not have the financial resources to care for all. Martini, *Agent Orange*, 29.

107. Diplomatic efforts to establish US responsibility were initiated under George W. Bush. Martini, *Agent Orange*, 207–208; Fuller, "4 Decades On, U.S. Starts Cleanup of Agent Orange in Vietnam."

108. J. R. McNeill, *Something New under the Sun: An Environmental History of the Twentieth-Century World* (New York: W. W. Norton, 2000), 224, also 223–226. For more on the Green Revolution's effect on nutrition in the developing world with the switch to high-yield-variety export crops, see Susan George, *How the Other Half Dies: The Real Reasons for World Hunger* (Montclair, NJ: Allanheld, Osmun & Co. Publishers, 1977), 92–97.

109. Shiva, *The Violence of the Green Revolution*, 98; Everest, *Behind the Poison Cloud*, 45.

110. Everest, *Behind the Poison Cloud*, 45; Bogard, *The Bhopal Tragedy*, 7. For related criticisms of the effects of the Green Revolution, also see Weir, *The Bhopal Syndrome*.

111. Whiteside, *The Pendulum and the Toxic Cloud*, 2.

112. Before being discredited, observed attorney Victor Yannacone, who was involved in the class-action suit on behalf of US vets, 2,4,5-T similarly enjoyed the reputation of being a "model herbicide—unlike DDT, it was specific, nontoxic to animals, and biodegradable." Cited in Schuck, *Agent Orange on Trial*, 60.

113. Activists such as Billee Shoecraft and Carol Van Strum began fighting to restrict domestic use of Agent Orange on public lands, and wrote about their

campaigns. Billee Shoecraft, *Sue the Bastards!* (Phoenix, AZ: Franklin Press, 1971); Van Strum, *A Bitter Fog.*

Chapter 5. The Twenty-Year Itch: Activists, Experts, and the Regulatory Era

1. Christopher J. Bosso, *Pesticides and Politics: The Life Cycle of a Public Issue* (Pittsburgh, PA: University of Pittsburgh Press, 1987), 188–189.

2. Details of this political revolution can be found in many sources, for example, Bosso, *Pesticides and Politics*; Richard L. Andrews, *Managing the Environment, Managing Ourselves: A History of American Environmental Policy* (New Haven, CT: Yale University Press, 1999); J. Brooks Flippen, *Nixon and the Environment* (Albuquerque: University of New Mexico Press, 2000); Samuel P. Hays, *Beauty, Health, and Permanence: Environmental Politics in the United States, 1955–1985* (Cambridge: Cambridge University Press, 1987); John Wargo, *Our Children's Toxic Legacy: How Science and Law Fail to Protect Us from Pesticides* (New Haven, CT: Yale University Press, 1996).

3. Quoted in "Introduction," Norman J. Vig and Michael E. Kraft, eds., *Environmental Policy in the 1980s: Reagan's New Agenda* (Washington, DC: Congressional Quarterly, 1984), 12.

4. As political scientist Christopher Bosso observed, the creation of the EPA was important in the growth of environmentalism because it "gave environmentalists somewhere to go" other than the USDA. Bosso, *Pesticides and Politics*, 153.

5. Thomas R. Dunlap, *DDT: Scientists, Citizens, and Public Policy* (Princeton, NJ: Princeton University Press, 1981), 93–97; Roderick Frazier Nash, *The Rights of Nature: A History of Environmental Ethics* (Madison: University of Wisconsin Press, 1989), 164.

6. Tying together his critiques of consumer values and abuse of the environment, social critic Vance Packard wrote in his 1960 book, *The Waste Makers*, "A person can't go down to the store and order a new park." Cited in Adam Rome, "'Give Earth a Chance': The Environmental Movement and the Sixties," *Journal of American History* 90, no. 2 (September 2003): 525–554.

7. Hal Rothman, *The Greening of a Nation: Environmentalism in the United States since 1945* (New York: Harcourt Brace College Publishers, 1998), 52. For more on the coalescing of environmental sensibilities and a movement in the 1960s and 1970s, see Kirkpatrick Sale, *The Green Revolution: The American Environmental Movement* (New York: Hill and Wang, 1993); Samuel Hays, *A History of Environmental Politics since 1945* (Pittsburgh, PA: University of Pittsburgh Press, 2000); Andrew Kirk, *Counterculture Green: The Whole Earth Catalogue and American Environmentalism* (Lawrence: University Press of Kansas, 2007).

8. Paul Ehrlich, *The Population Bomb* (New York: Ballantine Books, 1968). Popular concern about overpopulation had also been prominent in two best sellers twenty years earlier, Fairfield Osborn's *Our Plundered Planet* and William Vogt's *Road to Survival.* For a discussion of the connection between worry over population and environmentalism, see Thomas Robertson, *The Malthusian Moment: Global Population Growth and the Birth of American Environmentalism* (New Brunswick, NJ: Rutgers University Press, 2012), and Adam Rome, *The Genius of Earth Day: How a 1970 Teach-In Unexpectedly Made the First Green Generation* (New York: Hill and Wang, 2013), 26–28.

9. The film version depicted a dystopian future of 2022 in which 40 million people crowded into New York while nature outside urban centers had ceased to exist. Along with overpopulation, excessive pollution and global warming had led to severe food shortages so that people ended up subsisting on rationed, mass-produced wafers that—we learn by the end of the movie—were made from dead humans.

10. The authors argued that in order to survive, human society instead had to move to a state of equilibrium. Donella H. Meadows, Dennis L. Meadows, Jorgen Randers, and William Behrens III, *The Limits to Growth: A Report for the Club of Rome's Project on the Predicament of Mankind*, 2nd ed. (New York: Potomac Associates Book, 1974).

11. Christopher Bosso's *Environment, Inc.: From Grassroots to Beltway* (Lawrence: University Press of Kansas, 2005) is the most helpful study of various environmental organizations in the United States and the increasingly active political role that they began playing after 1970. Also helpful is Sale, *The Green Revolution.* On the history of the National Audubon Society, in particular, see also Frank Graham Jr. with Carl Buchheister, *The Audubon Ark: A History of the National Audubon Society* (Austin: University of Texas Press, 1990).

12. Statistics on Audubon taken from Bosso, *Environment, Inc.*, Tables 1.1, 2.2, 3.1, 3.2, 4.1, 4.2, and 4.4.

13. Graham with Buchheister, *The Audubon Ark*, 186–187.

14. Bosso, *Environment, Inc.*, 33–34; Graham with Buchheister, *The Audubon Ark*, 187. Subsequently, Baker invited both pro- and anti-DDT forces to speak at Audubon conventions. Draft statement, Roland Clement, "The Role of Audubon in the Demise of DDT," 9 July 1969, file—Clement, Roland, 1969–1971, box B-158, Papers of the National Audubon Society, New York Public Library (Audubon Papers).

15. Memorandum, Kenneth Morrison, National Audubon Society public relations director, to Florida Branches and Affiliates, 27 June 1956, folder—Poisons (1), box B-26, Audubon Papers.

16. For example, Charles Callison, conservation director, National Wildlife Federation, before House Committee on Appropriations, Agriculture Subcommittee, 24 March 1959, file—Poisons, box B-26, Audubon Papers; Bosso, *Pesticides and Politics*, 89–90.

17. Edmund Russell, *War and Nature: Fighting Humans and Insects with Chemicals from World War I to Silent Spring* (Cambridge: Cambridge University Press, 2001), 214.

18. Dunlap, *DDT,* 89–90.

19. John Baker to William Brown, Zoology Department, University of Arizona, 27 May 1959, Folder—Poisons, box B-26, Audubon Papers.

20. Pamphlet, National Academy of Sciences—National Research Council, July 1961, folder 1147, Clippings for 1962–3, Houghton Mifflin Defense, box 64, Series I, Rachel Carson Papers YCAL 46, Beinecke Library, Yale University (Carson Papers).

21. Statement from USDA, "Imported Fire Ant Control Program," Agricultural Research Service, Plant Pest Control Division, n.d.; Department of Health, Education, and Welfare, Public Health Service statement on fire-ant program, July 1958; John Cutler, assistant surgeon general, to secretary of agriculture re: visit of John Baker, 18 August 1958; "False Statements by USDA before Subcommittee of Agricultural Appropriation Bill," March 1959; and "Recent Events and News from Imported Fire Ant Control Program Which Should Be Used and Stressed by NAS," folder—Poisons, box B-26, Audubon Papers.

Reflecting Audubon attitudes toward the USDA, organization officials made attempts to play one agency off against the other, for example, praising HEW officials directly and criticizing the USDA. John Baker to Arthur Fleming, 25 November 1958, folder—Pesticides, box B-26, Audubon Papers.

22. Dunlap, *DDT,* 91; Russell, *War and Nature,* 214–215.

23. "The Hazards of Broadcasting Toxic Pesticides, as Illustrated by Experience with the Imported Fire Ant Control Program," Audubon booklet, 10 November 1958, presented at the 54th annual National Audubon Society convention by Harold Peters, file Pesticides, box B-453, Audubon Papers. In addition, Audubon criticized the USDA spraying program against Dutch elm disease and the Bureau of Land Management's aerial spraying of 1080-baited corn to control ants in the Southwest. Harold Peters, "Dutch Elm Disease and Birds," presentation at National Audubon Society convention, 28 October 1961, file—Pollution, box B-27; telegram, Carl Buchheister to Stewart Udall, 4 May 1961, and telegram, William Carr to Carl Buchheister, 3 May 1961, file—Stewart Udall, box B-122, Audubon Papers.

24. "The Hazards of Broadcasting Toxic Pesticides."

25. Historian Thomas Dunlap criticized Audubon's continuing reticence on the pesticides issue. He observed that "as late as 1961, in fact, [then-president Carl] Buchheister listed the wilderness bill, the national seashore, and preservation of wetlands ahead of a new bill to coordinate pesticide use and registration as goals for conservationists." Dunlap, *DDT,* 92.

26. Examples of this multipronged lobbying are in Charles Callison to Honorable Leonard Wolf, 1 September 1960; Kiwannis Club of Miami resolution, 12 August 1960; Callison to Robert Anderson, assistant surgeon general and chairman,

Interagency Pesticides Review Council, 29 November 1961; Callison to T. A. Thompson, chair of Subcommittee on Fisheries and Wildlife, House Committee on Merchant Marine Fisheries, 20 June 1963; and Callison to Dr. Walter Dykstra, Research Staff Specialist, Bureau of Sport Fisheries and Wildlife, Department of the Interior, 15 July 1964, Pesticides 1960–1965, box B-211, Audubon Papers.

27. Programs in files on annual conventions, 1962, 1963, 1964, box B-70, Audubon Papers. Along with his pledge of support, John Baker gently chided Carson for not being a member of Audubon and invited her to join, which she did. Roland Clement to Rachel Carson, 26 September 1958, file Carson, Rachel, 1958–1962, box B-67, Audubon Papers.

28. Graham with Buchheister, *The Audubon Ark*, 224–5.

29. John Baker to Rachel Carson, 16 April 1958; and Carl Buchheister to Rachel Carson, 21 November 1958, file Carson, Rachel, 1958–1962, box B-67, Audubon Papers.

30. See file Carson, Rachel, 1958–1962, box B-67, Audubon Papers.

31. Robert Burnap to Rachel Carson, 25 February 1959, file Carson, Rachel, 1958–1962, box B-67, Audubon Papers.

32. Paul Brooks to Carl Buchheister, 30 January 1962; and Carl Buchheister to Paul Brooks, 5 February 1962, folder 1493 National Audubon Society, 1962–3, box 85, Series I, Carson Papers; Anne Ford to Carl Buchheister, 16 July 1962, file Carson, Rachel, 1958–1962, box B-67, B. Buchheister 1. Name/Subject (c. 1959–1970), Section B, Audubon Papers.

33. Roland Clement to Rachel Carson, 27 November 1962, folder 1493 National Audubon Society, 1962–3, box 85, Carson Papers.

34. Carl Buchheister to Branch and Affiliate Officers, file Carson, Rachel, 1958–1962, box B-67, Audubon Papers.

35. Roland Clement to Miss Nellie Van Vorst, president, Schenectady Bird Club, 18 February 1963 ("Dear Friend" form letter), file Rachel Carson, 1963–1966, box B-67, Audubon Papers.

36. Dunlap, *DDT*, 92; Graham with Buchheister, *The Audubon Ark*, 225–232.

37. Roland Clement, "The Failure of Common Sense," file—Conventions—Annual, 1961 (2 of 2), box B-70, Audubon Papers.

38. Memorandum, Roland Clement to R. Watson Pomeroy, 29 October 1963, "Papers in a Symposium on Use and Effects of Pesticides," Albany, NY, 23 September 1963; and Roland Clement, "NAS—The Safe Use of Insecticides," 9 September 1963, file—Pesticides, box B-453; Roland Clement, "The Pesticides Controversy," to joint meeting of Society of Sigma XI and the Research and Engineering Society of America, 4 April 1963, folder—Callison, Charles, Speeches, 1960–1970, box B-151, Audubon Papers. In one November letter to Carson, Clement recounted how he had equipped himself in a public debate with Dr. Robert White-Stevens, spokesman for

the chemical lobby. Roland Clement to Rachel Carson, 27 November 1962, folder 1493 National Audubon Society, 1962–3, box 85, Carson Papers.

Other scientists shared Clement's concerns. For example, see papers from "The Effects of Toxic Pesticides on Wildlife" at the 54th annual convention of the National Audubon Society, 10 November 1958: John George, "Pesticides and Wildlife"; Daniel Speake, "Fire Ant Eradication and Fire Ants in Alabama"; George Wallace, "Insecticides and Birds"; Robert Rudd, "The Indirect Effects of Chemicals in Nature," file—Pesticides, box B-453, Audubon Papers.

39. Roland Clement to Charles Callison and J. Franson, 6 October 1970, file—Clement, Roland, 1969–71, box B-158, Audubon Papers.

40. This and subsequent citations from Carl Buchheister, "Meeting the Pesticides Problem," 2 October 1962, Washington, DC, file—Legislation File: Pesticides Coordination Bill, box B-129, Audubon Papers.

41. Charles Callison to Justus C. Ward, 14 February 1962, file—Pesticides, 1960–1965, box B-211, Audubon Papers.

42. Press release from National Audubon Society on proposed bill, 6 April 1960, and HR 11502 (86th Congress, 2nd session) in House of Representatives, 31 March 1960, file—Legislation file: Pesticides Coordination Bill, box B-129, Audubon Papers.

43. National Audubon Society Statement on HR 11502, 86th Congress, 3 May 1960, file—Legislation file: Pesticides Coordination Bill, box B-129, Audubon Papers.

44. Charles Callison to Hon. Leonard Wolf, 14 June 1960; and Wolf to Callison, 31 May 1960, file—Legislation File: Pesticides Coordination Bill, box B-129, Audubon Papers.

45. Carl Buchheister to Dr. Gustav Swanson, Department of Conservation, Cornell University, 6 April 1960, file—Legislation File: Pesticides Coordination Bill, box B-129, Audubon Papers.

46. Charles Callison to all state game, fish, and conservation directors, 17 June 1964, file—Pesticides 1960–1964, box B-211, Audubon Papers.

47. When one looks at programs for the annual conventions and titles of presentations, it is not clear exactly how much attention was paid to pesticides within the presentations because "pesticides" was not an explicit term in the titles in 1965, 1966, or 1967. Convention files for these years, box B-70, Audubon Papers.

48. Bosso, *Environment, Inc.*, 41.

49. Charles Callison to Dr. Maurice Goddard, secretary, Department of Forests and Waters, Commonwealth of Pennsylvania, 7 May 1965, file—Pesticides, 1960–1965, box B-211, Audubon Papers.

50. Robert Boardman, public information director, National Audubon Society, to Henry Rippe, 12 August 1969, file—DDT (1969–1971), box B-168, Audubon Papers.

51. Memorandum, John Franson to Charles Callison, 4 August 1969, file—DDT (1969–1971), box B-168, Audubon Papers. In the same file, see also assorted letters

from the National Audubon Society, especially Callison, to local regional activists about introducing bills in state legislatures to ban DDT.

52. Elvis Stahr, president, National Audubon Society, to Orville Freeman, 13 November 1968, folder F Pesticides, 1/1–2/28/1968, box 4851, RG 16, USDA, National Archives II (NARA).

53. Elvis Stahr to Clifford Hardin, 3 November 1969, folder 12/1/69 (1 of 3), box 5081, RG 16, USDA, NARA. Another example of Audubon lobbying was seen earlier in the year when Stahr wrote to Hardin, protesting the USDA policy of spraying airports with persistent pesticides ("drenching airports with Dieldrin") to block insects from entering the country. Elvis Stahr to Clifford Hardin, 14 July 1969, folder 8/69 (1 of 2), box 5080, RG 16, USDA, NARA.

54. Flippen, *Nixon and the Environment*, 31, 44.

55. Statement by Paul Howard, Western regional representative, National Audubon Society, to Senator Fred Marler, chair, Senate Agriculture Committee, 18 June 1969, file—DDT, box B-168, Audubon Papers.

56. Charles Callison to *New York Times Magazine*, 17 April 1974, file—US Department of the Interior, Fish and Wildlife Service, 1974, box B-229, Audubon Papers.

57. E. W. Kenworthy, "Court Orders New Unit to File Notice of DDT Ban," *New York Times*, 8 January 1971, 1; "Ag Department to Press Battle for Pesticide, Hardin Aide Says," *Illinois State Journal*, 30 November 1970.

58. For a brief example of the backlash among farmers and the chemical industry, see "Move to Curb E.P.A. on Pesticides Loses," *New York Times*, 5 September 1975.

59. For example, see Charles Callison to Milanne Rehor, assistant researcher, Planet Ocean Museum, International Oceanographic Foundation, 13 December 1974; John Franson, Southwest regional representative, National Audubon Society, to Russell Train, 27 February 1975; and Carlyle Blackeney Jr. to SC chapter presidents, 8 April 1976, file—DDT, 1972–1976, box B-168, Audubon Papers. Audubon worked on pesticide issues at different levels of government, for example, bringing suit against the state government for the use of toxaphene on rangeland in South Dakota in 1979. For example, National Audubon Society press release, 14 July 1979; Richard Madson, regional representative, National Audubon Society, to Clint Roberts, secretary, South Dakota Department of Agriculture, 29 August 1979; Madson, "Special Report," 6 August 1979, to South Dakota members, National Audubon Society; and National Audubon Society press release, 3 September 1979, file—Issues—Toxics, box B-429, Audubon Papers.

60. Cynthia Wilson to Elvis Stahr, Charles Callison, and Roland Clement, 12 April 1973, file—Tussock Moth, 1973 (1 of 2), box B-226, Audubon Papers. For an example of praise for the EPA in the press as a bulwark against industry interests, see Charles Quaintance, "The DDT–Tussock Moth Controversy: Calamity in the Forests," in *Proceedings for EPA Hearings on Request for Use of DDT to Control Douglas-Fir Tussock Moth*, Carton 1, 8-0048, RG 412, EPA, NARA.

61. Charles Callison to Washington and Oregon Audubon chapters, 22 August 1973; Roland Clement to Charles Callison, 13 April 1973; Roland Clement to Elvis Stahr, Charles Callison, Tom Wimmer, Robert Boardman, Paul Howard, R. Turner, Cynthia Wilson, Ian Nisbet, 19 November 1973, file—Tussock Moth, 1973 (1 of 2), box B-226, Audubon Papers.

62. Director, Bureau of Sport Fisheries and Wildlife, Fish and Wildlife Service, Department of the Interior, RG 412-80-00-48, Carton 2, unclassified papers, EPA, NARA.

63. Russell Train to Charles Callison, 27 January 1976, file—Pesticides, 1976–1978, box B-211, Audubon Papers.

64. Charles Callison to Russell Train, 26 February 1976; and Train to Callison, 26 April 1976, file—Pesticides, 1976–1978, box B-211, Audubon Papers.

65. "Summary of Activities," November–December 1977 and January–March 1978, file—Pesticides, 1976–1978, box B-211, Audubon Papers. For more on National Audubon Society lobbying efforts, see Cynthia Wilson's "Summary of Pesticide Legislation," 1972; "Statement of the National Audubon Society on HR 10729," 15 June 1972; and National Audubon Society memorandum, Cynthia Wilson to Charles Callison, 26 November 1975, file—Pesticide Control Act (1 of 2), box 262, Audubon Papers.

66. Maureen Hinkle, "A Citizen's Action Guide to FIFRA," file—Pesticide Legislation Manual, box B-554; "Getting the Bugs Out," 1981, file—Pesticides, box B-578, Audubon Papers.

67. Memorandum, 25 June 1969 (on National Audubon Society letterhead; author and recipient unknown); National Audubon Society memorandum, 25 June 1969; and press release, "Companies Appeal Cancellation of DDT Uses," 6 January 1970, file DDT (1969–1971), box B-168, Audubon Papers.

68. Roland Clement to Charles Callison, 13 April 1973, file—Tussock Moth, 1973 (1 of 2), box B-226, Audubon Papers.

69. Rachel Carson, *Silent Spring* (New York: Houghton Mifflin Harcourt, 1962), 22.

70. Steven Stoll observed of the department, "It became the Church of Information and Technology (with its own missionaries) for millions of modernizing farmers. Its experts eventually embraced any machine or chemical that promised increased production regardless of how technological change would affect farm families or the environment." Steven Stoll, *Larding the Lean Earth: Soil and Society in Nineteenth-Century America* (New York: Hill and Wang, 2002), 212.

71. Pete Daniel, *Toxic Drift: Pesticides and Health in the Post–World War II South* (Baton Rouge: Louisiana State University Press, 2005), 85; overall discussion of issue, 84–98.

72. Nyle Brady to the secretary, 3 April 1964; and Sec. Anthony Celebrezze,

HEW, to secretary, USDA, 14 May 1964, folder 4132, 4/28–6/5 (2 of 2), box 4132, RG 16, USDA, NARA.

73. Rod Leonard to the secretary, 14 May 1964, folder 4/28–6/5 (1 of 2), box 4132, RG 16, USDA, NARA.

74. John Finney, "Pesticide Caution Urged a Year Ago," *New York Times*, 7 April 1964, in folder 4/28–6/5 (2 of 2), box 4132, RG 16, USDA, NARA.

75. Interestingly, the same editorial critical of Freeman both reflected prevailing views of pesticide use ("important for farm production") and also challenged the idea of their necessity ("Some consumers might wonder whether producing still more surpluses is a good argument for unrestricted use of poisons"). Tom Hughes to the secretary, 24 April 1964, with clippings: "Spray Now, Pay Later," *Washington Post*, 19 April 1964, and "Ribicoff Plans Law on Plant Inspection in Fish-Kill Issue," *Washington Post*, 24 April 1964; Walter Sullivan, "Pesticide Maker Tied to Fish Kill," 23 April 1964; and John Finney, "U.S. Is Criticized on Pesticide Data," 24 April 1964, in folder 4/28–6/5 (2 of 2), box 4132, RG 16, USDA, NARA.

76. Memorandum, Jim Ward to undersecretary, USDA, 19 November 1964, folder—Insecticides, 9/23 to (3 of 4), box 4131, RG 16, USDA, NARA.

77. Memorandum, Rod Leonard to Tom Hughes, 24 November 1964, folder—Insecticides, 9/23 to (3 of 4), box 4131, RG 16, USDA, NARA.

78. A discussion of the hearings can be found in Daniel, *Toxic Drift*, 86–90.

79. B. T. Shaw, ARS, to the secretary through Nyle C. Brady, 27 April 1964, folder 4/28–6/5 (2 of 2), box 4132, RG 16, USDA, NARA.

80. Dennis Hayley, director of information, NACA, to "Dear Broadcaster," April 1964, and press release, NACA, after 26 April 1964, special for TV farm directors, folder 4/28–6/5 (2 of 2), box 4132, RG 16, USDA, NARA.

81. Press release, Shell Chemical Agricultural News, March 1964, folder 4/28–6/5 (2 of 2), box 4132, RG 16, USDA, NARA.

82. E. E. Saulmon to Arthur Godfrey, 22 June 1966; and E. E. Saulmon to Eddie Albert, 22 June 1966, folder 4–7/1966, box 4543, RG 16, USDA, NARA.

83. Celebrity pesticides spots 4 and 5 with Layne Beaty, chief, generic letters to public service director, May 1970; storyboard drawings for public service announcements (six sets), Office of Information, USDA, from unprocessed collection 313, National Agricultural Library (NAL), USDA.

84. Harold Lewis to G. L. Mehren, 29 June 1966, with attachment, folder 4–7/1966, box 4543, RG 16, USDA, NARA.

85. E. E. Saulmon to Ken Birkhead, 2 December 1966, folder 12/66, box 4542, RG 16, USDA, NARA.

86. Charles Sayre, president, National Cotton Council of America, to Clifford Hardin, 8 February 1971, folder 4–5/71, box 5460, RG 16, USDA, NARA.

87. Parke Brinkley to Clifford Hardin, 13 December 1969, folder 1/1–5/31, box 5271, RG 16, USDA, NARA.

88. Parke Brinkley to Earl Butz, 27 November 1972, folder 8/72–12/72, box 5604, RG 16, USDA, NARA.

89. Earl Butz to Parke Brinkley, 14 December 1972, folder 8/72–12/72, box 5604, RG 16, USDA, NARA.

90. Especially see Dunlap, *DDT*; and David Kinkela, *DDT and the American Century: Global Health, Environmental Politics, and the Pesticide That Changed the World* (Chapel Hill: University of North Carolina Press, 2011).

91. Gaylord Nelson to Orville Freeman, 13 June 1966; Ken Birkhead to secretary, 15 July 1966, with attachment, folder 4–7/1966; and Freeman to Nelson, 5 August 1966, 8–9/1966, box 4543, RG 16, USDA, NARA.

92. Gaylord Nelson to Clifford Hardin, 15 April 1969; telegram, Nelson to Hardin, 17 April 1969; and Ned Bayley to Gaylord Nelson, 5 May 1969, folder 5/1–6/30/69 (1 of 2), box 5080, RG 16, USDA, NARA.

93. Ned Bayley to Gaylord Nelson, 12 May 1969 and 15 May 1969, folder 5/1–6/30/69 (1 of 2), box 5080, RG 16, USDA, NARA.

94. Frank L. Graham, "Gathering Storm over DDT," *New Republic*, 24 June 1967, 15–17, in folder 4/1–7/31/67, box 4713, RG 16, USDA, NARA.

95. Victor Cohn, "U.S. Curbs DDT, Exempts Key Crops," *Washington Post*, 29 August 1970; Richard Lyons, "U.S. Widens Curb of Users of DDT," *New York Times*, 29 August 1970; "U.S. Widens Its Curbs on Uses of DDT," *Evening Star*, 29 August 1970; and "Registered Uses for Livestock, Lumber, Some Crops Cancelled," *Wall Street Journal*, 31 August 1970, in folder 8/1 (2 of 2), box 5271; see also "New Storm Brewing over DDT," *Business Week*, 8 March 1969, in folder 1/1–4/31/69 (1 of 2), box 5080, RG 16, USDA, NARA.

96. T. C. Byerly to N. D. Bayley, 2 September 1969, folder 9–10/17/69, box 5081, RG 16, USDA, NARA.

97. "Norman Borlaug, D.D.T.," *New York Times*, 26 November 1971, in folder (DDT) 1, box 5460, RG 16, USDA, NARA.

98. Herbert Lawson, "Forest Flap: Were Northwest Firms Saved from Moth, or Did DDT's Harm Outweigh Any Gain?" *Wall Street Journal*, 7 January 1975, in folder 1/1–12/31/75, box 6013, RG 16, USDA, NARA.

99. For examples of communications between USDA officials and Whitten, see Jamie Whitten to Dr. George Mehren, assistant secretary, USDA, 18 July 1966, folder 4–7/1966, box 4543; Jamie Whitten to George Mehren, 18 August 1967, folder 8/1–10/31/67, box 4713; and Ned Bayley to Jamie Whitten, 5 February 1968, folder F—Pesticides, 1/1–2/28/1968, box 4851, RG 16, USDA, NARA.

100. Orville Freeman to Aaron Bagg, president, Wilson Ornithological Society, 8 May 1967, folder 4/1–7/31/67, box 4713, RG 16, USDA, NARA.

101. Jamie L. Whitten, *That We May Live* (Princeton, NJ: D. Van Nostrand Company, Inc., 1966), 209, 39, 83, 215. Whitten also rejected Rachel Carson's understanding of a balance of nature, arguing that humans had to win the struggle over pests and thus control their environment. Around the same time, other authors also asserted that the struggle against insect pests remained a life-and-death contest. Wheeler McMillen, for example, warned that insects were "pervasive, persistent and persevering." Wheeler McMillen, *Bugs or People?* (New York: Appleton-Century, 1965), 5, 20–27, 87, 125.

102. "Fish, Wildlife, and Pesticides," Department of the Interior, Fish and Wildlife Service, 1966, file—Pesticides, box B-453, Audubon Papers.

103. Stewart Udall to Orville Freeman, 2 May 1964; and Freeman to Udall, 18 June 1964, folder 6/6–7/6, box 4132, RG 16, USDA, NARA.

104. Department of the Interior press release, "Dieldrin Pesticide Causing Increasing Number of Bald Eagle Deaths," file—US Dept of Interior, 1966–1972, box B-228, Audubon Papers.

105. "Secretary Hickel Bans Use of 16 Pesticides on Any Interior Lands or Programs," 18 June 1970, folder 6/17–7/22/70, box 5269, RG 16, USDA, NARA.

106. T. C. Byerly to John Dingell, 22 July 1970, folder 6/17–7/22/70, box 5269, RG 16, USDA, NARA.

107. John Dingell to Clifford Hardin, 22 June 1970, 6/17–7/22/70, box 5269, RG 16, USDA, NARA.

108. N. C. Brady to Sen. Richard Russell, 27 May 1964; and N. C. Brady to Charles Murphy, 22 May 1964, folder 4/28–6/5 (1 of 2), box 4132, RG 16, USDA, NARA.

109. Clifford Hardin, memorandum no. 1666, "USDA Policy on Pesticides," 23 October 1969 (superseding memorandum 1565 from 23 December 1964), folder 6/17–7/22/70, box 5269, RG 16, USDA, NARA.

110. "The Need for Pesticides," October 1974, handout from Agricultural Research Service, National Program Staff, USDA, NAL, USDA.

111. Dep. Asst. Sec. of Interior Curtis Bohlen to Hon. John Dingell, 23 September 1971, folder—Pest Part 1, Box 344, RG 48, Interior, NARA.

112. Fred Tschirley to Mrs. F. J. Coates, 18 November 1971, folder 11/3–12/31/71, box 5459, RG 16, USDA, NARA.

113. Nad Bayley to Patricia Petrowski, 13 April 1970; and Patricia Petrowski to Clifford Hardin, 10 March 1970, folder 1/1–5/31, box 5271, RG 16, USDA, NARA.

114. Austin Fox, Farm Pesticides Group, Farm Production Economics Division, Economic Research Service, to Fred Tschirley, 22 September 1971, folder (DDT) 1, box 5460, RG 16, USDA, NARA.

115. Ned Bayley to Gaylord Nelson, 12 May 1969 and 15 May 1969, folder 5/1–6/30/69 (1 of 2), box 5080, RG 16, USDA, NARA.

116. T. C. Bylerly to John Dingell, 22 July 1970, folder 6/17–7/22/70, box 5269, RG 16, USDA, NARA.

117. Diane Tempest to Orville Freeman, 7 February 1966, and Freeman to Tempest, 23 February 1966, folder 1–3/66, box 4543, RG 16, USDA, NARA.

118. Fred Tschirley to Earl Butz, 5 August 1974, folder 6/1–11/31/74, box 5886, RG 16, USDA, NARA.

119. Report of EPA, "The Control of Pesticides Released into the Environment," final draft, 15 March 1975, folder 4/16/75, box 6011, RG 16, USDA, NARA.

120. Clifford Hardin, secretary's memorandum no. 1666, "USDA Policy on Pesticides," 23 October 1969, folder 6/17–7/22/70, box 5269, RG 16, USDA, NARA.

121. "OTA's Pest Management Strategies in Crop Protection," 23 October 1979, file—Agricultural Practices, box B-557, Audubon Papers. For another example of agency support of IPM, see report of EPA, "The Control of Pesticides Released into the Environment," 15 March 1975, folder 4/16/75, box 6011, RG 16, USDA, NARA.

122. Assistant secretary of the interior (name illegible) to Russell Train, 10 May 1972, folder—Pest, Part 2, box 344, RG 48, Interior, NARA.

123. Helga and William Olkowski, "How to Control Garden Pests without Killing Almost Everything Else," Rachel Carson Center for the Living Environment, Inc., 1977, file—Pesticides 1976–1978, box B-211, Audubon Papers.

124. Perkins's discussion of pesticide debates in the 1970s and his portraits of the experts involved have informed the discussion that follows. John Perkins, *Insects, Experts, and the Insecticide Crisis: The Quest for New Pest Management Strategies* (New York and London: Plenum Press, 1982), esp. 58–72, 97–102.

125. Robert van den Bosch, *The Pesticide Conspiracy* (Garden City, NY: Doubleday & Company, 1978), 151–152.

126. Robert L. Rudd, *Pesticides and the Living Landscape* (Madison and Milwaukee University of Wisconsin Press, 1970), 41.

127. Perkins, *Insects, Experts, and the Insecticide Crisis*, 127.

128. Outline of speech, "New Trends and Objectives in Entomology Resarch," at USDA–Landgrant Inst. Luncheon, 1 June 1962, folder 1081, box 21, Series V, Papers of Edward Fred Knipling, NAL, USDA (Knipling Papers).

129. For contemporary as well as retrospective views from Knipling on the research into the sterile-male technique, see correspondence in folders 282, 285, 296, 297, 299, 301, 306, and 310, box 8, Series IV, Correspondence, Collection 210, Knipling Papers.

130. John H. Perkins, "Insights from the History of Pest Control for Public Policy," draft paper for AAAS meeting in January 1979, enclosed with letter, John Perkins to Edward Knipling, 21 November 1978, file 557 or 568, box 12, Collection 210, Knipling Papers.

131. Memorandum, Edward Knipling, director, to all branches and pioneering laboratories, 18 March 1960, folder 310, box 8, Series IV, Knipling Papers.

132. Memorandum, Edward Knipling to branch chiefs (Pesticides Chemicals, Cotton Insect Research, Fruit and Vegetable Insects Research, Grain and Forage Insects Research), 4 April 1966, box 9, Series IV, Knipling Papers.

133. Memorandum, Edward Knipling to R. G. Dahms, chief, Grain and Forage Insects Research Branch, 11 August 1966, folder 341, box 9, Series IV, Knipling Papers.

134. Edward Knipling to John H. Perkins, 18 August 1977, folder 509, box 11, Series IV, Knipling Papers.

135. Edward Knipling to John H. Perkins, 23 January 1979, folder 560, box 12, Series IV, Knipling Papers.

136. Memorandum, Edward Knipling to R. G. Dahms and T. E. Summers, 30 August 1966, with report, "Proposed Procedure and Estimated Requirements for an Integrated Cultural-Insecticide-Sterile Insect Program for the Complete Suppression of the Sugarcane Borer in Louisiana," 7 August 1966, folder 341, box 9, Series IV, Knipling Papers.

137. Donna Bonorden to Edward Knipling, January 1972; Knipling to Bonorden, 27 January 1972; copy of Bonorden oral report, 20 March 1972; Bonorden to Knipling, 11 October 1972; and Knipling to Bonorden, 2 November 1972, folder 1039, box 21, Series IV, Knipling Papers.

138. Perkins, *Insects, Experts, and the Insecticide Crisis*, 187.

139. Edward Knipling to C. S. Cotton, 2 July 1973, folder 413, box 10, Series IV, Knipling Papers.

140. Outline of Edward Knipling speech, "Monoculture, Pesticides, and Alternatives," 27 October 1976, in CA at ARS, folder 1197, box 23, Series IV, Knipling Papers.

When Knipling spoke of alternatives, he was sometimes referring to alternative chemicals, not just nonchemical methods. For example, see Edward Knipling to Roger W. Hallowell Jr., 14 December 1976, folder 508, box 11, Series IV, Knipling Papers.

141. Edward Knipling to John H. Perkins, 30 November 1978; see also Perkins to Knipling, 21 November 1978, with draft, "Insights from the History of Pest Control for Public Policy"; Knipling to Perkins, 6 December 1978; Knipling to Perkins, 20 December 1978 (twenty-one-page letter); and T. W. Edminster, deputy director of agricultural research, to Edward Knipling, 16 January 1979, with Perkins draft, "Boll Weevil Eradication," files 557 and 568, box 12. See also John Perkins manuscript, "Boll Weevil Eradication: Changing Technology and the Roots of a Public Policy Controversy," with handwritten comments by Edward Knipling, enclosed with letter, Perkins to Knipling, 8 November 1978, folder 551, box 11, Series IV, Knipling Papers.

142. Edward Knipling to John H. Perkins, 20 December 1978, folder 557 or 568, box 12, Series IV, Knipling Papers.

143. Perkins was both trying to smooth Knipling's ruffled feathers and to sincerely

learn from his criticisms. He wrote to Knipling at the end of December 1978, "I also hope that your disagreements with my manuscripts will not lead you to write me off as a mere prejudiced crank. I'm quite serious when I say that your challenges force me to re-evaluate and clarify my thoughts." John H. Perkins to Edward Knipling, 11 December 1978; also Perkins to Knipling, 8 January 1979, folder 560, box 12, Series IV, Knipling Papers.

144. Edward Knipling to T. W. Edminster and Thomas Mulhern, cc Waldemar Klassen, 5 January 1979; also Knipling to J. Ritchie Smith, 23 January 1979, folder 557 or 568, box 12, Series IV, Knipling Papers.

145. Edward Knipling to Mr. T. W. Edminster and Dr. Thomas Mulhern, 15 January 1979; also Knipling to J. Ritchie Smith, 23 January 1979, folder 560, box 12, Series IV, Knipling Papers.

146. Others at the USDA and in industry were also in communication with Perkins, giving their reactions to his drafts. Their reactions were usually very negative. See for example, J. Ritchie Smith to Edward Knipling, 15 December 1978; J. Ritchie Smith to John H. Perkins, 15 December 1978; and Perkins to Smith, 22 December 1978, folder 557 and 568, box 12, Series IV, Knipling Papers.

147. Edward Knipling to Mr. T. W. Edminster and Dr. Thomas Mulhern, 15 January 1979; also Edward Knipling to John H. Perkins, 23 January 1979, folder 560. For Knipling's continued critical views of Perkins along with his cordial interactions, see also Knipling to Perkins, 19 April 1979; and Knipling to Charles Parencia, 24 April 1979, folder 557 and 568, box 12, Series IV, Knipling Papers.

148. Edward Knipling, anonymous review of "Boll Weevil Eradication" for *Science*, 20 September 1979, folder 582, box 12, Series IV, Knipling Papers.

149. Edward Knipling to John H. Perkins, 11 December 1980, folder 557 and 568, box 12, Series IV, Knipling Papers.

150. Not all of the USDA staffers were as respectful—or forgiving—of Perkins. See Charles Parencia to John H. Perkins, 25 May 1982, folder 650, box 13, Series IV, Knipling Papers.

151. Edward Knipling to Herbert Oberlander, 23 July 1996, as well as similar letters to Charlie Rogers and Dicky Hardee, also dated 23 July 1996, folder 825, box 16; also Susan Offut to Edward Knipling, 16 October 1995; Knipling to Offut, 20 November 1995; and Knipling to Edgar King, 1 December 1995, folder 787; Knipling to Floyd Horn, 12 April 1996, folder 809; and Knipling to Carol Browner, 15 April 1996, folder 810, box 15, Series IV, Knipling Papers.

152. Edward Knipling to Susan Offut, Economic Research Service administrator, 11 March 1998, with report enclosed, folder 887, box 16, Series IV, Knipling Papers.

153. Ned Bayley to Jamie Whitten, 5 February 1968, folder F—Pesticides, 1/1–2/28/1968, box 4851, RG 16, USDA, NARA.

154. See Rome, *The Genius of Earth Day*, esp. 10, 116–117, 209, 272; also Michael

Egan, *Barry Commoner and the Science of Survival: The Remaking of American Environmentalism* (Cambridge, MA: MIT Press, 2007), 110; Christopher C. Sellers, *Crabgrass Crucible: Suburban Nature and the Rise of Environmentalism in Twentieth-Century America* (Chapel Hill: University of North Carolina Press, 2012), 7, 243–245.

155. Egan, *Barry Commoner and the Science of Survival*, 126; Barry Commoner, *The Closing Circle: Nature, Man, and Technology* (New York: Bantam Books, 1972), 297; see also Rome, *The Genius of Earth Day*, 22.

156. Historian Brooks Flippen, for example, describing criticisms from the National Academy of Sciences about TOSCA's emphasis on acute effects rather than long-term consequences, observed that "TOSCA represented another Train compromise, his praise [of the law] as much an indication of industry resistance as the actual protection the law afforded." J. Brooks Flippen, *Conservative Conservationist: Russell E. Train and the Emergence of American Environmentalism* (Baton Rouge: Louisiana State University Press, 2006), 175.

157. Egan, *Barry Commoner and the Science of Survival*, 139.

158. Article, May–June 1967, *Audubon*, as attachment to letter, Jamie Whitten to George Mehren, 18 August 1967, folder 8/1–10/31/67, box 4713, RG 16, USDA, NARA.

159. "Insecticide Seen as Possible Agent in Human Cancer," *Washington Post*, 7 August 1979.

160. "DDT Makers Must Look Ahead," *Chemical Week*, folder 12/1/69—(1 of 3), box 5081, RG 16, USDA, NARA.

Chapter 6. Love Is Blind: Chemical Disasters at Home and Abroad

1. As historian John Opie observed, "Environmental quality became an essential feature of the quality of life and standard of living that they [Americans] demanded as a birthright." John Opie, *Nature's Nation: An Environmental History of the United States* (Fort Worth, TX: Harcourt Brace and Company, 1998), 432. For examples of public opinion on Earth Day, see "After the Talkfest on Earth Day," *Chicago Tribune*, 22 April 1970, 20; see also Casey Burko, "Mass Action Sought for Earth Day," *Chicago Tribune*, 19 April 1970, N3; Gladwin Hill, "Man and His Environment," *New York Times*, 20 April 1970, 33; Gladwin Hill, "Nation Set to Observe Earth Day," *New York Times*, 21 April 1970, 36.

Support for environmental regulations coexisted with resentment about the role of government in other areas, including escalating taxes. Robert Cameron Mitchell, "Public Opinion and Environmental Politics in the 1970s and 1980s," in *Environmental Policy in the 1980s: Reagan's New Agenda*, ed. Norman J. Vig and Michael E. Kraft (Washington, DC: Congressional Quarterly, 1984).

2. One 1982 *Newsweek* poll showed that 40 percent of respondents disapproved of Reagan's environmental policies, and in a poll a year later, the number rose to 47 percent. Also, in 1983, several ABC News/*Washington Post* polls reported that 50 percent of respondents felt that the president cared more about protecting business violators than enforcing environmental laws. Mitchell, "Public Opinion and Environmental Politics," 57.

3. Ibid., 56.

4. Historian Samuel Hays wrote, for example, that regulations of toxic chemicals in the 1970s "energized the chemical industry to become a leader in the anti-environmental movement." Samuel P. Hays, *A History of Environmental Politics since 1945* (Pittsburgh, PA: University of Pittsburgh Press, 2000), 116.

5. Jonathan Lash, Katherine Gillman, and David Sheridan, *A Season of Spoils: The Reagan Administration's Attack on the Environment* (New York: Pantheon Books, 1984); Norman J. Vig, "The President and the Environment: Revolution or Retreat?" in Vig and Kraft, eds., *Environmental Policy in the 1980s*, 90.

6. For discussion of the shifts at EPA brought about by Gorsuch and others, and changes in the understanding of science, see Michelle Murphy, *Sick Building Syndrome and the Problem of Uncertainty: Environmental Politics, Technoscience, and Women Workers* (Durham, NC, and London: Duke University Press, 2006), esp. 117–199. See also Lash, Gillman, and Sheridan, *A Season of Spoils*, 148.

7. Lash, Gillman, and Sheridan, *A Season of Spoils*, 131, 148, 149.

8. Robert Proctor, *Cancer Wars: How Politics Shapes What We Know and Don't Know about Cancer* (New York: Basic Books, 1995), 97, 125, 140–141.

9. Lash, Gillman, and Sheridan, *A Season of Spoils*, 169, 190–192.

10. John Wargo, *Our Children's Toxic Legacy: How Science and Law Fail to Protect Us from Pesticides* (New Haven, CT: Yale University Press, 1996), 97–98. Joan Claybrook noted that in the first year of the Reagan administration, 505 emergency exemptions were granted, whereas 198 were granted in the last year of the Carter administration. The ratio of approved to denied exemptions: 10 to 1 under Reagan, 6 to 5 under Carter. Joan Claybrook and the Staff of *Public Citizen*, *Retreat from Safety: Reagan's Attack on America's Health* (New York: Pantheon Books, 1984), 157. See also Lash, Gillman, and Sheridan, *A Season of Spoils*, 179–180.

11. Wargo, *Our Children's Toxic Legacy*, 97–98.

12. Claybrook and the Staff of *Public Citizen*, *Retreat from Safety*, 72–73.

13. Lash, Gillman, and Sheridan, *A Season of Spoils*, 20, 57–58.

14. Claybrook and the Staff of *Public Citizen*, *Retreat from Safety*, 121–212; Vig, "The President and the Environment," 88.

15. The effect, observed environmentalist Joan Claybrook, was that the OMB and the White House, with no public consultation, ended up weakening or eliminating environmental standards, "often with only passing regard for the agencies'

statutory obligations." Claybrook and the Staff of *Public Citizen*, *Retreat from Safety*, xviii–xix, xxv–xxvi.

16. Lash, Gillman, and Sheridan, *A Season of Spoils*, 168–169; Claybrook and the Staff of *Public Citizen*, *Retreat from Safety*, 121–122.

17. Christopher Bosso, *Pesticides and Politics: The Life Cycle of a Public Issue* (Pittsburgh, PA: University of Pittsburgh Press, 1987), 199; Lash, Gillman, and Sheridan, *A Season of Spoils*, 168; Wargo, *Our Children's Toxic Legacy*, 95.

18. Lash, Gillman, and Sheridan, *A Season of Spoils*, 192–193.

19. Wargo, *Our Children's Toxic Legacy*, 95.

20. Ibid., 95; Bosso, *Pesticides and Politics*, 199; Lash, Gillman, and Sheridan, *A Season of Spoils*, 189, 193.

21. Claybrook and the Staff of *Public Citizen*, *Retreat from Safety*, 156.

22. Lash, Gillman, and Sheridan, *A Season of Spoils*, 170–172.

23. Claybrook and the Staff of *Public Citizen*, *Retreat from Safety*, 92–93. Thirty rescue workers and medical personnel who came in contact with the workers showed signs of ill health and continued to be monitored for effects from EDB. Lash, Gillman, and Sheridan, *A Season of Spoils*, 176–177.

24. Claybrook and the Staff of *Public Citizen*, *Retreat from Safety*, 93–94.

25. Ibid., 93; Lash, Gillman, and Sheridan, *A Season of Spoils*, 172.

26. Lash, Gillman, and Sheridan, *A Season of Spoils*, 169, 173–174, 176.

27. Ibid., 174–175.

28. Bosso, *Pesticides and Politics*, 239–240; Lash, Gillman, and Sheridan, *A Season of Spoils*, 179; Claybrook and the Staff of *Public Citizen*, *Retreat from Safety*, ix, 94–96, 159.

29. David Rosenbaum, "States' Actions on EDB in Food Resulting in Pattern of Confusion," *New York Times*, 18 February 1984, 1.

30. Ibid.; Martha Brannigan and Marilyn Chase, "Florida Relaxes Ban on Items with EDB," *Wall Street Journal*, 6 February 1984, 1; Steve Weiner, "Food Industry Faces States' Challenges over Levels of EDB," *Wall Street Journal*, 23 February 1984, 1; see also "EDB Pesticide Found in 15% of State's Stored Grain," *Chicago Tribune*, 28 Jan 1984, 2; Seth King, "Separating Wheat from the EDB," *New York Times*, 25 March 1984, E9.

31. For example, Terry Atlas, "EPA Puts Stricter Curbs on EDB," *Chicago Tribune*, 4 February 1984, 1; Kissette Bendy, "EDB, a Harmful Chemical EPA Wants to Control," *Philadelphia Tribune*, 28 February 1984, 3; Andy Pasztzor, "U.S. Crackdown on EDB Pesticide Aims to Avoid Disrupting Grain-Product Sales," *Wall Street Journal*, 6 February 1984, 1.

32. For example, James Worsham, "U.S. Toughens Curbs on EDB," *Chicago Tribune*, 3 March 1984, 2; Philip Boffey, "Experts Disagree on Pesticides Risk," *New York Times*, 4 February 1984, 9; Philip Boffey, "Some Experts Say EDB Risk Is Small," *New York Times*, 21 February 1984, A1.

33. "EDB: A Needless Cancer Crisis," *New York Times*, 21 January 1984, 20; "At Sixes and Sevens on EDB," *New York Times*, 3 March 1984, 22; Francesca Lyman, "Stopping Deadly EDB," *New York Times*, 13 February 1984, A21; Keith Barrons, "Prefer Worms to EDB in Your Cereal?" *Wall Street Journal*, 13 January 1984, 1; "Cancer! Cancer!" *Wall Street Journal*, 14 March 1984, 1.

34. Lash, Gillman, and Sheridan, *A Season of Spoils*, 180–181; Wargo, *Our Children's Toxic Legacy*, 134.

35. Angus Wright, *The Death of Ramón Gonzalez: The Modern Agricultural Dilemma*, rev. ed. (Austin: University of Texas Press, 2005), 196.

36. Lash, Gillman, and Sheridan, *A Season of Spoils*, 180. See also Wargo, *Our Children's Toxic Legacy*, 134.

37. Claybrook and the Staff of *Public Citizen*, *Retreat from Safety*, 158; Lash, Gillman, and Sheridan, *A Season of Spoils*, 182–183.

38. Claybrook and the Staff of *Public Citizen*, *Retreat from Safety*, 158; Lash, Gillman, and Sheridan, *A Season of Spoils*, 183.

39. Lash, Gillman, and Sheridan, *A Season of Spoils*, 185.

40. The last straw for his departure was an insensitive comment about the ethnic diversity of a particular commission. Norman Vig and Michael Kraft, "Environmental Policy from the Seventies and Eighties," in Vig and Kraft, eds., *Environmental Policy in the 1980s*, 3.

41. Environmentalist Joan Claybrook observed, "It took President Reagan two years to realize that public support for environmental laws is so strong that it is politically necessary to at least *appear* to be protecting the environment." Claybrook and the Staff of *Public Citizen*, *Retreat from Safety*, 161.

42. Ibid., 161–163.

43. David Weir and Mark Schapiro, *Circle of Poison: Pesticides and People in a Hungry World* (San Francisco, CA: Institute for Food and Development Policy, 1981). See also *For Export Only: Pesticides and Pills*, a two-part documentary by Robert Richter for PBS, 1981; Ruth Norris, ed., *Pills, Pesticides, and Profits: The International Trade in Toxic Substances* (Croton-on-Hudson, NY: North River Press, 1982).

44. See for example, Dan Kurzman, *A Killing Wind: Inside Union Carbide and the Bhopal Catastrophe* (New York: McGraw-Hill, 1987); Larry Everest, *Behind the Poison Cloud: Union Carbide's Bhopal Massacre* (Chicago: Banner Press, 1985); Anees Chishti, *Dateline Bhopal: A Newsman's Diary of the Gas Disaster* (New Delhi, India: Concept Publishing Company, 1986); Dominique Lapierre and Javier Moro, *Five Past Midnight in Bhopal*, trans. Kathryn Spink (New York: Warner Books, 2002).

45. Examples include Anil Agarwal, Juliet Merrifield, and Rajesh Tandon, *No Place to Run: Local Realities and Global Issues of the Bhopal Disaster* (New Delhi, India, and New Market, TN: Society for Participatory Research in Asia and Highlander Education and Research Center, 1985); *The Bhopal Gas Tragedy, 1984–?: A Report from the*

Sambhavna Trust (Bhopal, India: Bhopal People's Health and Documentation Clinic, 1998); Alfred De Grazia, *A Cloud over Bhopal: Causes, Consequences, and Constructive Solutions* (Bombay, India: Kalos Foundation for the India-America Committee for the Bhopal Victims, 1985); T. R. Chouhan et al., *Bhopal, the Inside Story: Carbide Workers Speak Out on the World's Worst Industrial Disaster* (New York and Mapusa, Goa, India: Apex Press and The Other India Press, 1994); Ward Morehouse and M. Arun Subramaniam, *The Bhopal Tragedy: What Really Happened and What It Means for American Workers and Communities at Risk* (New York: Council on International and Public Affairs, 1986); Brojendra Nath Banerjee, *Environmental Pollution and Bhopal Killings* (Delhi, India: Gian Publishing House, 1987).

46. Four examples are David Weir, *The Bhopal Syndrome: Pesticides, Environment, and Health* (San Francisco, CA: Sierra Club Books, 1987); Banerjee, *Environmental Pollution and Bhopal Killings*; Kim Fortun, *Advocacy after Bhopal: Environmentalism, Disaster, New Global Orders* (Chicago: University of Chicago Press, 2001); Ann Larabee, *Decade of Disaster* (Urbana and Chicago: University of Illinois Press, 2000).

47. See William Bogard, *The Bhopal Tragedy: Language, Logic, and Politics in the Production of a Hazard* (Boulder, CO: Westview Press, 1989); Paul Shrivastava, *Bhopal: Anatomy of a Crisis* (London: Paul Chapman Publishing, 1992); Lisa Newton and David Schmidt, *Wake-Up Calls: Classic Cases in Business Ethics*, 2nd ed. (Mason, OH: Thomson, Southwestern, 2004); Nandini Gunewardena and Mark Schuller, eds., *Capitalizing on Catastrophe: Neoliberal Strategies in Disaster Reconstruction* (Lanham, MD: Rowman Altamira, 2008).

48. Third World holdings were important, bringing in a little more than one-fifth of company profits in 1984. Everest, *Behind the Poison Cloud*, 20–21; Shrivastava, *Bhopal*, 29.

49. Shrivastava, *Bhopal*, 30.

50. Ibid., 30. For background on the Green Revolution and its impact, see David Kinkela, *DDT and the American Century: Global Health, Environmental Politics, and the Pesticide That Changed the World* (Chapel Hill: University of North Carolina Press, 2011). See also Jack Doyle, *Altered Harvest: Agriculture, Genetics, and the Fate of the World's Food Supply* (New York: Penguin Books, 1985), 255–270; Peter Pringle, *Food, Inc.: Mandel to Monsanto—the Promises and Perils of the Biotech Harvest* (New York: Simon and Schuster, 2003), 36–55.

51. Weir, *The Bhopal Syndrome*, 34–35.

52. Ibid., 35.

53. Fortun, *Advocacy after Bhopal*, xv; Everest, *Behind the Poison Cloud*, 46–47; Shrivastava, *Bhopal*, 3, 41–43.

54. Chandana Mathur and Ward Morehouse, "Twice Poisoned Bhopal: Notes on the Continuing Aftermath of the World's Worst Industrial Disaster," *International Labor and Working-Class History* 62 (Fall 2002): 69.

55. Shrivastava, *Bhopal*, 33, 35.

56. Everest, *Behind the Poison Cloud*, 33, 37–38.

57. Ibid., 33, 35; Weir, *The Bhopal Syndrome*, 40–41; *The Bhopal Gas Tragedy, 1984–?*, 9; Elizabeth Guilette, "The Foul Odor of Capital: The Union Carbide Disaster in Bhopal India," in Gunewardena and Schuller, eds., *Capitalizing on Catastrophe*, 175.

58. De Grazia, *A Cloud over Bhopal*, 54.

59. Everest, *Behind the Poison Cloud*, 50. Increasingly, these problems were known in Bhopal and other parts of India after a series of articles by journalist Raj Kumar Keswani. Workers and union officials began to issue their own warnings about plant safety. Weir, *The Bhopal Syndrome*, 40–41.

60. The public system had been deliberately disabled due to the embarrassment of frequent minor leaks. Morehouse and Subramaniam, *The Bhopal Tragedy*, 20–21.

61. Shrivastava, *Bhopal*, 119.

62. Exxon would later pay a $5 billion liability for the 1989 Valdez oil spill (in which no human lives were lost), and Dow set aside $2.2 billion in 2002 to pay for any potential litigation from asbestos production in the United States. Suketu Mehta, "A Cloud Still Hangs over Bhopal," *New York Times*, 2 December 2009. On the process of negotiations, see Shrivastava, *Bhopal*, 119.

63. Fortun, *Advocacy after Bhopal*, 26, 39.

64. Guilette, "The Foul Odor of Capital," 184.

65. Mathur and Morehouse, "Twice Poisoned Bhopal," 73, 74.

66. Sara Goodman, "Poisoned Water Haunts Bhopal 25 Years after Deadly Accident—Report," *New York Times*, 1 December 2009.

67. The following observations of press accounts are based on a survey of articles from the mainstream American press accessed through the Proquest database and nytimes.com; individual articles are cited throughout this chapter as needed. Observations here also draw on the analysis by a communications scholar of media from the first two months after the disaster: Lee Wilkins, *Shared Vulnerability: The Media and American Perceptions of the Bhopal Disaster* (Westport, CT: Greenwood Press, 1987). Also helpful were Larabee, *Decade of Disaster*, and Everest, *Behind the Poison Cloud.*

68. Wilkins, *Shared Vulnerability*, 45.

69. Ibid., 27.

70. Thomas J. Lueck, "Union Carbide Set for Damage Suits," *New York Times*, 7 December 1984, A10.

71. Wilkins, *Shared Vulnerability*, 56, 65, 80, 82; Larabee, *Decade of Disaster*, 92, 120.

72. Larabee, *Decade of Disaster*, 129.

73. For example, Michael Wines, "Firm Calls 'Deliberate' Act Possible in Bhopal Disaster," *Los Angeles Times*, 21 March 1985, 1; Barry Meier, "Carbide Suits May

Affect Industry Norms—Chemical Makers Look at Safety Overseas," *Wall Street Journal*, 5 April 1985, 1.

74. "Carbide to Give $5 Million for Bhopal Victims," *Houston Chronicle*, 18 April 1985, 4; "Union Carbide Agrees to Aid Bhopal Gas Victims," *Chicago Tribune*, 19 April 1985, 22.

75. Larabee, *Decade of Disaster*, 129–130; Everest, *Behind the Poison Cloud*, 86.

76. The Bhopal plant had not been inspected for thirty-one months before the tragedy. Meier, "Carbide Suits May Affect Industry Norms." For stories on the Union Carbide report, see "India Blasts Report on Bhopal Disaster," *San Francisco Chronicle*, 22 March 1985, 26.

77. Everest, *Behind the Poison Cloud*, 18–19.

78. Ibid., 19–20, 120; Weir, *The Bhopal Syndrome*, 60.

79. Examples include Steven Weisman, "Bhopal Is in Midst of Grim Recovery a Year after Leak," *New York Times*, 1 December 1985, 1; Sheila Tefft, "Cloud of Fear Lingers over Bhopal," *Chicago Tribune*, 1 December 1985, 8; "Bhopal Crowds Protest Gas Tragedy," *San Diego Union*, 3 December 1985, A4; "Foreign Firms Feel the Impact of Bhopal Most—a *Wall Street Journal* News Roundup," *Wall Street Journal*, 26 November 1985, 1.

80. Weisman, "Bhopal Is in Midst of Grim Recovery."

81. Larabee, *Decade of Disaster*, 126.

82. "Bhopal Disaster Deliberate Act of Worker, Carbide Claims," *Houston Chronicle*, 11 August 1986, 1. See also Wolfgang Saxon, "Union Carbide Says Upset Worker Set Off the Bhopal Plant Disaster," *New York Times*, 11 August 1986, A4.

83. Rajiv Desai, "An Ill Wind for the People of Once Prosperous Bhopal, the Horror of History's Worst Industrial Disaster May Never End," *Chicago Tribune*, 30 November 1986, H14.

84. Laurie Hays and Richard Koenig, "Dissecting Disaster: How Union Carbide Fleshed Out Its Theory of Sabotage at Bhopal—Its Investigators Scoured India Hunting for Ex-Workers, Rule Out Any 'Mistake'—but Indians Don't Buy Idea," *Wall Street Journal*, 7 July 1988, 1.

85. Stephen Labaton, "Bhopal Outcome: Trial Is Avoided," *New York Times*, 15 February 1989, D3; "The Ghosts of Bhopal," *Economist*, 18 February 1989, 70.

86. For example, Mark Fineman, "New Generation Hit Bhopal—Death Won't Leave City," *Los Angeles Times*, 13 March 1989, 1. See also "$470 Million Settlement OK'd in Bhopal Tragedy," *Houston Chronicle*, 15 February 1989, 1; Dube Siddharth, "Indian Town Agonizes in 5th Year since Gas Leak; Anniversary of Union Carbide Accident in Bhopal Brings Warnings of New Tragedy," *Washington Post*, 3 December 1989, A34.

87. Barbara Crosette, "The World: Bhopal's Tragedy Revisited; 10 Years after the Gas, No End to Tears," *New York Times*, 11 December 1994, E5. Another example,

Bill Dawson, "Decade after Bhopal Tragedy, New Consciousness in Place," *Houston Chronicle*, 2 December 1994, 29.

88. Two years later, the *Village Voice* published an article more critical of Union Carbide (doubting the sabotage theory and observing that company shareholders and executives were financially better off ten years after the disaster) and the lack of resolution for victims. Suketu Mehta, "After Bhopal," *Village Voice*, 10 December 1996. For more on Union Carbide insurance paying much of the company's settlement costs, see Ingrid Eckerman, "Chemical Industry and Public Health," *Master of Public Health* (2001): 24, http://www.lakareformiljon.org/images/stories/dokument/2009/bhopal_gas_disaster.pdf.

89. Moni Basu, "Bhopal Doctor Remains on Case," *Atlanta Journal-Constitution*, 1 December 2004, 1F; Charlene Crabb, "Revisiting the Bhopal Tragedy," *Science* 306, no. 5702 (3 December 2004): 1670–1671; Mian Ridge, "India: Bhopal Disaster Lingers, 25 Years Later," *Christian Science Monitor*, 3 December 2009, 6; Yogesh Vajpeyi, "15 Years On, Bhopal's Deadly Silence," *World Press Review* 47, 3 (1 March 2000): 44–45; Mehta, "A Cloud Still Hangs over Bhopal"; Goodman, "Poisoned Water Haunts Bhopal 25 Years after Deadly Accident"; "NYC Students 'Die' on 25th Anniversary of Bhopal Chemical Disaster," *Gothamist*, http://gothamist.com/2009/12/04/nyc_students_die_on_25th_anniversar.php#photo-1.

90. For example, Amy Waldman, "Some Bhopal Gas Victims Still Seeking Vengeance," *Pittsburgh Post-Gazette*, 23 September 2002, A1.

91. Banerjee, *Environmental Pollution and Bhopal Killings*, 10–12; Everest, *Behind the Poison Cloud*, 69–71.

92. For stories that were the exception, discussing the cyanide association, see Tefft, "Cloud of Fear Lingers over Bhopal"; "Bhopal Crowds Protest Gas Tragedy," *San Diego Union*, 3 December 1985, A4; Everest, *Behind the Poison Cloud*, 75–76, 77.

93. One article actually used the term "mishap," but this gross understatement was clearly an exception. "India Affirms Bhopal Settlement, Reopen's Carbide's Criminal Case," *Christian Science Monitor*, 7 October 1991, 4.

94. For example, Lueck, "Union Carbide Set for Damage Suits"; "Carbide to Give $5 Million for Bhopal Victims"; Siddharth, "Indian Town Agonizes in 5th Year since Gas Leak"; Mehta, "A Cloud Still Hangs over Bhopal." Other estimates were even higher. One journal article, for example, said that the recognized mainstream figure was more than 5,000 deaths, although some activists put it near 20,000. See Mathur and Morehouse, "Twice Poisoned Bhopal."

95. Kinkela, *DDT and the American Century*, 128–129.

96. Lapierre and Moro, *Five Past Midnight in Bhopal*, 72.

97. Ibid., 74–75.

98. Chouhan, *Bhopal, the Inside Story*, 19.

99. Kurzman, *A Killing Wind*, 22.

100. Everest, *Behind the Poison Cloud*, 129–130, 133.

101. Shrivastava, *Bhopal*, 63.

102. For example, Wines, "Firm Calls 'Deliberate' Act Possible in Bhopal Disaster."

103. One estimate from the 1980s put the annual release of known carcinogens at 676 tons, with 10,000 tons of other chemicals also released into the air. Everest, *Behind the Poison Cloud*, 36–37.

104. Ibid., 35, 37.

105. De Grazia, *A Cloud over Bhopal*, 88; Shrivastava, *Bhopal*, 64; Agarwal, Merrifield, and Tandon, *No Place to Run*, 11.

106. Shrivastava, *Bhopal*, 64.

107. Everest, *Behind the Poison Cloud*, 35–36; Shrivastava, *Bhopal*, 64.

108. For discussion of Love Canal and its impact, see Lois Marie Gibbs, *Love Canal and the Birth of the Environmental Health Movement*, 3rd ed. (Washington, DC: Island Press, 2010); Adeline Gordon Levine, *Love Canal: Science, Politics, and People* (Lexington, MA: DC Heath and Company, 1982); Allan Mazur, *A Hazardous Inquiry: The Rashomon Effect at Love Canal* (Cambridge, MA: Harvard University Press, 1998); Amy Marie Hay, "Recipe for Disaster: Chemical Wastes, Community Activists, and Public Health at Love Canal, 1945–2000" (PhD diss., Department of History, Michigan State University, East Lansing, 2005). See also Murphy, *Sick Building Syndrome and the Problem of Uncertainty*; Craig E. Colten and Peter N. Skinner, *The Road to Love Canal: Managing Industrial Waste before EPA* (Austin: University of Texas Press, 1996).

109. Murphy, *Sick Building Syndrome and the Problem of Uncertainty*, 102–103.

110. Mazur, *A Hazardous Inquiry*, 121–141.

111. Gibbs, *Love Canal and the Birth of the Environmental Health Movement*, 210.

112. Mazur, *A Hazardous Inquiry*, 9–11.

113. Bosso, *Pesticides and Politics*, 225–227.

114. Guilette, "The Foul Odor of Capital," 173.

Chapter 7. Recommitment: Endocrine Disruptors, GMOs, and Organic Food

1. John Opie, *Nature's Nation: An Environmental History of the United States* (Fort Worth, TX: Harcourt Brace and Company, 1998), 440–441.

2. Ian Burton, Robert Gates, and Gilbert White, *The Environment as Hazard* (New York and London: The Guilford Press, 1993), 47–48.

3. Environmental writer Mary O'Brien observed, "Environmental risk assessments are overwhelmingly used to construct a scientific-looking claim that an unnecessary, hazardous activity or substance is 'safe,' or poses 'insignificant harm,' or, when dead

bodies clearly belie this, is 'acceptable.'" Mary H. O'Brien, "When Harm Is Not Necessary: Risk Assessment as Diversion," in *Reclaiming the Environmental Debate: The Politics of Health in a Toxic Culture*, ed. Richard H. Hofrichter (Cambridge, MA: MIT Press, 2000), 116. If many environmentalists believed that risks were underestimated, others, of course, argued the opposite, such as entomologist Robert Snetsinger, whose history of the pest-control industry likened ordinary laymen to women and children who didn't really understand pesticides. Robert Snetsinger, *The Ratcatcher's Child: A History of the Pest Control Industry* (Cleveland, OH: Franzak & Foster Company, 1983), esp. 286–287.

4. The issue of attitudes about milk contamination was discussed by Kendra Smith-Howard in "Perfecting Nature's Food: A Cultural and Environmental History of Milk in the United States, 1900–1975" (PhD diss., Department of History, University of Wisconsin–Madison, 2007).

5. Howard Raiffa, "Concluding Remarks," in *Societal Risk Assessment: How Safe Is Safe Enough?* ed. Richard Schwing and Walter Albers Jr. (New York and London: Plenum Press, 1980), 339.

6. Robert N. Proctor, *Cancer Wars: How Politics Shapes What We Know and Don't Know about Cancer* (New York: Basic Books, 1995), 153.

7. Ibid., statistic on incidence and death rates, 249; see also, 1, 34, 69; on Ames, 133–148.

8. Theo Colburn, Dianne Dumanoski, and John Peterson Myers, *Our Stolen Future: Are We Threatening Our Fertility, Intelligence, and Survival? A Scientific Detective Story* (New York: Penguin Publishing, 1996), 202–208.

9. Ibid., 207.

10. McKay Jenkins, *What's Gotten into Us? Staying Healthy in a Toxic World* (New York: Random House, 2011), 17–18.

11. Sandra Steingrabber, *Living Downstream: A Scientist's Personal Investigation of Cancer and the Environment* (New York: Vintage Books, 1997), 112, 119, 120; Jenkins, *What's Gotten into Us?* 168–170.

12. Scientists began investigating the link between chemicals and estrogenic responses in the 1930s, though their warnings were ignored as the postwar chemical revolution took hold. Nancy Langston, "Gender Transformed: Endocrine Disruptors in the Environment," in *Seeing Nature through Gender*, ed. Virginia J. Scharff (Lawrence: University Press of Kansas, 2003), 143. See also Nancy Langston, *Toxic Bodies: Hormone Disruptors and the Legacy of DES* (New Haven, CT: Yale University Press, 2010).

13. Langston, "Gender Transformed," 151–152.

14. Steingrabber, *Living Downstream*; Linda Nash, *Inescapable Ecologies: A History of Environment, Disease, and Knowledge* (Berkeley: University of California Press, 2006).

15. See Langston, *Toxic Bodies*, 135, 136–143. See also the forum edited by Jody

Roberts and Nancy Langston published in *Environmental History* in October 2008, especially Linda Nash, "Purity and Danger: Historical Reflections on the Regulation of Environmental Pollutants," 651–658; Sarah Vogel, "From 'the Dose Makes the Poison' to 'the Timing Makes the Poison': Conceptualizing Risk in the Synthetic Age," 667–673; and Arthur Daemmrich, "Risk Frameworks and Biomonitoring: Distributed Regulation of Synthetic Chemicals in Humans," *Environmental History* 13, no. 4 (October 2008): 684–694.

16. Quoted in Langston, *Toxic Bodies*, 152. Some critics strongly rejected the precautionary principle as unscientific and a rhetorical manipulation. See for example, Aaron Wildavsky, *But Is It True? A Citizen's Guide to Environmental Health and Safety Issues* (Cambridge, MA: Harvard University Press, 1995), 428.

17. Vogel, "From 'the Dose Makes the Poison' to 'the Timing Makes the Poison,'" 670.

18. The survey of print press was done through Ebscohost (including Reader's Guide Retrospective, Business Source Premier, Academic Search Complete) and Proquest from 1980 to 2012. A survey of television news stories on the five largest networks (ABC, CBS, NBC, Fox, and CNN) was done through Vanderbilt Television News Archive from 1968 to 2012.

19. These numbers are estimates based on the indexing of the media databases used. I have found scattered other stories outside these databases.

20. Kara Sissell, "Industry Disputes Findings of Cleaning Products Study," *Chemical Week* 174, no. 8 (March 2012): 33; Philip Clarke, "Product Limitation Is a Real Threat," *Farmer's Weekly* 147, no. 17 (26 October 2007): 56.

21. Gina Kolata, "Chemicals That Mimic Hormones Spark Alarm and Debate," *New York Times*, 19 March 1996, C1.

22. Michael Fumento, "Truth Disruptors," *Forbes* 162, no. 11 (16 November 1998): 146–149.

23. For example, Amara Rose, "Hot Flashes: Hormone Mimics Wreak Havoc on Women's Health," *E: The Environmental Magazine*, January–February 2006, 40.

24. Mindy Pennypacker, "Plastic Containers for Water and Food," *World Watch* (March–April 2004): 8; Adam Voiland, "More Problems with Plastics," *U.S. News & World Report*, 19 May 2008, 14, 54; Linda White, "Childhood Obesity Tied to Some Plastics," *New York Times*, 18 April 2009, A18; Linda White, "Plastics: What's Dangerous, What's Not," *Mother Earth News*, August–September 2009, 70–73; Janet Raloff, "Plastics Ingredients Raise Concerns," *Science News*, 5 June 2010, 14; Harriet Weinstein, "Canned Chemicals," *E: The Environmental Magazine*, January–February 2011, 40–41; Elizabeth Kolbert, "Is There Poison in Our Food?" *Mother Earth News*, February–March 2012, 14–15.

25. Francine Stevens, "Natural Options," *E: The Environmental Magazine*, September–October 1997, 42–43; Becky Gillette, "Premature Puberty," *E: The

Environmental Magazine, November–December 1997, 42–43; Tracey Rembert, "Bringing Up Baby—Naturally," *E: The Environmental Magazine*, September–October 1999, 48; Jordan Rothacker, "The 10 Most Wanted," *Vegetarian Times*, June 2001, 12; Sherrill Sellman, "What Women Must Know," *Total Health*, November–December 2006, 20–22; Lisa Turner, "Find Hormonal Harmony," *Better Nutrition*, May 2009, 34–38; "How to Avoid Chemical Reactions," *Men's Health*, December 2009, 10, 146; Lisa Turner, "Good Enough to Eat," *Better Nutrition*, February 2010, 38–41; "Health Worries over Antibacterial Soap Additive," *New Scientist*, 17 April 2010, 4; Sarah Mosko, "You Are What You Eat," *E: The Environmental Magazine*, September–October 2011, 32–33.

26. Full-page advertisement from Center for Children's Health and the Environment, Mount Sinai Hospital, 17 June 2002, fourth in a series of ads in *New York Times*, A5; see also Lindsey Berkson, "Hormone Deception," *Total Health*, November–December 2002, 18–20; Mike Weilbacher, "Toxic Shock: The Environment-Cancer Connection," *E: The Environmental Magazine*, May 1995, 28; Alyssa Burger, "Sex Offenders," *E: The Environmental Magazine*, March 1996, 44.

27. Adam Voiland, "More Problems with Plastics," *U.S. News & World Report*, 19 May 2008, 54; Sherrill Sellman, "What Women Must Know," *Total Health*, November–December 2006, 20–22; Judith Shulevitz, "The Toxicity Panic," *New Republic*, 28 April 2011, 11–15; advertisement from Mount Sinai, "What's Getting into Our Children?" *New York Times*, 4 August 2009, A23; Jennifer Lee, "Child Obesity Tied to Some Plastics," *New York Times*, 18 April 2009, A18; Amara Rose, "Hot Flashes," *E: The Environmental Magazine*, January–February 2006, 40; Jennifer Bogo, "Brain Storm," *E: The Environmental Magazine*, July–August 1999, 42–43; advertisement from Environmental Working Group, "Something to Chew On," *New York Times*, 23 February 1999, C22; Stevens, "Natural Options."

28. Kolbert, "Is There Poison in Our Food?"; Nicholas Kristof, "Cancer from the Kitchen," *New York Times*, 6 December 2009, WK11; Kathleen O'Grady, "Early Puberty for Girls," *Women's Health Activist*, September–October 2009, 4–5; Darshak Sangahavi, "Preschool Puberty," 17 October 2006, F1; Becky Gillette, "Premature Puberty," *E: The Environmental Magazine*, November–December 1997, 42–43.

29. "Intersex Fish Are Found at High Rate in a Region," *New York Times*, 7 September 2006, A24; Nikhil Swaminathan, "Stealth Attack," *Psychology Today*, October 2012, 78–86; Felicity Barringer, "Hermaphrodite Frogs Found in Suburban Ponds," *New York Times*, 8 April 2008, F2; Fred Guterl, "What's Killing the Frogs?" *Newsweek*, 13 May 2002, 46.

30. William Souder, "It's Not Easy Being Green: Are Weed-Killers Turning Frogs into Hermaphrodites?" *Harper's Magazine*, August 2006, 59–66.

31. Steingrabber, *Living Downstream*, 6, 160, 161.

32. The biologist Tyrone Hayes continued to be one of the best-known atrazine researchers whose strong denunciations of the herbicide made him the object of

Syngenta efforts to discredit his work—and, he argued, derail his career. Rachel Aviv, "Annals of Science: A Valuable Reputation," *New Yorker*, 10 February 2014, 52–63.

33. Nicholas Kristof columns in the *New York Times:* "It's Time to Learn From Frogs," 28 June 2009, WK9; "Chemicals and Our Health," 16 July 2009, A27; "Cancer from the Kitchen," 6 December 2009, WK11; "How Chemicals Affect Us," 3 May 2012, A31; "Big Chem, Big Harm?" 26 August 2012, SR11; "Warnings from a Flabby Mouse," 20 January 2013, SR11.

34. Souder, "It's Not Easy Being Green," 61; see also Swaminathan, "Stealth Attack."

35. "Tulane Withdraws Paper That Prompted Health Fears," *New York Times*, 22 August 1997, A12.

36. William Stevens, "Reproduction May Be Disrupted, but Experts Differ on Damage," *New York Times*, 23 August 1994, C1.

37. Swaminathan, "Stealth Attack."

38. Langston, *Toxic Bodies*, 162–163.

39. Juliet Eilperin, "EPA to Require Tests on Pesticides to Determine Risk to Humans and Animals," *Washington Post*, 16 April 2009, http://www.washingtonpost.com/wp-dyn/content/article/2009/04/15/AR2009041501960.html.

40. George Irving Jr., administrator, ARS, to T. C. Byerly, assistant director, science and education, "Pesticides Research, Regulation and Action: Programs of the Department of Agriculture," 21 September 1970, folder 8/1–9/22 [1 of 2], box 5269, RG 16, USDA, National Archives II (NARA).

41. Alfred D. Chandler Jr., *Shaping the Industrial Century: The Remarkable Story of the Evolution of the Modern Chemical and Pharmaceutical Industries* (Cambridge, MA: Harvard University Press, 2005), 30.

42. Jack Doyle, *Altered Harvest: Agriculture, Genetics, and the Fate of the World's Food Supply* (New York: Penguin Books, 1985), 71; Jack Ralph Kloppenberg Jr., *First the Seed: The Political Economy of Plant Biotechnology, 1492–2000*, 2nd ed. (Madison: University of Wisconsin Press, 2004), Gore quotation 198.

43. Kloppenberg, *First the Seed*, 198, 196, 198, 210, 296–298. See also Peter Pringle, *Food, Inc.: Mandel to Monsanto—the Promises and Perils of the Biotech Harvest* (New York: Simon and Schuster, 2003), 93–94. For further discussion on the corporate evolution of biotech, see Doyle, *Altered Harvest*, 25, 109, 214–215 footnote, 218, 352–353; and Robert Gottlieb, *Environmentalism Unbound: Exploring New Pathways for Change* (Cambridge, MA: MIT Press, 2001), 216–224.

44. For an overview of the Green Revolution and its relationship to biotech, see Pringle, *Food, Inc.*, 36–55; Doyle, *Altered Harvest*, 255–270.

45. Pringle, *Food, Inc.*, 51. As historian Robert Gottlieb observed, biotech advocates self-consciously seized on this legacy, "using language reminiscent of the promotion of green revolution technology." Gottlieb, *Environmentalism Unbound*, 217–218.

46. Kloppenberg, *First the Seed,* 295–296; Pringle, *Food, Inc.,* 69, 77.

47. Kloppenberg, *First the Seed,* 296.

48. Ibid., 191, 296.

49. Pringle, *Food, Inc.,* 190; Kloppenberg, *First the Seed,* 305–306, 316.

50. Mark Schapiro, *Exposed: The Toxic Chemistry of Everyday Products and What's at Stake for American Power* (White River Junction, VT: Chelsea Green Publishing, 2007), 91; *Food, Inc.* (documentary), directed by Robert Kenner, 2008–2009, 91 minutes; Doyle, *Altered Harvest,* 214, 215–6; Kloppenberg, *First the Seed,* 247, 316; Chandler, *Shaping the Industrial Century,* 67.

51. Kloppenberg, *First the Seed,* 303–305; Pringle, *Food, Inc.,* 101; Schapiro, *Exposed,* 86, 91–92; Gottlieb, *Environmentalism Unbound,* 222.

52. Schapiro, *Exposed,* 98–100.

53. Kloppenberg, *First the Seed,* 304–305; Pringle, *Food, Inc.,* 3, 184–187.

54. Schapiro, *Exposed,* 94.

55. Gottlieb, *Environmentalism Unbound,* 219.

56. Joseph Mendelson III, "Untested, Unlabeled, and You're Eating It: The Health and Environmental Hazards of Genetically Engineered Food," in *The Fatal Harvest Reader: The Tragedy of Industrial Agriculture,* ed. Andrew Kimbrell (Washington, DC: Island Press, 2002), 152–153.

57. Activists such as Jeremy Rifkin instead launched a "pure food campaign" and called for a moratorium on GMO technology. Pringle, *Food, Inc.,* 64–68.

58. Ibid., 136–138.

59. Ibid., 109–111.

60. Mendelson, "Untested, Unlabeled, and You're Eating It," 155.

61. Michael Pollan, *The Botany of Desire: A Plant's-Eye View of the World* (New York: Random House, 2001), 207, 209; Mendelson, "Untested, Unlabeled, and You're Eating It," 154.

62. Mendelson, "Untested, Unlabeled, and You're Eating It," 157.

63. For discussion of the whole episode, see Pringle, *Food, Inc.,* 122–134, 138–139.

64. Gottlieb, *Environmentalism Unbound,* 223; Hope Shand, "Intellectual Property: Enhancing Corporate Monopoly and Bioserfdom," in Kimbrell, ed., *The Fatal Harvest Reader.* See also Debi Barker, "Globalization and Industrial Agriculture," in Kimbrell, ed., *The Fatal Harvest Reader.*

65. Gottlieb, *Environmentalism Unbound,* 223. Although they forswore marketing plants that made sterile seeds, the companies instead used genetic use restriction technologies to design plants with certain genetic traits (such as herbicide resistance) that would be inactive unless they were treated with a proprietary chemical activator. Pollan, *The Botany of Desire,* 233–234.

Beginning in the mid-1990s, Monsanto worked hard to police access to and use of its seeds, investigating farmers and bringing some to court. Pringle, *Food, Inc.,*

177–182; *Food, Inc.* (documentary). In her exposé of Monsanto, the French writer Marie-Monique Robin devoted much attention to the company's emphasis on GMOs and its pressure on farmers to adopt them. See *The World According to Monsanto: Pollution, Corruption, and the Control of Our Food Supply, an Investigation into the World's Most Controversial Company* (New York: New Press, 2008).

66. Gottlieb, *Environmentalism Unbound*, 224.

67. Pringle, *Food, Inc.*, 26–27. For more on the international effects of GMOs and industrial agriculture, see Raj Patel, "Better Living through Chemistry," *Stuffed and Starved: The Hidden Battle for the World Food System* (Brooklyn, NY: Melville House Publishing, 2007, 2009), 119–164.

68. Kloppenberg, *First the Seed*, 255.

69. Related to the industry argument that GMOs were natural was the one that they should also be allowed under organic food guidelines. See Rekha Balu, "Monsanto Asks USDA to Delay Decision on Whether Genetic Crops Are Organic," *Wall Street Journal*, 17 April 1998, A6.

70. Kloppenberg, *First the Seed*, 308; quotation from Barker, "Globalization and Industrial Agriculture," 262.

71. Pringle, *Food, Inc.*, 25; Barker, "Globalization and Industrial Agriculture," 262; Patel, "Better Living through Chemistry," 136–137.

72. Pollan, *The Botany of Desire*, 189.

73. Kloppenberg, *First the Seed*, 302–303; Pollan, *The Botany of Desire;* Amy Harmon and Andrew Pollack, "Battle Brewing over Labeling of Genetically Modified Food," *New York Times*, 25 May 2012, A1.

74. Harmon and Pollack, "Battle Brewing over Labeling of Genetically Modified Food"; Mark Bittman, "Buying the Vote on G.M.O.'s," *New York Times*, 23 October 2012; Michael Pollan, "Vote for the Dinner Party: Is This the Year that the Food Movement Finally Enters Politics?" *New York Times Magazine*, 14 October 2012; Anna Almendrala, "Prop 37 Defeated: California Voters Reject Mandatory GMO Labeling," *Huffington Post*, 7 November 2012, http://www.huffingtonpost.com/2012/11/07/prop-37-defeated-californ_n_2088402.html.

75. Stephanie Strom, "Connecticut Approves Labeling Genetically Modified Foods," *New York Times*, 3 June 2013; "Vermont Passes Bill to Require Warning Labels for Genetically Modified Foods," *Guardian*, 24 April 2014, http://www.theguardian.com/environment/2014/apr/24/vermont-bill-gm-food-health-labels.

76. Pollan, *The Botany of Desire*, 214–216.

77. Schapiro, *Exposed*, 87–89; Julia Moskin, "Modified Crops Tap a Wellspring of Protest," *New York Times*, 7 February 2012.

78. Carl Zimmer, "Looking for Ways to Beat the Weeds," *New York Times*, 16 July 2013, D1, D3.

79. Kloppenberg, *First the Seed*, 316.

80. The organic farms, CSAs, farmers' markets, and food co-ops tended to be concentrated in the politically "blue" areas of the Northeast, Pacific Coast, and upper Midwest. Warren J. Belasco, *Appetite for Change: How the Counterculture Took on the Food Industry*, 2nd ed. (Ithaca, NY: Cornell University Press, 2007), 247, 250.

81. On the relationship between the origins of organic food and environmentalism, see Christopher C. Sellers, *Crabgrass Crucible: Suburban Nature and the Rise of Environmentalism in Twentieth-Century America* (Chapel Hill: University of North Carolina Press, 2012), 80–82.

82. Kathleen Doheny, "Organic Produce: What It Means and How to Find It," *Los Angeles Times*, 14 March 1989, 1; Robin Goldwyn Blumenthal, "Trade Group Seeks to End Confusion over What Exactly Is Organic Farming," *Wall Street Journal*, 7 August, 1989, 1; Maria LaGranga, "Demand for Organics Wilting," *Los Angeles Times*, 15 June 1990, 1; Connie Chung, *NBC Evening News*, 14 March 1989. When "organic" was not yet the standard terminology, one NBC News story used "natural farming" more as a contrast to "use of chemicals." Ann Rubenstein, *NBC Evening News*, 7 December 1989.

As food writer Michael Pollan observed years later, with the panic over alar, "Middle America suddenly discovered organic." Michael Pollan, *The Omnivore's Dilemma: A Natural History of Four Meals* (New York: Random House, 2006), 153.

83. Denise Gellene, "'Organic Milk' Makes Debut Here," *Los Angeles Times*, 24 September 1993, 3.

84. Russ Parsons, "Organic, It's Not Easy Being Green," *Los Angeles Times*, 8 July 1993, 8.

85. Gottlieb, *Environmentalism Unbound*, 239; Pollan, *The Omnivore's Dilemma*, 154–155; Martha Groves, "USDA Rules May Be Slow in Coming," *Los Angeles Times*, 1 May 1998, 3; "How Not to Define 'Organic,'" *Consumer Reports*, July 1998, 11.

86. For example, see Laura Shapiro, "Is Organic Better?" *Newsweek*, 1 June 1998, 54–57; Brandon Mitchener, "U.S. Sets Standards for 'Organic' Foods in Move to End Hodgepodge of Rules," *Wall Street Journal*, 27 December 2000; "A New 'Organic' Food Label," *Consumer Reports*, March 2001, 10; Geoffrey Cowley, "Certified Organic," *Newsweek*, 140:14, 30 September 2002, 50–55; "USDA Labeled Organic Foods Appear in Supermarkets October 21," *New York Beacon*, 9 October 2002, 11; Betsy McKay, "The Organic Myth—That Pesticide-Free Product Isn't Always Healthiest Pick; Anyone for 'Natural' Cheetos?" *Wall Street Journal*, 26 December 2002, B1.

87. Starre Vartan, "Happy Eggs: 'Free Range,' 'Cage Free,' 'Organic'—What's the Story?" *E: The Environmental Magazine*, May–June 2003, 42.

88. Max Withers, "The Many Meanings of 'Organic': Demand for Certified Produce Is Up, but So Is Confusion over Farming Standards," *Los Angeles Times*, 4 May 2005, F8.

89. José Rose, "Soaring Sales of Organic Foods Squeeze Supermarket Suppliers," *Wall Street Journal*, 30 August 2006, B3A; "When It Pays to Buy Organic," *Consumer Reports*, February 2006, 12–17; "Great Organic Debate: The Label Is Everywhere, but Controversy Rages over Its Value—and What It Really Means," *Chicago Tribune*, 24 March 2010, 36.

90. Bryan Keogh, "If Label Says Food Is Organic, It Must Be," *Chicago Tribune*, 17 April 2003, 1.18; "USDA Drops New Organic Rules," *Los Angeles Times*, 27 May 2004, C3.

91. Kimberly Kindy, "Debate Grows over 'Organic' Label," *Los Angeles Times*, 3 July 2009, B2.

92. Belasco, *Appetite for Change*, 4, 15, 32, 56–57. Also for the countercultural context for organic food, see Gottlieb, *Environmentalism Unbound*, 233–234; Adam Rome, *The Genius of Earth Day: How a 1970 Teach-In Unexpectedly Made the First Green Generation* (New York: Hill and Wang, 2013), 44–46.

93. Steven Stoll, *Larding the Lean Earth: Soil and Society in Nineteenth-Century America* (New York: Hill and Wang, 2002), 5; Pollan, *The Omnivore's Dilemma*; *Food, Inc.* (documentary).

94. Belasco, *Appetite for Change*, 158–160, 166.

95. Robert Greene, "Big Firms Gobble Organics as USDA Hashes Out Rules," *Los Angeles Times*, 11 September 1996, 7; Dan Berger, "Organic, the Big Business of Organics," *Los Angeles Times*, 8 July 1993, 8; Beth Botts, "Organic Evolution," *Chicago Tribune*, 3 June 2001, 1; Cowley, "Certified Organic."

96. Blumenthal, "Trade Group Seeks to End Confusion over What Exactly Is Organic Farming"; Laura Shapiro, "Is Organic Better?" *Newsweek*, 1 June 1998, 54–57; Cowley, "Certified Organic."

97. McKay, "The Organic Myth." Some articles still hinted that those who bought organic did so for irrational reasons; see "Organic Foods," *NBC Evening News*, 21 October 2002.

98. Dennis Rodkin, "Beyond Veggies: Organic Gardening Magazine Steps Out to Take on the Whole Yard," *Chicago Tribune*, 13 December 1998, 5; Beth Botts, "Organic Evolution: The Latest Generation of Organic Gardeners Embraces Old Methods, New Motives," *Chicago Tribune*, 3 June 2001, 1.

For a profile of J. I. Rodale and changing organic culture, see Andrew N. Case, "Looking for Organic America: J. I. Rodale, The Rodale Press, and the Popular Culture of Environmentalism" (PhD diss., Department of History, University of Wisconsin–Madison, 2012).

99. Rob Kaiser, "Farmers Make a Natural Progression," *Chicago Tribune*, 13 October 2002, 5:1. See also Starre Vartan, "Happy Eggs," *E: The Environmental Magazine*, May–June 2003, 42.

100. Pollan, *The Omnivore's Dilemma*, 158.

101. Susanne Freidberg, *Fresh: A Perishable History* (Cambridge, MA: Belknap Press of Harvard University Press, 2009), 155.

102. Belasco, *Appetite for Change*, 76.

103. Berger, "Organic, the Big Business of Organics." For another example listing the mergers and acquisitions among natural food and conventional corporations, see Greene, "Big Firms Gobble Organics as USDA Hashes Out Rules."

104. Mitchener, "U.S. Sets Standards for 'Organic' Foods in Move to End a Hodgepodge of Rules."

105. Richard Kahlenberg, "Supermarket Chain Becomes Major Source of Organic Food with Little Fanfare," *Los Angeles Times*, 6 July 1995, 17; Kirby Lee Davis, "Riding the Organic Wave," *Journal Record* (Oklahoma City), 28 September 2011; Alissa Gulin, "Organic Products Expo to Draw 20,000 to Baltimore," *Daily Record* (Baltimore), 16 September 2012; Spencer Jakab, "Organic Growth Limited, Even at Whole Foods," *Wall Street Journal*, 12 February 2013.

106. "Organic Food Regulations," *CNN Evening News*, 15 December 1997; "Organic Food," *NBC Evening News*, 15 December 1997; Cowley, "Certified Organic." See also McKay, "The Organic Myth"; Max Withers, "Farmers Markets, Behind the Labels," *Los Angeles Times*, 4 May 2005, F8; "Organic Food," *NBC Evening News*, 4 November 2005; Kindy, "Debate Grows over 'Organic' Label"; Kim Severson, "More Choice, and More Confusion, in Quest for Healthy Eating," *New York Times*, 8 September 2012, A18.

107. The large chains kept the name and image of the natural food company, downplaying their ownership so as not to hurt the organic brand. Rose, "Soaring Sales of Organic Foods Squeeze Supermarket Suppliers"; Steven Gary, "Organic Food Goes Mass Market," *Wall Street Journal*, 4 May 2006, D1; "Target Offers Organic Food," *Los Angeles Times*, 29 September 2006, C3; Aarti Shah, "Food Giants Mull How Far to Push Organic," *PRweek*, 24 March 2008, 6; Laurie Budgar, "Conventional Stores Go Organic," *Natural Foods Merchandiser*, August 2007, 1.

108. *Food, Inc.* (documentary). For more on industry growth, see "Recession Not Hurting Organic Agriculture," *USA Today*, August 2011, 7; Matt Hoffman, "Organic Growth," *La Crosse Tribune* (WI), 12 April 2013, A1; Severson, "More Choice, and More Confusion, in Quest for Healthy Eating."

109. "Organic Food Proves Sustainable in Bad Economy," *Chicago Tribune*, 22 December 2009, 1, 2.

110. Pollan observed that the board ended up "ignor[ing] the 1990 law, drawing up a list of permissible additives and synthetics, from ascorbic acid to xanthan gum." Pollan, *The Omnivore's Dilemma*, 156, 183. Hershberg made his case in the documentary film *Food, Inc.*

111. Patel, *Stuffed and Starved*, 246.

112. Doheny, "Organic Produce"; Blumenthal, "Trade Group Seeks to End Confusion over What Exactly Is Organic Farming"; LaGanga, "Demand for Organics Wilting."

113. Cowley, "Certified Organic."

114. Maggie Shea, "Majority of American Shoppers Prefer Organic," *Modern Baking*, 15 August 2011.

115. Three segments on "Food, Pesticides, and Water," *NBC Evening News*, 12 and 18 October 1994 and 11 August 1997; Gellen, "'Organic Milk' Makes Debut Here"; "Pesticides/Congressional Report," *NBC Evening News*, 27 June 1993; Marla Cone, "Going Organic Can Shield Children from Pesticides," *Los Angeles Times*, 3 September 2005, A10; Andrea Petersen, "Report Supports Organic Produce, but Not Milk," *Wall Street Journal*, 23 October 2012, D4; "Medicine, Parkinson's," *NBC Evening News*, 5 November 2000; "ADHD and Pesticides," *NBC Evening News*, 17 May 2010.

116. Within a few years, top chefs were also embracing organic food as better-tasting. Richard Kahlenberg, "Consumers Catching onto the Organic Cause," *Los Angeles Times*, 27 July 1995, 18; Cowley, "Certified Organic."

117. Withers, "The Many Meanings of 'Organic.'"

118. Shapiro, "Is Organic Better?"; "Pesticide Is No Stranger to Organic Produce," *Los Angeles Times*, 8 May 2002, A27; Cone, "Going Organic Can Shield Children from Pesticides."

119. Laura Sayre, "Is Organic Food Really Better for You?" *Mother Earth News*, December 2007–January 2008, 24; Paul Kita, "The Organic Edge," *Men's Health*, September 2010, 34; Karen Kaplan, "Organic Strawberries Are Superior," *Los Angeles Times*, 2 September 2010, AA4.

120. "Can You Be Sure It's Organic?" *Sun Reporter* (San Francisco), 8 July 1972, 17.

121. Maureen Salamon, "Organic Foods Not Healthier or More Nutritious," *U.S. News & World Report*, September 2012, 1; Elizabeth Weise, "Study Sees No Nutritional Edge in Organic Food," *Miami Times*, 5 September 2012, 16B; "Food/Organics," *NBC Evening News*, 4 September 2012.

122. Kenneth Chang, "Parsing of Data Led to Mixed Messages on Organic Food's Value," *New York Times*, 15 October 2012.

123. "The Case for Organic Food," *Los Angeles Times*, 5 September 2012, A16; Mark Bittman, "That Flawed Stanford Study," *New York Times*, 2 October 2012. See also Dan Charles, "Are Organic Vegetables More Nutritious after All?" *National Public Radio*, 11 July 2014, http://www.npr.org/blogs/thesalt/2014/07/11/330760923/are-organic-vegetables-more-nutritious-after-all.

124. Shapiro, "Is Organic Better?"; Cowley, "Certified Organic."

125. "Can You Be Sure It's Organic?"

126. Belasco, *Appetite for Change*, 119.

127. "Organic Farming Can Feed the World, U-M Study Shows," *La Prensa* (San Antonio, TX), 20 July 2007, 15.

128. John R. Block, "A Reality Check for Organic Food Dreamers," *Wall Street Journal*, 24 December 2012, A11; letters to the editor, *Wall Street Journal*, Nick Maravell, 8 January 2013, and Ron Dudley, 17 January 2013.

129. Jonathan Foley, "A Five-Step Plan to Feed the World," *National Geographic*, May 2014, 43.

130. Tracie McMillan, *The American Way of Eating: Undercover at Walmart, Applebee's, Farm Fields and the Dinner Table* (New York: Scribner, 2012), 8. McMillan observed that the amount spent on food varied by income level so that families earning less than $30,000 in 2009 spent 21–36 percent of income on food, whereas those earning more than $70,000 spent 9 percent on food (254).

131. "When It Pays to Buy Organic." Lists such as this were common in news articles in the 1990s and 2000s; for another example, see Stevens, "Natural Options."

132. Betsy McKay, "When Buying Organic Makes Sense—and When It Doesn't," *Wall Street Journal*, 16 January 2007, D1. Skepticism about the health value of organic foods was still common in 2012, for example, "Food/Organic," *NBC Evening News*, 4 September and 22 October 2012; also on *NBC Evening News*, "Organic Food," 24 June 2010.

133. For example, see Gregory Karp, "A Careful Eye Keeps Organics Affordable," *Chicago Tribune*, 18 May 2008, 6; "When to Buy Organic," *Consumer Reports*, September 2008, 8; Karen Springen, "Best Organics for the Buck," *Newsweek*, 13 October 2008; "Frugal Shoppers Forgoing Organic," *Los Angeles Times*, 10 December 2008, C2; "Great Organic Debate," *Chicago Tribune*, 24 March 2010, 36; Sopriya Doshi, "Break into Organic, Don't Break the Bank," *Chicago Tribune*, 10 April 2010, 18; "How to Save Cash While Shopping Organic," *Chicago Tribune*, 7 March 2012, 6.4; "Personal Best: A Nightly Guide to Fitness," *NBC Evening News*, 2 March 2010.

134. "Organics: Health Food or Hype?" *Good Housekeeping*, October 2002, 58; McKay, "The Organic Myth." See also "Junk Is Junk," *Chicago Tribune*, 4 December 2006, 40; Monica Eng, "'Natural' Isn't Always Organic," *Los Angeles Times*, 11 July 2009, B4.

135. Lisa H. Newton and David P. Schmidt, *Wake-Up Calls: Classic Cases in Business Ethics*, 2nd ed. (Mason, OH: Thomson, Southwestern, 2004), 13.

136. Langston, *Toxic Bodies*, 160; Allan Mazur, *A Hazardous Inquiry: The Rashomon Effect at Love Canal* (Cambridge and London: Harvard University Press, 1998), 50–51.

137. Marcy Darnovsky, "Green Living in a Toxic World: The Pitfalls and Promises of Everyday Environmentalism," in *Reclaiming the Environmental Debate: The Politics of Health in a Toxic Culture*, ed. Richard Hofrichter (Cambridge, MA: MIT Press, 2000), 221, 226.

138. Even Michael Pollan, whose environmental analysis was well researched and complex, owed some of his popularity to this formulation. Pollan wrote environmental

analysis as personal memoir, even structuring his books based on his own meals or garden projects. Many contemporary environmental books are designed as personal explorations; see, for example, Jenkins, *What's Gotten into Us?*

139. Belasco, *Appetite for Change*, 252.

Conclusion

1. On increased pesticide use in the last three decades of the twentieth century, see David Pimental, "After *Silent Spring*: Ecological Effects of Pesticides on Public Health and on Birds and Other Organisms," in *Rachel Carson: Legacy and Challenge*, ed. Lisa Sideris and Kathleen Dean Moore (Albany: State University of New York Press, 2008), 190–191. Many sources have documented the increased use of pesticides through the second half of the twentieth century, for example, Pete Daniel, *Toxic Drift: Pesticides and Health in the Post–World War II South* (Baton Rouge: Louisiana State University Press, 2005), 112; Bruce Gardner, *American Agriculture in the Twentieth Century: How It Flourished and What It Cost* (Cambridge, MA: Harvard University Press, 2002), 25.

2. Christopher J. Bosso, *Pesticides and Politics: The Life Cycle of a Public Issue* (Pittsburgh, PA: University of Pittsburgh Press, 1987), 141.

3. McKay Jenkins, *What's Gotten into Us? Staying Healthy in a Toxic World* (New York: Random House, 2011), 171–172, 172–180. Advertisement for TruGreen from *Clipper Magazine*, 2012. For more on the evolution of lawn culture and its environmental impact, see Paul Robbins, *Lawn People: How Grasses, Weeds, and Chemicals Make Us Who We Are* (Philadelphia, PA: Temple University Press, 2007); Virginia Scott Jenkins, *The Lawn: A History of an American Obsession* (Washington, DC, and London: Smithsonian Institution Press, 1994); Ted Steinberg, *American Green: The Obsessive Quest for the Perfect Lawn* (New York and London: W. W. Norton & Company, 2006).

4. David Kinkela, *DDT and the American Century: Global Health, Environmental Politics, and the Pesticide that Changed the World* (Chapel Hill: University of North Carolina Press, 2011), 166.

5. Many scholars have addressed the evolution of attitudes toward risk and its place in industrial and postindustrial society. For the foundational work, see Ulrich Beck, *Risk Society: Towards a New Modernity*, trans. Mark Ritter (London: Sage Publications, 1992). For an example of how the concept is used in the history of technology, see Arwen P. Mohun, *Risk: Negotiating Safety in American Society* (Baltimore, MD: Johns Hopkins University Press, 2013).

6. Robert Rudd, "The Indirect Effects of Chemicals in Nature," National Audubon Convention, 10 November 1958, file—Pesticides, box B-453, Papers of the National Audubon Society, New York Public Library.

7. Butz didn't realize that the vastly expanded agricultural infrastructure would lead in the 1980s to a farm crisis when international grain production recovered and fuel and credit costs went up for American farmers. Warren Belasco, *Appetite for Change: How the Counterculture Took on the Food Industry*, 2nd ed. (Ithaca, NY: Cornell University Press, 2007), 133.

8. Orville L. Freedman, "Perspectives and Prospects," *Agricultural History* 66, no. 2 (Spring 1992): 4, 5.

9. Jonathan Foley, "A Five-Step Plan to Feed the World," *National Geographic*, May 2014, 27.

10. Michael Pollan, *The Botany of Desire: A Plant's-Eye View of the World* (New York: Random House, 2001), 225. In another observation about the downsides of monoculture, historian Joshua Blu Buhs observed in 2004, "Pests are not born; they are made." Joshua Blu Buhs, *The Fire Ant Wars: Nature, Science, and Public Policy in Twentieth-Century America* (Chicago: University of Chicago Press, 2004), 38.

11. David Weir, *The Bhopal Syndrome: Pesticides, Environment, and Health* (San Francisco, CA: Sierra Club Books, 1987), 22–23. On patterns of herbicide use, see Clinton Evans, *The War on Weeds in the Prairie West: An Environmental History* (Calgary, Alberta: University of Calgary Press, 2002), 166, 171. For the estimated number of species resistant to pesticides in 2008, see Pimental, "After *Silent Spring*," 192.

12. Angus Wright, *The Death of Ramón Gonzalez: The Modern Agricultural Dilemma*, rev. ed. (Austin: University of Texas Press, 2005), 275. See also, with slightly different figures of crop losses, Paul Hawken, Amory Lovins, and L. Hunter Lovins, *Natural Capitalism: Creating the Next Industrial Revolution* (Boston, MA: Little, Brown and Company, 1999), 196. Warren Belasco, writing about crop losses in the mid-1980s, said they were about 20 percent, the same as in 1945. Belasco, *Appetite for Change*, 118, 139. For an example of yields, see Steven Stoll, *Larding the Lean Earth: Soil and Society in Nineteenth-Century America* (New York: Hill and Wang, 2002), 220–221.

13. Hawken, Lovins, and Lovins, *Natural Capitalism*, 194.

14. Pollan, *The Botany of Desire*, 226.

15. Aaron Wildavsky, *But Is It True? A Citizen's Guide to Environmental Health and Safety Issues* (Cambridge, MA: Harvard University Press, 1995), 55.

16. Steven Maguire, "Contested Icons: Rachel Carson and DDT," in Sideris and Moore, eds., *Rachel Carson: Legacy and Challenge*, 194–195; Kinkela, *DDT and the American Century*, 4–5.

17. James L. A. Webb Jr., *Humanity's Burden: A Global History of Malaria* (Cambridge: Cambridge University Press, 2009), 153–154. For background history on American and international efforts to battle mosquitoes, including those that carry malaria, see Andrew Spielman, ScD, and Michael D'Antonio, *Mosquito: A Natural History of Our Most Persistent and Deadly Foe* (New York: Hyperion, 2001); Gordon

Patterson, *The Mosquito Crusades: A History of the American Anti-Mosquito Movement from the Reed Commission to the First Earth Day* (New Brunswick, NJ: Rutgers University Press, 2009); and Amy L. S. Staples, *The Birth of Development: How the World Bank, Food and Agriculture Organization, and the World Health Organization Changed the World, 1945–1965* (Kent, OH: Kent State University Press, 2006).

18. Webb, *Humanity's Burden*, 174.

19. Agreement on these terms of use was reached at the 2001 Stockholm Convention on Persistent Organic Pollutants. Ibid., 185–186.

20. For discussion of the issue, see Mark Hamilton Lytle, *The Gentle Subversive: Rachel Carson, Silent Spring, and the Rise of the Environmental Movement* (New York: Oxford University Press, 2007), 220–225; John Quiggin and Tim Lambert, "Rehabilitating Carson: Why Do Some People Continue to Hold Rachel Carson Responsible for Millions of Malaria Deaths?" *Prospect*, 24 May 2008, http://www.prospectmagazine.co.uk/magazine/rehabilitatingcarson; Naomi Oreskes and Erik M. Conway, *Merchants of Doubt: How a Handful of Scientists Obscured the Truth on Issues from Tobacco Smoke to Global Warming* (London: Bloomsbury, 2010). For an example of the anti-Carson charges, see Roger Meiners and Andrew Morriss, "Silent Springs and Silent Villages: Pesticides and the Trampling of Property Rights," in *Government vs. Environment*, ed. Donald Leal and Roger Meiners (Lanham, MD: Rowman & Littlefield Publishers, 2002), 26–30.

21. McKay Jenkins, *What's Gotten into US?* 170.

22. Linda Nash, *Inescapable Ecologies: A History of Environment, Disease, and Knowledge* (Berkeley: University of California Press, 2006), 159–160.

23. One environmental issue linked to pesticides became a more frequent topic in the press by the early twenty-first century: the collapse of bee and pollinator populations. Scientists were increasingly worried about this development, which might endanger the pollination of many commercially raised crops. There was growing evidence by 2012 that colony-collapse disorder and declining pollinator populations were linked to chronic pesticide exposure. For example, Susan Millius, "Pesticide-Dosed Bees Can Lose Royals, Way Home," *Science News*, 5 May 2012, 8.

24. Wright, *The Death of Ramón Gonzalez*, 139.

25. For discussion of the lack of UFW support from environmental organizations, see Robert Gordon, "Poisons in the Fields: The United Farm Workers, Pesticides, and Environmental Politics," *Pacific Historical Review* 68, no. 1 (February 1999): 51–77. On effects of pesticides on agricultural workers (and the role of Chavez), see Wright, *The Death of Ramón Gonzalez*, 21.

26. Wright, *The Death of Ramón Gonzalez*, 355.

27. In addition, biologist Sandra Steingrabber lobbied for another corollary principle: "least toxic alternative," which would prohibit the use of toxic substances if a goal could be accomplished without them. Sandra Steingrabber, *Living Downstream:*

A Scientist's Personal Investigation of Cancer and the Environment (New York: Vintage Books, 1997), 270.

28. Robert Long to Dr. T. Colin Campbell, Department of Biochemistry and Nutrition, Virginia Polytechnic Institute, 1 March 1974, folder 1/1–3/29/74, box 5886, RG 16, USDA, National Archives II (NARA).

29. Fred Tschirley to Dr. Rene J. Dubos, professor emeritus, Rockefeller University, 8 January 1974, folder 1/1–3/29/1974, box 5886, RG 16, USDA, NARA.

30. McKay Jenkins, *What's Gotten into Us?* 186.

31. Ibid., 141.

32. Statistic cited in Michael Egan, *Barry Commoner and the Science of Survival: The Remaking of American Environmentalism* (Cambridge, MA: MIT Press, 2007), 4.

33. Jim Guest, "Chemical Reaction," *Consumer Reports*, September 2013, 6.

Bibliography

Archives

Harry S. Truman Library, Independence, MO
Papers of Charles Brannan
Papers of Harry S. Truman Official File

National Agricultural Library, United States Department of Agriculture, Beltsville, MD
Collection 182, USDA History
Collection 210, Edward Fred Knipling Papers
Collection 313 (unprocessed)

National Archives II, College Park, MD
Record Group 16, United States Department of Agriculture
Record Group 48, Department of the Interior
Record Group 166, Foreign Agricultural Service
Record Group 412, Environmental Protection Agency

National Audubon Society—Manuscript Division, New York Public Library, New York, NY
Section B: Presidents, Vice Presidents, and General Files

Othmer Library, Chemical Heritage Foundation, Philadelphia, PA
Dow Collection
Hercules Collection

Rachel Carson Papers, Beinecke Library, Yale University, New Haven, CT
Series I
YCAL 46

Vanderbilt Television News Archive, Nashville, TN
News programs 1968 to present, consulted on-line.

Newspapers and Magazines

American Mercury
American Sociological Review
Audubon Magazine
Barron's National Business and Financial Weekly
Better Nutrition
Bismarck Tribune
Business Week
Chemical Week
Discover
Dollars & Sense
E: The Environmental Magazine
Ecologist
Farmers Weekly
Forbes
Harper's Magazine
Illinois State Journal
Issues
Men's Health
Mother Earth News
Land Economics
Los Angeles Times
Nation
New Republic
New Scientist
Newsweek
New Yorker
New York Times
New York Times Magazine
Onearth
Popular Science
Prospect Magazine
Psychology Today
Science News
Science World

Scientific American Earth
Skeptic
Sports Illustrated
Time International
Times Standard
Total Health
U.S. News & World Report
Vegetarian Times
Washington Post
Women & Environments International Magazine
Women's Health Activist
World Health Forum
World Watch

Television News and Films

ABC News
CBS News
CNN News
Fox News
NBC News

The American Experience: Rachel Carson's Silent Spring, reporter and producer, Neil Goodwin, 1993, 55 minutes.
CBS Reports: The Silent Spring *of Rachel Carson*, 1963, 60 minutes.
Food, Inc., directed by Robert Kenner, 2008–2009, 91 minutes.
For Export Only: Pesticides and Pills. PBS television, reporter and producer, Robert Richter, 1981, 120 minutes.
Living Downstream, directed by Chanda Chevannes, 2010, 82 minutes.

Books

Ackerman, Frank. *Poisoned for Pennies: The Economics of Toxics and Precaution.* Washington, DC: Island Press, 2008.
Agarwal, Anil, Juliet Merrifield, and Rajesh Tandon. *No Place to Run: Local Realities and Global Issues of the Bhopal Disaster.* New Delhi, India, and New Market, TN: Society for Participatory Research in Asia and Highlander Education and Research Center, 1985.

Allan, Stuart, Barbara Adam, and Cynthia Carter, eds. *Environmental Risks and the Media.* London and New York: Routledge, 2000.

Anderson, J. L. *Industrializing the Corn Belt: Agriculture, Technology, and Environment, 1945–1972.* DeKalb: Northern Illinois University Press, 2009.

Andrews, Richard L. *Managing the Environment, Managing Ourselves: A History of American Environmental Policy.* New Haven, CT: Yale University Press, 1999.

Banerjee, Brojendra Nath. *Environmental Pollution and Bhopal Killings.* Delhi, India: Gian Publishing House, 1987.

Beck, Ulrich. *Risk Society: Towards a New Modernity.* Translated by Mark Ritter. London: Sage Publications, 1992.

Belasco, Warren J. *Appetite for Change: How the Counterculture Took on the Food Industry,* 2nd ed. Ithaca, NY: Cornell University Press, 2007.

The Bhopal Gas Tragedy, 1984–?: A Report from the Sambhavna Trust. Bhopal, India: Bhopal People's Health and Documentation Clinic, 1998.

Bogard, William. *The Bhopal Tragedy: Language, Logic, and Politics in the Production of a Hazard.* Boulder, CO: Westview Press, 1989.

Bosso, Christopher. *Environment, Inc.: From Grassroots to Beltway.* Lawrence: University Press of Kansas, 2005.

———. *Pesticides and Politics: The Life Cycle of a Public Issue.* Pittsburgh, PA: University of Pittsburgh Press, 1987.

Brooks, Paul. *The House of Life: Rachel Carson at Work.* Boston, MA: Houghton Mifflin Company, 1972.

———. *Speaking for Nature.* San Francisco, CA: Sierra Club Books, 1980.

Buhs, Joshua Blu. *The Fire Ant Wars: Nature, Science, and Public Policy in Twentieth-Century America.* Chicago: University of Chicago Press, 2004.

Burton, Ian, Robert W. Gates, and Gilbert F. White. *The Environment as Hazard,* 2nd ed. New York and London: Guilford Press, 1993.

Carson, Rachel. *Silent Spring.* New York: Houghton Mifflin Harcourt, 1962.

Cecil, Paul Frederick. *Herbicidal Warfare: The Ranch Hand Project in Vietnam.* New York: Praeger, 1986.

Chambers, David Wade. *Worm in the Bud: Case Study of the Pesticide Controversy.* Victoria, Australia: Deakin University, 1984.

Chandler, Alfred D., Jr. *Shaping the Industrial Century: The Remarkable Story of the Evolution of the Modern Chemical and Pharmaceutical Industries.* Cambridge, MA: Harvard University Press, 2005.

Chishti, Anees. *Dateline Bhopal: A Newsman's Diary of the Gas Disaster.* New Delhi, India: Concept Publishing Company, 1986.

Chouhan, T. R., et al. *Bhopal, the Inside Story: Carbide Workers Speak Out on the World's Worst Industrial Disaster.* New York and Mapusa, Goa, India: Apex Press and The Other India Press, 1994.

Claybrook, Joan, and the Staff of *Public Citizen*. *Retreat from Safety: Reagan's Attack on America's Health*. New York: Pantheon Books, 1984.

Colburn, Theo, Dianne Dumanoski, and John Peterson Myers. *Our Stolen Future: Are We Threatening Our Fertility, Intelligence, and Survival? A Scientific Detective Story*. Foreword by Vice President Al Gore. New York: Penguin Publishing, 1996.

Colten, Craig E., and Peter N. Skinner. *The Road to Love Canal: Managing Industrial Waste before EPA*. Austin: University of Texas Press, 1996.

Commoner, Barry. *The Closing Circle: Nature, Man, and Technology*. New York: Bantam Books, 1972.

Conkin, Paul K. *A Revolution down on the Farm: The Transformation of American Agriculture since 1929*. Lexington: University Press of Kentucky, 2008.

Cook, Timothy E. *Governing with the News: The News Media as a Political Institution*, 2nd ed. Chicago: University of Chicago Press, 2005.

Corbett, Julia B. *Communicating Nature: How We Create and Understand Environmental Messages*. Washington, DC: Island Press, 2006.

Cullather, Nick. *The Hungry World: America's Cold War Battle against Poverty in Asia*. Cambridge, MA: Harvard University Press, 2010.

Daniel, Pete. *Lost Revolutions: The South in the 1950s*. Chapel Hill and London: University of North Carolina Press for Smithsonian National Museum of American History, 2000.

———. *Toxic Drift: Pesticides and Health in the Post–World War II South*. Baton Rouge: Louisiana State University Press, 2005.

Doyle, Jack. *Altered Harvest: Agriculture, Genetics, and the Fate of the World's Food Supply*. New York: Penguin Books, 1995.

Dunlap, Thomas R. *DDT: Scientists, Citizens, and Public Policy*. Princeton, NJ: Princeton University Press, 1981.

Dux, John, and P. J. Young. *Agent Orange: The Bitter Harvest*. Sydney, Australia: Hodder and Stoughton, 1980.

Egan, Michael. *Barry Commoner and the Science of Survival: The Remaking of American Environmentalism*. Cambridge, MA: MIT Press, 2007.

Ehrlich, Paul. *The Population Bomb*. New York: Ballantine Books, 1968.

Ekbladh, David. *The Great American Mission: Modernization and the Construction of an American World Order*. Princeton, NJ: Princeton University Press, 2010.

Engerman, David C., Nils Gilman, Mark H. Haefele, and Michael E. Latham, eds. *Staging Growth: Modernization, Development and the Global Cold War*. Amherst and Boston: University of Massachusetts Press, 2003.

Evans, Clinton L. *The War on Weeds in the Prairie West: An Environmental History*. Calgary, Alberta: University of Calgary Press, 2002.

Everest, Larry. *Behind the Poison Cloud: Union Carbide's Bhopal Massacre*. Chicago: Banner Press, 1985.

Fitzgerald, Deborah. *Every Farm a Factory: The Industrial Ideal in American Agriculture.* New Haven, CT: Yale University Press, 2003.

Flippen, J. Brooks. *Conservative Conservationist: Russell E. Train and the Emergence of American Environmentalism.* Baton Rouge: Louisiana State University Press, 2006.

———. *Nixon and the Environment.* Albuquerque: University of New Mexico Press, 2000.

Fortun, Kim. *Advocacy after Bhopal: Environmentalism, Disaster, New Global Orders.* Chicago: University of Chicago Press, 2001.

Freeman, Martha, ed. *Always Rachel: The Letters of Rachel Carson and Dorothy Freeman, 1952–1964.* Boston: Beacon Press, 1995.

Freidberg, Susanne. *Fresh: A Perishable History.* Cambridge, MA: Belknap Press of Harvard University Press, 2009.

Gardner, Bruce L. *American Agriculture in the Twentieth Century: How It Flourished and What It Cost.* Cambridge, MA: Harvard University Press, 2002.

Gartner, Carol B. *Rachel Carson.* New York: Frederick Unger Publishing Co., 1983.

George, Dr. John L. *The Program to Eradicate the Imported Fire Ant, Preliminary Observations; A Report to the Conservation Foundation and the New York Zoological Society.* New York: Conservation Foundation, 1958.

George, Susan. *How the Other Half Dies: The Real Reasons for World Hunger.* Montclair, NJ: Allanheld, Osmun & Co., Publishers, 1977.

Gibbs, Lois Marie. *Love Canal and the Birth of the Environmental Health Movement,* 3rd ed. Washington, DC: Island Press, 2010.

Gilman, Nils. *Mandarins of the Future: Modernization Theory in Cold War America.* Baltimore, MD: Johns Hopkins University Press, 2003.

Gottlieb, Robert. *Environmentalism Unbound: Exploring New Pathways for Change.* Cambridge, MA: MIT Press, 2001.

Graham, Frank, Jr., with Carl W. Buchheister. *The Audubon Ark: A History of the National Audubon Society.* Austin: University of Texas Press, 1990.

Grazia, Alfred de. *A Cloud over Bhopal: Causes, Consequences, and Constructive Solutions.* Bombay, India: Kalos Foundation for the India-America Committee for the Bhopal Victims, 1985.

Gunewardena, Nandini, and Mark Schuller, eds. *Capitalizing on Catastrophe: Neoliberal Strategies in Disaster Reconstruction.* Lanham, MD: Rowman Altamira, 2008.

Hawken, Paul, Amory Lovins, and L. Hunter Lovins. *Natural Capitalism: Creating the Next Industrial Revolution.* Boston, MA: Little, Brown and Company, 1999.

Hays, Samuel P. *Beauty, Health, and Permanence: Environmental Politics in the United States, 1955–1985.* Cambridge: Cambridge University Press, 1987.

———. *Explorations in Environmental History.* Pittsburgh, PA: University of Pittsburgh Press, 1998.

———. *A History of Environmental Politics since 1945.* Pittsburgh, PA: University of Pittsburgh Press, 2000.

Herber, Lewis (real name Murray Bookchin). *Our Synthetic Environment.* New York: Alfred Knopf, 1962.

Hersh, Seymour M. *Chemical and Biological Warfare: America's Hidden Arsenal.* Indianapolis, IN: Bobbs-Merrill, 1968.

Hofrichter, Richard, ed. *Reclaiming the Environmental Debate: The Politics of Health in a Toxic Culture.* Cambridge, MA: MIT Press, 2000.

Hynes, H. Patricia. *The Recurring* Silent Spring. New York: Pergamon Press, 1989.

Institute of Medicine of the National Academies. *Veterans and Agent Orange, Update 2006.* Washington, DC: National Academies Press, 2007.

Jackson, Kenneth. *Crabgrass Frontier: The Suburbanization of the United States.* New York: Oxford University Press, 1985.

Jenkins, McKay. *What's Gotten into Us? Staying Healthy in a Toxic World.* New York: Random House, 2011.

Jenkins, Virginia Scott. *The Lawn: A History of an American Obsession.* Washington, DC, and London: Smithsonian Institution Press, 1994.

Kimbrell, Andrew, ed. *The Fatal Harvest Reader: The Tragedy of Industrial Agriculture.* Washington, DC: Island Press, 2002.

Kinkela, David. *DDT and the American Century: Global Health, Environmental Politics, and the Pesticide That Changed the World.* Chapel Hill: University of North Carolina Press, 2011.

Kirk, Andrew G. *Counterculture Green: The Whole Earth Catalog and American Environmentalism.* Lawrence: University Press of Kansas, 2007.

Kloppenberg, Jack Ralph. Jr. *First the Seed: The Political Economy of Plant Biotechnology, 1492–2000,* 2nd ed. Madison: University of Wisconsin Press, 2004.

Kurzman, Dan. *A Killing Wind: Inside Union Carbide and the Bhopal Catastrophe.* New York: McGraw-Hill, 1987.

Langston, Nancy. *Toxic Bodies: Hormone Disruptors and the Legacy of DES.* New Haven, CT: Yale University Press, 2010.

Lapierre, Dominique, and Javier Moro. *Five Past Midnight in Bhopal.* Translated from the French by Kathryn Spink. New York: Warner Books, 2002.

Larabee, Ann. *Decade of Disaster.* Urbana and Chicago: University of Illinois Press, 2000.

Lash, Jonathan, Katherine Gillman, and David Sheridan. *A Season of Spoils: The Reagan Administration's Attack on the Environment.* New York: Pantheon Books, 1984.

Lear, Linda, ed. *Lost Woods: The Discovered Writings of Rachel Carson.* Boston, MA: Beacon Press, 1998.

———. *Rachel Carson: Witness for Nature.* New York: Henry Holt and Company, 1997.

Leopold, Aldo. *A Sand County Almanac, with Essays on Conservation from Round River.* Illustrated by Charles W. Schwartz. New York: Ballantine Books, 1966.

Lester, Libby. *Media and Environment.* Cambridge: Polity Press, 2010.

Levine, Adeline Gordon. *Love Canal: Science, Politics, and People.* Lexington, MA: DC Heath and Company, 1982.

Longgood, William. *Poisons in Your Food.* New York: Simon and Schuster, 1960.

Lytle, Mark Hamilton. *The Gentle Subversive: Rachel Carson,* Silent Spring, *and the Rise of the Environmental Movement.* New York: Oxford University Press, 2007.

Marco, Gino J., Robert M. Hollingworth, and William Durham, eds. Silent Spring *Revisited.* Washington, DC: American Chemical Society, 1987.

Martini, Edwin A. *Agent Orange: History, Science, and the Politics of Uncertainty.* Amherst and Boston: University of Massachusetts Press, 2012.

Mazur, Allan. *A Hazardous Inquiry: The Rashomon Effect at Love Canal.* Cambridge, MA: Harvard University Press, 1998.

McCarthy, Richard D. *The Ultimate Folly: War by Pestilence, Asphyxiation, and Defoliation.* New York: Alfred Knopf, 1969.

McCay, Mary. *Rachel Carson.* New York: Twayne Publishers, 1993.

McMillan, Tracie. *The American Way of Eating: Undercover at Walmart, Applebee's, Farm Fields and the Dinner Table.* New York: Scribner, 2012.

McMillen, Wheeler. *Bugs or People?* New York: Appleton-Century, 1965.

McNeill, J. R. *Something New under the Sun: An Environmental History of the Twentieth-Century World.* New York: W. W. Norton, 2000.

——— and Corinna Unger, eds. *Environmental Histories of the Cold War.* Washington, DC, and Cambridge: German Historical Institute, 2010.

McWilliams, James E. *American Pests: The Losing War on Insects from Colonial Times to DDT.* New York: Columbia University Press, 2008.

Meadows, Donella H., Dennis L. Meadows, Jorgen Randers, and William Behrens III. *The Limits to Growth: A Report for the Club of Rome's Project on the Predicament of Mankind,* 2nd ed. New York: Potomac Associates Book, 1974.

Mohun, Arwen P. *Risk: Negotiating Safety in American Society.* Baltimore, MD: Johns Hopkins University Press, 2013.

Morehouse, Ward, and M. Arun Subramaniam. *The Bhopal Tragedy: What Really Happened and What It Means for American Workers and Communities at Risk. A Preliminary Report for the Citizens Commission on Bhopal.* Foreword by Les Leopold and Anthony Mazzocchi. New York: Council on International and Public Affairs, 1986.

Murphy, Michelle. *Sick Building Syndrome and the Problem of Uncertainty: Environmental Politics, Technoscience, and Women Workers.* Durham, NC, and London: Duke University Press, 2006.

Murphy, Priscilla Coit. *What a Book Can Do: The Publication and Reception of* Silent Spring. Amherst: University of Massachusetts Press, 2005.

Nash, Linda. *Inescapable Ecologies: A History of Environment, Disease, and Knowledge.* Berkeley: University of California Press, 2006.

Nash, Roderick Frazier. *The Rights of Nature: A History of Environmental Ethics.* Madison: University of Wisconsin Press, 1989.

Neilands, J. B., G. H. Orians, E. W. Pfeiffer, A. Vennema, and A. H. Westing. *Harvest of Death: Chemical Warfare in Vietnam and Cambodia.* New York: Free Press, 1972.

Newton, Lisa H., and David P. Schmidt. *Wake-Up Calls: Classic Cases in Business Ethics*, 2nd ed. Mason, OH: Thomson, Southwestern, 2004.

Norris, Ruth, ed. *Pills, Pesticides, and Profits: The International Trade in Toxic Substances.* Croton-on-Hudson, NY: North River Press, 1982.

Opie, John. *Nature's Nation: An Environmental History of the United States.* Fort Worth, TX: Harcourt Brace and Company, 1998.

Oreskes, Naomi, and Erik M. Conway. *Merchants of Doubt: How a Handful of Scientists Obscured the Truth on Issues from Tobacco Smoke to Global Warming.* London: Bloomsbury, 2010.

Osborn, Fairfield. *Our Plundered Planet.* Boston: Little, Brown and Company, 1948.

Outwater, Alice. *Water: A Natural History.* Illustrations by Billy Brauer. New York: Basic Books, 1996.

Packenham, Robert A. *Liberal America and the Third World: Political Development Ideas in Foreign Aid and Social Science.* Princeton, NJ: Princeton University Press, 1973.

Patel, Raj. *Stuffed and Starved: The Hidden Battle for the World Food System.* Brooklyn, NY: Melville House Publishing, 2009.

Patterson, Gordon. *The Mosquito Crusades: A History of the American Anti-Mosquito Movement from the Reed Commission to the First Earth Day.* New Brunswick, NJ: Rutgers University Press, 2009.

Perkins, John H. *Geopolitics and the Green Revolution: Wheat, Genes, and the Cold War.* New York: Oxford University Press, 1997.

———. *Insects, Experts, and the Insecticide Crisis: The Quest for New Pest Management Strategies.* New York and London: Plenum Press, 1982.

Pollan, Michael. *The Botany of Desire: A Plant's-Eye View of the World.* New York: Random House, 2001.

———. *The Omnivore's Dilemma: A Natural History of Four Meals.* New York: Penguin Books, 2006.

Pringle, Peter. *Food, Inc.: Mendel to Monsanto—the Promises and Perils of the Biotech Harvest.* New York: Simon and Schuster, 2003.

Proctor, Robert N. *Cancer Wars: How Politics Shapes What We Know and Don't Know about Cancer.* New York: Basic Books, 1995.

Robbins, Paul. *Lawn People: How Grasses, Weeds, and Chemicals Make Us Who We Are.* Philadelphia, PA: Temple University Press, 2007.

Robertson, Thomas. *The Malthusian Moment: Global Population Growth and the Birth of American Environmentalism.* New Brunswick, NJ: Rutgers University Press, 2012.

Robin, Marie-Monique. *The World According to Monsanto: Pollution, Corruption, and the Control of Our Food Supply, an Investigation into the World's Most Controversial Company.* New York: New Press, 2008.

Rome, Adam. *The Bulldozer in the Countryside: Suburban Sprawl and the Rise of American Environmentalism.* Cambridge: Cambridge University Press, 2001.

———. *The Genius of Earth Day: How a 1970 Teach-In Unexpectedly Made the First Green Generation.* New York: Hill and Wang, 2013.

Rothman, Hal K. *The Greening of a Nation: Environmentalism in the United States since 1945.* New York: Harcourt Brace College Publishers, 1998.

Rudd, Robert L. *Pesticides and the Living Landscape.* Madison and Milwaukee: University of Wisconsin Press, 1970.

Russell, Edmund. *War and Nature: Fighting Humans and Insects with Chemicals from World War I to* Silent Spring. Cambridge: Cambridge University Press, 2001.

Sale, Kirkpatrick. *The Green Revolution: The American Environmental Movement.* New York: Hill and Wang, 1993.

Schapiro, Mark. *Exposed: The Toxic Chemistry of Everyday Products and What's at Stake for American Power.* White River Junction, VT: Chelsea Green Publishing, 2007.

Schuck, Peter H. *Agent Orange on Trial: Mass Toxic Disasters in the Courts*, enlarged ed. Cambridge, MA: Belknap Press of Harvard University Press, 1987.

Schwing, Richard C., and Walter A. Alberts Jr., eds. *Societal Risk Assessment: How Safe Is Safe Enough?* New York and London: Plenum Press, 1980.

Sellers, Christopher C. *Crabgrass Crucible: Suburban Nature and the Rise of Environmentalism in Twentieth-Century America.* Chapel Hill: University of North Carolina Press, 2012.

Shiva, Vandana. *The Violence of the Green Revolution: Third World Agriculture, Ecology and Politics.* London and New Jersey: Zed Books, and Penang, Malaysia: Third World Network, 1991.

Shoecraft, Billee. "*Sue the Bastards!*" Introduction by Frank Egler. Phoenix, AZ: Franklin Press, 1971.

Shrivastava, Paul. *Bhopal: Anatomy of a Crisis*, 2nd ed. London: Paul Chapman Publishing, 1992.

Sideris, Lisa H., and Kathleen Dean Moore, eds. *Rachel Carson: Legacy and Challenge.* Albany: State University of New York Press, 2008.

Snetsinger, Robert. *The Ratcatcher's Child: A History of the Pest Control Industry.* Cleveland, OH: Franzak & Foster Company, 1983.

Soluri, John. *Banana Cultures: Agriculture, Consumption, and Environmental Change in Honduras and the United States.* Austin: University of Texas Press, 2005.

Spear, Robert J. *The Great Gypsy Moth War: The History of the First Campaign in Massachusetts to Eradicate the Gypsy Moth, 1890–1901.* Amherst: University of Massachusetts Press, 2005.

Spielman, Andrew, ScD, and Michael D'Antonio. *Mosquito: A Natural History of Our Most Persistent and Deadly Foe.* New York: Hyperion, 2001.

Staples, Amy L. S. *The Birth of Development: How the World Bank, Food and Agriculture*

Organization, and the World Health Organization Changed the World, 1945–1965. Kent, OH: Kent State University Press, 2006.

Steinberg, Ted. *American Green: The Obsessive Quest for the Perfect Lawn.* New York and London: W. W. Norton & Company, 2006.

Steingrabber, Sandra. *Living Downstream: A Scientist's Personal Investigation of Cancer and the Environment.* New York: Vintage Books, 1997.

Stoll, Steven. *Larding the Lean Earth: Soil and Society in Nineteenth-Century America.* New York: Hill and Wang, 2002.

Taylor, Bron. *Dark Green Religion: Nature, Spirituality, and the Planetary Future.* Berkeley: University of California Press, 2010.

Van den Bosch, Robert. *The Pesticide Conspiracy.* Garden City, NY: Doubleday & Company, 1978.

Van Strum, Carol. *A Bitter Fog: Herbicides and Human Rights.* San Francisco: Random House, 1983.

Vig, Norman J., and Michael E. Kraft, eds. *Environmental Policy in the 1980s: Reagan's New Agenda.* Washington, DC: Congressional Quarterly, 1984.

Vogt, William. *The Road to Survival.* New York: William Sloane Associates, 1948.

Waddell, Craig, ed. *And No Birds Sing: Rhetorical Analyses of Rachel Carson's* Silent Spring. Foreword by Paul Brooks. Carbondale and Edwardsville: Southern Illinois University Press, 2000.

Wargo, John. *Our Children's Toxic Legacy: How Science and Law Fail to Protect Us from Pesticides.* New Haven, CT: Yale University Press, 1996.

Webb, James L. A., Jr. *Humanity's Burden: A Global History of Malaria.* Cambridge: Cambridge University Press, 2009.

Weir, David. *The Bhopal Syndrome: Pesticides, Environment, and Health.* San Francisco, CA: Sierra Club Books, 1987.

——— and Mark Schapiro. *Circle of Poison: Pesticides and People in a Hungry World.* San Francisco, CA: Institute for Food and Development Policy, 1981.

Westing, Arthur H., ed. *Herbicides in War: The Long-Term Ecological and Human Consequences.* London: Taylor and Francis, 1984.

Whiteside, Thomas. *Defoliation: What Are Our Herbicides Doing to Us?* New York: Ballantine Books, 1970.

———. *The Pendulum and the Toxic Cloud: The Course of Dioxin Contamination.* New Haven, CT: Yale University Press, 1979.

———. *The Withering Rain: America's Herbicidal Folly.* New York: Dutton, 1971.

Whitten, Jamie L. *That We May Live.* Princeton, NJ: D. Van Nostrand Company, 1966.

Whorton, James. *Before* Silent Spring*: Pesticides and Public Health in Pre-DDT America.* Princeton, NJ: Princeton University Press, 1974.

Wilcox, Fred A. *Waiting for an Army to Die: The Tragedy of Agent Orange.* Cabin John, MD: Seven Locks Press, 1989.

Wildavsky, Aaron. *But Is It True? A Citizen's Guide to Environmental Health and Safety Issues.* Cambridge, MA: Harvard University Press, 1995.

Wilkins, Lee. *Shared Vulnerability: The Media and American Perceptions of the Bhopal Disaster.* Westport, CT: Greenwood Press, 1987.

Wright, Angus. *The Death of Ramón Gonzalez: The Modern Agricultural Dilemma*, rev. ed. Austin: University of Texas Press, 2005.

Zierler, David. *The Invention of Ecocide: Agent Orange, Vietnam, and the Scientists Who Changed the Way We Think about the Environment.* Athens: University of Georgia Press, 2011.

Journal Articles and Book Chapters

Anderson, J. L. "War on Weeds: Iowa Farmers and Growth-Regulator Herbicides." *Technology and Culture* 46, no. 4 (2005): 719–744.

Buhs, Joshua Blu. "Dead Cows on a Georgia Field: Mapping the Cultural Landscape of the Post–World War II American Pesticides Controversies." *Environmental History* 7, no. 1 (January 2002): 99–121.

Cooper, Frederick, and Randall Packard. "Introduction." In *International Development and the Social Sciences: Essays on the History and Politics of Knowledge*, edited by Frederick Cooper and Randall Packard. Berkeley: University of California Press, 1997.

Daemmrich, Arthur. "Risk Frameworks and Biomonitoring: Distributed Regulation of Synthetic Chemicals in Humans." In "Toxic Bodies/Toxic Environments: An Interdisciplinary Forum," *Environmental History* 13, no. 4 (October 2008): 684–694.

Egan, Michael. "Toxic Knowledge: A Mercurial Fugue in Three Parts." "In Toxic Bodies/Toxic Environments: An Interdisciplinary Forum," *Environmental History* 13, no. 4 (October 2008): 636–642.

Freeman, Orville L. "Perspectives and Prospects." *Agricultural History* 66, no. 2 (Spring 1992): 3–11.

Gardner, B. Delworth. "Some Issues Surrounding Land and Chemical Use in Agriculture." In *Agriculture and the Environment: Searching for Greener Pastures*, edited by Tevy L. Anderson and Bruce Yandle. Stanford, CA: Hoover Institution Press, 2001.

Gordon, Robert. "Poisons in the Fields: The United Farm Workers, Pesticides, and Environmental Politics." *Pacific Historical Review* 68, no. 1 (February 1999): 51–77.

Hay, Amy M. "Dow Chemical vs. 'Coercive Utopians': Constructing the Contested Ground of Science and Government Regulation in 1970s America." *Business and Economic History, On-Line* 9 (2011), http://www.thebhc.org/publications/BEHonline/2011/hay.pdf.

Hazlett, Maril. "Voices from the *Spring: Silent Spring* and the Ecological Turn in American Health." In *Seeing Nature through Gender*, edited by Virginia J. Scharff. Lawrence: University Press of Kansas, 2003.

Kroll, Gary. "The 'Silent Springs' of Rachel Carson: Mass Media and the Origins of Modern Environmentalism." *Public Understanding of Science* 10 (2001): 403–420.

Langston, Nancy. "Gendered Transformation: Endocrine Disruption in the Environment." In *Seeing Nature through Gender*, edited by Virginia J. Scharff. Lawrence: University Press of Kansas, 2003.

Lutts, Ralph H. "Chemical Fallout: Rachel Carson's *Silent Spring*, Radioactive Fallout, and the Environmental Movement." *Environmental Review* 9, no. 3 (Autumn 1985): 210–225.

Maguire, Steven. "Contested Icons: Rachel Carson and DDT." In *Rachel Carson: Legacy and Challenge*, edited by Lisa H. Sideris and Kathleen Dean Moore. Albany: State University of New York Press, 2008.

Mathur, Chandana, and Ward Morehouse. "Twice Poisoned Bhopal: Notes on the Continuing Aftermath of the World's Worst Industrial Disaster." *International Labor and Working-Class History* 62 (Fall 2002): 69.

McCord, Peter. "Divergences on the Left: The Environmentalisms of Rachel Carson and Murray Bookchin." *Left History* 13, no. 1 (Spring–Summer 2008): 14–34.

McVety, Amanda Kay. "Pursuing Progress: Point Four in Ethiopia." *Diplomatic History* 32, no. 3 (June 2008): 371–403.

Meiners, Roger E., and Andrew P. Morriss. "Silent Springs and Silent Villages: Pesticides and the Trampling of Property Rights." In *Government vs. Environment*, edited by Donald R. Leal and Roger E. Meiners. Lanham, MD: Rowman & Littlefield Publishers, 2002, 15–37.

Nash, Linda. "Purity and Danger: Historical Reflections on the Regulation of Environmental Pollutants." In "Toxic Bodies/Toxic Environments: An Interdisciplinary Forum," *Environmental History* 13, no. 4 (October 2008): 651–658.

Norwood, Vera. "How to Value a Flower: Locating Beauty in Toxic Landscapes." In *Rachel Carson: Legacy and Challenge*, edited by Lisa H. Sideris and Kathleen Dean Moore. Albany: State University of New York Press, 2008.

Pimental, David. "After *Silent Spring*: Ecological Effects of Pesticides on Public Health and on Birds and Other Organisms." In *Rachel Carson: Legacy and Challenge*, edited by Lisa H. Sideris and Kathleen Dean Moore. Albany: State University of New York Press, 2008.

Rome, Adam. "'Give Earth a Chance': The Environmental Movement and the Sixties." *Journal of American History* 90, no. 2 (September 2003): 525–554.

Sharpless, John. "Population Science, Private Foundations, and Development Aid: The Transformation of Demographic Knowledge in the United States, 1945–1965." In *International Development and the Social Sciences: Essays on the History and Politics of Knowledge*, edited by Frederick Cooper and Randall Packard. Berkeley: University of California Press, 1997.

Sideris, Lisa H. "The Secular and Religious Sources of Rachel Carson's Sense of Wonder." In *Rachel Carson: Legacy and Challenge*, edited by Lisa H. Sideris and Kathleen Dean Moore. Albany: State University of New York Press, 2008.

Smith, Michael. "'Silence, Miss Carson!': Science, Gender, and the Reception of *Silent Spring*." In *Rachel Carson: Legacy and Challenge*, edited by Lisa H. Sideris and Kathleen Dean Moore. Albany: State University of New York Press, 2008.

Smith-Howard, Kendra. "Antibiotics and Agricultural Change: Purifying Milk and Protecting Health in the Postwar Era." *Agricultural History* 84, no. 3 (June 2010): 327–351.

Vogel, Sarah A. "From 'the Dose Makes the Poison' to 'the Timing Makes the Poison': Conceptualizing Risk in the Synthetic Age." In "Toxic Bodies/Toxic Environments: An Interdisciplinary Forum," *Environmental History* 13, no. 4 (October 2008): 667–673.

——— and Jody A. Roberts. "Why the Toxic Substances Control Act Needs an Overhaul, and How to Strengthen Oversight of Chemicals in the Interim." *Health Affairs* 30, no. 5 (May 2011): 898–905.

Westing, Arthur H. "Herbicides in War: Past and Present." In *Herbicides in War: The Long-Term Ecological and Human Consequences*, edited by Arthur H. Westing. London: Taylor and Francis, 1984.

Zierler, David. "Against Protocol: Ecocide, Détente, and the Question of Chemical Warfare in Vietnam, 1969–1975." In *Environmental Histories of the Cold War*, edited by J. R. McNeil and Corinna Unger. Washington, DC, and Cambridge: The German Historical Institute and Cambridge University Press, 2010.

Unpublished Manuscripts and Dissertations

Brooks, Karl. "A Legacy Cast in Concrete: The Truman Presidency's Transformation of America's Natural Environment, 1945–1953." Unpublished paper presented at A Conference on the Historical Significance of the Truman Presidency, Harry S. Truman Presidential Library, July 2003.

Case, Andrew N. "Looking for Organic America: J. I. Rodale, The Rodale Press, and the Popular Culture of Environmentalism." PhD dissertation, Department of History, University of Wisconsin–Madison, 2012.

Hay, Amy Marie. "Recipe for Disaster: Chemical Wastes, Community Activists, and Public Health at Love Canal, 1945–2000." PhD dissertation, Department of History, Michigan State University, East Lansing, 2005.

Smith-Howard, Kendra. "Perfecting Nature's Food: A Cultural and Environmental History of Milk in the United States, 1900–1975." PhD dissertation, Department of History, University of Wisconsin–Madison, 2007.

Vail, David D. "Guardians of Abundance: Aerial Application, Agricultural Chemicals, and Toxicity in the Postwar Prairie West." PhD dissertation, Department of History, Kansas State University, Manhattan, 2012.

Index